To Jon a

Thank You for Your
friendship and kind
support. Best wishes,
always!

Kurtz Brock

Lucky Life

A novel

Kirk Brocker

For Pam, Celia, Halley and Claire.

Cover artwork by Kirk Brocker – 2016
Copyright © 2017 Kirk Brocker
All rights reserved.
ISBN 978-1542631457

Prologue

Marley's Chains

"People seem not to see that their opinion of the world is also a confession of character."
Ralph Waldo Emerson

A sullen, round-faced deputy sheriff pushed open the door allowing the slender woman in a neat gray suit to brush past into the tiny waiting room.

"Five minutes, Mrs. Albright," was all he said before closing the heavy metal door, producing a noticeable and disconcerting "click" of the lock.

Her first thought was how remarkably empty the room was save the worn wooden desk and its three tired chairs. Unless it was well hidden there was nothing else in the space but a fresh coat of white paint and a relentless antiseptic odor leaching from the lavatory across the hall.

She placed her leather purse on the floor next to the table. Folded discreetly in the side panel was a copy of yesterday's local Freeland newspaper. There along with the funeral notices, school menus, and bowling league scores appeared a short article (page 3) under the curt banner: **Albright Found Guilty.** Even now after two days in the courtroom and weeks of preparation, it seemed impossible. Still, the newspaper had it mostly right.

Albright Found Guilty

Freeland, Iowa - Dallas Albright, sixteen, of Freeland, was found guilty in Southern Iowa District Court yesterday of aggravated assault, burglary, and illegal use of a handgun. Sentencing will take place on July 28, 1987 by Judge Arthur Pendleton.

Albright, along with Douglas Capernick, Gordon Gordonski, and William Stetson was charged in connection with a May 18th 1987 altercation that left both Albright and Capernick hospitalized. A .38 caliber handgun stolen earlier from the Freeland Chief of Police was recovered at the scene.

Local authorities, including the County Sheriff's office, were able to link Albright and Capernick to a series of unsolved robberies that took place during the summer of 1984. The items stolen, including rare coins and an antique sword dating back to the Civil War, have yet to be recovered. Douglas Capernick's trial is scheduled to begin November 9, 1987.

Left alone with the monotony of the small space her mind began to drift; back, always back, never forward. In that quiet moment, she allowed herself to linger over a pleasing memory of father and sons cuddled together on the sofa, laughing madly over the Sunday comics. On those beautiful mornings the boys would insist on having their apple juice in a coffee cup; it made them feel grown-up, they said, "Big like Dad." Then whenever he laughed they would laugh, joyful and unruly, always too loud, and at the silliest things. It was wonderfully sweet and real, but too soon gone those Sunday mornings.

The jingle from what had to be a very large ring of keys preceded the release of the lock. Emily Albright automatically pushed over to the side of the desk as the portly deputy, and an equally round partner, led the small young man into the tiny space. Pointing a chubby index finger toward the chair behind the desk, the shorter rounder one demanded, "Sit there."

While the tiny prisoner dutifully shuffled around the desk, Emily whispered an earnest prayer that the lawman might remove the chains that shackled the boy's small hands and feet. It was the sound, the constant clanking of metal on metal that bothered her most; it seemed to amplify the drama of what had already been an overwhelming morning. Predictably, the callous guard made no effort to free his prisoner, which left Emily to wonder whether the Lord had been too busy to oblige or if He'd purposefully chosen to disregard her small request.

Turning to retreat, the one with the keys said to no one, at least he was looking at no one, "Five minutes."

What can a mother possibly say to a sixteen-year-old son who has just been convicted of crimes that will send him to prison for the next five years?

"Why isn't he frightened," she wondered?

Searching for somewhere safe to begin, Emily Albright asked, "Do you need anything? Is there anything I can get you?"

The beautiful boy laughed quietly, but still loud enough for her to hear.

"No, Mother," he replied. "I'm pretty sure they'll give me everything I need."

"Four minutes and fifteen-seconds," Emily thought as she sat down on the wooden chair directly across from her prisoner. "I need to say something, but what? Of course, he'll never write. I know he'll never write. And Anamosa is so far. He may not even want me to visit."

"God, please. Please help me," she silently pleaded.

Emily Albright recognized that she was praying again, and even though it had changed nothing she continued, grateful for someone with whom to talk.

"I don't know what to think. Without Charles what can I do for this boy, our boy? Help me, please."

Terribly, the beautiful boy said nothing. As he had for the past three days, her son sat rigid on the hard wooden chair, stone-faced and unyielding. His shackled hands now rested motionless in his lap. Then as if to further abuse her kindness, he had cocked his head to the side, revealing in those gorgeous blue eyes a vacant expression which she mistook for disinterest or possibly boredom. Under the circumstances, it seemed a remarkable pose for someone with such an unfortunate future.

"Did Mr. Arbite say anything more about the possibility for an appeal?" she asked, already fully aware of the answer.

Across the table the small boy in the oversized orange prison jumpsuit remained quiet.

"Well, I'll come to visit next week, maybe Friday, to see how you're getting along."

Still he did not reply.

For about the billionth time, she asked herself, "What have we done to this child?"

"You know," the boy mumbled, "if you want to go you can just knock on the door and the guard will let you out."

"No. I want to stay," Emily replied, but then hastily added, "Do you want me to go?"

"I don't care. I was just thinking that it might be better if we said good-bye and got on with it."

Emily wondered who that suggestion was intended to benefit. For a moment, she allowed herself the indulgence of pretending he was being kind and offering this as a way to make the final break easier on her. But years of disappointment warned her that it wasn't true. The moment, along with her rush of hope, evaporated in his silence.

"I'll stay until they come back, dear."

"Are you expecting something more?" he asked the floor.

It was Emily's turn to remain silent.

"Do you want me to say I'm sorry, again?" he added, and then as if for effect dramatically placed his manacled hands back on the wooden desk.

"How about something like, no one got hurt. Or, hey, I'll come back a changed man. It'll be good for me. What about this one: Don't worry, Mother, I still have my whole life in front of me. I'll make Dad proud of me, yet. I promise."

There was a short pause before he added in a quieter, less confrontational tone, "Did I get that right for you? Do you feel better?"

"No, Dallas. I don't feel any better."

Three minutes and thirty-seconds.

Leaning back into the chair made his chains rattle like Marley's on Christmas Eve. Then in a voice she was sure she'd never hear again, the timid and sorrowful one, the one that always came after his confession but before the punishment, he whispered, "There were a lot of mistakes weren't there?"

She fought back the urge but said nothing, hoping that for just a little longer he'd continue to be her boy, the little boy that needed her.

"If he would only just open and show me that there's still something good, something honest. What happened to the boy with the apple juice and the funny papers? What have we done? Please, I need to know that I'm not this person, that I couldn't do these things. Please."

When she returned to the moment her son was looking directly into her eyes.

"I don't get it," he whispered. "Why is everyone the enemy to me?"

She replied without thinking, "I don't understand what you mean. Am I the enemy? Is your father? Andy?"

He raised his hands as if in self-defense.

"No, that's not what I mean. It's just that I can't say anything you'll understand. I know I don't have any friends, but that's the way I want it. It's weird, I know. And maybe it's a problem, but not for me."

He started to withdraw again, but when he saw the sadness in her eyes quickly added, "But you've been great to stay with me, really. It must have been hard, especially without Dad."

"Yes," she thought, "it is very hard without your father. But is he saying that just to play us off one another? Has he taken sides, too?"

Two minutes fifteen-seconds.

"Don't visit me for a while, okay? I don't want to think about you, or Andy, or Debbie. I need time to get it together. I'll call you, or write, or something. I'll let you know when I'm ready."

One minute forty-five seconds.

"It'll be okay," he laughed, but not because he'd said anything funny. Then in what she assumed was an effort at sincerity, he quickly added, "You know this wasn't about you, right?"

She turned away from her oldest son to concentrate on the stark white wall above his head. If she was going to ask, she had to ask now.

"Dallas, did you intend to kill that boy?"

Both heard the key turning in the lock.

"They're a minute early," she thought, wondering whether to say the three words out loud before it was too late.

The door swung open, but before the deputies could enter Emily Albright stood and heroically held out her hands, beckoning her son to stand and embrace her.

8

PART ONE

Chapter One

Lucky Life

"Every judgment stands on the edge of error."
The Ascent of Man - Jacob Bronowski

Dallas Albright has a recurring dream that he lives in a different universe. Whenever he visits one of these iterative worlds he will experience a new and distinct version of his own life.

Sometimes the differences between the life he is living and the one he is visiting are subtle and small. He might, for example, live a life where instead of brown eyes his will be blue. In another, he might be eight feet tall and hail from the planet Frunobulax. It is impossible to predict. The inscrutable universe will provide Dallas an infinite number of adaptations where each new life will be, must be, unique from the one he is now living. Failing to see the irony, Dallas Albright considers these experiences a kind of *lucky life*.

The idea for *lucky life* came from a book, one that he admittedly could never quite understand or finish. *Holes in the Infinite* had been a birthday gift from his mother who bought the book hoping that some thought provoking reading might inspire her son during his "time away." She was partly right.

On its release the scientist/author was generously praised by both his colleagues and the media for making the complex physics of a "multiverse" more accessible to the layman. But times change; today that same covetous crowd openly disparages his personal and professional credibility for having the temerity to gloss himself a "popular scientist"; that is, a scientist who imagines himself an entertainer.

To get the most out of his full fifteen minutes, the scientist/author will further strain his tenuous links back to academia by retaining the counsel of Blandon and Ernest, a stylish Hollywood talent agency better known in the trades for their excesses than their successes. The team's first order of business ("Because at B&E, we're all about family.") was to land their new boy an appearance on a well-known, late night talk show. Cast as the brainy wunderkind, he is judiciously slotted between the confused young starlet and the trendy musical act. Once on the sofa the smart-ass host encourages him to say outrageous things, things like, "There are an infinite number of universes, each with an infinite number of us, all living infinite versions of our lives."

Dallas Albright could understand that notion well enough to imagine his first version of *lucky life*. Sadly, this remarkable mental leap turns out to be a small consolation since he must always return to this reality and the life that he has ruined.

Deep in the southwest corner of Iowa is the small town of Freeland, Dallas Albright's childhood home. The current population is 6,845, but that will change.

While Lee was offering his sword to Grant on the Appomattox Court House lawn, the President of the Chicago and Northwestern Railroad, Mr. Marvin Hughitt was busy hiring a pair of fraternal twin brothers to ramrod his western survey crew. Arnold and Abbott Ehrmann were given the important job of mapping and acquiring the most advantageous route for the C & N's proposed new line between Dubuque and Council Bluffs. Along the way these shrewd opportunists also managed to exploit their advanced knowledge of the territory's future by making highly successful real estate and livestock investments.

It seems remarkable that someone as straight-laced as Marvin Hughitt, an honorable man among the loathsome robber barons, would have ever engaged two such disreputable people. The shameful Ehrmann brothers of Indianapolis, Indiana were in every way ugly men. Along with their utter lack of personal hygiene, both were confirmed bachelors with no scruples and an avaricious lust for money. In short order, the greedy siblings laid the ground work for what would one day become a trail of fledgling communities; small independent villages that took deep root across the Iowa prairie. Like the noxious buckhorn (*plantago lanceleola*) they flourished alongside the Chicago and Northwestern's shiny, new silver tracks. As Arnold Ehrmann would later confirm in his unappreciated biography, *Roll West*, "Buying land wasn't so much about who you knew, but more about when you got there."

There was a time when a town existed solely because of the railroad. Today, Freeland lies only three miles south of the most travelled interstate highway in the United States, but the four or five trains that still rumble through town every day never stop.

Like most of rural America, Freeland, Iowa had become a relentlessly shrinking spot on a well-worn map, a map that has been folded and refolded many many times. The few folks left waiting to turn out the lights remain defiantly loyal, obstinately loyal, to something - a time, a place, a style - that had once offered them considerable comfort and fulfillment.

10

Dallas Albright will grow up **from** the same place, but not **of** the same place as the good people of Freeland.

Chapter Two
Charles Albright

"Our life evokes our character."
The Power of Myth - Joseph Campbell

Charles William Albright - Dallas Albright's future father - will be the single most influential person in the boy's life; you might say that his fingerprints are permanently imprinted upon his son's back. Like Dallas, he too was born in Iowa. This is Charles' story.

In 1939, while at the University of Iowa, Charles' father Gordon will meet, court, and marry a stunning young sorority girl by the name of Charys Belle Campbell; a triumphant example of his *lucky life*. Charys was a Pi Phi who had come to Iowa from the posh North Shore of Chicago where her people were socially and politically well-connected. Her father was none other than Otto Darius Campbell, the most powerful and longest serving Attorney General in Illinois history.

Otto Campbell's first political success came in 1928 when he was elected to represent Cook County in the Illinois House of Representatives. Before his election, young Campbell was an up-and-coming North Side defense attorney with a rich pedigree and a *cum laude* diploma from Yale. Then as a newcomer to Chicago politics, he effectively blindsided the four-term incumbent, Andersen J. Boneventure by executing a vicious, no-holds-barred attack campaign, one that took dead-aim on Boneventure's notorious history for missed votes, and an unseemly predilection for younger (much younger) women. Boneventure publicly blamed his startling defeat on what he considered the "extraordinary amount of money that young Campbell spent on his campaign." The "extraordinary amount of money" to which former Representative Boneventure referred was slightly more than $7,000, most of which was fronted by Campbell's new father-in-law, Dr. Douglas Englander.

"Doc" Englander knew a good bet when he saw one. A brilliant surgeon and a bold entrepreneur, Englander recognized the potential in his handsome Ivy League son-in-law, and used his considerable influence to identify additional financial supporters from within the Chicago medical community, likeminded men of medicine who saw the value of having a left-leaning legislator in the Illinois House.

It was during his sophomore term on the hill that Otto Campbell befriended another Representative on the rise, the future mayor and undisputed boss of Chicago, Richard J. Daley. Interestingly - perhaps ironically - for their first campaigns the two lifelong Democrats disguised their true party affiliations and were elected as Republicans. Despite their different backgrounds and perspective this political subterfuge became the foundation for a lifelong friendship, one that encouraged and sustained both men's insatiable political ambitions.

As an institution for their only child's higher education, the University of Iowa would not have been on either Otto or Lillian Campbell's short-list. It was generally assumed that the bright and vivacious young woman from Evanston would be attending a private school equal to her social status, like Smith, or perhaps Wellesley, at the least Bennett. Instead, Charys Campbell's unilateral decision to attend the University of Iowa - her first, but not her last deviation from their wishes - guaranteed that her parent's well-designed master plan was about to go off the rails. Adding insult to injury was the infuriating detail that Charys' choice of schools had nothing to with academic rigor; she had enrolled at Iowa to follow a young man.

It was a beautiful spring evening, Charys wanted to believe it was the perfect spring evening. In this version of her *lucky life* a sliver of golden moon hung perfectly balanced above the horizon. A gentle breeze lightly touched her skin as Ray Noble and his orchestra softly provided her favorite tune - *The Very Thought of You*. But best of all, most important of all, there was no one for miles to interrupt this decision. Then afterwards, as the couple lay reclining in the backseat of his father's 1934 Ford, the boy sincerely pledged his "forever love." Apart from the situation's inherent awkwardness and discomfort from the topography, Charys Campbell was certain that this was indeed the "magical moment" her friends had promised.

Sadly, soon after their arrival in Iowa City, the young Lothario's testosterone overwhelmed both his better judgment and commitments. In this new environment rich with opportunity, the excitable boy found himself greedily drawn to every fresh passing skirt. Like a skittish mouse in a maze, the unfaithful preppy would first race off in one direction, only to have another pretty face take him down a different path. Of course, it didn't take long before word of his silly dalliances made their way back to the good sisters in the Pi Phi house, but in spite of all their well-intentioned warnings and unsolicited advice, by November, Charys Campbell had become the proverbial sadder but wiser girl.

Charys' future husband, Gordon Albright came from a far more humble place.

With the constant carping of a twice-widowed mother still braying in his ears, Gordon's future father, Wilhelm (Bill) Jems Albright abandoned Hapsburg in 1906 to join his cousin Günter Albright who had managed to make it as far west as the coal mines of Dubuque, Iowa. Then in 1910, this version of Bill's *lucky life* has him marry a bright, diminutive school teacher, Miss Sarah Allen Pitsque. Four years later, they return to her parent's farm near Cedar Rapids where they will make three babies and help the family to grow its fledgling dairy business. By 1915, Gordon, the middle child, is born and the Albright Dairy opens its doors at 309 Locust, right in the heart of downtown Cedar Rapids.

During its many years of service, the Albright Dairy becomes something of an institution in Cedar Rapids. People come to depend upon the fresh dairy products that are delivered right to their door, twice a week, by those nice men in their crisp white shirts and bright blue trucks.

In the fall of 1937, the Albright's will proudly send Gordon the fourteen miles south to Iowa City where he will attend the University of Iowa. Their plan was for him to study business. Once properly schooled, he was to then return home and help his older brother Thomas manage the dairy operations. But like many of the best laid plans, Bill and Sarah Albright's were spilled when their boy unexpectedly announced his intense aversion to the smell of sour milk. This distressing olfactory obstacle, which out of respect for his parents he'd kept secret for nearly five years, made his long-term future in the dairy industry problematic. The day he left Cedar Rapids and the Albright Dairy, Gordon vowed to never return. Instead, he struck out to use his good looks and personality to find his own alternate program.

A hardworking student and a passable football player, Gordon Albright also found Iowa City ripe with opportunity. Lanky and slightly undersized for a Big Ten tight end, he would spend the better part of his freshman and sophomore seasons riding the pines, watching as the Hawkeyes suffered two abysmal campaigns. But as every loyal Iowa football fan knows, 1939 turns out to be one for the record books, and arguably the greatest single season in the school's history.

Thanks to the exceptional talent of Nile Kinnick - the Christian Scientist from Adel, Iowa - the Iowa Ironmen will come out of the cellar just long enough to give the Black and Gold a stunning six win season. Although Gordon wasn't quite good enough to steal a spot from the two outstanding senior tight ends (Evans and Prasse) first-year coach, Dr. Eddie Anderson would freely substitute him throughout the line-up, unintentionally making Gordon one of the first platoon players in college or professional football history. Of those different roles, Gordon's favorite position turned out to be the blocking back on punt returns. There his only job was to give the great Kinnick that extra second, a single step, which helped to send him on his way to history.

Later that fall, Niles Kinnick deservedly won the Heisman Trophy. Other newsworthy items included the Nazi's successful invasion of Poland, and Albert Einstein's letter to President Roosevelt encouraging him to move forward with the production of a nuclear weapon. These unique but connected strings will soon play a significant role in everyone's *lucky life*.

Gordon's senior season found the Ironmen slipping backwards to finish with a disappointing four-and-four record. Thanks to the departure of Kinnick and the tight ends, Gordon now had a spot on the starting line-up. Even though they didn't live up to the expectations of their fans, Gordon always thought of the 1940 season as a success, after all, he caught five touchdown passes - two in one game against Illinois - and the attentions of the cute Pi Phi and future wife, Charys Campbell.

To his credit, Gordon parlayed his Saturday gridiron success into a position as a loan officer with the Hyland Bank and Trust of Cedar Rapids, Iowa. Although Bill and Sarah were still confounded by their son's lack of interest in the family business, they were placated when he and their beautiful new daughter-in-law moved into a charming Cape Cod three doors down the street from them on West Addams.

In this version of his *lucky life,* Charles Arthur Albright (Dallas Albright's future father, the one with the heavy fingers) will arrive early on the morning of March 15, 1941 - the Ides of March. In spite of the joy and hope that the child would bring to his family, the outside world was unsettled and confusing. Just the week before, Hitler's army had boldly marched into Czechoslovakia, sending hundreds of thousands of Jews fleeing south into exile, and making Chamberlin's bold promise to protect central Europe utterly worthless.

The letter that the Albright's had dread but certainly anticipated came in the morning mail on April 2, 1943.

The Selective Service and Training Act allowed the United States government to "conscribe" young men to support the war efforts in Europe and Japan. Gordon's letter insisted that he promptly report for induction at Camp Dodge in Des Moines, Iowa. On the day he departed, Gordon and Charys had been married only eighteen months; their son Charles was seventeen days old.

Soon after getting off the Camp Dodge bus, Gordon was mysteriously separated from the others by a baby-faced lieutenant, who then quietly ushered the newbie into a small private room featuring only a wooden desk, two chairs, and a fresh coat of white paint.

"You know, Albright," Lieutenant Paul Avery declared as he lit a Pal Mal cigarette from the one he'd been smoking, "you might wanna give some serious thought to a military career." Then looking out the window over Gordon's freshly shaved head to where a second bus of recruits was now unloading, he added, "It sure as hell beats the life of a boot." Lieutenant Avery - Iowa State University class of 1938 - emphasized the merit in his suggestion by pointing through the window at a group of green civilians, soon to be soldiers, as they stumbled to a rather amateur form of attention.

Although he certainly had qualities that would have made him a leader of men, Gordon did not hesitate to inform the Lieutenant that he would prefer to, "Respectfully decline the Lieutenant's offer, Sir." and instead remain an enlisted man.

Gordon had come to Des Moines with a straightforward plan to survive the war, one from which he refused to stray. His private strategy was to make himself as small as he could, say as little as possible and never ever volunteer for anything. After his three years, five months, and ten days of service to the 3rd battalion of the 329th regiment of Major General Robert C. Macon's 83rd "Thunderbolt" infantry division, this version of Gordon's *lucky life* will see him returning to Iowa with his mind and body parts more-or-less intact.

It is worth noting that in another fifty years it will be Gordon Albright's grandson, Dallas Albright, who will be the first of his kin to give serious consideration to the optimistic combination of adjective and noun in the expression *lucky life*. During his incarceration there will be a wealth of time for such academic considerations. However, back on that terrible morning in June when his grandfather charged out of the assault craft and on to the bloody beaches of Normandy, it's likely that Gordon Albright would have missed the unintended irony imbedded in the expression. Its alternative meaning is especially relevant to that particular experience, since in this version of Gordon's *lucky life* he is one of the fortunate survivors of that gruesome offensive.

So what if the humorist/scientist is correct and there are an infinite number of alternative versions of our *lucky life*? With limitless possibilities there will be ones where Gordon Albright is not so lucky. There will even be episodes where he is one of the five thousand who won't make it across the beach. *Lucky life* does not repeat, design, or judge. If you chose to believe that parallel to this time and place there are an infinite number of alternative versions, all operating simultaneously and completely distinct from each other, then you must also appreciate that in some of them, many of them, there will be lives we desire, as well as those that offer pain and heartbreak. The profound question of what the scientific proof of *lucky life's* reality would do to one's *lucky life* is something that will one day engage all of Dallas Albright's imagination.

Thankfully, Gordon Albright returns home to Cedar Rapids bringing with him three new and permanent opinions: an enthusiasm for Bordeaux (particularly the 1928 Chateau Latour), a fascination for paintings by the seventeenth century Flemish master, Teniers the Younger, and an everlasting hatred for the cruelties of war. Although seemingly unrelated, these considerations have already triggered life-changing consequences to this particular version of Gordon Albright's *lucky life*.

On April 11, 1945, it is Gordon and his compatriots of the 83rd that will liberate the Langenstein-Zwieberg concentration camp. The history books refer to Langenstein-Zwieberg as an "under-camp" of the larger Buchenwald. In this case, "under camp" is a useless distinction. By the time Gordon and the Thunderbolt broke down the gates and put an end to the daily parade of horse drawn carts heaped with bodies on their way to the furnaces in Quedlinburg, more than five thousand people had pointlessly died of starvation and disease.

Along with his newfound enthusiasm for French wines and Dutch paintings, Gordon returns to Iowa with some especially unwanted baggage; permanent memories that will include his own firsthand knowledge of the Nazis' unspeakable cruelties. There was no training from Lieutenant Paul Avery that could have possibly prepared Gordon for war's harshest reality, which is, simply stated: man is both capable and willing to see his fellow man as something less than human.

In this version of his *lucky life*, Gordon's plan to survive the war was a success. Then on a blistering hot afternoon in August, he returns to Cedar Rapids and a well-earned hero's welcome. With appropriate fanfare, he is reinstated to his former position at the Hyland Trust. Six years later, Gordon's personal fortunes improve when he's named President of the bank, a station of respect and reward from which he capably serves the community until that terrible afternoon in April of 1967.

While Gordon was busy marching across France his son Charles would grow into a bright, serious little boy. It was during those long anxious evenings, the giant Philco radio humming quietly in the background, that grandmother Sarah lovingly, skillfully, began to teach Charles to read and write. By four, he had reached a level of proficiency that children twice his age will not have mastered.

Along with her passion for reading, Charles also received a fair share of his grandmother's DNA. Like Sarah, the child was small; a model roughly three-quarters the size of children his own age. To be smaller is always a problem for a boy, but it was made worse by the fact that Charles was clearly brighter than his peers. His intellect was generally mistaken as aloofness, which he was not, and then turned against him by both adults and children. His serious nature confused people and created the false impression that he was strange. The fact that he came from a well-respected and prominent family only forced people to gossip more quietly behind Gordon and Charys' back.

Long before reaching his seventeenth birthday, Charles Albright was ready to forsake the confining narrative of Washington High School and

Cedar Rapids, Iowa. An early graduation where he was named valedictorian helped persuade Northwestern University to extend him a full academic scholarship. By 1963, Charles had completed his undergraduate course work and was accepted at the Northwestern School of Business.

Although he was always small (at his high school graduation, he was 5'- 4" and weighed only 118 pounds), Charles loved sport and welcomed every opportunity to compete. Sadly, the hard reality of most team sports is that there's rarely a spot for the small man. There have been, however, notable exceptions.

Tommy Burns (5'- 4") was heavyweight champion of the world until he went twelve rounds with (6'- 1") Jack Johnson. Bob Cousy - the "Houdini of the Hardwoods" (5'- 11'') made the NBA all-star team twelve straight years, and led the Celtics to six championships. And then there was Yankees short-stop, Phil Rizzuto - "the Scooter" - (5'- 6") who played his entire thirteen-year career with the Yankees, helping them to win ten American League Championships and seven World Series rings. In spite of these remarkable exceptions, Charles Albright's athletic endeavors were stifled not by a lack of hustle, but from inferior height.

There were many in Cedar Rapids who could still remember his father Gordon's successful grid iron career at the University of Iowa, including old Bud Legett, Washington High's longtime and highly successful football coach. But Legett was a no-nonsense kind of man and pulled no punches with Charles. Looking down on the boy's fresh enthusiastic face, Legett let fly a stream of brown chew that dribbled down his chin. Then wiping his broken gnarled left hand across a whiskered face, the old coach shook his head and announced without reservation, "You're welcome to help with the equipment, son, but there'll be no place for you on the team."

When he reported for basketball try-outs, he was jeered by his taller classmates and sent home before touching a ball. Coach Riley Patterson's pitiful apology began, "Sorry, Charles. You should stick to things you're good at."

Track and field seemed like a possibility, but his short legs were incapable of keeping pace with the longer and ganglier athletes.

The tough training regimen of a wrestler appealed to him, but in one of her rare ultimatums Charys forbid him from grappling. That unexpected and strenuous objection was mostly centered on her concern for his small size; she refused to listen to the argument that there were weight classes. But truth be told, that specific line of reasoning was mostly subterfuge to mask the more strident position that her handsome son should not go through life with cauliflower ears.

By the time he was accepted at Northwestern, Charles had given up on team sports altogether. Told that golf would be useful for a future business career, he played with modest success on the Washington High golf team

18

where he qualified for regional competition, but failed to make the state tournament. Like many a weekend golfer, Charles Albright would come to discover that there was something appealing about the leisurely pace and quiet of the game. A casual walk on those fabulously manicured lawns seemed like time well spent.

Chapter Three

Emily Krist Loses Her Pinkie

"Taking a new step, uttering a new word is what people fear most."
Fyodor Dostoyevsky

Emily Anne Krist was born in the Freeland Community Hospital to Johanna and Jacob Krist on July 25, 1945. Twenty-two years later, on a spectacular fall afternoon in Cedar Rapids, Iowa, Emily Krist will marry Charles Albright. Then through an unlikely combination of circumstances that involve a brutal ice storm, a disagreeable aunt, and an expectant mother's amazing courage, Emily Albright will give birth to our protagonist, Dallas Albright, on Christmas Eve, 1969.

When little Emily Krist joined the waking world at seven forty-five A.M. the temperature inside the hospital's operating room was only eighty-one degrees. This ordinary summer morning was in welcome contrast to what had been two weeks of stifling ninety-plus degree days.

Despite of the fact that William Havilland Carrier had been selling his commercial air conditioning equipment since the late '20s, it would not be until 1958 (thirteen years after Emily Krist was born) that the frugal and hardheaded Freeland Community Hospital Board would reluctantly agree to its installation at the Freeland Community Hospital. So on this temperate morning, all the hospital staff, especially the delivery nurses and Doctor Walter Lund, were grateful when Johanna and Emily conducted their miracle at a time of day when the temperature was slightly more forgiving.

Johanna enthusiastically credited the welcome cooler conditions to her diligence at prayer, she was certain that God had wanted her first and only childbirth to be consummated under His best possible conditions. For months afterwards, Johanna lived to retell her story to anyone that she could corner, after all, to have the Almighty hear your prayers and end the hellish heat wave of 1945 was - at least in her mind - a remarkable measure of distinction; a blessing that set her apart from the other devoted members of Saint John's Lutheran Church, a congregation that proudly boasted of being southwest Iowa's most conservative of the Missouri Synod churches.

To learn the needed skills of a new mother, Johanna naturally defaulted to her own clan. Her people were Henriksen's; hard, God-fearing Lutheran farmers who took a deep perverse pleasure in berating and beating their children for what they called, "holy transgressions." It would be this harsh treatment at the hands of a dull and insensitive father that later helped Johanna rationalize her own bitter behavior. As a consequence, Emily's shaky opinion of her own self-worth would borrow more from the nurture than the nature camp.

Although he would never know it, Jacob Krist was one of the last of his kind; he was a blacksmith. In keeping with times and traditions, Jacob's small shop on west Main looked as if it had come straight out of a Samuel Carr painting. Along with a beloved hound stretched out on the hard-packed dirt floor, there was generally a steady stream of casual onlookers and curious children peering through the open front door. From somewhere deep in those dark shadows a worn leather bellows exhaled a steady rush of air. The furnace provided a bright orange glow that would backlight the smith as he patently labored over the anvil. An intense biting aroma of bituminous coal hung like a scratchy blanket, flavoring the air and clouding the lungs. It was here in this medieval world that Jacob Krist diligently labored at his craft.

In those days the blacksmith was as valuable to a small rural community as the doctor or the preacher. This was a time when people still repaired things, the blacksmith's stock and trade. Jacob Krist's days were mostly busy with the task of rebuilding a wooden wheel for a horse cart, mending a leather harness, or fabricating a small metal part for some broken farm machinery. His labors were honest hard work that required as much finesse as they did force. Sadly, the big man's own timidity and lack of any real business savvy meant that he never charged enough for his work, leaving the family with what they needed and little more.

For those first seventeen years, Emily Krist lived with her parents at 519 Locust Street in a small four-up/four-down. The tiny gray house sat among a warren of tiny gray houses, all evenly spaced along the rough brick road and the eastern side of the great hill. Sometimes at the end of a hard day, Jacob would haul his weary bones back up that steep grade, all the time thinking that somehow they'd gotten it wrong: shouldn't the reward come at the end of the workday and not be downhill in the morning? Since his labors were mostly solitary there was considerable time - Johanna believed too much time - to reflect on such things. Among the "things" that troubled him most was how an ignorant man could reclaim an eroding faith in an uncompromising church.

Despite his own heavy-handed religious education, one that had filled his head and heart with vivid disturbing images of heaven, hell, God and Satan, Jacob Krist discovered soon after his beautiful Emily was born that he no longer took any comfort or joy from their long Sunday rituals. Afraid to share his irreverent feelings with anyone, he silently grew more and more impatient with what he felt were the harsh and uncompromising doctrines of the Missouri Synod Lutheran Church. It wasn't that he'd lost his faith, exactly. Only this angry God (the Old Testament one that Pastor Frederickson demanded he embrace) the one that had no patience, no tolerance for man's weakness, seemed to Jacob a contradiction with what he saw as the softer more sensible New Testament message of love and understanding. His lack of confidence left him alone to struggle with the kind of questions that if spoken aloud would have caused more than just consternation between a husband and wife.

Unlike her future husband, Emily Krist was not a great reader. Because her parent's formal education had been limited to what they would pick up in six short years at a one-room school house, and, of course, the King James Bible, the two Danes remained quietly ignorant of the possibilities a public education could offer their little girl.

In her new role as a homemaker, Johanna was constantly complaining about all the demanding household labors she alone was forced to endure, chores made even more tiresome by the presence of the child. But in spite of her incessant carping, Johanna could generally be found sitting at the kitchen table with a cup of strong black coffee and the daily crossword; in the background the Motorola never stopped playing the hit-parade.

As for her silent husband, the big man truly loved the child but gladly left for the shop at dawn, rarely returning before supper time. Notwithstanding Jacob's obvious and sincere feelings for the girl, the notion of inviting Emily to visit him at work would have never crossed his mind.

Given these limited perspectives and rigid religious dogma, it should come as no surprise that Emily Krist was largely left to her own devices. It was in those quiet solitary hours that she first discovered the gift of a bold and vivid imagination, the kind of dreamy introverted perspective that often comes from being ignored. In time, Emily's stories and make-believe would become so consuming that when summoned to help with dinner or a chore, she could be found contentedly oblivious, lost in her own exquisite world far from Freeland.

Like most neighborhoods in the 1950's, the Krist's was overflowing with children; a confident sign of a postwar optimism. Emily, however, had little direct contact with any of these children. On the rare occasion that she was asked to play, she would invariably stand on the outside of the game, a timid and immobile observer hopelessly unsure of herself. Her insecurities were interpreted by many of the children as strange, and perhaps even unfriendly. She had few toys to share, and the Krist backyard was small and without the attraction of swing sets, sand piles, or slides. Even those children who were urged by their mother's to include "the little Krist girl" quickly lost interest with the mousy child who always had nothing to say.

On a bright and beautiful September morning in 1950, the children of Freeland returned for their first day of school and Emily Krist lost the pinkie from her left-hand.

Peering out from behind the dusty gray muslin curtains in the Krist's front room, Emily watched with confusion and concern as the neighborhood children inexplicably began to flee their homes.

"Where are they going," she wondered, recalling a frightening story that her mother had once told her about a piper? Unfortunately for the five-year-old Emily Albright, so little had been said about school that she had no idea what was happening, let alone that someday soon she would be expected to join them.

Once the last stragglers had passed from sight, she silently slipped out the backdoor, making sure to close it as quietly as possible, and then spritely ran across the small backyard to a tired and weather-beaten shed that sat in the corner of the lot. This small unpainted building was Emily's secret hiding place, her magic carpet and fairy castle all in one. In among the tools and equipment that Jacob Krist kept so neatly arranged on the shelves and walls, Emily had found her own perfect private world. The kind of place where no one ever came; a place where her imagination could take her wherever she wanted to go.

She was sitting on the shed's dirt floor enjoying a wonderful mindless drift when an almost imperceptible knock came upon the door. At first Emily questioned whether she'd really heard it, but when the knock happened a second time she realized that someone, or something, was outside the door.

A panic overwhelmed her so that she could not move or speak.

"What will I do if it's Mother," she wondered?

Then, slowly, the door opened a wee crack, and through that tiny slit Emily could see one pale blue eye peeking in at her.

Had her emotion's allowed her to think more clearly, she would have immediately realized that the eye could not possibly be her mother's. In the first place, this eye was blue, her mothers' were green. Then there was the issue of height, this eye was much closer to the ground than her mother's would have been.

Another moment passed, and then the door opened just far enough that Emily could see the full face of a young child boldly staring in at her. This face was almost perfectly round and sat atop a small body clothed in denim britches, a collared shirt of bright orange, and a brand new pair of Red Ball Jet shoes.

"Hello," said the round face.

Emily sat perfectly still hoping that it would go away.

"I said, hello. Can't you talk? I can."

The panic that had driven the breath from Emily's chest was slowly settling, and with its welcome release came three connected thoughts: First, it was clear that this face belonged to a girl. Second, the girl appeared to be smaller and perhaps younger than she. And third, she could talk.

As obvious as these insights might seem, Emily felt a new and startling rush of satisfaction from these important conclusions. This new pleasure and feeling of pride allowed the child to do something that she'd been unable to do before, she spoke.

"Yes, I can talk," she replied in a thin and timid whisper.

This was an enormous victory for someone who had until just that moment found it impossible to talk to strangers.

Startled but emboldened by her first sentence, Emily heard herself say, "Who are you?"

Although Emily did not welcome an intrusion into the magic world of the shed, the little moonfaced girl audaciously entered the hut and sat down on the floor right in front of her. The wooden door closed behind her, leaving the room's only light to come from a small, four-pained window directly above the workbench. The bright September sun poured through the dirty glass producing four bold splashes of pure light on the ground between the two girls.

The new girl smiled at Emily before saying, "My name is June. What's yours?

"Emily."

"Is this where you live? Where is your bed?" asked the child.

Surprised by what she thought an odd question, Emily replied, "No, I live in the house. I've got a bed upstairs, and a doll, too."

Emily Krist felt quite satisfied with that answer and lifted her chin in a bold display of confidence. The new girl nodded enthusiastically, confirming that living in a house with a bed and a doll was indeed an extraordinary accomplishment.

The two young conversationalists then embarked on a wonderful dialog which revealed that June, who had just turned four on August 2nd, lived in the green house directly behind Emily's. June went on to explain that her older brother, Phillip had just left their home on his way to the first day of school; Phillip was a third-grader and not especially kind to his little sister. To join his friends and leave his baby sister behind, Phillip had run away from June as fast as he possibly could. While trying to pursue the older boys, June found herself mixed-up and abandoned in the Krist backyard. Spotting Emily going into the shed, she felt compelled to follow hoping that this unknown girl might have a treat for her. Why she thought Emily might have a treat was never explained and struck Emily as misguided.

After explaining that she had no treats, Emily suddenly realized that she also had nothing else to say to the new girl. Afraid that her silence might cause June to go away, Emily began to look around the shed in hopes of finding something that might be of interest to this new acquaintance.

The Krist's shed was filled with garden and carpentry tools. There was a ladder, tin cans half-filled with nails and bolts, saws and hand tools, spools of wire, an old truck tire, and piles of newspapers bound tightly with a brown string. Emily feared that none of these items would work into conservation, but with a sense of desperation now crawling up her throat, she spotted the push mower hanging from a hook on the wall opposite of the door. This push mower did not have an engine, but was instead a long-handled machine with a series of blades attached to the wheels. When you pushed the mower forward the spinning wheels would turn the blades, and if the blades were kept very sharp they would cut the grass.

"My father cuts the grass with that," Emily erupted, hoping that lawn mowers, or grass, or dads, would be of some interest to June.

June thought for a moment, and then replied, "I like candy. Do you like candy?"

Emily was taken aback by the *non-sequitur*. Why would she ask about candy? It didn't have anything to do with lawn mowers, or grass, or dads.

"I said that my father cuts the grass with this."

Emily got up from the floor and walked over to point at the machine, hoping that a more direct approach would steer the conversation away from candy and back to lawn mower, and dads, and grass.

"See," Emily demonstrated, "if you spin the wheels this turns."

"Let me see," June said, getting up from the dirt floor.

As a blacksmith, Jacob Krist took the care and maintenance of tools seriously; after all, he made his meager living repairing them, cleaning them, and always keeping them razor sharp. For a push mower like this one to work properly it required that the blades have an extremely good edge. One way to test the edge was with a piece of newspaper; it was considered appropriately sharp if the paper was cut by merely running a small piece along the length of the blade. This mower had very sharp blades.

Emboldened by her new friends apparent interest, Emily proudly showed June the push mower, and even demonstrated that by turning the big wheels it would make the blades spin.

Why Emily wanted to stop the spinning blade is unimportant. What is important is that June announced, "Let me try" just as Emily reached in to grab the blades.

The second that the wheel began to move Emily knew that she had hurt her finger, but the extent of her injury wasn't immediately understood by either girl. It was the blood that made June start to scream, and there was a great deal of blood coming from the severed pinkie of Emily's left-hand.

While June shrieked and hopped wildly from one foot to the other, Emily sat down on the dirt floor gently cradling her bloody hand in her lap.

The weight of the sharp blades had been enough to cleanly, almost surgically, cut Emily's pinkie off just above the knuckle. The little stub of her former finger had fallen on the floor and now lay naked in the dirt next to the truck tire.

Frightened that her mother would be angry for the offense of playing in the shed, she could feel herself reverting back to the old Emily; the meek and timid one. Meanwhile, June had stopped screaming by sticking her right thumb into her mouth, thereby lapsing back to a behavior she had stopped just three months before. Given the situation's remarkable drama, Emily was grateful for the calm, but didn't bother to thank the girl. Instead, she sat silently in the dirt wishing that her father might unexpectedly come home to retrieve something that he needed from the shed, and finding her there would hold her in his arms and magically make everything good again. Although he'd never done this before, such was the state of Emily's anxiety.

The blood continued to flow and had soaked the front of her britches. June, who had been loudly working on her thumb, peered down into Emily's lap to inspect the damage. Without another word the little girl ran out of the door at top speed leaving poor Emily alone in the shed.

Thanks to the steady rotation of the earth, the morning sun was now in a position where a blaze of light, something like a perfect spotlight, poured through the shed's four tiny window panes, brightly illuminating the little girl and her wounded hand. For poor little Emily Albright, it seemed that God himself was shining the dazzling light of heaven upon her so that the whole world could witness her foolishness.

As the child bravely looked down on her bloody hand, she hoped that someone, even her mother, might come and take her away from this horrible place.

She began to cry.

It was not a loud or wailing kind of cry, but in silent sobs the tears flowed down her face making her mouth salty and blurring her vision.

Suddenly, the whole room was filled with light. A beautiful woman was kneeling next to her, gently touching the injured hand while quietly speaking words that Emily could not understand.

"God has sent an angel in the light," Emily thought to herself. The sense of relief was so intense that she gave herself over completely to the angel, who in this case was June's mother, Ingrid Steffens.

June had done what children always do in these situations - she ran home and got her mother. When she slammed through the back door of the Steffen's house and frantically raced into the kitchen, there was the predictable moment of confusion between mother and daughter. Eventually, Ingrid was able to interpret from the frantic broken clues that somewhere a little girl was hurt, and that it was the "mowers fault."

With an apron for a bandage, Ingrid lifted tiny Emily Krist from the dirt floor of the shed and carried her toward the house. June was sent ahead to, "Knock on the door and call for the mother."

It is certainly an unusual way to meet someone, that is, while carrying their injured child, one covered in a frightening amount of blood, into their kitchen. Still, Johanna managed a reasonable degree of open-mindedness and hospitality while holding the door open to allow Ingrid and the children to enter. Emily was surprised that the women could clean and inspect her left-hand without asking the obvious question, "Where is your finger?" That realization would not occur until all four of them were in the Krist's '48 Ford coupe and headed toward the Freeland Community Hospital. Lacking a quick or unanimous solution for locating the missing digit, it was agreed that getting Emily to the Emergency Room and stopping the bleeding was more important. Once they were there and situated it was decided that Ingrid should return with June to locate the finger.

In the 1950's, hospital's had a particular odor that was so pervasive, so dominate, that for certain people it would become the distinguishing memory of their visit. That singular remarkable smell was ether. For Emily Krist, ether will forever be synonymous with hospitals, her lost finger, and the unanticipated death of her father.

At nine-thirty in the morning, the temperature in the hospital was a pleasant seventy-three degrees. The last time Emily had been there, and she knew this only because of the incessant reminders from her mother and the women of the church, the temperature had been much warmer. But unlike that first hospital experience, on this trip she would take away several lifelong memories: memories of the fantastic whirl of people, the throbbing pain that came from what was left of her little finger, and the deep and sickening smell of the ether.

Normally, the Freeland Community Hospital's Emergency Room did not reek of ether, but only twenty minutes before Emily's arrival a farmer named Julius Olsen had been admitted to the same (the only) emergency room. While Emily and June were learning about sharp blades in the shed, Mr. Olsen was being rushed to the hospital by his youngest son, Gerald. Emily's exposure to the sickening ether occurred because Mr. Olsen's injuries were so severe that he required a heavy dose of the anesthesia before being admitted to the operating theater. The circumstance that made such a dramatic procedure necessary was that Mr. Olsen's left-hand had just been severed at the wrist when the grain auger he was operating caught the sleeve of his shirt and dragged his innocent arm into the terrible machine.

While Emily and Johanna sat through the thousand-and-one-questions associated with the detached finger of a five year-old girl, Ingrid and June had taken the Ford and were headed back to retrieve the lost appendage. With June's help they quickly located the tiny stump directly below where the mower was hanging on the wall, right next to the bald truck tire. Fifty minutes later, mother and daughter rushed into the emergency room of the Freeland Community Hospital with a blue Kleenex wrapped around the miniature digit.

What slowed the Steffens return to the hospital was that the borrowed Ford ran out of gas.

Jacob had always been the primary driver for the Krist family, and, as it was in his frugal nature to try to squeeze every last drop of gasoline out of the vehicle before going to the filling station, he had allowed the car to run perilously low on fuel. In this case, his thrift left him a lifetime - albeit a short one - of regret. He went to his grave lamenting that if he'd only kept the tank full of gas his "beautiful Emily" would have five full fingers on her left-hand.

Of course, Jacob Krist's perspective about Emily's finger was all wrong. By the time the petrified digit was retrieved and brought to the emergency room, it was useless. Even if the technology and medical skill had been available at the Freeland Community Hospital, the dirty little stub had become hard and a bit crusty around the edges. When the local surgeon - Dr. Robert LaRue, the same surgeon who had just moments before ministered to Julius Olsen and his lost hand - finally got around to unwrapping the Kleenex, what remained of Emily's little finger was more fossil than flesh.

Although it would have been impossible to have anticipated it at the time, the trauma of Emily's severed finger did offer one positive outcome: both Emily and her mother had made a new and valuable friend.

June and Emily's friendship flourished into one so special and complete that it will last a lifetime. Because Emily's small stature and shaky confidence were enough to hold her back from starting kindergarten when she was five, the two girls began their formal education the following fall, and stayed together until their graduation from Freeland High School in the spring of 1963. Emily would be the first to admit that without June she would surely have become a very different person.

As for Ingrid and Johanna, the women had little on which to build a relationship other than their children's friendship, the proximity of their homes, and a complete distaste for the Y-chromosome. It didn't matter the species, it was the very quality of being male that offended both women to the point that after the sex that produced their daughters neither would ever again offer themselves as a willing partner. The many hours that the two women spent around the Krist's kitchen table was filled by a droning condemnation for all men and the ruination that they had wrought upon the planet. The two women agreed on one thing: if some aspect of life was amiss, incorrect, broken, or poorly planned it will have been the result of a man's involvement.

As often as the two women were together, which turned out be pretty much every day, their husbands never met.

In his role as the town's trusted blacksmith, Jacob was well-known and respected by the good people of Freeland. However, among the leaders of the local business community there was a running joke about why this pleasant giant man always refused their requests to participate in civic or volunteer activities. It turns out that his strident position wasn't about any true lack of public spirit, but was more about his lifelong anxiety of interacting with people outside of his shop. Johanna's armchair psychoanalysis was only slightly off the mark; she attributed his reticence to the obvious truth that a blacksmith can never quite get his hands clean.

Ingrid's husband, David Steffens was the proverbial traveling salesman for the Homeland Mutual Insurance Company, that is, until nineteen seventy when he will open his own successful independent agency in the nearby community of Greenfield. At the time of Emily's accident he was keeping an office and small apartment in Shenandoah, Iowa, where he spent two days a week. The rest of the time, David Steffens cheerfully wandered the highways of southwest Iowa searching for new clients in need of protection from life's inevitable miseries.

Chapter Four

The Never Ending Life of Need

"Exit pursued by a bear."
The Winter's Tale - William Shakespeare

Thanks in large part to June's friendship and steady heartfelt encouragement, Emily Krist does learn to speak; in fact, when her imagination and confidence are properly mixed, Emily becomes a remarkably witty young woman. To be sure, she will always struggle with her childhood anxieties, particularly when engaged in conversation with a large group. But in this specific version of her *lucky life,* a moment of well-timed encouragement will help Emily to discover that she can channel both the creative and temperamental qualities of a fine dramatist.

It was during the fall of her senior year in high school that Emily Krist finds her muse. Thanks to the encouragement of Miss Gretchen Gleason, a bright young instructor fresh out of the teaching college at the University of Northern Iowa, Emily will be forever transformed by the fabulous opportunity of the theater.

It is Miss Gleason who recognizes Emily as a kindred spirit. Like Emily, Gretchen Gleason was also a natural target; a small mousey woman with remarkably long and thin appendages, an apparent disinterest in all things associated with make-up, and a slight stutter that most often appeared when confronted or confused. Among the pixie woman's many quirks was the curious habit of placing a piece of chalk, usually the one she'd just finished using, behind her ear. Unlike a lead pencil, this decision often left the right side of her face and hair blemished by streaks and smudges of white. The Freeland High faculty soon came to recognize those days in which Miss Gleason was active at the board.

As often happens in small rural schools, Miss Gleason was hired on short notice. It seems that the man she was to replace, Mr. Harold Ackerman had surprised the superintendent when he submitted his resignation from Freeland High School in late June. On the day he accepted the higher paying position at the larger school district of Harlan, the thirty-four year-old English teacher imagined himself moving up. Except in this version of Harold's *lucky life*, his large and remarkably loud wife, Gladys had secretly taken up with another man, a Mr. Earnest Teals, the Vice President of the Nishnabotna Savings and Loan. While the ink was still drying on Harold's new and lucrative teaching contract, Gladys was filing for divorce; so much for moving up.

As for Miss Gleason, along with her teaching responsibilities for the mostly maligned but mandatory Senior English, she was also made the faculty advisor for the Freeland High School Drama Club. It would be in this simple noble act of encouraging students to participate in an art form with which most had no experience, and therefore the uninformed preference to avoid, that Gretchen Gleason will shine the brightest.

What first alerted Miss Gleason to Emily's potential was her unanticipated interest in the Senior English class project associated with Thornton Wilder's chestnut, *Our Town*. Unlike the majority of seniors in Senior English, Emily not only came to class prepared for the daily work, but would stop by Miss Gleason's desk afterwards to inquire more deeply into the staging and production of the play. This is, of course, why teachers teach, and the blessing was not wasted on the young. Seizing the opportunity, the new Drama Teacher persuaded Emily to help her put on two student productions. That fall it was to be Thornton Wilder's, *Our Town*, and in the spring a new Freeland tradition was born by sending-up Meredith Wilson's brilliant new musical, *The Music Man*.

But what will become a far more important personal accomplishment, again attributable to the kindly encouragement of Gretchen Gleason and June Steffens, is that little Emily Krist will discover her own voice by writing and directing, what is by all accounts, a remarkable play entitled, *Once Last Summer*. It is this inspiration that brings Emily and her work to the attention of the scholarship committee at the Goodman School of Drama in Chicago, Illinois.

Several of the especially enthusiastic locals thought it unfortunate that *Once Last Summer* was written and produced in Freeland, Iowa because this truly original play saw only three performances. It was agreed by all who were lucky enough to have attended that the play was unlike anything they'd ever seen before. Admittedly, Freeland is a bit sheltered from the more daring theatrical presentations of playwright's like Beckett, Ionesco, and Foreman. Still, a well-told and dramatic story hardly requires a pedigree.

On its most simple level, *Once Last Summer* is the story of a young girl coming of age in a small town somewhere in the Midwestern United States. One could accuse Emily of mining her story fairly close to home, but somehow, "With a skill beyond her experience, the playwright builds an original and poetic device that transports her characters away from the provincial town to an utterly unique dimension. Surprisingly, Miss Krist finds a way to weave the magic of her dreams into a common language that we all can embrace.", or so said Mr. William Penn Arthur, part-time critic and arts reporter for the Omaha World Herald after seeing the third and final production of *Once Last Summer*.

The play is built in three acts, each set in a different part of the small community called Berryton. Act I takes place in the home of the protagonist, Uma. Act II is in an open field of tall grass; it is night and the stars are especially vivid. Act III is centered on a bench that is located in front of the Berryton post office; this bench also acts as the communities' bus stop.

There is a particularly effective speech midway through the third and final act where Emily's protagonist - Uma - is confronted by an angel. This angel is well known to Uma, she is her Aunt Sylvia - her mother's sister - who had died of tuberculosis just three years before.

Stage Direction: (The sound of bus brakes followed by the opening of a door and a man's voice announces: "Berryton." ANGEL, with a suitcase in her right hand, walks out (stage left), stands close to UMA who is seated on the bench with two bags at her feet; UMA has her head down looking for bus ticket in her bag. UMA stands, picks up the two bags (one in each hand) and starts toward the waiting bus nearly running into ANGEL. There is a moment of recognition in UMA's face for ANGEL.

From offstage the Driver announces "All aboard, Omaha." UMA is startled by ANGEL, and retreats behind the bench where she speaks...)

UMA: Aunt Sylvia.... is it you?

ANGEL: Yes, dear.

UMA: (Surprised) I don't know what to say. It can't be you.... can it?

UMA moves around the bench and attempts to hug ANGEL, but ANGEL quickly moves away (behind bench) and speaks...

ANGEL: Why not? Besides you're the one who called for me. Sit down for a minute, won't you? (ANGEL walks over and sits on the bench furthest from audience, UMA moves stage left, ANGEL pats on the seat to coax UMA to sit.)

UMA: I can't. I have to go. The bus will leave without me.

(The sound of a door closing and the bus pulling away can be heard.)

UMA: Oh, no. Look what you've done! That was my bus. I needed to go.

(UMA drops her bags, but continues to stare at the ANGEL who appears to be looking off into the distance, smiling broadly and enjoying the view.)

UMA: What are you looking at? Why are you doing that? Why are you here?

ANGEL: So many questions, but then you always had plenty of questions.

(ANGEL again pats on the seat motioning for UMA to sit, but she still refuses.)

ANGEL: I had forgotten how pleasant Berryton can be at this time of day. Nice place really, but then you're leaving aren't you?

(UMA now appears suspicious of the ANGEL, but not afraid. UMA kicks her bags toward the bench and then goes to sit down with her back to ANGEL and facing audience.)

UMA: I hate this place, Aunt Sylvia; it's killing me. I can't stay.

(While UMA speaks ANGEL rummages around in her bag before pulling out a tall vanilla ice cream cone which she begins (loudly) to eat. UMA still has her back to the ANGEL, but looks over her shoulder longingly at the ice cream. The ANGEL continues to enjoy the cone before finally saying...)

ANGEL: Would you like some ice cream?

UMA: No thanks. Besides, how did you get it; is there something in your bag?

ANGEL: You might say that. Sure you don't want some ice cream, its real good. I think I have strawberry.

UMA: I can't stay here – really, I can't. Strawberry? Really? That's my favorite. Okay, but only if you have strawberry. And when the next bus comes, I'm gone.

(The ANGEL reaches down in her bag and produces a strawberry ice cream cone and a napkin, then hands it to UMA; as UMA reaches out to take the cone the ANGEL pulls it away...this happens several times before the ANGEL finally gives over the cone to UMA...this should be played for laughs.)

UMA: Well, thanks. That's a neat trick. Do you have any more?

ANGEL: Not really.

(ANGEL and UMA sit in silence eating the ice cream.)

ANGEL: What makes you think that your cousin Kristine and that no-good husband of hers will take you in when you get to Omaha? You know that child of mine has been working lots of extra hours trying to get ready for the baby. Heaven knows that deadbeat won't do anything but lay around all day, drinking beer, and watching television... all the time she's five months pregnant with my only grandchild.

(ANGEL has a far-off look as she considers the grandchild she will never know.)

ANGEL: Besides, it will be late. I know for a fact that they she goes to bed early. Maybe you should call first.

UMA: I just want to stay for the night, and then tomorrow I'm moving on. She always said to visit anytime.

ANGEL: Uma, for someone so smart that is a very stupid plan. Don't you think your cousin is going be the first place that your mother calls? Then what...

UMA: I don't and she won't. Anyway, we're through. I told her that I was leaving, and all she said was "Go" and then she called me a bunch of names.

ANGEL: They say that the kids that live in California come from all over the world. I'm told that it's a very cool scene (extend the word cooooool for a laugh).

UMA: Yeah, that's where I'm going; for sure. Get out of this hick town and go someplace where I don't always feel so (long pause) stupid (pause) and sad... and lonely. (Deliberate pause between stupid... sad... lonely...).

Later in the scene...

ANGEL: Uma, I want you to try and hear what I'm about to say. (The ANGEL sits back down on the bench; UMA stands by the bus stop sign, arms crossed with her back to the ANGEL). You think no one can feel like you do. You're all alone, right? Nobody gets you. Well, that's exactly true, honey.

(UMA turns in surprise at the ANGEL's remark.)

Now, you didn't hear this from me, but here's the thing... (ANGEL looks around exaggerating that no one is listening.)

People are God's big mistake. (Dramatic pause) It's true. See, there is no other creature on this planet that can feel as bad as a human. You ever seen a robin act the way you're acting? You won't ever see a cat carryin' on like that. How 'bout an ant; you think an ant would ever get himself worked up like this?

You take all that guilt, and fear, and hate, and then you spread it around real good so that everybody gets a little taste, and pretty soon all you've got are problems.

Want to know what's really funny? (UMA shrugs her shoulders.) Well, I'll tell you what's funny. You know right from wrong, but you don't do anything about it.

And HE's all the time lookin' the other way. HE says it's because you know you're gonna die and that's what makes you so crazy.

Well, some of us think that's taking the forgiveness thing a little too far.

But Uma, it's not as hopeless as it seems. You've got one thing going for you, you've got each other. You won't be here long, so try looking for the good things.

Sorry for the bad news kid, but there's no secret answer that's going to make your life work out. There's just you and about four billion others, all trying to make sense out of something that doesn't make any sense."

Once Last Summer ran for three nights. With each performance the size of the audience grew, until on Saturday additional chairs were needed to accommodate the overflow. Part of what inspired this remarkable turnout was that word had gotten round town that there was something quite different, maybe too different, going on at the local high school. Then there was the additional surprise and confusion about its author; no one would have ever predicted such a remarkable success from such an unlikely source. The little Emily Krist that people thought they knew seemed incapable of conjuring such a story, especially the part about the free-spirited angel, the one who apparently had no problem questioning the Lord's divine purpose.

But *Once Last Summer* had more than just a cryptic angel, it had merit. In fact, on Saturday night, along with the one hundred-fifty locals and the World Herald reporter, the sanctimonious Pastor Fredrickson could be conspicuously seen taking a seat in the front row. Even he seemed to approve of the drama, going so far as to acknowledge the successful play during his announcements at worship service the next morning.

"I believe congratulations are in order to Miss Emily Krist. As you may know, she has written and directed a play for our local high school. A rather bold and provocative effort that, I must say, came as a bit of a surprise. Still, it is an original and thoughtful program, especially considering the family's recent tragic loss. Emily, may the Lord continue to inspire all your efforts."

The passing reference to a "tragic loss" was not lost on anyone attending the ten-thirty worship service. Though Pastor Fredrickson's comments were certainly well-intended, they did not have a positive effect upon Emily Krist. Truth be told, his remarks stole what little joy she had gained from his acknowledgement.

Until that very moment, Emily Krist had purposefully put away her "loss", and had instead focused on her new found passion. Through the long and challenging five months that it took to write and produce *Once Last Summer*, Emily would come to understand that something new and important was happening in her life, something that seemed to give it purpose and meaning. For the first time, ever, she felt satisfied. Even though it would take some time to fully appreciate, one thing had become clear: her play's passion and soul had been inspired by the chocking fear left behind by her father's unexpected death.

After the accident that severed her finger at the knuckle, Emily and her mother would never grow any closer. Emily believed that her mother was a "harsh and small-minded woman who only tolerated her time here on Earth," while Johanna regarded her daughter as a "never ending life of need." Then a mere eight months before Emily's remarkable success of *Once Last Summer*, both mother and daughter were confronted with a life-changing calamity when Jacob Krist was introduced to the choir invisible.

Jacob was a powerful man who often worked in his blacksmith shop for twelve hours at a stretch. In this version of his *lucky life*, Jacob ignorantly suffers from a proud Danish lifestyle, one that includes a diet rich with gravy and sweets. It is this unhealthy regimen that puts a tourniquet around his weak and obstructed heart (technically speaking, a myocardial infarction) strangling the giant man of blood and oxygen, and leaving him in a heap on the dirt floor of his shop. The trusty Labrador, Gert was found lying calmly beside her master, her head resting quietly on his lifeless chest.

As one of *lucky life's* countless ironies it will be Gerald Olsen who discovers Jacob's dead body prostrate on the floor. It had been eleven years since that sunny day in September when his father Julius had lost his hand in the elevator accident at the exact same time Emily was losing her finger to the blades of the lawn mower. Since that day, the pragmatic Dane's frequently, and without any outward signs of prejudice or personal remorse, took advantage of the blacksmith's skills by having Jacob repair their damaged farm implements; this included the very auger that Julius' hand had broken during his unfortunate entanglement.

In the years to come, the Olsen's same practical perspective caused a uniquely personal and disturbing situation for young Emily. Because the Olsen's and Krist's both attended Saint Johns, Emily and Julius would often see one another at Sunday services. On those mornings, Mr. Olsen would always acknowledge the anniversary of their common amputations by a knowing nod to the young girl and a friendly wave of his stump. Although she was always respectful, Emily considered this behavior both unnecessary, and a bit creepy.

In those months following the death of her husband, Johanna took little comfort from either her daughter or friend Ingrid. The winter had come especially early and by Christmas southern Iowa was covered with snow that wouldn't leave the ground until mid-April. The relentless grey skies and colorless fields of that bleak Midwestern winter were perfect for the two now solitary women as they grieved for the only thing that they ever had in common.

Chapter Five

From Freeland to Chicago

"Life can only be understood backwards; but it must be lived forwards."
Søren Kierkegaard

June Steffens and Emily Krist stood holding hands while anxiously anticipating the arrival of the Greyhound bus for Chicago. It was Monday, August 25, 1963. From across the empty street, Brenda Lee's popular and pitiful tune *Break It to Me Gently* could be heard lilting out of the Krist's family Ford station wagon. While the girl's stood fidgeting among their bags, Johanna Krist sat quietly, she imagined stoically, behind the wheel considering the woeful tune.

"Break it to me gently; let me down the easy way.
Make me feel you still love me, even if it's just for one more day."

Suddenly, June was standing beside the open car window. With a tremendous burst of energy and enthusiasm, the young girl announced, "Thanks for the ride, Mrs. Krist."

Just fifteen minutes before June and Ingrid Steffens were saying their final good-bye's in the driveway of their home. Johanna, of course, thought them too long, but to help the girls with their heavy luggage she had offered to drive them the three blocks down to the Post Office/bus stop. Now robbed of her thoughts by the girl's intrusion, Johanna smiled back, and then, with what seemed to June a rather melodramatic effort, opened her car door and slowly got out.

"Break it to me gently, so my tears won't fall too fast.
If you must go then go slowly, let me love you to the last."

June had scampered back to where Emily was still standing in front of the bus stop's bench. Their bags were scattered around their feet as they clutched their purses and each other in anticipation. Off in the distance, all three could hear the sound of the bus as it turned the corner and started down Main.

Johanna reached out for her daughter with the hope that something special and lasting might happen. Emily returned the awkward gesture with an uncomfortable hug and a meek smile of farewell.

"Don't get off the bus until you get to Chicago," Johanna warned her daughter. "Sit next to each other. And try not to talk to boys."

As the bus came to a stop in front of the Post Office, Johanna understood that in a few seconds she would be completely and forever alone. This cruel inevitable day had been on her calendar for eighteen years, and now it was here.

The driver climbed down the steps to open the large hatch on the side of the bus, where he then quickly stowed the girl's luggage. June offered a final wave and a smile to Johanna before she climbed the steps to disappear down the aisle.

"I'm happy for you Emily. Do good work. Be safe."

"Thanks, Mom. I will. I'll write as soon as we get there."

From inside the bus, the driver asked, "You ready, Miss?"

"Yes," she answered, offering a final tiny farewell wave.

Johanna stood by the door anticipating, but the girl did not look back.

The door closed.

With a loud roar the bus pulled out onto Main and headed east toward the highway, the one that would take them to Chicago and beyond.

Johanna stood watching until the bus was well out of sight. The nagging *voice* from within took advantage of the moment to remind her that the little girl had surpassed both of their expectations. Without any help from either of them, the child had a chance at a life completely outside of their own experiences and understanding. How Emily had found herself was a mystery that they jealously coveted but would never discover.

Supporting herself with her hand on the hood of the car, Johanna Krist's pride was all that kept her from crying.

Out of the window, Brenda Lee sang,

> *"Break it to me gently; give me time to ease the pain.*
> *Love me just a little longer, 'cause I'll never love again."*

Chapter Six

A Premier at the Goodman

"It was love at first sight, at last sight, at ever and ever sight."
Lolita - Vladimir Nabokov

It was Saturday, April 21, 1966, and Charles Albright had been summoned by his grandmother, Lillian Campbell.

"It's for your own good, Charles," she told him. "You need to get out more often."

Her handwritten invitation had instructed him to arrive at her apartment for "cocktails at five-thirty." The note also stressed that he should, "Dress for the theater. A tuxedo is not required."

After Otto Campbell's death from lung cancer in 1955, Lillian Campbell sold the family's North Shore estate in Evanston and retired to a lakeside apartment at 880 North Lake Shore Drive. Sometimes known as the Glass House, Lillian's building is both an architectural masterpiece and one of the city's more prominent landmarks; its location and distinctive design has made it one of the most photographed buildings in all of Chicago. Her corner veranda, which lies directly off the perfectly appointed living room, offers a breathtaking view of both Lake Michigan and the city skyline.

Lillian Campbell loved to entertain; her strategic move into one of Chicago's most dramatic properties would only improve her already considerable social standing. As both an enthusiast for the arts and a potential major donor, Lillian eagerly accepted the many invitations to join the city's elite cultural boards, including her greatest love, the Art Institute of Chicago. Thanks to her considerable largess and stupendous view of the lake, Lillian Campbell rarely found an invitation to one of her fundraising party's declined.

Checking his watch as he entered the Glass House lobby (5:28 P.M.), Charles allowed the bellman to open the doors.

"Miss Campbell is expecting you," he said, motioning toward the elevator while offering a sympathetic smile. "Eighteen," he reminded Charles with a tip of his cap.

Stepping off the elevator and into the hallway, he could see that the door to his grandmother's apartment was open. In anticipation of his arrival, a small black woman in a prim, light blue dress was standing just inside the doorway.

"Good evening, Mr. Albright. Miss Campbell asked for you to wait in the living room. She'll be with you in a minute." Then closing the door behind him, she asked, "May I get you something to drink?"

"Thank you, Mary," Charles replied, walking through the door and into the hallway. "What is she having?"

"She asked me to chill some champagne, but I can get most anything you'd like."

Charles would have "liked" a bottle of beer, but here at the Glass House beer would have probably been frowned upon.

Charles Albright had received his graduate degree from the Northwestern School of Business a year ago in May; his diligent work there had made him *cum laude*. As a graduation present, Grandmother Lillian had insisted on giving him a "Soiree, one that will be attended by all the right people."

For the occasion, she enthusiastically opened her apartment to a group of her closest personal friends, including many of Chicago's social and political elite. Charles lasting recollection of the evening was the amazing cross-section of handsome confident people who all quickly found their way to the bar.

"Judge Brandies, allow me to introduce you to my grandson."

"Charles, let me present William Downe, the President of the Chicago National Bank."

"Oh, you must meet Alan Ryerson of the Ryerson Gallery."

"Congressman Sawyer, I'd like you meet one of Chicago's up-and-coming young men."

"Maya, you must meet my talented grandson."

And on, and on, and on it went until the crowd of privileged people had consumed all that they wanted; because, after all, enough is rarely enough.

"Charles, my boy, it is so good of you to join me this evening. How are you?"

At seventy-two, Lillian Campbell could still make an entrance. Dressed impeccably in a black Dior dress and heels, it was obvious that his grandmother had both style and nice legs.

"Mary," she commanded in a pleasant but precise voice.

When the maid returned from the adjoining room, Lillian motioned toward the table and the two crystal champagne glasses. Planned to perfection, the Veuve Clicquot had been opened moments before his arrival. The two tall, thin Waterford champagne flutes were filled with the golden liquor and set alive by a thousand tiny effervescent bubbles.

"To us," Lillian announced before taking a polite swallow.

Setting her glass down on the table, she motioned for Charles to join her on the sofa. As he took his seat on the long and rather hard piece of modern furniture, Lillian casually glanced over in Mary's direction. From her wordless directive the housekeeper returned to the kitchen, immediately producing a tray of assorted hors d'oeuvres, which she then lightly placed on the glass coffee table.

It was well known among both her friends and detractors that Lillian Campbell was as skillful at repartee as she was interior decorating. Although Charles didn't really mind their exchanges, he understood that they would be mostly one-sided with his grandmother asking the questions, ones centered on his work, the opportunity to improve his position in the community, and his mother. Charles preferred the latter topic.

He had just placed a cracker covered with a remarkably pungent white spread and dotted with tiny red berries into his mouth, when Grandmother Lillian announced, "I'm so pleased that you could join me this evening. As a Board member, I'm compelled to attend these sorts of things, but I thought that since we'll be seeing the works of young people, people more your age, you might find it interesting. Who knows, perhaps we'll meet the next Chekov tonight."

Under the pretext of fulfilling her responsibilities as an Art Institute board member, Lillian Campbell attended many openings, galas, and community functions. Within her considerable social circles, she was generally recognized as a great lover of the arts; in fact, she'd made a career of proving it with both her time and checkbook. But it was also true that Lillian Campbell liked going to places where she would be recognized. Thanks to her prominent position and personal ability to make significant financial contributions, the staff and artists she met were always anxious to fawn and dote upon her. Charles had twice before been asked to accompany his grandmother to openings at the museum, and in both cases it was clear that she was in her element: knowledgeable, confident, and unassailable.

Tonight they were to attend the premier of three, one-act plays by promising students at the Goodman School of Drama.

The Goodman Theater and School of Drama had been made possible by the great and protracted sorrow of Erna and William Goodman. Their son, Kenneth Sawyer Goodman was a playwright and producer of some modest success. But, unfortunately, during the influenza epidemic of 1918, the young Kenneth died. In this version of Ken's *lucky life*, his untimely demise rather dramatically confirms the well-known cliché that money can't buy everything.

As a condition of the Goodman's substantial generosity, it was agreed that the theater would honor Kenneth and carry the family's name; to insure

42

its longevity, the school and theater would be professionally managed, operated, and ultimately owned by the Art Institute of Chicago.

Curtain was at 7:30.

To insure that she received a proper reception, Lillian Campbell had directed one of the secretaries at the Art Institute to inform the Dean of the Goodman School, Doctor Richard Schnakel, that she and a guest would be attending the evening's performances. This last minute news of an unexpected dignitary, especially one as important as Lillian Campbell, had sent Dr. Schnakel into a heightened state of anxiety, which by association left the faculty dreading any interaction with either Dr. Schnakel or the unknown big shot.

As the Yellow cab (#822) pulled up in front of the Goodman Theater, Lillian reached over the seat to hand the driver a twenty dollar bill for a twelve-fifty fare, adding, "I would like to have you return for us at precisely ten o'clock. Will that be possible?"

The driver, an extremely short thin man with a Middle Eastern caste, nodded his head in apparent affirmation, but said nothing. As he got out of the cab and went round to open his grandmother's door, Charles considered the possibility that the cab driver might not speak English, thereby making the request for a ten o'clock pickup uncertain. To further amplify his concerns, he had no more than closed the cab door when #822 hit the gas and sped west on Randolph. Charles considered sharing his doubts, but by that point Lillian Campbell was already moving with considerable alacrity up the stairs toward the theater's main entrance.

The moment that grandmother and grandson entered the Goodman Theater through its great, gilded front doors, they were confronted by two polite and highly energetic students. The youngsters, a tall bony boy in need of a haircut, and a stunning strawberry blond, who by her every movement made it clear that she did not wish to be seen with the boy, wore identical green ribbons with the word "HOST" imprinted in gold upon the lapels of their matching blue blazers. Dr. Schnakel had left specific written instructions for the two of them to, "Wait for our VIP's near the ticket office, and then escort them with as little conversation as possible to the theater's Green Room."

After this properly inflated welcome, Dr. Schnakel's strategy called for his timorous faculty, armed only with their advanced degrees and a steadily warming plastic cup of cheap chardonnay, to engage the distinguished patron with clever small-talk about the school and the student's productions. At the time, no one paid much attention when a small and rather distracted young woman offered Lillian Campbell "a glass of wine, perhaps?" Lillian took a hard look at the girl, the bottle she was holding, and, of course, politely declined.

For the record, it was at that specific moment that Emily Krist and Charles Albright, our protagonist's future parents, meet for the first time.

As a form of student recognition the Goodman School made a habit each spring of hosting a special event using the staid title: **The Goodman School of Drama Presents: An Evening of One-Act Plays**

The commission to write these small one-act plays was awarded in February to "graduating seniors with great potential." This meant that the recipient needed to write, cast, and direct their play in approximately sixty days. Not surprisingly, the quality of the final work was commensurate with the abbreviated time to produce.

Emily Krist was one of the three recipients of the 1966 Goodman School of Drama's high honor. As a part of the evening's festivities, she and the other winners were invited to the Green Room to dispense wine and administer cheese to the attending dignitaries and faculty. Dr. Schnakel considered this one of the prize's "perks", and even insisted that each of the winners join him for a "brief, forty-five minute discussion" on how to make the most of this "important opportunity." Now just minutes before curtain, Emily nervously wandered among the small group, doling out the wine while anxiously anticipating the presentation of her one-act entitled, *Just Small Enough.*

Long before *Just Small Enough* went up there were already serious concerns among the Goodman School of Drama's prestigious faculty selection committee. It seems that after reading the first draft, many of the professors, including Dr. Schnakel, were left with considerable confusion and concern for Emily's concept.

"Why, for this prestigious opportunity," they asked, "did you choose to produce a children's play, particularly one that features such an extraordinary character?"

Dr. Schnakel and his staff were partly right, Emily had conceived *Just Small Enough* in the form of a children's play. It was the author's hope that by using a parable it might offer an interesting quality to her narrative and liven up the stage work. As far as the "extraordinary character" was concerned, the play's most interesting creature was a beautiful and an utterly cynical fairy named Tomorrow. In the disparaging words of the committee, "Your lead character gives an ominous and adult-quality to the narrative, something you may wish to reconsider."

In this case, the committee was right; unlike Mary Martin's charming Peter Pan who had gracefully flown across the Broadway stage and into the hearts of America, Tomorrow was a fairy of a very different persuasion. Throughout the fifty-minute production, Tomorrow would regularly descend from above, sitting in a cross-legged yoga position, where she then hovered

44

menacingly over the other characters (a mule, a chicken, a cat, a young boy and an elderly grandmother) while vigorously pontificating in exaggerated Shakespearian-tones about the evil nature of mankind - particularly the man in mankind.

The following line of dialog offers a glimpse of what concerned the selection committee. Here, Tomorrow considers the future relationship between the chicken and the cat:

Tomorrow: "It seems our grand and foolish cock has once again misjudged the fair pussy."

The Goodman Theater and School of Drama was not, as a matter-of-course, opposed to biting satire or provocative drama. Over the years, this venerable cultural institution had offered a wide variety of important - and less important - leading-edge plays, including: *Pal Joey, Fanny*, and *Carmen Jones*. However, the confidence of the school's selection committee had been shaken by what they considered "references inappropriate for the intended audience." These pointed comments, and the overall lack of support from her instructors, had seriously damaged Emily's already shaky confidence. Earlier that night as she and June prepared to leave the apartment for the theater, Emily informed her faithful friend that the play would either be recognized for the qualities that she knew were obvious, at least to everyone but the selection committee, or else she would be returning to Freeland on the Sunday morning bus.

There remains a long standing disagreement between Emily and Charles over the question of which of them noticed the other first. Emily's claim is largely based upon the considerable shadow cast by Lillian Campbell. What seems indisputable is that, in spite of her anxieties about the premier of *Just Small Enough*, Emily Krist certainly would have remembered Lillian Campbell's imperturbable demeanor and utter disinterest in her warm chardonnay. Emily contends that although it was Lillian who first captured her attention, she did experience a passing awareness of a short but handsome young man who seemed in some way to be affiliated with the grand dame.

Charles perspective was much simpler; he thought then, and always will, that Emily Krist was a "beauty." "Naturally," goes his claim, "I would remember that face."

Grandmother Lillian's curt dismal of the wine was all that was needed for the young playwright to quickly move on to another prospect. It seems likely that had Emily Krist understood the notion of a *lucky life,* she would have welcomed the opportunity to visit one different from the one she was currently living. Instead, Emily was now suffering those final awful moments of anticipation before her art was made public. For the past eight weeks, she had dedicated herself to the details of making *Just Small Enough* worthy of its premier upon the fabled boards of the Goodman Theater. Now as the chimes gently sounded, drawing the audience to their seats, Emily was left standing alone in the Green Room doorway, still holding the pathetic chardonnay, and wondering if anyone would miss her if she left?

Later that evening on the drive back to the Glass House, neither Grandmother Lillian nor Charles could recall much about either of the first two plays. It was instead the remarkable experience of seeing *Just Small Enough* and meeting the playwright afterwards that would stay with the two of them for the remainder of their lives.

Chapter Seven

#822

"Gravitation is not responsible for people falling in love."
Albert Einstein

Just Small Enough had only the one performance.

Though all the actors had delivered their lines and hit their marks perfectly, the lighting and sound were impeccable, even the program spelled everyone's name properly, the play was not good.

In spite of what had seemed like such an important idea back in April, one that Emily felt sure was chock-full of mature literary merit and deep social significance, in the end proved a titanic disaster. The notion of using a children's parable to project this screeching feminist doctrine was both bad theater, and in the eyes of some a setback to the cause. The absurd jargon and phony delivery made it obvious to even the most impartial observer that the play was not entertaining. Instead of a free-thinking spirit that offered enlightened prose and amusing anecdotes, Tomorrow comes across as a boorish nubile; a malcontent who floats precariously above the audience shrieking an amalgamation of rambling feminist dogma that ran the gamut from Joan of Arc to Betty Friedan. Her noisy rhetoric even went so far as to include some of Johanna and Ingrid's angry observations concerning the ruination of the planet by the men that they had married. Later that night in her letter home to her mother, Emily confessed, "I tried my best, Mother. And though people were mostly nice, I think I might have tried a little too hard."

Indeed, Emily had bravely attempted something that, in this case, just didn't fit her very well.

While the evening's dignitaries and guests would leave the theater mostly confused, the arrogant selection committee knew, of course, that *Just Small Enough* was doomed even before the curtain went up. In fairness to Emily's considerable talent and efforts, there were a small number of women who found Tomorrow's candor mildly amusing; in fact, there was one young lady who was so moved by the production that when the curtain fell she energetically jumped to her feet, stomping and applauding with overzealous gusto. It was only after she realized that no one shared her enthusiasm that the now red-faced girl quietly shrank back into her seat to wait for an appropriate moment when she might inconspicuously slide out the side door.

In the end, most women found the play misguided, while the men were glad that it only lasted fifty minutes; a lecture from a feminist fairy on a string seemed a waste of a perfectly good Saturday night.

The curtain calls were the shortest in the Goodman's storied history. Afterwards, Emily made her way backstage to offer her thanks to each of the cast and crew, hoping that they didn't sound too much like condolences. She had even prepared a short speech, one that congratulated them "for their hard work and cooperation in making *Just Small Enough* a great success," but once among the crew and actors, she realized that such a speech was not necessary. Unlike Emily and the exuberant young woman in the audience, her classmates were now busy tearing down sets or washing off their makeup. They had, in fact, paid little attention to the play or the audience's reaction; for them, *Just Small Enough* was more a matter of academics than art. Students at the Goodman School were expected to participate in their peers productions and were graded by the producer on the quality of their efforts. A triumph or flop meant little; it was, after all, the final grade that counted.

June sat patiently alone in the back row and waited for her friend to appear.

Over the years, she'd faithfully been to everything that Emily had done as a writer, director, or actor, and even though she'd read some of the script, she really had no idea what the play was about.

"I loved it when the fairy kept coming down out of the sky," she told her friend as they walked through the Goodman lobby. "Was the actress, what was her name, Tomorrow, was she scared to fly around on that thing?"

Emily was not entirely surprised by June's silly questions, it felt like her friend had been asking silly questions since that first time they'd met back in her father's shed. But there was still a sizable crowd in the lobby waiting for cabs or rides, and under the circumstances she preferred not to be recognized by any of these people. With her head down, she grabbed June by the hand and began moving quickly through the crowd. The theater clock above the box office window read: **10:12**.

"Let's go home. I've had enough for one day."

Outside and near the street, Dr. Richard Schnakel had managed to gain a death grip on Lillian Campbell's right wrist. So firm and committed was his hold that that the question of how she might extricate herself from the excitable nincompoop was causing serious concern.

"Like I was saying, Mrs. Campbell, it is always such an honor when you can join us. We're so grateful to you, and all that you do for the Goodman. You know your presence here means so very much to these young people."

48

"Yes, well, thank you, Doctor. Charles, have you seen that cab?"

To avoid any further conversation with the smarmy Dr. Schnakel, Charles was now looking back down Randolph toward the lake, all the time hoping that cab #882 would magically reappear and take them away from this ridiculous man. Charles knew from personal experience that in Lillian Campbell's world cab drivers, waiters, and civil servants gladly performed their tasks in a timely and courteous manner. He also recognized that in everyone else's world they were cab drivers, waiters, and civil servants.

"I don't know where he is, Grandmother. Perhaps, Dr. Schnakel can have someone call another cab. Wait a minute."

Across the street in front of the Chicago City Hall, an empty Checker cab had pulled out onto Randolph and was heading east on the busy four-lane. Hoping to catch the driver's attention, Charles suddenly turned to jog a few steps in the cab's direction when he crashed headlong into (yes) Emily Krist.

Ignoring the hectic street traffic and theater patrons, Charles politely bent down to offer his assistance and a strenuous apology to the unknown victim. Still slightly confused, Emily Albright looked up at the stranger only to realize that the contents of her tired brown briefcase (which included: her directing notes, a well-worn bus schedule, a copy of Richard Brautigan's, *In Watermelon Sugar*, a package of Dentyne chewing gum, $3.58 in change, a tube of Chapstick, and the master script for *Just Small Enough*) were now strewn across the sidewalk.

Fortunately for the future of the Albright's, the Checker cab driver either ignored Charles or didn't spot his exaggerated efforts to hail him. Instead, the two were granted their moment, the one universal moment which has inspired great art, won and lost massive fortunes, and set man against man - brother against brother.

As Phebe would wonder in *As You Like It*, "Who ever loved that loved not at first sight?"

Once Dr. Schnakel realized that it was Emily Krist, the author and director of the evening's problematic finale, who had caused this alarming collision, a collision with one of his theater's most important patrons, no less, the energetic administrator instantly jumped into action by first releasing his death grip on Lillian Campbell's wrist, and then spastically prancing over to try to assist with Charles' rescue. Charles needed no help from the clumsy Dr. Schnakel.

"I am terribly sorry. I wasn't watching where I was going," Charles offered as he bent to help Emily up from the ground.

Caught completely off-guard by Charles mad dash for the Checker cab, Emily Krist now found herself sitting on her backside trying to gather her wits and belongings. June, who had spent a good portion of her life a step or two behind Emily, was now running back toward the Goodman to capture a runaway orange that had also escaped from Emily's bag.

"My goodness, Miss Krist, you should be more careful than to barge into one of our guests," Dr. Schnakel shouted at Charles back.

While Emily and Charles were enjoying their moment, Grandmother Lillian had had enough; she was tired and wanted badly to be shed of these people and the evening.

"Charles," she asked with a noticeable measure of impatience, "is the girl injured?

"I don't think so, Grandmother. Are you hurt?" Charles inquired with what he hoped was not a ridiculous smile.

In spite of her special moment with Charles, and Dr. Schnakel's unkind remarks, once she heard the phrase "Is the girl injured?" Emily Krist instantly remembered Lillian Campbell; she would, in fact, never be able to forget Lillian Campbell.

So the five actors stood for a rather long and protracted moment, each considering their own unspoken desires. Lillian Campbell desperately wanted cab #822 to reappear and take her away from the irritating Dr. Richard Schnakel. Charles, on the other hand, preferred to linger and learn more about the attractive woman that he had just knocked to the ground, the one with which he had shared a moment like he'd never known before. Although intrigued by the kindness of the man, and confused by her moment with him, Emily also knew that she was frightened by the imposing woman in the Dior. Though it would be many years before she would understand the unlimited opportunities that a *lucky life* can offer, in this particular version she sincerely wished that she'd just stayed home. While sweet June Steffens, the one person who had always been best at reading Emily and encouraging her, even when she was least brave, stood silently beside her friend certain in her heart that this was a special night, one that was meant to be.

Cab #822 was driven by Fahran Loond, a twenty-two year-old Afghan refugee who had been in the States for a grand total of sixty-eight days. As a fresh immigrant to Chicago, this driver-émigré had an extremely limited understanding of how to assist his Western patrons, especially a wealthy, heavy-tipping white woman. Other than the pleasure he got from driving his rattletrap machine at the highest rate of speed possible around the pitted streets of the Chicago loop, there was precious little that his previous experience could offer his new clientele; after all, there were very few tips in Kandahar, and even fewer white women.

His job as a driver-for-hire began two years before when he briefly served in that capacity to Sant Fateh Singh. Sant Fateh was a notorious Sikh holy man, who in his heyday had gained people's attention with his loud and frequent pronouncements. The most notable of these declarations claimed that should his followers fail to support the free Punjabi Suba movement, he, Sant Fateh Singh, would be joining Allah through the unpleasant process of self-immolation. In spite of the drama inherent in such a pledge, this would not have been the first time that Singh had played such a theatrical card. Apparently, whenever Singh's ability to draw an audience waned he would liven-up the act with even louder and more flamboyant declarations. Over time, some of his less-patient supporters began to secretly yearn for him to finally go through with the deed, but, of course, he never lit the match. He did, however, visit Loond's hometown of Kandahar, where for an afternoon Fahran drove him around the city in his father's 1958 Ford.

As the "new kid in town," Loond came to rely almost exclusively upon his American relatives to help untangle the complex ins-and-outs of this bizarre new culture. One those relatives, Delbar Chowdhari, a mildly challenged cousin who also drove for the Yellow Cab Company (#308), was especially free with his dubious counsel. For example, before his first day on the job, Delbar recommended that should a fare "take on a loud voice, or complain, you should click your tongue and take no shit." So far this flawed advice had provided uniformly poor results.

As far as the wealthy, heavy-tipping white woman was concerned, Fahran Loond was competent enough to return to the Goodman Theater at the agreed upon hour of ten o'clock, he was just not particularly punctual. So it was at ten twenty-two when his Yellow cab (#822) stopped in front of the Goodman Theater, precisely where he'd left his fare two hours and fifty-two minutes earlier. Fahran Loond reached over and flicked off the light switch indicating to anyone seeking a cab that his was now engaged.

In those three minutes between the time Charles Albright accidentally leveled Emily Krist and the arrival of cabdriver Loond in #822, a significant amount of both real and imagined information was shared between the two of them. Despite Dr. Schnakel's less than enthusiastic introduction, Charles had cleverly deduced that this young woman was not only a student at the Goodman School, but she was also the author and director of one of the evening's plays.

It was this conclusion that the anxious administrator feared the most. As far as he was concerned, there was no reason to draw attention to the fact that the school's most prestigious award had just been undermined by a play of such obvious inferior quality, not to mention the very real possibility that this theatrical travesty could affect future financial contributions from someone as obviously cultured and intelligent as Lillian Campbell.

This arrogant perspective turns out to be another of Dr. Schnakel's blunders; Lillian Campbell was anything but a harsh critic, particularly of new or experimental ideas created by young people. Lillian fervently believed that most contemporary art was by definition, "self-indulgent imitation." At cocktail parties or galas, she could be heard to say, "When it comes to modern art, there's no such thing as plagiarism. It is from the forgeries of the naïve that we'll find the next new ideas, the provocative one's that will likely never know an audience." Savoring her role as both a patron to the arts and as a board member of the Art Institute, she saw it as her personal responsibility to encourage young people to strike out, to be bold and innovative, knowing full well that most of their work would soon be disparaged by people twice their age and with half their talent.

It was during those three fateful minutes - the time between the knockdown and the cabs arrival - that the astute Lillian Campbell recognized that this young woman, someone who had clearly captivated her grandson while managing to offend most of the evening's theater patrons, was the artist who had created the Goodman School of Drama's award-winning production, *Just Small Enough.*

As they turned the corner on Lake Shore Drive and began to head south toward the Glass House, Lillian Campbell asked, "Did you inquire after the girl's phone number?"

There was a brief debate between Charles *cum laude* brain and his mind your own business brain about whether it was in his best interests to truthfully answer such an intrusive question.

"No," the *cum laude* side replied, "but I was thinking that she was pretty, and interesting, and that maybe I would try to find a way to give her a call sometime."

"If it would help you, I could have someone phone Dr. Schnakel's office and inquire?"

"That's okay," replied the mind you own business brain. "I can take care of it myself."

By the middle of the next week, Charles had hatched so many convoluted plans for getting Emily Krist's phone number that he was beginning to regret not accepting his grandmother's offer. Out of frustration, he finally committed to a clumsy multistep dance with the Goodman School's administrative staff.

It began with a series of poorly played lies. Charles, masquerading as the Executive Director of the Richardson Playhouse in Terre Haute, called the Goodman's administrative offices claiming that he had "heard of Ms. Krist's wonderful play, and needed to contact her regarding a possible position with the theater."

The secretary with whom Charles spoke, a Miss Jane Mansfield (really, Jane Mansfield) was dubious of the caller's true intent from the get-go.

In one of this *lucky life's* amusing ironies, Miss Mansfield had been born in Greencastle, Indiana, a small community fifteen miles from Terre Haute. She was well aware that there was no Richardson Playhouse in Terre

Haute; in fact, there was no playhouse in Terre Haute, Indiana. Still, the youthful voice and lack of guile had betrayed Charles so thoroughly that Miss Mansfield had no reservation suggesting, "You might try the phone book, honey."

Chapter Eight

Thinking What I'm Thinking

All You Need is Love.
John Lennon

To say that Emily Krist was surprised by Charles Albright's phone call asking if she'd like to go on a date would be to understate her reaction.

Emily Krist looked considerably younger than someone who was twenty-one years-old. Her petite size and youthful face often led people to mistake her for a teenager, a very young teenager. Although she was now old enough to legally purchase liquor, the only time that she'd ever tried had proven to be such a disaster that it permanently affected both her self-confidence and shopping habits.

Earlier that fall, Emily had enjoyed a small personal triumph in her *lucky life* when she was cast as Juliann Tesman, the aunt in Ibsen's classic *Heda Gabler*. Thanks to their high spirits and poor judgement, Emily and June innocently agreed to the backstage pleadings of a cute first-year boy who desperately wanted to accompany them to the cast party. It was this self-centered underage boy who had urged the girls to buy a bottle of wine.

The problems started in the check-out line of Dudek's Grocery. Dudek's was a convenient and unremarkable little market on the corner of Armitage and Halsted, just a few doors down from the girl's apartment. Although the wine was especially cheap, it still cost more than Emily had in her pocket book. While rummaging through her purse, she suddenly realized that not only did she lack the funds but also had no way to prove her age. In a panic, she remembered that her seldom-used driver's license was at the bottom of her spare purse back at the apartment.

The grocery clerk, a tall Polish man whose name tag read: **Wita Brodzik**, was now eyeing the three children with humorless suspicion; the boy, of course, had no money. Flustered and confused, Emily began to stammer an unintelligible explanation for why she had no proof of her identity to a man who spoke little English. As her world imploded, it was June who again graciously stepped forward to provide the needed money, a valid form of ID, and sweet comfort to her fretful friend.

As for the party and the boy, his dreams of a grand entrance went unrealized. The wine - a sugary New York Riesling - was so saccharine that the girls gladly bestowed the bottle upon the scheming freshman. In a foolish effort to appear the sophisticate, he quickly consumed what was left of the syrup. Although his social status could plummet no lower, his losing battle with the cheap liquor would leave him permanently branded with the humiliating nickname, Barfy.

Charles purposefully arrived early for their first date, hoping that her roommate June would be home alone and conveniently available to answer his questions about Emily's history and interests. She did not need much encouragement.

"Well, Emily's always been small, but she's so kindhearted," June began. "I think she's pretty, even if she does have thin hair. She's smart, I guess. Oh, yes, she reads, but she likes movies better. What's her favorite color? I think it's blue. She can't really cook anything, but her favorite meal is macaroni and cheese with hamburger. I've always told her everything, but she keeps some secrets. No, Emily's never been in love, but like I said, she doesn't tell me everything."

The couple's first date was for dinner and a movie; a pizza at Aurelio's on West Harrison and Alfred Hitchcock's, *Torn Curtain*. As it turned out the pizza was good, the conversation tentative, the movie fair, and the evening unforgettable.

Neither of them had a great deal of dating experience; both had tried during their high school years, but with unremarkable results. In one of their earliest conversations, they confided to one another that their limited social experience wasn't so much from a lack of interest as it was a wariness of inflated expectations.

In Emily's home town of Freeland, Iowa, the junior-senior prom had evolved into such an important social occasion that the entire community would enthusiastically participate in its planning and production. To be left home for lack of a date was considered unacceptable and not something that young people from Freeland did. Emily's scripted solution to this social dilemma required that she produce another play, one whose plot turned on its heroine telling a series of small white-lies.

Act One: Emily strategically confides in June, who will then tell most of the second period gym class, that she has accepted an invitation to the prom from a senior boy who lives in the distant community of Red Oak. In her play he is a handsome and popular fellow, someone that she'd met the previous summer during a weekend visit to her grandmother Ruthie's. In reality, Randy Marsden was a skinny stooping sophomore who's most attractive feature was that he lived twenty-three miles south of Freeland; close enough to attend the prom, but far enough away to be anonymous to Emily's classmates.

Act Two: During a telephone interview that consummated the terms for the date, Randy agrees to several fabrications, including: adding two years to his age, embellishing his social status by being cast as the Red Oak High School yearbook editor, and assuming the role of lead guitarist in a rock band called **THE ANNINHILATORS**. It was Randy who offered the last suggestion. He was, in fact, a very fine trumpeter who would later go to Iowa State University on a music scholarship, but like so many others, he would never realize his heart's true desire of fronting a rock 'n' roll power trio.

June Steffens invitation to the prom came as a complete surprise to both June and the Freeland High School student body.

It was near the end of fifth-period typing class and almost everyone was focused on the last timed-test of the day. Out of the corner of her eye, June spotted Connie Tripty unexpectedly leaning across the aisle to shove a note onto the corner of her desk. June's puzzled reaction was answered when Connie discreetly pointed in the direction of Jason Schneider. Risking the possibility of being discovered by Mrs. Hammond ("Hammond the Hammer" as she was known to her students), June glanced over at Jason who had stopped pecking on his manual Olivetti Linea typewriter and was now staring directly at her. Although she'd never noticed it before, but at that particular moment his pale complexion and pouting lips made him look a little like Rickie Nelson.

In a juvenile script, the note read, *"Want to go to the prom."*

Despite the grammatical and punctuation issues, this single sentence started June's heart pounding and mind racing with two pertinent questions: Was Jason Schneider asking her to go to the prom with him, or was he merely inquiring if she wanted to go to the prom, but not with him?

Jason leaned back in his chair and shamelessly offered his best James Dean, cocking his head slightly to the right and smiling out of the corner of his mouth. Although his efforts reminded June more of Tony Dow than James Dean, she felt certain that this inspired pose meant that he was asking her if she would like to attend the prom with him. She smiled and nodded her acceptance, hoping that her blush didn't make her look too much like Sandra Dee.

Jason Schneider was considered by some, especially the freshmen, to be one of Freeland High's cool guys. A good looking boy with sandy hair and reasonably clear skin, he was regarded by most adults as "harmless," a status no seventeen-year-old boy would ever want.

Jason's father, Art Schneider owned the local hardware store. Since the youngest of his three boys was now a senior, Art felt it was only right that he finally take his turn as President of the Freeland High Booster Club. Sadly, the basketball squad's two-and-twelve record came as a disappointment to the boosters, and no small embarrassment to its President. In his official capacity, Art was compelled to enthusiastically support the team even during their worst moments, and there had been many.

At his father's insistence, Jason Schneider was rarely seen without his blue-and-white letterman's jacket. On that jacket, Art had conspicuously pinned to the large white letter F a small silver medal, signifying that his son had been voted to the Second Team - All-Conference. This modest distinction was not Jason Schneider's most remarkable accomplishment; he had been, at least until the previous Friday night, dating one of the more popular girls in Freeland - Miss Stephanie Eckhardt.

By lunchtime Monday, the word around Freeland High School was that Stephanie and Jason's unexpected breakup had been instigated by Stephanie, possibly to open the door for other boys to invite her to the prom. There were many that suspected Jason's sudden invitation was more about his embarrassing social status than a sincere desire to take a nice girl like June Steffens to the prom. Emily silently shared this opinion but kept her concerns to herself, outwardly sharing in her friend's happiness, while hoping that Jason Schneider was not the cad she believed him to be.

For the next two weeks, Jason played his cards very close to the vest. Most mornings he would stop by June's locker to chat her up, never offering anything but encouragement and enthusiasm for their date. With only a few days left until the biggest event of 1963, all things looked good for June and Jason.

Except Jason Schneider was a weak, silly boy, and Stephanie Eckhardt a determined, manipulative young woman. When she learned that her heart's true desire (Connor McCarthy - Freeland High's quarterback, and arguably the most handsome kid in school) had finally chosen a date, and it was not her, plan B was put into motion. With a well-timed phone call by one of Stephanie's confederates, she and Jason would unexpectedly meet at the Freeland Bowl on Sunday afternoon. By the end of third frame the spineless Jason Schneider had two dates to the prom. Meanwhile, on the other side of town, mother and daughter were joyously laboring over the Chevron stitching featured around the bateau collar and raised waistline of June's lovely, handmade prom dress.

News of Stephanie's triumphant return raced through the halls of Freeland High. By third period, the camps were evenly split between those hoping to avoid any contact with June, and another more sinister group scheming to be somewhere nearby when Jason dropped his bomb.

Only Jason Schneider was not forthcoming with his news, and instead spent Monday afternoon skulking and slinking around the school. Even with his well-rehearsed speech, the coward could not muster the courage to confront the innocent June with his bad news.

Tension began to grow. By fifth period on Tuesday, June and Emily may have been the only people at the Freeland Community High School who did not know of the impending calamity.

Then, finally, at the closing bell on Tuesday afternoon, eleven days before the prom, Jason Schneider confronted June with the news "that there has been a misunderstanding." When he had asked her to the prom, he didn't know "Stephanie had already accepted his invitation." Surely, June couldn't expect him "to cancel on her now."

At that moment, the hallway in front of June's locker was jam-packed with kids eager to get out of the building and into the warm spring afternoon. It was a loud and frantic place, perfect for this kind of unpleasant business.

June Steffens was completely blindsided by Jason Schneider's cruel lies; not so for her friend Emily Krist. As Emily made her way through the crowded hallway toward June and Jason, it was clear what had just happened. In that cinematic, slow-motion moment when Jason turned to walk away, Emily considered striking the villain in the face; but her friend June had dropped her books and was now slumped against the locker door. In spite of her anger, this was not the time to deal with the traitorous coward; she needed to be there for her friend. As Emily reached to embrace the now catatonic June Steffens, the craven Jason Schneider slunk away and was lost to the hallway's craze of noise and moving bodies.

Despite her insistence that Emily keep her date with Randy Marsden, Emily called him the next day to cancel their plans. Randy seemed to take the news reasonably well, his only question was to inquire if they were having a band, and if so what was their name?

On the other hand, Ingrid Steffens was wounded almost as badly as her distraught daughter. So upset by the unexpected heartbreak, Ingrid did something that she'd never done before, and would never do again, she telephoned her husband.

At that moment, David Steffens (the traveling insurance salesman) was in Des Moines at an Independent Insurance Agent's conference. Feeling like she had nowhere else to turn, Ingrid screwed-up her courage and called his room at the Fleur Drive Holiday Inn just before eight A.M. Confused and mildly hung-over, the best advice David could offer was for June to seek a date with an underclassman; a reasonable suggestion that fell on deaf ears. As Ingrid miserably pointed out, the girl was inconsolable and making their home as cheerless as the Ettenberg Funeral Parlor.

By Monday most of Freeland was so excited by the nearness of the big event they had forgotten about poor June Steffens' appalling treatment at the hands of the despicable Jason Schneider. With only four days until the prom, the first decorations were beginning to appear in the gymnasium. Last minute purchases of corsages and boutonnieres were being called into the florist. Plans to procure liquor were confirmed with the local hooligans, or a distant cousin of legal age. Cars were washed, waxed, and detailed, while the final finishing touches were being applied to the girl's gowns.

June and Emily had been bringing their sack lunch to school since the seventh grade. The wisdom in a brownbag lunch meant that not only did they not have to eat the school's hot meal, but as a "senior privilege" the two girls could find a spot outside of the building and away from all the painful pre-prom excitement. Their favorite place was on the East side of the building where they could sit in silence and let the weak May sunshine warm their backs.

"Excuse me," said a quiet voice. "Sorry to bother you, but, June, could I speak to you, please?"

From behind them an unidentified presence cast a giant shadow that covered the ground in front of the girls. Both turned at the same moment, squinting up into the sun.

Keith Traugott was the biggest boy at Freeland High School. That fall, the football program suggested he was 6 foot 4 inches tall, and weighed 250 pounds, but to see him in person you might think that they had underestimated his true proportions.

Keith was a junior, and if it weren't for his amazing size he might have been invisible. He was a conspicuously quiet and well-mannered boy; in fact, so quiet that some mistook his lack of presence as a description of his intelligence. This was not completely fair.

Confounded and confused, June and Emily instinctively stood.

"I was wondering, June," Keith asked in what was clearly a well-rehearsed phrase, "if you might go with me to the prom this Saturday?"

The 1963 Freeland High School's prom theme, *"An Evening in Paradise"* was a well-intended tribute to the glorious South Seas, conceived and created by beautiful Midwestern children who had never seen an ocean.

It was a longstanding Freeland tradition that as a tribute to the graduating seniors the prom's theme and decorations would be created by the junior class. This year most of the town's people felt like the students had done an especially good job of capturing the spirit of the occasion when they manufactured several life-sized, artificial palm trees, equipped with the requisite fronds and coconuts. With some last minute help from their art teacher (Mr. Nolton) the North wall of the gym had been decorated with a charming but conspicuously crooked mural, one depicting a hazy yellow moon hovering over a tranquil blue sea. It seems the only setback to the junior's wonderful plans happened when the school's superintendent, Don

Kerpacheck, quietly squashed their hopes for flooding the gymnasium floor with sand.

June, Keith, Randy, and Emily would enjoy the kind of special night that you would wish for your own children. Since he'd already paid for the corsage, Randy had no real problem with the second change in plans, and gladly drove up from Red Oak in his parent's 1962 Chevy station wagon.

The essential photographs were taken outside the Steffen's home in front of a large budding lilac bush, now rich in fragrant purple blossoms. As she peered through the Kodak viewfinder, it felt to Ingrid that no matter how far back she stepped, and she was nearly in the street, she always seemed to be cutting off the top of Keith's head. Still, the photos of June and Emily (the ones showing their broad beaming smiles, arms wrapped tight around each other, dressed in long handmade gowns with a well-intentioned corsage strapped to their shoulders) remain one of their most cherished childhood treasures.

In what had to be a bad prank, Jason Schneider and Stephanie Eckhardt were seated only a few tables away from June and the group, but easily within earshot. From their slurred thick speech and silly behavior it was obvious that their poor judgement and bad manners were strongly influenced by the pint of Jim Beam whiskey hidden inside Jason's rented tuxedo jacket.

The King and Queen of the *Lost Paradise* were officially crowned between the main course and desert. Conspicuous in their sudden absence were Stephanie and Jason, along with their toadies, Gretchen Gamble and Ryan Gunderson. The four loudly returned from their collective trip to the washroom just in time to miss the coronation of the popular couple, Miranda Hossteder and Bill Warrington. Many believed that the foursome's rowdy and poorly timed return to the gymnasium was coordinated out of jealousy, but for those unfortunate enough to share their table it was obvious that the group's absence was more about sour mash than sour grapes.

The desert course was over and the first of the dining tables were being torn down to make way for the dance when Emily felt the first blush of anxiety. The evening's entertainment, a hot four-piece combo from south Sioux City called the **Teen Beats,** was now mindlessly fiddling with their knobs and strings in anticipation of an introduction. Meanwhile, over in a dark corner, a stumbling-drunk Jason Schneider had his arms draped around several boys in a kind of weaving football huddle. Along with the loud backslapping and stupid grab-ass, it was clear that something sinister was being considered.

Emily wasn't the only one who had noticed.

People might think that being the biggest boy in school would have kept Keith Traugott out of the sites of most bullies; unfortunately, it was that very quality that made him the target for some of their worst pranks and harshest hazing. Years of personal experience had taught Keith that it was rarely just one boy who sought after trouble, loud talk and fights always seemed to want for an audience. Yet, in spite of all their cruel treatment, only once had Keith Traugott been pushed far enough to fight back.

It was in the fall of his sophomore year when two older thugs (Bill Tilton and A.J. Keilor) cornered Keith in the boy's locker room and threatened to throw his clothes in the shower unless he gave them his meal card. When he refused, Keilor's brilliant advice was to "Shut up. Don't ever mouth-off to seniors." His verbal attack was followed by a hard shove to the chest that sent Keith stumbling backwards against the locker door, cutting a deep gash in the back of his head. With an astonishing roar, Keith Traugott madly rushed his assailant, violently shoving him backwards. The ferocity and unexpectedness caused the punk to trip and fall over the nearby bench, resulting in a substantial wound to the back of his head. Without further premeditation, Keith then swatted Keilor with the back of his hand, effectively breaking the bully's nose, and starting a fountain of blood that would silently spread across the locker room floor to mingle with his buddy Tilton's.

There were a handful of the more vocal Freeland students who felt that Principal Donald Rattenberg had inequitably dispensed his punishment for the locker room scuffle. By way of a supportive protest several handwritten signs arguing Keith's unfair treatment were scotch-taped in conspicuous locations around the building. But as these things usually go, between classes all the protests were quietly removed with no further comment from the Principal's Office.

As for his part in the fracas, Keith was suspended from school for two days. This "public embarrassment," as his father Ottman Traugott called it, gave the old man open season on his only child. Mr. Traugott's idea for a fair and just punishment, one in which he happily took full advantage, was for Keith to spend two long days cleaning manure from the cattle barn.

As a reminder that one's *lucky life* can often be quite unfair, the two senior no-accounts were punished with only an afternoon of in-school suspension, which they served in the school library reading magazines and drinking cokes. They carried out the weak sentence openly scoffing at their ridiculous restitution, while nursing a broken nose and a head full of stitches.

Sadly, the real damage was neither to Keith's head, nor the truant's reputation. From that point forward, Keith Traugott was mostly ignored by the older boy's hazing, but the real price that the gentle boy paid - the invisible one - was his deep retreat into himself; a solitary path that left him even more distant from his classmates and teachers.

The **Teen Beats** were a tight four-piece guitar band that had been playing western Iowa since their graduation from high school in 1959. This meant that the **Teen Beats** were no longer teens, but were now young men in their early twenties. Their modest age advantage, along with the sideburns and flashy matching burgundy suits, made them seem sharp and experienced. They opened the evening and filled the dance floor with *Wipe Out* by the Surfaris. By the third tune, (the Isley Brothers, *Twist and Shout*) almost everyone was either on the dance floor or crowding the stage to get closer to the music.

It took June a great deal of pleading before Keith Traugott would dance, but when the band finally offered a slow song, (Ben E. King's, *Stand by Me*) and the floor filled with some of the other reluctant dancers, June was finally able to coax him off his seat. They were both beautiful and comic. Anxious and stiff, Keith towered over the tiny June as she happily struggled to lead her giant around the dance floor. There were a fair share of snickers and smirks, but, thankfully, the couple was so engrossed in their own *lucky life* that they hardly noticed their amused classmates.

It came as a complete surprise to Emily, but Randy Marsden turned out to be a terrific dancer. To look at the gangly kid you might not have expected much, but once the music started he showed both a great sense of rhythm, and a kind of goofy presence that translated well to the dance floor. Before long, Emily's classmates were taking note of this new boy, the one that they didn't know but of whom they were more than just a little jealous.

Meanwhile, the alcohol had made a mess out of Jason Schneider.

Confident that his classmates found him both charismatic and a leader of men, the drunken boy stumbled from group to group, shouting madly about the "dork from Red Oak who's got no business at our prom." Since most of Jason's male friends had no particular interest in either Emily Krist or the harmless dweeb she was protecting, they silently tolerated this abusive behavior, hoping he'd move on before the chaperones decided to descend. On the other hand, Jason's female classmates were beside themselves, taking cruel delight in the fact that Jason Schneider was not only a drunken mess, but that his prom date was nowhere to be seen.

The **Teen Beats** were killing a version of Del Shannon's *Runaway* when Jason and Ryan Gunderson staggered across the dance floor toward Emily and Randy. It was Emily who saw them first and strategically positioned herself between her date and the drunken boys.

Overwhelmed with bourbon's confidence, Jason demanded, "Who's this loser?"

Under normal circumstances, everyone, especially Jason Schneider, expected that the meek Emily Krist would fade at his first words. But on this amazing night she surprised them all, including herself, when she responded to the boy's abuse by shouting back, "Mind your own business, Jason."

Like it had been cued, the loud music suddenly stopped. In that frozen moment, no one moved or spoke; Emily's brave command hung like a cloud in the unexpected silence. Without trying to, without wanting to, she and Jason were now the prom's new center of attention. Naturally, this shocking explosion inspired the curiosity of the other dancers near them and motivated everyone to press in tighter around the action.

That is until the **Teen Beats'** lead singer mindlessly shouted down from the stage, "Hey, we're gonna take a short break, but we'll be right back. Remember, the punch bowl's been spiked, so you might wanna go easy on it."

With only a halfhearted wave, the jaded singer turned to join the other musicians as they lit up their smokes and aimlessly wandered toward the exit. As was their habit, a signature of sorts, the **Teen Beats** purposefully left two banks of bright red stage lights on to illuminate the still crowded dance floor.

It was obvious to everyone in the circle that Jason Schneider did not need another visit to the punch bowl; by this point, the effects of the alcohol had left the novice struggling to maintain his balance. As he tried to take a step toward Emily and Randy, the boy suddenly teetered sideways and bounced off the shoulder of the newly crowned Prom King, Bill Warrington.

Fed up with Jason's foolishness, Warrington growled, "Get lost, Schneider.", then purposefully shoved the drunk back into the center of the circle and flat on his nose.

With most of Freeland High School now looking down on him, Jason Schneider - the prom clown - now lay sprawled out on the familiar gymnasium floor, bathed in blood-red stage lights. As the room began to pitch and spin around him, the pitiful inebriate could feel the frightening brown bottle nausea wretch up from his stomach. Blindly hoping to get to his knees before it was too late, Jason Schneider grabbed for the nearest person in the crowd - Connie Tripty.

"Hey, Jason," the tall girl howled down at him. "Where's your date?"

Reeling completely out of control, the drunken boy squinted up at his nemesis. Pointing her long wicked finger toward the stage, Connie cackled hysterically, "There she is Jason."

In his alcohol-fueled hallucination, Jason Schneider peered out from beyond the circle to where Connie Tripty was now wildly gesturing toward the thick burgundy curtains that hung beside the stage. There, peeking out from behind the drapery - stage left - the miserable fool could make out what appeared to be his date, the equally intoxicated Stephanie Eckhardt. Enjoying an amateurish puff from the bass guitar player's cigarette, Stephanie giggled uncontrollably while waving down to her screaming classmates. Tightly wedged between two of the lecherous *Teen Beats*, the legless girl then staggered through the emergency exit and out into the night.

On the way home from their first date, Charles politely asked Emily if she would like to "Stop for a beer, or coffee, or something?" Emily politely declined, noting the late hour, and offering the excuse that she had a "busy day tomorrow."

Emily's decision to decline the nightcap wasn't so much about the late hour, or the fact that she was "busy" - she wasn't. In this case, it was more about her anxiety over the age-old question of whether to kiss this man on a first date? She had indeed kissed a boy (four, to be precise) and she'd even kissed one on the first date. But this person, this Charles Albright person, seemed so different from the other boys she'd known. This was a man; a man with a job, although at the time of their first date she did not know what it was; a man with an important grandmother; a man who had seen *Just Small Enough*, and still called her. This, she hoped, was someone who might be more than a first date.

As they approached Emily's apartment building, she sensed that he had become tenser and more rigid in his gait.

"Perhaps," she wondered, "he's thinking the same thing that I'm thinking?"

Charles was thinking precisely the same thing that Emily was thinking, except his thoughts were liberally seasoned with anxiety and a hefty dash of panic. He was excited about this girl, and found her attractive in ways he'd never experienced with the other girls. But what about the questions of a good night kiss; should he attempt to kiss her, only to find her offended, and then be rejected? This thought proved too much.

Thankfully, Emily assumed a role she would serve in their relationship for years to come, and made it easy for the tentative Romeo by gently taking his hand before giving him a short sincere kiss on the cheek.

From that evening forward neither dated another, nor did they care to. Like couples do, they soon created their own common qualities of timing, empathy, and compassion, quickly growing to love and need the comfort of their own company.

Chapter Nine

So what happens next?

"And with that, she dared the bravest thing she'd ever done;
she looked right into his eyes."
The Princess Bride – William Goldman

"Why do you keep doing that? You look great."

Charles snuck a quick glance over at Emily in the passenger seat of his 1964 Camaro and smiled. She was still anxiously fussing with her hair and make-up in anticipation of her second meeting with his grandmother, Lillian Campbell. Although he didn't mention it, Charles both understood and shared her anxiety; Grandmother Lillian was intimidating.

For Charles, his grandmother's invitation was impossible to turn down; for Emily, however, Lillian Campbell's party promised an unexpected opportunity for improved employment. During an earlier conversation, Grandmother Lillian had mentioned to Charles that her friend, Mr. Carl Grove (the Tribune Company's Vice President for Radio and Television Operations) was expected to attend. In a tone that Charles felt fairly certain was intended to be supportive of his relationship with Emily, she went on to suggest "that an introduction would certainly be a good opportunity for your new friend."

Since her graduation from the Goodman School of Drama in May, Emily had worked hard to balance the thrill of her new relationship with the practical need for money. As a student on scholarship, Emily had taken a part-time position as a cashier at the beautiful Patio Theater on Irving Park and Austin. The job paid poorly, not even minimum wage. The one legitimate perk was a reciprocal free admission to most of the other movie theaters in the city. June and Emily kept tally on a calendar taped to the refrigerator; in the nineteen months that she had worked at the Patio they had seen twenty-eight different films. Counting the matinees and evenings, Emily was working less than thirty-five hours a week, which meant that after taxes she was bringing home around $65.

Then quite of the blue, Dr. Schnakel contacted Emily offering her a "small job in our properties offices." If she was interested, there was an opening on Tuesdays and Thursdays where she would clean, mend, and inventory the school's costumes and props.

"It won't pay much, dear. But who knows, it may help you to find other opportunities."

Of course her new position at the Goodman had nothing to do with the property department's needs, but everything to do with the fact that she was now dating the grandson of Lillian Campbell. If nothing else, Dr. Schnakel was a speculator. He confided to his secretary Janice Iiams that, "By keeping Emily Krist close, we may buy some points with the grand dame."

The doorman welcomed the couple with his usual understated enthusiasm. "Eighteen, Mr. Albright," he advised.

Along with the Tribune's Vice President, Grandmother Lillian had also mentioned that the guest list would include a small gathering of local notables who were coming to honor the retiring Tribune columnist and art critic, Cliff Terry. For the past twenty-two years, Mr. Terry's wit and encyclopedic knowledge of the more tawdry side of Chicago's social elite had made him a popular companion for many of the city's more affluent hostesses. Truth be told, the aging Mr. Terry had been asked to resign back in March, but by continuing to make strategic appearances at events around the city he was able to prolong his inevitable social demise and enjoy a free meal.

Emily knew of Mr. Terry's reputation firsthand.

During her first year at the School of Drama, she had worked as one of the unpaid minions for the Goodman's highly anticipated revival of *Macbeth*. This important production would feature the Tony Award winner, Judith Anderson in a reprise of her stellar performance as Lady Macbeth. The scale of the production, along with the artistic skills of the professional actors and union crew, had been a revelation to the young girl from Iowa. Hundreds of hours and tens of thousands of dollars had been committed to its success, but in a single blistering dismissal Mr. Terry single-handedly soured the public to the production, shortening the run by three weeks, and costing the show's financial backers a fortune. Despite her permanent grudge against the callous critic, Cliff Terry was the least of Emily's concerns.

Mary met them at the door. "Good evening, Mr. Albright. It's nice to see you again. May I take your coat, Miss?"

Emily handed over her raincoat remembering that her mother had bought it for her to wear at her father's funeral. Looking at the maid now holding the thin gray jacket, she wondered why she thought she needed a coat on a clear night in June.

"Charles, I'm so glad that you could come."

With that innocent phrase, Emily Krist turned to face her greatest fear.

Lillian Campbell floated majestically across the crowded room, perfect in her stunning emerald green dress. She dominated the space in a way that made everyone near her shrink and fade.

"She is magnificent," Charles thought, as he leaned forward to kiss her cheek, a practice she had insisted upon since he was old enough to remember.

"It's good that you could join us tonight, Emily," Lillian offered while reaching out to shake hands.

Emily accepted her hostess' hand, noting it to be cool, dry, and perfectly manicured. She hoped that hers did not feel as clammy as she feared.

"Oh, thank you Mrs. Campbell. You have a lovely home."

"Yes. Well, enjoy yourself, dear. Charles, have you spoken with your mother? All is well in Iowa, I trust?"

The couple found a quiet corner near the kitchen where they could discreetly observe the other guests without the need to interact. It was only seven-thirty, but the promised "small party" had already turned out to be a sizeable crowd. Everyone there seemed to be someone, and they all loved Lillian Campbell.

In spite of her nerves, Emily Krist was fascinated by the hostess. By hiding inconspicuously in their little corner, she could observe firsthand the tremendous amount of energy that Lillian Campbell spent to deliver her grand and gracious style. It was remarkable; she knew every person by sight, and then greeted them as if they were the one and only person in this great crowd that she wanted to see. She addressed all of them by their titles, by their professions, by their status, their family history, and, of course, from the most recent event that they had both just attended. Emily imagined her as both director and star of a fabulously complex and improvised play; one in which she - Lillian Campbell - played the part of the regal host. Displaying her commanding style and gracious presence, she would skillfully maneuver the characters and dialog through the evening's intrigue, always gliding away at the perfect moment to leave her audience utterly satisfied and longing for more.

For some time the hesitant couple hid in the corner of the living room, sipping their red wine, and making up fantastic stories about the party guests. In Charles and Emily's make-believe world the room was filled with Hollywood movie directors, millionaires, and spies; in reality, the room truly **was** filled with Hollywood movie directors, millionaires, and spies.

"Enough you wallflowers."

In a startling move, Grandmother Lillian had firmly taken hold of Emily by the arm. Then as they began to walk away, she held up her other hand, motioning for Charles to stay where he was. A flash of panic washed across Emily's lovely face before she was lost to the crowd.

"Carl, I'd like you to meet someone."

Lillian and Emily were now standing outside a small group of two gentlemen and three women who had been occupying the corner directly across the room from the one that Emily had just left. A short stout man with very little hair and a broad infectious smile looked up and announced, "Ladies and gentleman, our hostess, Lillian Campbell." The group collectively turned to acknowledge their host with great appreciation and all the appropriate pleasantries. Lillian played her part perfectly by smiling and recognizing each person with a hug or a handshake. After the obligatory small talk, Lillian deftly hooked Carl Grove by the arm and softly extracted him from the group.

"As always, Lillian, it's just a beautiful party. I am sorry, but I'm going to need to leave soon. Duty calls, something at the station that apparently can't be solved without me."

"Not to worry my friend, but before you go I want you to meet someone. Carl, this is Miss Emily Krist, a friend of my grandson, Charles. Emily this is Mr. Carl Grove of the Tribune Company. I do consider him a good friend, in spite of the fact that he is solely responsible for what you see on the television. Carl, Miss Krist recently graduated from the Goodman and is currently considering her options. I was hoping that you might take a moment to visit and perhaps share some of your wisdom about the world of television. If you're lucky, Emily, he might even offer you some of that sage advice he promises to those of us who own stock in the Tribune Company."

Before Carl Grove could protest, Lillian had excused herself and was off to tend to the needs of her guests.

Content to remain invisible in his corner, Charles watched as his grandmother introduced Emily to the small group of party guests. Delighted that it was she who was now being passed around, Charles enjoyed another deep swallow of the rich cabernet, while encouraging the wine to continue its good work. Naturally, he was thinking only about Emily and how happy he was since they had met just four months before. It wasn't until a voice interrupted his reverie that he realized a man was standing in front of him; a pleasant enough looking man, impeccably dressed in a black blazer and gray slacks, his thinning silver hair perfectly swept back. His steel blue eyes and steady gaze gave him the unmistakable quality of seriousness.

"Excuse me for interrupting. You looked as if you were thinking great thoughts," the man said in a calm and deeply confident tone.

Charles instantly returned to the party in the Glass House.

The man continued, "I believe I have the advantage, Charles. You see we've met once before, but that was some time ago. It was at you grandfather's funeral. My name is William Byrne."

Charles was understandably confused by this stranger's introduction, his Grandfather Campbell had been dead for eleven years and his recollection of that sad time was mostly lost to his youthful memory. Barely fourteen, Charles was still attending Cedar Rapids High School when his grandfather passed away from lung cancer. The relentless malignancy took nearly six-months before it finally killed Attorney General Campbell. His only lasting memory of that experience was how grim an ordeal the illness had been for his mother, Charys. It's one thing to be the only daughter of a famous man, but to be the daughter of a famous man and purposefully chose a life of self-imposed absence in Iowa was quite another.

The funerals were magnificent. And why wouldn't they be, Lillian had been planning them most of her married life. In his position as Illinois' longest serving Attorney General, Otto Campbell had gathered a substantial number of influential friends, and likely an equal number of powerful enemies. So in keeping with what Lillian insisted were "Otto's last wishes" there would be both a formal service at Saint Anthanasius in Evanston, and then a week later a private memorial at the Campbell's North Shore estate. The spiritual service at Saint Anthanasius was as well-attended as the ten o'clock mass on Easter Sunday. As for the more secular event, it was held in Lillian's formal gardens on a stunning day in May. When asked by the Chicago Tribune reporter, the widow Campbell estimated that the number of well-wishers that afternoon had exceeded four hundred.

Although he'd never given it any thought, but at this point in his life Charles had no real personal experience with death or dying; Grandfather Campbell was the only relative to have passed in his first twenty-five years. He did, however, have one vivid memory of the events surrounding that funeral, and it did not include William Byrne. Before the start of what turned out to be a rather lengthy and pious funeral mass, Lillian had privately whispered to Charles that he must sit between her and his mother. To the hundreds in attendance this seating arrangement appeared to have a certain charm; that is, a widowed grandmother comforted by her brave and only grandson. However, for Gordon Albright this seating arrangement was yet another reminder of what he perceived as his mother-in-law's purposeful manipulation and control of his family. To use the boy as a prop in her well-staged drama was more than he could bear.

Once Grandmother Lillian learned that Gordon had expressed strong reservations about the boy's return to Evanston for the memorial event, she confronted him directly, insisting, "Otto's friends and admirers will expect that his entire family be present for his wake."

"I do not wish to sound insensitive, or show a lack of respect, Lillian, but neither the boy, nor I, will be attending the memorial."

That was the last time Lillian Campbell ever spoke to or of her daughter's husband, Gordon Albright.

"So your grandmother tells me you graduated from Northwestern last year; *cum laude* wasn't it? An excellent achievement; tell me, did you have the chance to take any of your course work with my good friend, Elliott Saul?"

Elliott Saul, Ph.D. was well known to every person, be they student, faculty or staff, on the Northwestern University campus. Along with a storied academic career as an economist, Saul's vitae also included serving as a member of President Roosevelt's "Brain Trust" both during and after World War II. It was Secretary of State, George Marshall who had chosen Saul to be both a consultant, and one of the primary authors for what was to eventually become the postwar Marshall Plan. Since joining the faculty in 1955, his courses were eagerly sought by serious students.

"Yes, Sir," Charles replied. "I was lucky enough to get into his International Studies Seminar last spring. It was challenging in every way, but one of my best experiences. If you don't mind me asking, how is it that you know Dr. Saul?"

After a long swallow of dark brown liquor from his highball glass, the tall man replied, "Oh, we were classmates before the war. Brilliant man, really; wicked sense of humor, and a fair backhand. Probably not something he shares with many students. Still, he is a remarkable fellow."

After another pull from the glass, Byrne looked Charles over closely and asked in a surprisingly pointed way, "So, young man, what happens next?"

"I beg your pardon?"

"I'm curious how you're getting along at Bear Sterns." Byrne replied, all the time keeping direct eye contact with Charles.

For the second time in their brief conversation, William Byrne had the advantage.

"Fine, I guess. How do you know that I work for Sterns?"

"Your grandmother's apartment has an extraordinary view of the city. Would you care to join me on the veranda?"

The way he said it sounded more like a command than a request.

Outside two stunning young women in fashionable evening clothes were sitting back-to-back on a brightly upholstered bench, intently engaged in what appeared to be an especially intimate conversation. When Charles and William Byrne walked through the open glass doors, the darker of the two spotted the men and instantly turned back to whisper in the blonde's ear. Like frightened doves flushed from deep grass, the two picked up their wine glasses, and without bothering to look back ambled arm-in-arm into the apartment.

"I do enjoy your grandmother's parties," the tall man said as he smiled at the retreating women. "She certainly has a knack for putting just the right people together, don't you think?" He paused before adding, "But just between you and me, I come mostly for the view."

William Byrne set his empty glass down on the small table next to the bench, and then with his back to Charles and the other guests grabbed hold of the veranda's sturdy black railing with both hands. As the sun set behind the city's magnificent skyline, great shafts of orange, blue, and purple light shot between the buildings and out onto Lake Michigan. Eighteen stories below, the traffic on Lake Shore Drive stopped and started as it frenetically wound its way along the edge of the dark water.

"Your grandfather was a great man, Charles. Did you know him well?"

Charles looked out over the city while considering his answer.

"Yes, at least as well as a boy can from three hundred miles away. We would visit Chicago three or four times a year. I stayed with them for a week during the summer at their home on Lake Geneva. There were the holidays, of course, and always letters and telephone. Grandmother and my mother are close. Both Mom and I are only children, so I suppose we may have been a little..."

Charles struggled for a word other than "spoiled" to describe his relationship with the women in his family, but the sentence was left dangling when none came to mind.

Byrne took advantage and pressed the point.

"I was fortunate to know your grandfather quite well. In fact, he was a close friend, one of the best I've ever known. You might not fully appreciate it, but Otto Campbell was a brilliant lawyer. He had a way to see people for what they were, both the good and the bad. A tireless man who loved this city..." A brief pause followed with Byrne picking up his empty glass before concluding, "... and this country."

Charles looked out across the dark waters of Lake Michigan and tried to conjure an image of his grandfather. The Otto Campbell he remembered was a tall and lanky man, always clean shaven, with close-cropped hair. The family photographs from his younger days at Saint Ignatius prep school showed a handsome boy with a confident gaze and a mature smile. His time at Yale had produced an erudite and formal man; so much so, that even at the most casual of family events he always wore a white shirt and bow tie. He never used aftershave or perfumes, but pleasantly smelled of talc. Grandfather's voice was melodic and gentle; generally calm, never rushed, never angry. The patriarch enjoyed family gatherings and vacations, but was rarely far from the phone. It was hard to remember an occasion that didn't include a visit from one of grandfather's men, too soon followed by a brief farewell, and an unapologetic departure.

"Charles, let me get to the point. A year ago your grandmother mentioned you to me. She told me of your successes at Northwestern."

A dramatic pause, and then Byrne continued. "It is possible that you might have certain skills that could be helpful to an organization like the one I represent. If you're interested, perhaps we could meet sometime to discuss it?"

"Excuse me, Sir, but interested in what?" Charles replied.

"I work with the State Department, mostly in matters regarding security. Your knowledge of finance and business are valuable tools, particularly if they're applied to the kind of operations that I deal with. Then there's also the matter of your personal background. You come from a remarkable and patriotic family. That's something to be very proud of."

Byrne continued. "You do understand that your student deferment ended with your graduation from Northwestern? A bright guy like you is surely aware of the increasing number of young men that are being drafted. By the end of the year, the Army will have drafted more than four hundred thousand, and I can assure you that they are all headed straight for Southeast Asia. I don't wish to cause any great concerns, it's such a pleasant evening, but at some point, perhaps sooner than you think, you may be called to serve."

Charles was stunned by what he was hearing, but before he could form a cogent question Byrne rattled the ice in his empty glass and concluded, "Charles, there are many ways to serve your country. Some of them are beyond the purview of the Cedar Rapids draft board. What I'm suggesting is that you might consider a role where you can use your talents to their best end. I'm confident that the thought of you lying in a fox hole west of Dong Ha would be a worry for your grandmother and, frankly, it would be a disappointment to the memory of your grandfather."

"Mr. Byrne, I don't think I understand what you're driving at. I registered for the draft when I turned eighteen and got my student deferment. I read the papers and can see that the Army is calling more guys every day. But do you know something I don't know? Am I being drafted?"

The tall man waved his hands and replied, "No, that's not what I'm talking about, Charles. Let me try to be more direct. I work for the Central Intelligence Agency."

Byrne could see from Charles reaction that he was startled by the bluntness of his comment, so quickly added, "I have an office in Washington, and one here in Chicago." Then in lighter tone, he added, "But Charles, in spite of all you hear about those dimly lit hallways, I can assure you that we keep the lights on all the time."

Charles smiled out of politeness, but even with Byrne's apparent effort at humor he found himself chilled to the bone.

"Part of my job is to identify talented young men who want to help their country. I like what I see. If you're interested in learning more about what we do, I'm offering you an opportunity to meet and get better acquainted. Here's my card. Call my secretary and she'll be able to provide you some dates that work in your calendar. No pressure. In fact, I'll tell you a couple of good stories about your grandfather if you like."

Byrne reached into his jacket pocket and produced a business card, which he handed to Charles.

"It was good to meet you, Charles. I hope you'll call."

With that, he walked back into the living room and was instantly lost among the party guests.

"I can't believe it. I mean he didn't actually offer me a job or anything, but he said that he knew there was going to be an opening for a Production Assistant, and then he told me to make an appointment to come in for a personal interview. Charles, it's like a dream. I can't believe that I might be able to get a job working at WGN."

Charles heard most of what Emily was saying, but between the heavy traffic on Lake Shore Drive and his own news he was having trouble staying focused. For the thirty minute drive back to her apartment, Emily uncharacteristically dominated the conversation.

"I'm going to need your help, Charles. I mean, I have to write a resume and... Oh, I can't believe what just happened."

He did catch the last sentence, and at least on this one point he knew what she meant.

They found a parking spot close to the building and were walking toward Emily's front door when Charles asked, "Emily, let's go down to the Tip Top and have a drink. I need to talk with you about something."

The Tip Top was a small neighborhood bar two blocks west of Emily's apartment building. On those nights when June was home, the couple found the quiet tavern a comfortable and convenient hideaway; nothing fancy, just eight bar stools, six booths, twenty-five cent draw beer, and a juke box that hadn't seen a new release since 1960.

Fearing the worst, Emily now walked along in silence with Charles tightly holding her hand. He'd still given no indication of his thoughts when they entered the bar and found a spot in a booth near the back door. Once the barman returned with two draft beers, Charles reached across the table and took Emily's hand.

"Emily, I'm not altogether sure what happened tonight, but I want to tell you something and hear what you think."

This certainly didn't sound like he was about to break up with her, but Emily also recognized the stress in his voice and serious look on his face.

"What is it?" she asked, with what she hoped was a reassuring squeeze to his hand.

Charles reached into his pocket and then slid the business card across the table. The simple white piece of paper revealed nothing, offering only William Byrne's name, a street address on West Congress, and a phone number.

After a quick look at the card, Emily suggested lightly, "I guess if you're a spy you probably wouldn't have a card that said you were a spy."

"I'm not sure what he is, but what does concern me is what I should do? Part of me wants to go and meet with him, if nothing more than to hear what he's offering. But another part of me wants to stay as far away as possible, and hope that I don't get drafted. Or worse, that he gets me drafted."

Now confident that tonight was not going to be their last, Emily got up from her seat and went around to slide into the booth beside him. He gladly put his arm around her and kissed the top of her head.

"I don't want to go to the Army, Em. I mean, I will if I get drafted, but I've never thought of myself as a patriot. All the men in my family have served. Dad was in Germany; Grandfather Campbell too. But I guess I always hoped that it would somehow just miss me."

He looked up at the ceiling and muttered mostly to himself, "Not very good planning, huh?"

They sat for a moment in silence listening to Jo Stafford's version of *"You Belong to Me."*

"Just remember, darling all the while, you belong to me."

He kissed her again on the top of the head. "All I know is that I don't want to leave you now, or ever."

Emily snuggled in even closer and closed her eyes, hoping for the moment to shut out everything and everyone but the man beside her. Before this evening, Emily had secretly wondered how she would know if she was in love. Now, thanks to these crazy circumstances, it was perfectly clear: she knew that she loved Charles, and always would.

"What just happened?" Emily Krist wondered.

With the very real possibility that they might soon be separated, perhaps forever, her youth and innocence were receding like an image in the rearview mirror. Up ahead was all foggy and unclear. This was where all the hard decisions waited, the ones that adults make.

Somewhere in the background the needle lifted from the record. In that gap, that interlude, there was a silent moment of acknowledgment for the end of her childhood. Then just as quickly the sound of a metal needle on vinyl offered a new reality, her *lucky life*. In this one she had finally left Freeland for good.

Chapter Ten

I Can Tell You One Thing...

"Engage people with what they expect; it is what they are able to discern and confirms their projections. It settles them into predictable patterns of response, occupying their minds while you wait for the extraordinary moment - that which they cannot anticipate."

The Art of War - Sun Tzu

A full week had passed since Grandmother Lillian's party. Both Emily and Charles had decided to act upon their invitations to meet with Carl Grove and William Byrne.

Emily's experience could not have been scripted better had she written it herself. Grove's secretary was anticipating her call and promptly set up a meeting between Emily and the Assistant News Director, Stanley Dalton.

Grove was right. The news department was going to be needing a Production Assistant, and even though Emily's qualifications were far from what Dalton would have normally consider appropriate for the job, he did understand who had recommended her for the interview. Later that night over dinner, Dalton confided to his wife, "She's bright and will learn the staging and direction, but she knows nothing about television production or news. She's a cute kid who got a break."

Charles procrastinated until the following Wednesday before he finally called the number on William Byrne's business card. Like Emily's experience, the woman who answered the phone had been informed that Charles might be calling for an interview. She was pleasant enough, but provided no additional insights into William Byrne or his work. She offered him a meeting for three o'clock on Friday afternoon at the West Congress address.

"I'm pleased to see you, Charles. What made you decide to take this meeting?"

Byrne shook Charles hand and motioned for him to take a seat in one of the two straight-back chairs directly in front of a dark wooden desk. He closed the office door, and then walked around to take a seat behind the desk. Over his shoulder, the window looked out on to Chicago's south side with its many industrial buildings and heavy truck traffic. By standing next to the window and looking toward the east, you could just catch a view of the southwest corner of Soldier Field.

Charles warily glanced around the office as he considered Byrne's question: stark white walls, two gray file cabinets, the straight-backed chairs, a nondescript sofa, and Byrne's small wooden desk; a room as plain as his business card. On top of the desk were three manila folders, a copy of the Chicago Tribune, and a black rotary phone. Clearly, William Byrne spent little time in his Spartan quarters.

'Well," Charles began, "I've been thinking about our conversation and felt like I needed to get some more information. Besides, I'd be lying if I said I wasn't intrigued."

Byrne nodded his head that he understood, but showed no sign of enthusiasm.

"This is the Central Intelligence Agency," he stated matter-of-factly, his hands passive on the desk in front of him. "Our job is to manage the nation's intelligence activities. You'll find us operating in nearly every county around the world. We are the eyes and ears of our government, and believe me, without us the world would quickly become an even more dangerous place."

For the next twenty minutes, Byrne delivered a well-rehearsed history lesson on "the Agency," starting back after World War II with the Office of Strategic Services, and ending with a surprisingly impassioned commentary on the current Administration's "dependence upon our skills."

"It won't surprise you that today we're heavily involved in our diplomatic and military efforts in Southeast Asia. It would be inappropriate for me to say much more, but it is fair to say that we will be needed there for some time. But that's not what I had in mind when I suggested you might have a role with the Agency."

Charles had been sitting in the same position for nearly half an hour, but now sensed the payoff.

"There are a substantial number of people in this country who do not support United States efforts in Viet Nam. During the past eighteen months, these people have gotten better organized and much louder. They are making more and more noise about policy that they do not understand. This noise has been distorted and eagerly reported by our liberal media. What now passes for news confuses people. This can cause us to take our eye off the target."

"That's interesting," said Charles, "but what is it that you think I can do to help your agency?"

William Byrne slowly pushed his chair away from the desk and then purposefully walked around to sit on the corner nearest Charles.

"It's a good a question," Byrne replied. "I'm not sure that there is a role for you with the Central Intelligence Agency. If we decide to pursue this further there are several tests that we can give you to determine your aptitudes and abilities. There would be a security screening, and some

76

background tests beyond those that we've already run. And, of course, there is some specialized training required. Someone with your education and business savvy would certainly have value..." Byrne's voice trailed off as if he was thinking about something completely different.

"Why is it that I feel that there is a 'but' coming on here?" Charles asked.

"No. No. Not a 'but', exactly, although I do have a question for you: What are your thoughts about our involvement in Viet Nam?"

Charles had come prepared for this question. Since agreeing to the meeting, he had anticipated that his thoughts about what was euphemistically being called the "conflict in Viet Nam" would surely be of interest to a guy like William Byrne.

Charles Albright was neither a pacifist, nor someone seeking to avoid his patriotic responsibilities, but as the summer of 1966 came to an end less than half of the American people supported the handling of the war. Charles Albright was certainly in that camp. Thanks to the evening television news programs, American's had their own front row seat to the gruesome images of young men fighting a relentless enemy, an enemy that seemed indistinguishable from the very people that we were trying to help. As he considered William Byrne's question, Charles wondered if there was anyone left who didn't know of at least one person who'd already died in Viet Nam.

"Mr. Byrne, I don't believe we should be increasing the number of American troops in Viet Nam. General Westmoreland is surely a capable leader, but last year's air strikes, the Rolling Thunder, convinced me that the Viet Cong are never going to give up. The jungles of Viet Nam are their jungles. A lot of good men have died for what may be unwinnable."

"Go on," Byrne said, as he returned to his chair and lit a Pal Mall cigarette.

"Well, I'm afraid there's not much more to say. These are just my ideas from watching the news. I'm sure there are other perspectives that I don't understand, but it seems pretty clear that the war has divided our country."

Byrne swiveled around to look out the window, his back now to Charles.

"I think you're right about one thing," he said. "This country is divided over this war."

A cloud of blue smoke surrounded the man's head as he turned his chair back around to face Charles.

"I think there are several reasons why good Americans, like you, Charles, are coming to believe that this war is 'unwinnable.' Damn, I hate that phrase; what the hell do people know about winnable wars? But I suppose there are enough freethinkers out there. Clever bastards who've learned how to manipulate the media almost as effectively as we do, spouting their own propaganda for pacifism and free love. I can assure you that it is both necessary and right for us to take the offensive. Without an aggressive posture, we'll find our strength fading and our resolve lost to a group of eggheads and rowdies who haven't a clue about what to do with their power. You see, Viet Nam is only the start. Next it's Cambodia, Laos, and then Thailand..."

Byrne trailed off again, as if distracted by another intrusive thought. Charles waited in silence for his return.

"There is a department within the Agency that concerns itself with, well, let's just say a domestic agenda. Given your family history, it struck me that you might welcome a role where you could use your skills to help discourage some of the more vocal antiwar protestors. I think you would agree that there are certain entertainers, academics, and public figures that have become very newsworthy lately, all because of their anti-war rhetoric."

His eyes never left Charles as he continued, "To insure that accurate information is getting to the American people, it can be beneficial to have certain groups and individuals silenced, or at least quieted. With the support of other government agencies, say, the Internal Revenue System, it is possible that those who would purposefully mislead or confuse the issues will find themselves with their own new set of problems."

Another long pause followed before Byrne concluded, "Clearly there are certain people in this country who have abused their right to the First Amendment. There's no mystery here, it's their spoken goal to manage a campaign of misinformation. Those efforts must be stopped before they permanently damage our leaders will. It is to this purpose that I thought of Otto Campbell's grandson."

Two hours later in the corner booth of the Tip Top, Charles confided the story to Emily, concluding with the comment, "I can tell you one thing, I will never join William Byrne's CIA."

What he didn't say but secretly feared was how this decision could easily come back upon both he and Emily.

For Charles, there remained the nagging question of his grandmother's involvement in the William Byrne episode. On the one hand, he loved his grandmother and was grateful for her continued interest in his affairs; it was clear she wanted to help him, at least with her own version of what she thought his life should be like. Still, he couldn't shake the fact that it was at her party where he'd first met William Byrne. Was there some connection? Surely, she didn't share his point-of-view about the government making trouble for those who opposed the war; after all, it hadn't been that many years since the country suffered the uncertainty and intolerance of the McCarthy business.

Instead of directly confronting the situation, Charles Albright foolishly spent the weekend fretting and stewing about his situation, wasting what turned out to be two beautiful summer days in Chicago.

It wasn't until Sunday afternoon that June and Emily could finally persuade the brooding Charles to join them for an afternoon of swimming and lounging at Fullerton Beach. Ironically, the amazing view from Fullerton's not only includes the great expanse of Lake Michigan, but also a splendid panorama of downtown Chicago, including one of its most notable landmarks - the Glass House.

By noon on Monday, Charles decided that if Grandmother Lillian had not called by close of business on Wednesday, he would call her. It was after six-thirty and he had just gotten home from the office when the phone rang.

"It's me. Did she call?' asked Emily.

"No, but I think I'll try her. Are you guys still going to the movies? Maybe we could meet for a beer or something after?"

"I'd like to see you. How about we meet at the Tip Top at ten?"

"Okay. See you then. Oh, what are you going to see?"

"I want to go to the new Michael Caine picture, but June is holding out for something called *Georgy Girl*. You know, like the song. I guess we'll figure it out when we get there. See you at ten. Love you!"

He hung up the phone, but before he could lose his resolve dialed Grandmother Lillian's number. After several rings a rather somber but tinny version of her voice came on the line, announcing, "Hello, this is a recording machine. I am unable to answer your call. Please leave a message." There was a metallic click, followed by a short electronic beep.

Charles was surprised by the idea of a recorded message on the telephone, but after a moment of confused silence he managed to spit out, "Hello. Yes, Grandmother? This is Charles phoning, but you're not there. Well, if you hear me would you call when you can? Please? Oh, yes. Well, could you make it tomorrow? I'll be out for a while. Thank you. Good bye." Then not exactly sure what to do next, he listened thinking that there would be another beep or some instructions for how to end the call. Of course, none came.

"Charles?" the office intercom asked in a tone that sounded as if it was not really sure he was at his desk. "Will you take a call from Lillian Campbell?"

Nine-thirty on a Thursday is a particularly hectic time at the offices of Bear Stern's. By midmorning the markets are moving and adjusting at a breakneck pace, to be off on personal business, even for a few moments, would not be something that a broker would choose. In this case, Charles quickly snatched the phone from its cradle and answered, "Hello, Grandmother. How are you this morning?"

The click of a button turning on Lillian Campbell's telephone intercom could be heard just before she came on the line. "Fine, Charles. Thank you for asking. I trust all is well with you?"

Charles could picture his grandmother in her drawing room, seated at the antique Franklin writing desk, her social calendar by her side, oblivious to the inconvenience that any small talk might have on his schedule.

"What do you think of my new toy, the telephone machine?" she asked.

"Very handy for someone as busy as you, I expect."

Charles thought he could hear the muffled voices of people talking in the background. "Are you entertaining so early?" he asked.

"Oh, no, there are some people here who are taking pictures for a magazine. A bit of an inconvenience, really, but you called me last night, yes?"

"Yes, I did." Maddeningly, the entire pre-planned dialog had fled his mind like a canary who finds the door to its cage open. "Well, yes, anyway," he stammered. "I was calling because I was curious about a man that I met at your house the other night."

Before he could say the name, Lillian interrupted, and in her matter-of-fact tone stated, "William Byrne."

"Yes, exactly," he replied. At this point, Charles was rarely surprised by his grandmother's uncanny prescience.

"I'm sure you know his occupation?"

He regretted the clumsy remark as soon as it came out of his mouth.

Lillian paused for a moment, and then spoke, but not directly to Charles. "Would you excuse me for a moment, please? I'll join you when I'm finished here. Thank you."

After a few seconds, Charles could hear the door to her bedroom close and then the sound of the receiver being lifted from its cradle.

"Of course I know his occupation. He has been a friend of your grandfather and mine for nearly thirty-five years." After another short pause, she continued, "I understand that you visited Bill in his office."

Another pregnant pause followed as she waited for Charles to re-enter the conversation.

"I did," he stated in what he hoped was an upbeat and positive tone. "Mr. Byrne's suggested that I might wish to consider a change in careers. He said I have skills that might be valuable to his business."

Charles paused, waiting for Grandmother Lillian to react to their cat-and-mouse conversation. He knew, of course, with which of the two mammals he was more closely aligned.

"Charles, as my only grandson I have tried to be as helpful and supportive as you and your mother will allow. I trust that you know I have only your best interests in mind."

There was a short break where Charles suspected she was taking a sip of her Earl Grey.

"Months ago I was at a dinner party that Bill and his wife Evelyn were attending; lovely woman, Evelyn. We had a moment alone, and he asked me about you. At the time, I remember thinking that it had been quite a while since he'd last seen you, probably at Otto's funeral. I told him that you had just finished your degree from Northwestern and that you had taken a position with Sterns. That was that, we didn't speak again until he called to invite me to join them for dinner. Unfortunately, it was to be on the same night that I was hosting my event here at the apartment. I told him I couldn't go, but would they care to change their plans and stop by for a drink? He asked who else was on the guest list, and I must have shared several names with him. I believe I mentioned that you would be here as well. He seemed interested and promised to get back to me after he'd spoken with Evelyn. I didn't think much about the fact that he had come alone, but, of course, I did notice that the two of you were visiting on the veranda."

Charles was doing his best to keep from reading anything sinister into this new revelation of Byrne's inquiry about the guest list. Under the circumstances, he was beginning to feel that his paranoia was earned; after all, it was a fact that the CIA had done a check on his background, Byrne's admitted as much.

"Charles, are you still there?"

"Yes, I'm still here," he answered. "Grandmother, I told Mr. Byrne that I wasn't interested in joining his organization."

"Yes, dear, I know," she replied.

"I guess I need to know if that's going to be a problem."

"How do you mean?"

"Well, Mr. Byrne appears to be a very powerful man. If he is disappointed or angry with me…well, I'm anxious about what he might do."

"Charles, what are you talking about?"

"Grandmother, I can be drafted."

Lillian's voice took on a warm and motherly tone. "Dear, you needn't worry that William Byrne would ever do anything to harm you. I told you that he's a friend of mine."

There was another brief pause, and then, "You see, Charles, although Bill and I have always had very different perspectives, particularly when it comes to politics, he is an honorable man. I can only guess at what he shared with you about his business, but you must appreciate that there are remarkably powerful forces working outside of our sphere. It's true that he controls some of those forces, and it is also a fact that they conduct their business in ways that some of us might consider questionable. But you should keep in mind that Bill Byrne has now worked through four different administrations, which I must say is quite an accomplishment.

Grandmother Lillian continued, "If you think about it, you've been afforded a rather unique opportunity. Under the circumstances, I think I would agree with your decision; it appears to me that you're quite busy with your own work, and your new life."

Charles recognized that his grandmother was offering her own subtle commentary on his relationship with Emily, but the context and softness in her voice let him believe, at least for the moment, she was satisfied with him.

"As a friend, Bill called me yesterday to tell me that the two of you had spoken. Just so you know, he also told me that I should be proud to have such a fine young man as a grandson. I told him that he was correct. I am proud."

Chapter Eleven

For Heaven Sakes

"Think you're escaping and run into yourself.
Longest way round is the shortest way home."
Ulysses - James Joyce

Autumn in Chicago is extraordinary; the crisp clean air and the natural beauty of the changing leaves make a walk through one of the city's many neighborhood parks a pleasure. But despite the fabulous weather, Charles Albright could not forget his encounter with William Byrne, or the real possibility that he might soon be drafted. Mostly because he had no control over these life-changing possibilities, he grew more distant, anxious, and fatigued. If he slept his worries would only return in the morning, further amplified by the headlines that broadcast a constant escalation of the war and the unrelenting conscription of new men. Across the country, student resistance was becoming louder and more violent, yet the Johnson administration's singular response was to draft more people. Charles did not doubt William Byrne's declaration that, "Most of them will be headed for Southeast Asia." He only knew that he did not want to be one of them.

By Thanksgiving it was clear that he needed a change of scenery. So, in spite of his anxieties, or perhaps because of them, he decided to undertake one of the most worrisome trips a young man will ever make - taking the girlfriend home to meet the parents.

"My grandparents live just down the block a couple of houses," Charles said, as they pulled into the driveway of his parent's home, a three-bedroom Tudor that appeared to Emily as a suburban palace. "It's always been nice to have them so close." As he spoke, Charles realized that he was commenting on both the physical and emotional distance that his grandparents had in his life.

The five-hour drive from the city had been quiet and reflective, small-talk mostly unnecessary. The larger and more obvious issues were left unspoken leaving the couple to either listen to the fading radio or enjoy their communal silence.

Charles got out of the Camaro and walked around to open Emily's door. He had performed this same small offering of chivalry many times before, but today as he reached to take her hand he thought he recognized both anticipation and the pleasant buzz of optimism. Her smile was real, but around her eyes he could see a kind of tenseness that he knew came from this their moment of truth. For reasons he couldn't yet explain, he was glad for it, and anticipated that this anxiety would be well-received by his people. As she stood, he kissed her lightly on the cheek, and whispered, "Thank you. I know they'll love you."

Instead of ringing the bell, Charles instinctively pushed open the oversized, wooden front door. Hanging from its center was an impressive cornucopia, expertly decorated with tiny gourds, miniature pumpkins, and colorful leaves.

Crossing the threshold into the foyer, he announced, "Is anybody home?"

The house was warm and smelled of cinnamon, sage, and all the other wonderful homecoming aromas that help make Thanksgiving the best of all human holidays.

"They're here, Sarah!" Grandpa Bill shouted as he jumped up from his chair in the living room.

From out of the nearby kitchen came Charles' family. Grandmother Sarah, a small almost miniature woman with a head full of beautiful white hair tenderly reached out to touch his face with both hands. His mother, Charys waited her turn, and then embraced her son not bothering to hide the small tear that touched his cheek and heart. Grandpa Bill was there pumping his hand and clapping him on the back. And then Gordon, standing in the kitchen doorway wearing both an apron and a welcome-home grin, waited patiently for his son to approach and embrace.

Stepping back next to Emily, all Charles could see were eight eager eyes, each filled with the questions and anticipation that had captured their imagination since the announcement that their young man was "bringing a girl home for Thanksgiving."

"Well, aren't you going to introduce us to this beautiful young woman?" Grandpa Bill insisted.

"For heaven's sake, give them a moment," Sarah scolded, as she lightly punched an elbow into his side.

"Yes. Well, Emily, I'd like you to meet my family. This is my mother, Charys, my grandparents, Sarah and Bill Albright, and that man back there, the one holding up the house, is my father, Gordon. Everyone, I'd like you to meet my friend, Emily Krist."

All went well that day for the young couple. Because it was one of the few things that mother and grandmother could do in anticipation of the couple's visit, the Thanksgiving feast was prepared with far more enthusiasm and scale than ever before.

In contrast to the women's diligent efforts, during those three days of advanced preparation, the Albright men employed every possible maneuver to stay away from the kitchen; it was clear that should they linger they would be put to work or sent to the store. Never before had they seen their spouses take on such an amazing and complex variety of Thanksgiving dishes. By Wednesday evening the meal had grown into multiple courses, requiring dishes, crockery, and utensils that neither of the men had ever seen before.

After the feast, the family retired to the living room for coffee, desert, and conversation. Earlier in the afternoon, Emily had made the happy discovery of an antique rocking chair, an Albright family heirloom that sat next to the sofa. She anticipated correctly that this was the same chair that Sarah and Charys had used while comforting the baby Charles. She found the aged oak rocker with its well-worn cushion especially appealing. Not only could she imagine the two Albright women sitting in the dark anxiously listening to the radio for any kind of good news, but this comfortable piece of furniture also reminded Emily of her own safe spot: Grandmother Saffii's rocking chair. This one sat close enough to the hearth for her to be able to enjoy the fire's warmth, but still removed from the others so that she could remain discreetly out of the family's conversation. It made for the perfect spot; courteously distant, but close enough to listen as the Albright's relived some of their favorite holiday memories, memories considerably different from her own.

As everyone enjoyed their pumpkin pie, Emily allowed herself the moment to take in the comforts of the room. Around the well-appointed space were a number of charming family photographs, including several faded black-and-whites. Earlier, Emily had spent time studying each image, trying to memorize the faces and imagine the circumstances in which the pictures were taken. She was especially drawn to one that she assumed was Sarah and Bill's wedding photo. The snapshot was easily forty years old, taken as an ecstatic young couple danced down the aisle of a small country church. In sharp contrast, there was a smaller picture of Otto Campbell, one hand in the air and the other on a Bible, as he was sworn in as Illinois' Attorney General. It did not go unnoticed that a somber, perfectly dressed Lillian Campbell stood by his side.

The room also featured several remarkable, oversized oil paintings, the largest of which hung above the fireplace and was brightly illuminated by flood lights recessed into the ceiling. All three were landscapes, presumably of Iowa fields and farms, but done in highly exaggerated and mildly off-putting colors. The lack of technique and artist's indecision imposed upon the finished work an obvious amateur quality.

Emily later learned from a judiciously worded question that the artist was a close friend of the family. Ellen Kingsley, now Mrs. Ellen Krammer, had been one of Charys' college sorority sisters and a bridesmaid at their wedding. While at Iowa, she studied painting and earned what would turn out to be an unused Bachelors of Fine Arts.

Like many Pi Phi's, Ellen married well. She and her husband, Anderson Krammer still lived in Iowa City. Doctor Krammer was a surgeon and instructor of cardiology at the University of Iowa's prestigious medical center. Fortunately for his patients, Dr. Krammer's skills as a surgeon were more highly developed than his wife's were as a painter. The three large canvases that held such a place of importance in the Albright living room had been a present to Charys on her forty-first birthday. Originally, Ellen had consigned all eight of the paintings, which she referred to as her "fall romance collection", to the Trundle Art and Antique Gallery in Coralville, Iowa. Six years later, five of the large canvases were still hanging in various corners of the shop, while Ellen and Arthur Trundall awaited their first sale.

It was during an earlier reconnaissance of the room that Emily discovered a smaller, almost modest, framed canvas. Its placement between a heavily curtained window and a built-in set of bookshelves made it inconspicuous enough that a casual visitor might have overlooked it altogether.

In a stunning contrast to the Krammer canvases, this small picture made the most of subtle shades and precise brushwork. Set in what might have been the seventeenth century, it warmly depicted a festival where a large group of people had congregated in an open public space surrounded by several buildings, perhaps homes or shops. Many of the guests were seated, while others danced around a central figure that enthusiastically played the bagpipes. Under closer examination, the picture reveals itself as both sophisticated and highly detailed with more than a dozen well-defined characters, each face telling their own unique and personal story.

This picture was a puzzle to Emily. It seemed clear that if it was an original it was not done by a contemporary painter. Which begged the question, why was it here, and why in such an unappreciated space?

"If I sit here any longer I'm going to turn into a pumpkin," announced Grandpa Bill as he hauled himself out of the easy chair. "Who wants to play some cards? Emily, come be my partner and we'll teach these fella's a lesson."

"Oh, I don't think you'd want me as a partner," replied Emily. "I've never been much of a card player."

That last sentence was true; the Krist's were not card players. On holidays and family gatherings, the children were never included in any adult activities, especially card games. Instead, the adults preferred to spend their time sitting at the mammoth dining room table, drinking gallons of highly sweetened ice tea, and complaining bitterly about the obvious "decline in the American way of life."

The men would occupy the north end of the table where their patriarch, Alder Dyer Krist, would hold court. Jacob's brothers (Stephen and Glen, along with their brother-in-law, Curt) would sit dutifully on those severe, straight-backed wooden chairs, railing against the government's "strangle hold" on commodity prices, the stupidity of their elected county supervisors, and those galling Kennedy's. As a man of few words, Alder seldom spoke, but when he did it generally took the form of a single declarative sentence. For example, he might espouse the virtues of hard work by demanding, "Don't you dare pray for a lighter load, you pray for a stronger back." One of his favorites themes was to admonish the failings of science, while praising the "good Lord's handiwork." "What value is it going to the moon?" he would ask. "Will it bring you any closer to God?"

The women were assigned the south end of the table for their pity parties. In one of his few acts of chivalry, Alder insisted that Grandmother Saffii be spared the severity of the dining room chairs and was instead enthroned in her well-worn rocker at the nadir of the table. It would have been Saffii who had just spent the past five hours on her feet both preparing and cleaning up after the family's noon meal. From this spot of distinction, she would mostly listen and crochet while the other women enthusiastically disparaged their children's teachers, Pastor Frederickson's wife, and, of course, their husbands.

Meanwhile, the Krist kids were expected to be invisible and silent. Regardless of the season or current weather conditions, the children were expected to play outdoors and as far away from the house as possible. There was no patience for any child who would come to the table hurt, hungry, or bored.

On a rare occasion, Grandmother Saffii would get out her box of double-twelve dominoes from a drawer in the sideboard and offer to play a hand or two with her grandchildren. The game was always held in the kitchen, and never once included another adult. As the youngest grandchild by more than six years, Emily's older cousins made no effort to involve her in any of their games, or conversation; however, this cold indifference did offer one positive: instead of being asked to play, Emily was allowed to observe the game from Grandmother Saffii's knee. From this happy spot she could watch her grandmother match and move the colored tiles out onto the pattern. Occasionally, she would even allow Emily to retrieve her penny from the "train" (Saffii played a mean game of Mexican Train) after which the two of them would face the other children and shout, "Back in business, boys."

Unlike the Krist's, most children learn their family's favorite card games by standing at the elbow of a parent or relative. It's a wonderful tradition that teaches the observant child more than just a game; a hotly contested and well-played hand offers a glimpse into the valuable adult skills of guile, subterfuge, and patience. Whether its canasta, pitch, pinochle, euchre, whist, five hundred, hearts or gin rummy, the pleasure found in fifty-two paste boards and a cold drink cannot be overvalued. There are those that prefer to play blind tiger, red dog, schafkopf, pig, slap jack, or straight draw poker, but regardless of the game, the time a child spends observing and playing cards should be viewed as a valuable life lesson and enthusiastically encouraged.

The Albright's played a spirited game of ten-point pitch. Mr. Hoyle says, "There is a large family of games in which the object is to win high, low, jack, and game." Originally an English diversion called All Fours it was brought to the United States by the first colonists. Over time it evolved into Seven Up, sometimes called Old Sledge. Today, pitch can be played as five-point, seven-point, or the Albright's preference, ten-point. Because you only use trump cards, pitch is fast-paced and benefits from fearless bidding. A relatively simple game to learn, it is rich with subtleties. Ten-point pitch appreciates luck, but rewards the ruthless.

The four card players retired to the Albright kitchen table to do battle. As Gordon went to retrieve a deck of cards and a pad of paper, drink orders were taken and filled. Charles tended bar while Grandpa Bill did his best to quickly teach his partner the rules. By the time everyone was seated and the drinks delivered, Emily understood just enough of the game to know that she was getting nine cards and "that the three is the key."

Thanks to Grandpa Bill's skill and bravado, the two made a good showing in the first game, losing thirty-eight to fifty-two. By midway through the second set, Emily was becoming more confident and aggressive, even winning an eight-bid from Charles.

It was during a break when Grandpa Bill had stepped out of the room that Emily screwed-up her courage and asked about the picture in the living room.

"Mr. Albright, I was enjoying that wonderful little painting that hangs in your living room. Can you tell me about it? It looks like it might be quite old?"

Gordon continued to shuffle the cards as if he hadn't heard her, or was ignoring the question. This pause was certainly no longer than ten-seconds, but its effect on Emily was to set her heart pounding with the fear that she'd somehow said something wrong.

Finally, Gordon replied, "There's not a whole lot I can tell you about that old thing. Years ago, when we first moved into this house, Charles was probably two or three, Charys found it in the attic. I guess we both liked it. It's been hanging on the wall there in the living room ever since."

He smiled and began to deal the cards as Grandpa Bill sat down.

"Okay, partner," he cheered. "Bid 'em up."
Nothing more was said about the picture.

The next morning as Charles carried the bags out to the car, Emily stole away for a last look at the painting. After the card game she had retired to the guest bedroom where she laid awake wondering why such a wonderful work of art had received such a short shrift from the Albright's. Everything about their home and appointments, except perhaps the unfortunate Krammer pictures, confirmed that Charys Albright had admirable taste. How could she not recognize the qualities of this little painting and give it a better more visible spot in her home?

Emily was standing close to the painting, intently studying the detail and pondering how she was going to bring it up with Charles, when from behind her Gordon Albright suddenly announced, "I'm glad you like the painting."

"Yes, it's charming," she stuttered, while turning so that she could face both Mr. Albright and the painting.

For a moment neither said anything, but then Gordon Albright surprised her as he stepped closer to the picture, and offered, "I'm especially drawn to these characters."

He pointed to the lower left corner of the canvas where a young and handsome couple is making their way toward the celebration. There is a stunning woman in a beautiful golden dress highlighted by brilliant white sleeves and setoff with a large red brooch. Beside her is an especially handsome young man sporting a rich tan jacket and carrying a top hat; he serenely looks at the young woman whose gloved hand he holds in his right. Behind them appear two ladies-in-waiting, each beautifully dressed but with the obvious look of envy on their faces. A young boy labors behind the couple. From his expression you can see he is trying his best to hold the regal woman's dress off the ground, but is distracted by a small white dog that is busy barking and wagging its tail. All of this extraordinary detail was in a section of the canvas that would measure less than four-inches square.

"They're fabulous," Emily whispered, knowing full-well that Gordon Albright was studying her reaction.

A gust of cold wind accompanied Charles through the front door.

"I guess that's everything. Are you ready?" he asked.

As it turned out, Emily did not need to think of a way to bring up the painting. They weren't out of the neighborhood before Charles asked, "What did Dad say to you?"

"You mean about the painting?" Emily replied. "He just said that he was glad I liked it, and then showed me a little detail that he admired. It's a very nice painting."

"I suppose it is." Charles replied. "It's always been there. In that spot, I mean. Guess I forgot about it."

Chapter Twelve

"I carry your heart..."

"Here is the deepest secret nobody knows."
e.e. cummings

Still savoring the success of their visit to Cedar Rapid, the return trip to the city was filled with excited conversation and grand plans for their first Christmas together. Emily's new job at WGN provided her the perfect out for not going home to Freeland; due to her lack of seniority, she was virtually guaranteed to be one of those working in the newsroom on Christmas and New Year's Day. There was a genuine moment of remorse where Emily almost felt bad enough about her mother being alone for the holidays that she considered inviting her to come to Chicago. But with the grueling work schedule and limited time that they could be together, she rationalized that it made no sense to inject her mother into what she hoped would be her best Christmas ever.

Charles plans were more dramatic. Armed with the unspoken blessings of his family, he had decided to propose to Emily on Christmas Eve. The location and amenities had yet to be resolved.

This exhilarating decision was accompanied by a host of complications, including how to inform his family that he would not be coming home for Christmas without telling them why. Had he been able to see it from his parent's point of view, he might have recognized how quickly they would see through his poor deception. By not returning to Cedar Rapids for Christmas - something he'd always done before, and right on the heels of bringing a girlfriend home to meet them - would certainly provide substantial evidence that matrimonial considerations were in the works.

For the next three weeks, Charles quietly, and with surprising stealth, planned their once-in-a-lifetime moment. What may seem like a simple straightforward task actually demands a number of strategic decisions and clever subterfuge. For instance, if you plan to propose marriage, you must have in your possession at the time of the request an engagement ring. To purchase what is a very personal, not to mention expensive item, requires both fortitude and the size of the woman's finger. And there lies the problem: how does one discover the size of the woman's finger without informing the intended of your intentions?

Charles briefly considered taking June into his confidence with the hope that she could provide the crucial information, but after thinking about it, he remembered an episode that had taken place only a few weeks before which put both her loyalties and ability to keep a secret into question.

It happened that Grandmother Lillian had given Charles her symphony tickets for a Sunday matinee performance of Mahler's Fifth. When he called to invite Emily to join him, June answered the phone.

"She's still at work," June informed him.

In Emily's absence, Charles chose to take advantage of the situation and asked June, "Do you think Emily would like to go to a symphony concert?"

June was confident that she would.

Armed with this information, Charles impulsively decided to surprise Emily.

He instructed June to "not say a word about the tickets." He added, "Just tell Emily it's a surprise, and that we're going someplace where she should wear a nice dress."

At some point in their relationship most men come to understand that women universally hate this kind of "surprise", preferring to have as many specific details as possible for any adventure in which they have been asked to "wear a nice dress." At this moment in their courtship, Charles was innocent of this important information.

On the afternoon of the concert, as he waited in their apartment for Emily to finish dressing, he happened upon a remarkable book lying beside the sofa. The book, which was really more like a large textbook, lay on the floor next to the sofa, mostly hidden by a copy of the October 1966 Vogue magazine; one that featured George Harrison's glamorous wife, Patti Boyd. The magazine's cover prominently displayed Miss Boyd's beautiful face, (a face that has a striking resemblance to June's rounded features) artfully lodged beneath an enormous and utterly ridiculous fur hat. In spite of the distracting photo, Charles discovered the book and its substantive title, *The Concert Companion - A Comprehensive Guide to Symphonic Music* by Robert Bagar and Louis Biancolli.

One could jump to the conclusion that to help Emily through her first experience at the symphony, good friend June had ignored her promise to Charles, and had instead informed her roommate of their secret destination. It is also possible that she'd gone so far as to acquire the Bagar and Biancolli. An additional scrap of circumstantial evidence appeared when Charles discovered a slip of paper, perhaps a bookmark, coincidentally lodged in the section dedicated to Mahler's Fifth Symphony. Regardless, it was clear to Charles that it was both unfair and too much of a burden to entrust June with such important information.

Emily Krist owned very little jewelry. Before her relationship with Charles the only people who would have ever considered giving Emily jewelry would have been either her father or June. The one ring that she did enjoy wearing was a gold band so thin and diminutive that its value was purely sentimental. This tiny ring, with no setting or ornamentation, had been one of a pair that each friend had given the other at the time of their graduation. It was June's sentimental idea that they each buy the other's ring. For the next four years this charming memento never left Emily left hand.

With both hands now deep in the soapy dishwater, and Charles capably standing by with the soggy dish towel, Emily absent-mindedly fished around in the sink for the remaining silverware. Instead of finding the two butter knives that lay hidden under the suds, Emily painfully discovered the surgically sharp, forged utility knife. Although not a terribly deep cut, by the time she drew her hand from the dishwater there was already a significant amount of blood seeping from the wound on her left hand ring finger.

"Oh, please," she muttered, snatching the towel from Charles, and then quickly wrapping it around her bleeding digit.

"What is it?" he asked.

Carefully peeling back the towel to peer at the wound, she answered, "I just cut myself on that darned knife. I wonder if we have any Band-Aids in the medicine cabinet."

"Do you want me to go look?"

"No. I'll go. I can probably find it quicker," she said while taking off the now bloody ring and placing it on the windowsill above the sink. "I'll be right back," she said rewrapping her hand in towel.

The very thing that Charles needed to happen had just happened. There lying on the windowsill was the template for his marital happiness. The question was how to take advantage of Emily's misfortune?

His first thought was to locate a piece of paper and pencil, so that he could make a tracing of the ring. Armed with an accurate stencil, it would be simple for the jeweler to learn the ring's true size.

As Charles began thinking about where he could quickly locate pencil and paper, the sound of a key opening the front door signaled June's return. Glancing around the small space, an alternative presented itself in the form of a bag of carrots that still lay on the kitchen table waiting to be returned to the refrigerator.

"Hello. Anyone home?" she shouted from the hallway.

Emily called back from the bathroom, "I've cut myself. Do you know if we have any Band-Aids?"

"Let me see," June said, as she hurried down the hall to the bathroom. "Hi, Charles," she offered, racing past the kitchen door still wearing her winter coat. "Did you look under the sink, Em?"

Charles seized the opportunity and quickly pulled a carrot from the bag. Snatching the bloody ring from the sill, he slid it over the vegetable, and then sliced off the top of the carrot right at the mark where vegetable touched gold. The knife was then quickly returned to the sink, the ring to the windowsill, and the unnecessary stub of carrot was disposed by popping it into his mouth. As he walked out to the hall closet to put the carrot into his overcoat pocket, he contentedly asked, "Are you okay, Emily?"

Poeta Bianchi could not resist the temptation to laugh as Charles responded to her question, "Do you know the size of ring that she wears?" by extracting a carrot from his overcoat pocket. The elegant Miss Bianchi had been employed at Campagna's Fine Jewelry for more than twelve years, and in that time she had helped many men purchase an engagement ring. Among the entertaining methods that these future husbands employed to identify the proper size for their beloved's ring, she was amused to admit that this was the first time she had ever worked with a vegetable.

On December 24, 1966, Charles Albright proposed to Emily Krist over lunch at Jacques. The menu featured a spectacular spinach quiche and a bottle of Chablis Vaudesir Grand Cru – 1963.

It had been exactly two hundred and ten days since their collision in front of the Goodman Theater. Like that unexpected moment on Randolph Street, Emily had no forewarning of Charles' intentions and was happily taken by surprise at his well-rehearsed and successful proposal. She was so unaware of his intentions that as they took their seats in the restaurant, Emily imagined this romantic moment was more about convenience than commitment, Jacques being only a short cab ride from WGN studios.

Charles will always take great pleasure from surprising his wife. This evergreen quality comes mostly from deep love, but also because she never anticipates an unexpected kindness. Emily's innocence was shaped by the regrettable fact that her people did not appreciate the joy that comes from the expression of a selfless act; during her formative years, there were no spontaneous acts of love, or fun. Instead, the Krist's were cynical souls, hardened by work, and their fervent commitment to a demanding God. Their one outward indulgence was the rigorous celebration for the coming reward, the one that was not of this Earth.

The proposal had a wonderful cinematic quality that suffered only slightly from Charles rushed delivery. He had searched for a long time to find a poet or writer who shared his sentiments without overreaching. Turned out it was e.e. cummings perfect poem, *i carry your heart* that expressed both his conviction and confidence.

i carry your heart with me (i carry it in

my heart) i am never without it (anywhere

i go you go, my dear; and whatever is done

by only me is your doing, my darling)

i fear no fate (for you are my fate, my sweet) i want

no world (for beautiful you are my world, my true)

and it's you are whatever a moon has always meant

and whatever a sun will always sing is you

here is the deepest secret nobody knows

(here is the root of the root and the bud of the bud

and the sky of the sky of a tree called life; which grows

higher than soul can hope or mind can hide)

and this is the wonder that's keeping the stars apart

i carry your heart (i carry it in my heart)

"I love you Emily and want to spend the rest of my life with you. Will you marry me?"

As he spoke these words, Charles anxiously fumbled to open the ring box that he'd been hiding in his jacket pocket. There was a tearful nod of acceptance and the rush of an impassioned kiss, followed by the placement of the perfectly-sized engagement ring upon her left-hand ring finger. They clung to one another oblivious to anything outside of their own moment.

Eventually, Emily held up her hand to admire the ring. As she studied the stone, a small almost imperceptible look of concern passed across her face. If Charles hadn't been observing her reaction so closely it would have likely gone unnoticed.

But it was there.

Charles screwed up all of his courage, and asked, "Is there something wrong?"

"Oh, no; it's perfect. You, the proposal, and the ring; everything," she quickly replied.

"I don't know," he said. "It felt like there was something, something bothering you?"

Emily held out her hand. Then turning to look at Charles, she smiled the smile that only comes from genuine love, and added, "I was just thinking…"

"What?" Charles anxiously asked.

"Well, do you think you'd mind if I didn't wear the ring on my left hand. It's such a beautiful ring, and my hand is so ugly. If it's okay with you, I think I'd rather wear it on my right hand."

Notwithstanding her abbreviated pinkie, Emily's left hand was an identical match with her right; long shapely fingers that were both elegant and strong. Only it was clear to Charles that an engagement ring on this ring finger, the one next to her littler little finger, would never do.

"Of course," he said, taking her left hand in his and then gently pulling the ring from her finger. "Will you marry me?" he asked again.

"Yes, I will," she replied as he slid the ring on to her right ring finger.

Chapter Thirteen

312 Kemper Hall

"I never let my schooling interfere with my education."
Mark Twain

The wedding was set for May 28, 1967. The date itself held no special meaning or magic for either of them, but was treated more like a target on the calendar. It was decided that not only would there not be a church service, but they would also forgo the traditional trappings of flowers, dresses, tuxedos, and the extravagant reception, feeling them indulgent and unnecessary. They preferred instead a civil ceremony to be attended by their families, followed by an intimate dinner. In spite of this simpler approach there were still many arrangements and details that needed to be worked out. The one that troubled Emily the most was how to manage Lillian Campbell's expectations.

Selecting a civil servant to perform the wedding ceremony turned out to be one of the simpler details on Charles' to-do list. Associate Judge Jonah Rothstein of the Municipal Division for the Cook County Judicial Circuit Court was ideally suited for the role. Along with his official title and robes, Judge Rothstein was also a special friend of Charles, one that went back to his undergraduate days at Northwestern University.

Steiner, as he was known to the fifty-four young men who lived on the third floor of Kemper Hall, was employed by Northwestern University as the dormitory's floor monitor. Charles first encounter with Jonah "Steiner" Rothstein would have been at a freshman orientation in the Kemper commons.

Standing before his charges dressed in a pair of crudely hacked-off blue jean shorts, a red bowling shirt that read **Grand Lanes, Brooklyn, NY**, and black, high-top Converse tennis shoes - sans socks - he held up his hands for quiet.

"My name is Jonah Rothstein and I'm the floor monitor. Some people call me Stein, but you can call me Mr. Rothstein. I've been doing this job for two years. I do it because I like the free rent. But to get my free rent, the University says I've got to enforce all the dormitory policies. That paper in your hand will tell you what they are. It also says I'm supposed to be a "mentor," which might suggest that if you've got a question or a problem you can ask me."

Rothstein paused to look around the room before adding, "Only here's the thing, boys… I don't give a rat's ass about your problems, so don't bother me with 'em."

The unexpected audacity in Rothstein's remark left the newcomers seriously confused. For most of these privileged young men such a startling and callous greeting was unprecedented. But with his new charges now badly off balance, Rothstein coyly added, "There are, however, certain services that I am happy to provide… and my prices are reasonable."

When a young man begins his college career, along with his new found freedom comes certain desires, sometimes misinterpreted as needs. Many, perhaps most, of these desires are unavailable to minors. It is possible that a more seasoned student, one with an aggressive entrepreneurial spirit, can assist a younger, less-experienced boy by helping him acquire those desires

Steiner's dormitory room was known to the young men of Kemper Hall as the General Store. There one could procure the kind of contraband that they were unable to legally acquire for themselves. If, for instance, you were in the predicament of needing a mid-term paper in Freshmen Literature, you could purchase from the General Store an appropriately brilliant essay (i.e. **Nick Caraway's Pursuit of the 'American Dream' in Fitzgerald's *The Great Gatsby***) that was guaranteed to receive a passing grade or your money back. Say you were looking to play poker; Steiner generally had at least two tables and a reasonably well-stocked bar working in his personal dorm suite. Or if you had the right kind of date, he was happy to sell you a bottle of slow gin and a package of Trojan's. Cigarettes, liquor, pornography, false identification, lottery tickets, fireworks, and personal loans were all available at significantly inflated prices. Steiner was a merchant, banker, grocer, and in his own way a kind of mentor. Although hardly what Northwestern officials or their parents would have condoned, Steiner was certainly as memorable a character as any member of the university's esteemed faculty.

Graduating a year early from high school, Charles Albright was just seventeen when he arrived on the Northwestern campus that fall. Thanks to his outstanding academic work at Cedar Rapids Washington, he had been invited to attend the prestigious university on an academic scholarship; this also made his rent free.

Despite his age and youthful appearance, Charles was hardly what you'd call prudish; what the Iowa boy lacked was real-world experience. Instead of being distracted by those first adult opportunities, Charles chose to take his responsibilities to his scholarship seriously. So seriously, that during his first semester he took little time for anything but study. That kind of personal commitment meant he had no real need to avail himself of Steiner's services, in fact, until Christmas break, Jonah Rothstein would have been unable to identify Charles Albright as one of the young men assigned to the third floor of Kemper Hall.

When he thought about it, and he thought about it a lot, the young Jonah Rothstein did not especially like his given name. Under the category of "Isn't life difficult enough?" a person who has been tagged with the name of someone especially famous also inherits the additional challenge of making their own identity distinct from their namesake's.

If taken literally the story of Jonah and the whale is a puzzler for any kid, Jew or Gentile. Everyone knows the basics: God has told Jonah to take a message to the people of Nineveh, informing them that they've got to change their evil ways - or else. Hoping to flee from his responsibilities to both God and man, Jonah runs away and hides on board a boat headed for Tar shish. God is now unhappy, so, He stirs the seas and sends a raging storm upon Jonah, who we learn has inexplicably fallen asleep in the bow of the boat. When awakened by the anxious sailors, Jonah bravely tells the men that the only way to appease God will be for them to cast him overboard; it seems there was little disagreement with the proposed solution. Jonah is now adrift and alone in a tempestuous sea. While looking back upon the city of Jaffa, and wondering how he ever got himself into this spot, he is unkindly swallowed by a giant sea creature, perhaps a whale. Somehow undigested but still inside the monster's gut, Jonah spends the next three days pleading his case with God before he's finally expelled.

For two thousand eight hundred years this wonderful story has provided children their first opportunity to critique the plausibility for a literal interpretation of an Old Testament miracle; heady stuff for an eight-year-old. In Jonah's case, his Rabbi (Rabbi Boim) was the kind of young-at-heart teacher who hadn't yet grown weary of questions like, "Can God make a rock so big even he can't lift it?" Boim also appreciated that Jonah and his classmates were far more likely to discover the important message of personal redemption by spending their time contemplating Jonah **and** the whale, as opposed to Jonah **in** the whale. In this case, the modern-day Jonah would become the familiar operative noun.

"Why not, David, or Benjamin, or even Adam?" he often asked his mother.

Her perfect answer was always, "I was thinking about Moses, but changed my mind."

Steiner's people considered themselves lucky to be first-generation Brooklyn Jews.

In the spring of 1927, Taavi Rothstein and Freda Feldenkrais were forever joined as man, wife, and business partner; both considered their well-arranged marriage a bargain.

Among the old men and superstitious women of Erfurt, Germany, Freda had distinguished herself as both a practiced midwife and a reliable freelance psychic. Thanks mostly to the accuracy of her predictions (she claimed ninety-nine percent, although it was really closer to seventy), Freda had cultivated a considerable following among the area's expectant mothers. It was this steady stream of round and frightened women who would quietly make their way to the Rothstein's backdoor hoping for a cup of tea and some professional insight into the gender of their unborn babies that had made Freda Rothstein the primary breadwinner of the family.

Taavi, like his father and father's father, was an undertaker. A pragmatic and disciplined man, he paid little attention to his wife's prognostications; that is until the night she foretold Hitler's appointment as Chancellor. Although hardly a stretch of her psychic powers, it was enough to expedite their departure from Germany just weeks before Hitler closed shop on the Weimar Republic.

Soon after arriving in the United States, and armed only with a formal letter of introduction provided by Freda's cousin (Eliahu Cerfbeer), Taavi found himself in the offices of the prominent Brooklyn business man and undertaker, Mr. Joseph Morris. Even though Eliahu Cerfbeer and Joseph Morris would never meet, Taavi's letter was adequate introduction to warrant a first meeting; Eliahu and Joseph were cousins on their mother's side.

What brought Taavi to those Brooklyn offices was Mr. Joseph Morris' reputation as a brilliant enterprising man, and their common heritage as German Jews transplanted to America. Joseph's father, I.M. Morris had moved his family and a profitable shipping concern from Bremerhaven, Germany in 1898. Morris had found considerable success by being one of the first to incorporate Gustav de Laval's rotary-motion turbines into his small fleet of steel ships. The faster, quieter, and more reliable vessels lowered his costs and made him a fortune.

Joseph Morris was I.M.'s second son. As a young man his most fervent wish had been to escape his father's considerable shadow by distinguishing himself in his own unique way. His epiphany came one afternoon while on the docks watching the flood of Jewish immigrants stagger off one of his father's ships. As he stood there thinking about all that these poor people had left behind, he realized that their faith, his faith, would make specific demands of these Jews. Leaving their European homes meant leaving the machinery of their religion. For instance, who would organize and manage their new synagogues? Back home the shopkeepers could rely upon the mutual protection societies, but who would see to that here? And when it came time for the *bagroben*, who would provide the *chevra kadisha*? To accommodate these beautiful needs, Morris built the first formal Jewish funeral home. In spite of his father's reticence, business boomed.

For the next twenty-five years, Taavi Rothstein faithfully worked for I.M. Morris, Inc. as their chief embalmer. By saving every penny they could, Taavi and Freda were able to help his younger brothers (Herman and Saul) emigrate from western Poland to the States. Thanks to Taavi's new associations in the Brooklyn business world, both brothers were able to secure jobs as salesmen for the Dodge & Huncke Chemical Company. Dodge & Huncke specialized in the sale of embalming fluid.

Now completely dedicated to the 1958 version of the American Dream, the Rothstein brothers began to look for ways to break out on their own. Thanks to a bit of insider information, they learned Dodge & Huncke would soon be on the market, largely because Thomas Huncke was about to be indicted for tax evasion.

The Rothstein's worked hard and invested wisely. In short order they would acquire four other chemical companies, a chain of Acme Super Markets, a bowling alley in Trenton (Saul loved to bowl) and a share of the Sullivan Street Theater in Greenwich Village. From baby lotion to embalming fluid, the brothers Rothstein had it covered.

Taavi's middle-son, Jonah was in his second year at the Northwestern Law School. Along with his duties as a floor monitor and purveyor of vice, Steiner was also a very serious student. Seven days a week, rain or shine, he could be found deep among the stacks on the third floor of the law library consuming torts, contracts, and litigation. His energies and stamina were legendary among the boys of Kemper Hall. But Steiner was also a pragmatic businessman, profiting from the knowledge that people will always pay when they want something bad enough, especially if that something is forbidden.

As far as his personal life was concerned, Jonah Rothstein shared nothing with anyone; an East Coast enigma, happy to profit by providing teenage boys adult fare. He was utterly calculating and ruthless. No one was allowed credit. All sales were final. If ever approached by anyone outside the brethren of Kemper, he would indignantly feign ignorance of any such operation. As trustworthy as the great clock at Greenwich, every night at ten o'clock, and never a minute before, the doors to the General Store would open for business.

The first time that Charles Albright availed himself of the General Store's services was on a Friday night late in February. Charles and several of his friends had just finished a grueling week that was tipped-in by an unanticipated and ridiculously difficult exam in Dr. Amory Spellings, Soc. 101 class. With eight-inches of fresh snow on the ground and almost nothing to do, it was agreed that Charles would go to the General Store and buy some beer, preferably cold, and not Schlitz.

"I'd like to buy some beer, if you've got any?"

"What makes you think I would have any beer, or if I did, that I'd sell it to someone like you?" Steiner replied.

I don't know. I just heard that you might have some beer to sell."

"Does this look like a grocery?" he asked.

"No, nothing like a grocery."

The door was only partially open, still Charles could see into the smoke-filled room where six young men were playing cards. As he peered past Rothstein and into the haze, Steiner glanced back into the room. Then, slowly, he returned his gaze from the card players to Charles.

"Falstaff warm is two bucks; cold it's four."

"Two cold, please."

Charles roommate was a nitwit.

In 1960, Northwestern University required that all freshmen live on campus in university dormitories. On a pleasant enough afternoon in September, Charles had carried his luggage up two flights of stairs only to be confronted by a surly stranger who had already laid claim to the side of the dorm room that Charles preferred. This chubby problem was named Todd Seaton Kelly.

Todd Kelly's greatest sin was that he lived oblivious to the effect that his behavior had on the rest of the world. Born wealthy, Todd Kelly will always be wealthy. He will always be wealthy because his people are wealthy. It is out of conceit and contempt for the rest of the world that the Kelly's will make sure he stays that way, in spite of the boy's hurtful dangerous behavior.

In this case, Todd Kelly's improper conduct was influenced more by nurture than nature. His father was Robert Ryan Kelly, arguably Cook County's most successful and notorious attorney for the defense, and that is saying a lot in a town full of notorious attorneys for the defense.

Kelly made no effort to hide his considerable financial achievements. On the contrary, he understood that his future relied upon the parasitic agreements, outrageous scandal, wretched misery, and total disgrace of other wealthy people. If his law practice had a credo it would have been something simple like Sartre's observation that "like the wheel, we must be well greased."

It was no surprise that Robert Kelly loved seeing his picture in the paper.

"Best damn advertising you can get," he liked to say.

And the newspaper loved Robert Kelly. This was because wherever he went, so went rich and infamous felons. It also didn't hurt that Kelly was a handsome and strapping Irishman with an affected Irish brogue, a deep wardrobe of expensive Italian suits, and the manners of a pig. The camera loved him. Whether it was out at one of Chicago's late night spots surrounded by a bevy of beautiful women and professional athletes, or on the steps of the courthouse congratulating a relieved client, Robert Kelly was always available for a photo.

Photos of Kelly's son would also appear in the local fish wrap. During the first eight months of 1960, Todd Seaton Kelly had been arrested three times for trying to elude the Northbrook police department in one of his father's expensive automobiles. Along with speeding and resisting arrest, the younger Kelly was also charged with operating a motor vehicle while under the influence, public intoxication, and possession of alcohol by a minor. Todd's father did not like seeing his son's picture in the paper; but in spite of what were clear-cut cases of a wealthy young man doing reckless and foolish things, Todd Kelly spent a total of only ninety minutes behind bars - thirty minutes for each arrest - while paying traffic fines of just $450 dollars.

Clearly, *lucky life* does not dispense justice equally.

Todd Kelly was a nitwit and everyone who lived on the third floor of Kemper Hall knew it.

It was obvious from their first exchange that Charles Albright and Todd Kelly had nothing in common but a room in Kemper Hall. Charles was studious and quiet, Todd was loud and lazy. Todd was slick and aggressive, Charles was straightforward and sincere. One enjoyed school, the other saw it as a punishment. Besides their address, the only other thing they had in common was that neither liked the other.

Because they viewed school so differently, Charles went and Todd didn't, they rarely interacted. Within a week, Charles was seriously considering submitting a request for a change of roommates, but remembering Steiner's lack of empathy and the edict to never bother him with personal problems, he resigned himself to his bad draw and prayed nightly that Todd Kelly might be expelled or indicted.

Only Todd Kelly was not expelled. Instead, he was recruited, rushed, and pledged to the Tau Delta Phi fraternity. Unlike everyone else that Todd had ever known, the TD's saw him as a great catch and happily welcomed him into the brotherhood. Not only did their pledge have money, seemingly lots of money that he would lavishly spend on any and all of his comrades, but his well-known surname also offered the fraternity a seriously bankable cache. On that dark October night when Todd Kelly enthusiastically grabbed his ankles and pledged his devotion to the frat, it was understood that all of his new brothers could avail themselves to the professional legal services found at Kelly, Blake, and Ringwraith.

Pledge Todd Kelly lived for the TD's. He bought them beer, loaned them money, and volunteered for all of their insipid pranks. Later that November, Todd and two other suggestible initiates were told to don ski masks and run buck naked through the lobby of the Chi Omega sorority. Eyewitnesses reported that the girls were treated to very little.

Thanks to his open pocket book and complete lack of concern by the Kemper Hall floor monitor, by the semester break, Todd Kelly was, for all practical purposes, residing in the Tau Delta Phi fraternity house.

It was on Saturday, April 29, 1961 when Charles Albright and Jonah Rothstein became better acquainted.

Charles and two other fellows from Kemper had gone to the seven o'clock showing of the new John Wayne movie, *Rio Bravo*. After a visit to a local pizza place, the three returned to the dormitory where they stopped-off in the commons in hopes of finding a card game. Around eleven, Charles excused himself for a trip to the lavatory. On his way back to the commons, he passed his own room where he paused just long enough to hear unexpected noises coming from inside. Unsure what to do, he quietly tried the door and found it locked.

Hearing a strange and muffled voice coming from inside the room, Charles quickly dug out his key and flung open the door while snapping on the overhead light. A yelp of surprise came from a buck naked Todd Kelly as he madly stumbled to his feet exposing a limp and lifeless girl.

"What are you doing?" he screamed. "You're ruining it."

"You're an idiot. Why did you bring her here?"

Lying on the floor at Charles' feet was what had once been an elegant party dress, now a wadded-up ball of ruined yellow linen and crepe. Beside it was a mostly empty pint bottle of Four Roses whiskey and one black satin pump.

As Todd Kelly scrambled around on the floor in search of his pants, all the time cursing his roommates "shitty timing," Charles looked down on the girl who was still lying weirdly quiet on the bed. Nice looking, perhaps their age, she was slightly heavy in the hips with small girlish breasts. Her bra was still hooked in the back but had been callously pushed up under her chin. Her pink panties hung around her right ankle.

"Why isn't she moving," he wondered? "Why isn't she trying to cover herself?"

It was then he realized that the still body was unconscious.

"What's wrong with her?" Charles demanded.

"I don't know. Guess she can't hold her booze." Kelly offered while trying to pull on his black tuxedo trousers.

"Something's wrong with her. How long has she been this way?"

"I don't know. Long enough for me to get her panties off," he laughed.

The drunken boy reached over and pushed rudely on the girl's face. "Wake up, Trudi. Come on now, we gotta go. My roommate's here and he can see you naked."

Only the girl didn't move. She remained as still and white as a corpse; in fact, Charles feared that was what she was.

As if he were in slow-motion, Todd Kelly finally realized that the girl was not responding to his drunken nonsense. He knelt beside the bed and began to timidly slap at her cheeks. Like a mother singing to her sleeping child, he whispered, "Wake up, baby. Come on. We gotta go. It's time to go."

The girl lay cold and lifeless as a stone.

"Is she breathing?"

"I don't know," Todd whimpered. "What do you think we should do?"

Charles pushed Todd Kelly out of the way and bent over the girl's pale blue lips. After a long moment of silence, Charles barked, "Go get Rothstein. She isn't breathing."

The fat boy instantly bolted out of the door and down the hallway in the direction of the General Store.

Now on his knees beside the bed, Charles peered down onto the girl's ashen face. Later he would remember thinking that there had been no sign of life in the girl's face, and he wondered why that fact hadn't frightened him. But at that moment, he couldn't see or hear her breathing; her chest was still and refused to move. For all he knew she was already dead.

As if he feared he might wake her, Charles gently reached beneath the girl's head and removed the pillow, quietly laying it on the floor beside him. While lifting her chin, he realized that "officially" he'd never performed artificial respiration on anyone. Still, as a scout he'd dutifully memorized the procedures and knew exactly what needed to be done.

The girl smelled sour and tasted like liquor. When he pinched her nose and breathed into her mouth he could see the small pale chest expand slightly.

Again, but this time with a bigger breath. Again. And again.

Suddenly, the door flew open and there stood Jonah Rothstein.

"What the hell did you do to her?"

Charles took a moment between breathes to shout, "She's not breathing."

"Okay, god damn it, let me think. Keep it up Albright. Don't stop for anything. Kelly, throw a blanket over her."

Charles held the girl's nose and pried open her mouth before starting another round. As he bent down to administer the next breath, he could hear a definite rumbling from her stomach, followed by a violent fit of coughing and vomit that covered the bed, the girl, and Charles. Stunned by the horrible smell and shocking volume of the small girl's spew, Charles suffered a second dousing before he had the presence to get her on to her side and locate a wastebasket. By then there was little coming out of Trudi's mouth but a long thin line of drool and a whimpering cry for her mother.

As it became clear that the girl was not going to die, there was a passing moment of shared relief between Charles, Todd Kelly, and Jonah Rothstein. It didn't last long, no longer than it took to realize that they now had an audience of a dozen nineteen-year-old boys, all jockeying for position with the hopes of getting a peek at the drunken naked girl.

When Jonah Rothstein entered the men's lavatory carrying two cold bottles of Stroh's beer, Charles Albright was still standing in the center of three running showers with his arms hugging his chest, eyes closed as tight as he could manage, and still fully dressed - even his shoes. Charles was certain that the water could not get hot enough to wash off the smell, or the evening.

A nearly imperceptible smile crossed Steiner's face as he stood there in the doorway of the shower room looking at the pitiful condition of his charge and savior.

"Very ugly scene, Albright," Steiner observed.

Charles opened his eyes to find that Jonah Rothstein was now standing beside him in the shower, also fully dressed, and offering him a bottle of beer. For a second, he wondered if Rothstein was talking about him or the events in his dorm room.

After Rothstein slammed the door on the gaping dorm rats, he quickly took command of the scene.

"Kelly, get this girl in some clothes and then get her the hell out of here. You've got three minutes before I call the cops," he shouted. "Albright, you're going to have to clean this up. Here's the key to the custodian's closet."

Before he left to work the larger crowd control, Steiner offered the less than comforting remark, "You dumb bastards are lucky. If she would've died we'd all be eating breakfast in the Cook County jail."

As Charles, Todd, and Trudi considered that scenario, Steiner added, "Kelly for once be a mensch and take the girl home. Don't leave her on a doorstep somewhere."

Then the door closed behind him.

Poor, Trudi; by this point the miserable girl had sobered up enough to realize what a horrible mess she'd gotten herself into. Her solution was to sit on the edge of the bed wrapped in a vomit-soaked blanket while sobbing inconsolably into her hands; a trashed yellow party dress lay wadded-up in a ball on her lap.

106

Before word of the naked girl in room 312 spread any further, Steiner made sure that all of the boys returned to whatever it was they were doing. Along with his threats and cajoling came this advice, "Listen, boys... we are all in a hell of a lot of trouble here. If you don't believe me, think about what's going to happen if that girl goes to the police. I imagine it'll be tough to explain to your parents how you had nothing to do with it, especially if the police charge you with complicity to a rape. My advice is to say nothing about this... ever. Pleasant dreams, boys."

He knew it was a weak threat and that by breakfast the rest of the dormitory would be telling ridiculous, exaggerated versions of the story, but for the moment, he'd gotten his charges back into their rooms, the girl had been disposed of, and he now had time to figure out what to do next. He didn't need the shower, but it felt good to stand there beside the guy who might have just saved any chance he ever had of becoming a lawyer.

Steiner closed the General Store.

The next night at ten o'clock, Jonah Rothstein could be found deep in the stacks at the law library. From time to time someone seeking contraband would stop by and knock on his door, but no one ever answered. Without notice or fanfare, Steiner became just another student from the third floor of Kemper Hall.

In spite of his history as a cad, Todd Kelly did find Trudi a clean pair of his trousers and a T-shirt. Remembering Rothstein's threat to call the police, he quickly got the pathetic girl back to the Chi Omega sorority house; it was the Omega's Spring Formal that he had so effectively ruined for the naïve freshman.

Thankfully, Trudi did not go to the police. Mortified by her bad decisions and gullibility, she spent the remainder of the spring semester in hiding, coming out only for her American Literature final, and to be taken back home to Springfield, Missouri for summer break. If there was any positive that could come from such poor judgment, it was that Trudi's sisters would soon expose Todd Kelly as a potential rapist to every sorority on campus, thereby permanently ending his chances of dating another Northwestern co-ed.

That next fall, Charles occasionally spotted Trudi walking between classes, always surrounded by a gaggle of other girls who he assumed were her sorority sisters. Thankfully, she either ignored him, or was unable to remember the young man who on that awful night had most likely saved her life.

Jonah Rothstein and Charles Albright's extraordinary introduction acted as the catalyst for what was to become a lifetime friendship. Rothstein spent his last year of law school still enjoying free rent as the third floor monitor in Kemper Hall. Charles request for one of the floor's three private rooms was surprisingly approved; private rooms were seldom offered to underclassmen. It went unspoken, but Charles chose to believe that Steiner had somehow put in the fix.

In the spring of '62, Jonah Rothstein graduated from the Northwestern Law School in the top ten percent of his class. By then the entire Albright family had come to know and enjoy the one-of-a-kind, Jonah Rothstein. Charles took great pleasure in bringing Steiner back to Cedar Rapids for the holidays or long weekends. He knew that for Rothstein these trips were like excursions into a distant and foreign land, so different were the habits and attitudes of the Cedar Rapidians from his native Brooklyn.

After graduation, Rothstein was immediately employed by Graber, Lowberg, Horowitz, and Manning of Skokie, Illinois. His specialty was contract law, but he didn't stay with the firm for long. It took only three years before he was appointed as an Associate Judge for Cook County, the youngest in county history. It was there, ironically, in room 312, the same numbered room that Charles and Todd Kelly had shared, that he would direct the proceedings of Municipal Court.

Chapter Fourteen

Lightly Turns to Thoughts of Love

"And I still can see blue velvet through my tears."
Bernie Wayne and Lee Morris

"Really? The Lincoln Hotel?"

Grandmother Lillian picked up her sherry and directly drained the glass, leaving Emily and Charles to squirm on the hard sofa.

"The Lincoln?" she repeated. "You wouldn't consider the Drake, or perhaps the Saint Claire?"

"No, Grandmother," Charles replied, "the arrangements have all been made. We're excited about it. It's just what we want."

Their wedding plans may have been what the couple thought that they wanted, but from her reaction it was clear that they were not what Lillian Campbell preferred. On the drive over to the Glass House, the newlyweds had promised themselves that regardless of Lillian's reaction or generous promises, they would stay strong and hold with their original ideas. Understanding that with Grandmother Lillian it was a marathon and not a sprint, Charles hoped that they could get through this first meeting with only minor changes to their plans

"Well, I couldn't be happier for the two of you. It's wonderful news."

Lillian casually glanced over at the Waterford decanter. As if telepathically controlled, Mary suddenly appeared from the kitchen to stand by the living room doorway. After a crisp nod from her employer, Mary refilled the glass, adding perhaps a bit more sherry than a second "polite pour" at two-thirty in the afternoon would have called for.

"May twenty-eighth you say. I do love a spring wedding. You know, Charles, we really must have an appropriate engagement party. Please allow me the honor of presenting the two of you. We could do it here if you like."

Emily snuck a quick glance at Charles' reaction. It was clear from the far-off look on her face that Lillian was already thinking about the guest list and whether she should hire a piano player.

"I thought you might want to do something nice like that for us, but it's not necessary."

"Oh, but Charles, it is necessary, and it's my pleasure. My two up-and-coming young people need to be presented socially, and in a way that suits your future."

Charles took a deep breath and picked up Emily's hand.

"Really, Grandmother, we don't want an engagement party. Thank you for the offer, but both the engagement and wedding are going to be small and personal. That's what we want."

Emily considered adding something, but knew that most of the dialog she'd written for herself added little to the cause, and was more likely to provide Lillian a clear target for her disappointment.

In an unwanted flash of memory, Emily found herself back in front of the Goodman Theater sitting on her backside, her belongings scattered across the pavement, as her future fiancée peered down at her. Then from above came that unmistakable voice with its disdainful tone asking, "Is the girl injured?"

Even with that chilling memory still fresh in her mind, Emily bravely decided to add, "Thank you, Lillian. It is so kind of you, and we are grateful. It's just that we prefer that our wedding be smaller. I hope you can understand. We, that is, both of us, are grateful for your generosity and all that you've done to help me. But this is what we want. I hope you'll understand."

Lillian had reached out to pick up her sherry glass, but appeared to have a second thought and instead left it sitting on the glass table. There was a long and agonizing pause as she looked deeply into Emily's eyes - perhaps her soul - her expression frighteningly neutral and without any distinguishing features that might reveal her reaction.

"Very well then, she replied in a perfectly controlled and unemotional tone. "Obviously, if there is anything that I might do to assist with your exciting plans you will let me know won't you."

For now, Lillian Campbell had been restrained.

Seizing the moment, Charles pressed ahead. "Well, there is one thing that you could do for us."

"Certainly, dear; what is it?"

"It's about Dad, I mean… Gordon," Charles started. "I know this may be difficult, but we were hoping, I was hoping, that you and Dad might find a way to put aside some of your past issues, at least for the wedding?"

Lillian continued to show no outward sign of emotion at Charles' awkward request. Instead, she sat regally in her armchair with her hands folded quietly on her lap, all the time staring at the two of them in a way that made Emily feel that she was now prey.

After another particularly long minute, Lillian asked, "What is it exactly that you are asking of me?"

Anticipating this question, Charles had rehearsed his response, even practicing it once in front of Emily.

"Since we are such a small family, actually we're both from a small family, but I think it would be good for all of us to be together, to be a family, again."

Although his remarks were not as grammatically precise as he had rehearsed, they were certainly heartfelt, and conveyed his intent.

"I agree, Charles," Lillian offered, and then coyly paused to wait and see if he would rise to the bait.

When Charles did not respond, she continued, "Certainly, I would welcome the opportunity to work out any problems that your father might have. It's been a long time since I've spoken with him."

Eleven years to be precise; eleven years since their bad blood had come to a head at Otto Campbell's funeral. Since then neither had spoken a word to the other. So intense was their disdain that until this moment no one had dared to suggest a ceasefire.

In spite of the likely consequences - all bad - Charys continued to discreetly communicate with her mother by telephone, as well as the occasional trip to Chicago; her long weekends were thinly veiled as a "shopping excursion", or "an opportunity to get together with old friends." Although Gordon never outwardly objected to Charys' absence, he made it perfectly clear that there would be no chance for reconciliation. As far as he was concerned, his mother-in-law was a selfish and contemptuous woman, someone who could rationalize what he believed to be the worst of all sins: holding oneself above another. The normally mild-mannered Gordon Albright had but one antagonist on the planet, and that was his mother-in-law, Lillian Campbell.

"What do you propose, Charles?" she asked, while taking a smaller sip from her sherry.

"What do I propose" he thought to himself? "It's just like her to have someone else make the first move. I'm asking her to help here, heaven knows Dad won't, and she throws it back on me."

"I'm not sure," Charles offered. "Perhaps a phone call before the ceremony might work."

Lillian looked at the couple and smiled. "You're suggesting that I take a call from your father?"

"No," Charles replied down into his hands. "I was thinking, maybe, you might call him?"

Another pregnant pause followed, one which predictably offered no hint of what she was thinking.

"Perhaps," Grandmother Lillian responded slowly and carefully, her pace a reminder of how feline her temperament and movements could be, "it would be best if your father were to contact me."

Then after a short pause to let it sink in, she concluded, "Yes, I'm certain that's best. Now, let's talk about the wedding reception. What are your plans, Emily?"

April weather makes fools of young men.

With all due respect to Tennyson and his daunting, highly dramatic poetry, especially the one that proclaims, "In spring a young man's fancy lightly turns to thoughts of love," had he but known the young boys of 1968, he would've probably considered a rewrite. After all, how could Alfred ever anticipate the "lightly" in a thirty-five hundred pound Chevy Impala rushing pell-mell down a quiet neighborhood street at sixty-eight miles an hour?

It was the first Friday in April before Emily and Charles could get time away from her job at the television station to travel to Cedar Rapids for a weekend visit with his parents. The primary objective of the trip was to secure a commitment from his father that he would contact Grandmother Lillian and call a temporary truce to their hostilities. At this point, Charles had given up any hope for reconciliation, but at a minimum he needed some assurance from the two of them that there would not be a repeat of the open clash they'd had at his grandfather's funeral.

Most of the morning had slipped away before they were able to leave the city. By the time they made I-80, Charles was optimistic that they could still be in Cedar Rapids before five o'clock. Charys had promised a light evening meal, which meant that she and Grandmother Sarah had been cooking since Thursday morning.

Just west of Davenport, Emily looked up from her magazine, and asked, "Do you know what you're going to say to him, yet?"

So deep in his own thoughts, Charles hadn't spoken for the past twenty minutes. The Camaro's brand new 8-track tape machine was playing the Beatles latest hit, *Hey, Jude.*

> *"And anytime you feel the pain, hey Jude, refrain,*
> *Don't carry the world upon your shoulders."*

"Not really, but it'll probably sound a lot like what we said to Grandmother; hopefully with a bit more backbone."

Emily nodded, then added, "Are you going to tell him that we spoke with Lillian first? It might help if he thinks he's doing something for you that she wouldn't."

"That's a pretty good idea. I'll think about it and get back to you."

"You do that," she said, and then lightly kissed him on the cheek. "I'll be around."

Cedar Rapids Washington High School dismissed classes at three o'clock, but on those first fantastic days of spring most of the Warriors had mentally checked-out before lunch. By two-thirty, Kenny Cernik's thoughts

112

were limited to two things: cruising the streets of Cedar Rapids in his tricked-out '62 Chevy Impala, and his current girlfriend, Bobbie Vesley.

Kenny Cernik was a senior and scheduled to graduate from Washington High School in six weeks. The faculty and staff were delighted. After twelve years of public education, his only recognizable aptitude was his talent for pissing people off, and thanks to his surly attitude and false bravado he'd made the most of it. If the Washington administrators had kept detailed records for truancy, detentions, and fights, Kenny Cernik would have been the school's uncontested champion. It was Kenny Cernik who spiked the punch bowl at the homecoming dance. It was Kenny Cernik who simultaneously detonated two M-80's during the basketball pep rally. And it would have been Kenny Cernik who punched Mr. Dettenfaust (his biology teacher) in the nose for having the temerity to scold him for looking up the girl's skirts as they descended the stairs.

Bobbie Vesley was only a sophomore. Unbeknownst to most, including her parents, she was a very bright girl. An example of this well-disguised perspicacity was that she did not consider herself Kenny Cernik's girlfriend. She was clever enough to recognize that such a designation was truly a fool's errand; after all, he'd had at least three since Christmas. Still, Bobbi had a dream, a special dream, one that compelled her to put up with Kenny Cernik's bad behavior: she desperately wanted to go to the Washington High School junior-senior prom. And to realize that dream she was willing to pay a considerable price.

Part of her motivation was envy, amplified when her best friend Cindy Blaha smugly announced to the fifth-period sophomore English Lit class that she would be attending the prom with one of Kenny Cernik's good-for-nothing friends, Bruce Mueller. Another well-known Cedar Rapids reprobate, Mueller had only a slightly shorter criminal record than his pal, Kenny. It turns out that both Mueller and Cernik were co-conspirators in an evil scheme to woo and then deflower these two not-so-innocent young girls at their Junior-Senior prom. This big talk was their idea of a successful and memorable evening, thus confirming the old adage that "The pity of the poor can be found in the depth of their dreams."

With no destination in mind, Kenny Cernik and Bobbi Vesley lazily pulled the Chevy Impala out of the Washington High School parking lot and on to Second Avenue.

Then he stood on it!

The Impala's 327 cubic-inch V-8 ignited the Thrush Turbo mufflers like a bomb, simultaneously warming both his cold cold heart and his more prurient perspectives. There was nothing Kenny enjoyed more than the sound of that low baffled rumble as it bounced around a quiet neighborhood, especially if it was after midnight.

By the time they'd reached 25th Street, the white Impala was already making forty-five miles an hour, and still accelerating. Kenny had just glanced over to enjoy Bobbi's reaction to his macho driving skills, when he noticed that her loose fitting blouse had blown open in such a way as to provide a good clear look at her small right breast. This opportunity was no accident. Before getting into the car, Bobbi had knowingly, willfully, loosened the top two buttons on her gaudy, hot-pink chemise. By leaning slightly forward she hoped to provide Kenny the kind of stimulation that would guarantee her one true desire: an invitation to attend the junior-senior prom.

Impressed with his good fortune, Kenny Cernik took his eyes off the road for a second peek at his prey. The speedometer on his super-charged Impala had just reached sixty-eight miles an hour. Thoroughly thrilled with this *lucky life's* possibilities, Kenny Cernik and Bobbi Vesley were now less than two hundred feet from the stop sign at the corner of Second Avenue and 27th Street.

Charles' other grandfather, Grandpa Bill Albright, the one who started the Albright Dairy, had gone to his noon Rotary meeting at the Cedar Rapids Country Club. After lunch and the obligatory guest speaker, (an exchange student from Turkey named Abd Al-Karim) he made his way to the lounge to enjoy the usual spirited game of gin rummy with his pals. It was only when Grandpa Bill was finally ready to drive home that he discovered he was stranded by a dead battery in his car.

"Gordon? It's me. I'm in a bit of a spot. I'm out here at the Country Club and my car won't start. Feels like a dead battery. I've already called Al Cheddars down at his station, but he can't come out to look at it until later. Anyway, I was hoping that when you leave the bank you might drop by and pick me up? No, don't make a special trip. Well, okay, if you're leaving anyway. I can always play another hand or two of gin. Okay. See you at three."

Excited about the prospect of seeing his son and new fiancée, Gordon Albright had informed his office staff that he would be leaving the bank around two-thirty. Before work that morning, he had promised Charys that on the way home he would take time to run a couple of errands for her. His hope was to be finished by four o'clock, a full hour before Charles and Emily were expected to arrive from Chicago. Stopping by the Country Club was hardly out of the way.

Climbing into the passenger seat of his son's staid, '67 Cadillac Fleetwood, Grandpa Bill offered, "Sorry, Gordon. I must have left the damn lights on."

Despite the inconvenience of being stranded, Bill Albright still loved his car. And with good reason; the beautiful, ebony 1958 Coupe de Ville convertible was almost as well-known around the city of Cedar Rapids as its owner. The stunning monument to success, with its massive fins and ridiculous 365 cubic-inch V8 engine, had been impeccably maintained and remained in pristine condition. Treated like royalty, "the Coupe" had never left home without a brush-up to ensure that it looked its best. As a local tribute to its magnificence, every fall the kids from Washington High would contact Bill Albright with the same hopeful request, "Can we use your car for the Homecoming parade?" He never let them down. Unfortunately, Bill Albright's coupe had come fully equipped to escort a Homecoming Queen, but had no alarm to inform him that he'd left the headlights on.

"No problem, Dad. But before we go home I need to stop by Paramour's Pharmacy and pick up a couple things for Charys," Gordon explained. After making his turn on to Country Club Parkway, now heading for the corner of First Avenue and 27th Street, he added, "She said they'd have it ready, so it should only take a second."

Neither of the two men said anything. The magnificent spring weather had encouraged them both to roll down their windows and enjoy the fresh air. Bobby Vinton softly crooned the old Clover's hit, *Blue Velvet*. The posted speed limit in the residential neighborhood was thirty miles-per-hour, but, of course, everybody knew that.

At 27th Street, Gordon turned left to travel the last two blocks to the drug store, the only side street they would cross was Second Avenue. If he had noticed the deep throbbing sound off in the distance, he might have recognized it as the exhaust system from a high-performance car, but he didn't. Instead, Gordon Albright was enjoying his own thoughts and the beauty of a spring afternoon in Iowa; that is, until his car was violently broadsided by two children equally enthralled in their own unique versions of *lucky life*.

Kenny Cernik's Chevrolet Impala was traveling at sixty-eight miles per hour when it impaled Gordon Albright's Cadillac Fleetwood.

The accuracy of the strike was remarkable. The Impala hit the driver's side of the Fleetwood dead-center, like an arrow driven through the heart of a target. The force of the impact propelled both vehicles more than one hundred-and-eighty feet up into Paul and Althea Ackers' front yard, narrowly missing a massive century silver maple tree, but leveling forty feet of picket fence and a newly planted blue spruce.

Gordon Albright was dead from massive focal traumatic brain injuries before his car came to rest on the Acker's front stoop.

Bobbi Vesley was not so fortunate; the innocent girl lived on in horrific pain for nearly forty minutes, sliding in and out of consciousness from massive internal injuries that included traumatic aortic disruption and a ruptured spleen. She would finally succumb in the emergency room of Mercy Hospital surrounded by strangers.

Why did Gordon Albright and Bobbi Vesley need to die in a car crash at the crossroads of 27th Street and 2nd Avenue in Cedar Rapids, Iowa on Tuesday, April 18, 1967? Was this truly their only version of a *lucky life*?

Considering all the independent moving moments that must line up perfectly to allow for such a catastrophic injustice, the odds against it are almost inconceivable; a split-second one way or another and the accident does not - cannot - occur. The most subtle, inconsequential variance to their realities would have changed the outcome from a horrific fatality to something else unknown. Depending upon your perspective, for these two innocent humans to die on that beautiful sunny day in April was either Providence, or the remarkably specific organization of an astronomical number of unique variables.

Forty years into the future, the "popular scientist", the one that will help Gordon's grandson, Dallas Albright envision *lucky life,* will suggest a third option, and it is a doozy.

"Imagine," he'll say to the late night television audience, "that there are an infinite number of alternative universes out there, all of them existing simultaneously, but each one unique and invisible to the others."

As the talk show host rolls his eyes, signaling to the studio audience that they should laugh hysterically, the popular scientist will try one more time to deliver his point.

"What makes the physics work is the notion of infinite. See all these parallel universes, and there are an infinite number of them, must be self-contained and independent of each other's reality."

All that leads to this: If the popular scientist is correct, and there are an infinite number of universes with an infinite number of alternatives, then in some of these universes Gordon and Bobbi won't die.

That first night after the accident, Charles Albright lay awake in his childhood bedroom thinking about such things. This was not the first, nor would it be the last time, he was unable to turn off the machinery in his head.

On the nightstand beside his bed, the alarm clock's luminescent dial read **5:47 A.M.** Emily was safely tucked under his arm. His father was now stone-cold dead, his battered body resting at the Cranston Funeral Home. Grandfather Bill was adrift in a coma at the Mercy Hospital intensive care unit, his body thoroughly plugged with needles and wires, attended to by strangers. And the two children, youngsters that Charles had never met, one was now dead, the other miraculously alive but broken from head to toe.

In those first moments of growing light, the dawn of a new day, Charles tried again with all of his heart to find some sign of God's hand in the nightmare. He failed. As for this mind-boggling notion of a *lucky life*, Charles Albright won't live long enough to hear the phrase "string theory" or "multiverse." It's a shame, too, because Charles would have welcomed an alternative to what he believed were extremely limited options.

Quietly easing himself off the bed, Charles went ahead and pulled the comforter up over Emily's shoulder before silently slipping out of the room. Entering the kitchen, he discovered his mother talking softly, almost secretly, on the phone. As she furtively whispered into the receiver she would unconsciously wrap, and then unwrap, the long yellow telephone cord around her fingers. Every available space was littered with kitchen tools, dishes, and the half-prepared food that the two women had abandoned when the phone call had come.

With her back to her grandson, Grandma Sarah stood next to the sink, hovering over the coffeemaker, apparently trying to encourage its speedy progress. Surprised by the sight of her grandson in the doorway, she inexplicably yanked the carafe out of its holder, only to find that the machine was not yet done brewing. The steady stream of hot black liquid poured out over the gray marble countertop and down onto the tile floor. While Grandmother Sarah numbly watched the machine spew the remainder of its contents, Charys automatically reached under the sink to grab a roll of paper towels. Then handing Sarah the towels, Charys turned and spotted her son in the doorway, which caused her to jump as well. Both women were fully dressed and appeared ready to walk out the door.

"Yes. Cedar Rapids has an airport. Yes, Mother. Of course we have taxi cabs, but it might be better if someone would come and pick you up."

As she listened to her mother's reply, Charys continued to absently knead the long yellow phone cord. Then in a notably higher register, she responded, "Actually, it would be better if you waited until Sunday or Monday to come. I don't know all that I need to do, but, no, I think it would be better for me if you waited until Sunday. Thank you. I'll call later this afternoon when I know more. No. I don't know when I'll be home, but I promise I'll call you then."

Another lengthy pause followed; Charles presumed this would be Grandmother Lillian offering her daughter an alternative version of an itinerary.

The call concluded with Charys' bold lie, "Yes, Mother. I'm fine."

Saturday was split between the extremely well-lit waiting area outside of Mercy Hospital's intensive care unit, and making the arrangements for Gordon's funeral.

Upon their arrival, the family was dispassionately informed that there had been no change in Grandpa Bill's condition. The doctor on duty, a very young and sleepy looking fellow, Doctor Antonio Tomasello, assured them that this was a good thing.

"If it's such a good thing," Charles wondered, "why do they continue to keep an old woman from her husband?"

He had now endured this canned speech on the hospital's protocols, and the warning of his grandfather's "precarious condition" from three different doctors. Even though he was unwilling to accept their reasoning, especially if Grandpa Bill was that "precarious," he chose to remain quiet... for the moment.

It was agreed that Grandmother Sarah and Emily would keep vigil at the hospital, while Charys and Charles began the nightmare of making preparations for Gordon's funeral.

In a small windowless office just off the Cranston Funeral Home's main lobby, Samuel Cranston deliberately placed his giant coffee mug among the colorful sales brochures strategically spread across the desk. The oily man extended a steady, pale white hand across the table in a transparent effort to lend comfort to the widow. Staring vacantly back at the undertaker, Charys Albright automatically returned both hands to her lap and out of his reach. Charles, who had been carefully studying the colorful, multi-page brochure for the *King's Reward* coffin, looked up to observe his mother's peculiar reaction, but failed to notice the loud advertisement on the funeral director's oversized cup: **Grandview Savings and Loan – *Your Neighbor and Friend!*** Had the smarmy mortician considered his client's feelings, or the dead man's place of employment (the Hyland Trust) he certainly would have recognized that his ridiculous coffee cup was both an advertisement for a competing bank, and a tacky oversight to the man who now lay broken, cold, and lifeless in the adjacent room.

Samuel Cranston did not - could not - recognize his *faux pas*. Instead, he leaned back into his worn leather arm chair to better calculate the state of the bereaved. After a moment of what he planned as "sympathetic silence," he decided upon "Scenario Two," a trusted and effective strategy from the NFD's (National Funeral Directors) recent video short course: *"The Indirect Sell: Sympathy as a Motivator."* After almost twenty-two years in the business, Samuel Cranston knew, "the widow's stare" when he saw it.

"Charys," he declared, folding his own hands as if he were about to pray, "These next few days are going to be very difficult for you and Charles and Sarah, a real emotional roller coaster, yessiree. But I want you to know that we're going to do everything we can to help make this as simple as possible. We're just happy to be here for you."

Charys Albright had stopped listening to Samuel Cranston and was instead closely examining the palms of her own hands. She trusted her son would make all the decisions that this unpleasant man required to bury her

118

husband. Sitting there in that tiny claustrophobic room, overfilled with those hideous yellow chairs, Charys had discovered that unless she deliberately forced the horrible reality back into her consciousness, she was unable to remain focused for more than just a few seconds. Then as if to prove the point, Charles handed her a pen and she signed her name to several pieces of paper without a thought about what they said or meant.

Everyone stood. She thanked Cranston without shaking his hand and then allowed Charles to open the door for her. It wasn't until she was outside in the bright, clean April sunshine that she could remember where she was, or why she was there. Bending down to get into the passenger seat of the car, she asked herself, "How long do you think you'll be like this?"

The silent voice in her head replied, "Forever."

The negotiations at the funeral home had taken longer and cost more than Charles thought possible. It was nearly one o'clock before they returned to the house on their way back to the hospital.

Charys regretted it as soon as she checked the telephone answering machine; the impatient red digital number blinked that it had received twenty-one different messages. Wearily, she pulled a kitchen chair up next to the counter and began to listen. By the time she'd heard the fifth friend offering their condolences and willingness to "help in any way we can," Charys abruptly unplugged the recorder and took the phone off the hook. Looking up at her son, she did not seek his approval.

Alone now together in the kitchen, another of the unending waves of reality crashed over Charys Albright.

"I need your help," she said holding out her hands to her son.

Charles put down the dishes that he'd been clearing from the table and went over to kneel beside his mother's chair.

"Charles, I'm having some trouble thinking clearly. I don't know how to help you or Sarah. There's just so much... and I feel so useless... so lost."

The tears were honestly and unaffectedly streaming down both their cheeks as he pulled her out of the chair and into his arms.

It was nearing the end of the hospital's visiting hours and still the elusive Mercy doctors had offered precious little news of Grandpa Bill's condition. From what little that they'd been told nothing had changed in the last forty-eight hours: Bill Albright was still in a coma, but in stable condition. When, if ever, he would awaken was an unknown and impossible to predict. The family's only consolation was late that afternoon Sarah was finally allowed into the intensive care unit to sit with her husband.

At nine o'clock, Charys, Emily, and Charles were still maintaining their vigil when a silver-haired woman in a red-and-white checkered volunteer vest appeared at the door.

"Sorry to bother you, Mrs. Albright," the woman apologized. "There's an urgent call for you. The lady said it was an emergency and needs to speak with you right away. Yes, right away. She said her name was Campbell, Lillian Campbell. You can use the phone over there in the corner if you like."

Surprised to hear his grandmother's name coming from the stranger, Charles looked to see that his mother had slumped over with her chin now resting on her chest. She was staring down upon her visibly shaking hands.

"Mother?"

Like she'd been awakened from a deep and heavy sleep, Charys Albright slowly lifted her head and smiled politely at the woman, adding, "Thank you. I'll take that call now."

He was too far away to clearly hear what was being said, but when the short call ended, and she'd hung up the phone, Charys stood for a moment with her back to the three of them.

"What is it? What did she say?" Charles asked.

Charys finally turned to look at her son, and with a bit more anger in her voice than she might have preferred, replied, "Would you please drive out to the airport and pick up your grandmother."

Charles took the three women back to the house, but before he left to retrieve Grandmother Lillian from the airport, Charys gathered her little family together in the living room and offered the following words of perspective. Her meaning was both clear and preemptive.

"Regardless of my mother's presence here, we will continue our vigilance. Gordon is dead. That is a fact. But Bill is still with us, and we owe it to him to be there to fight for him."

So it began. Five straight days of beautiful springtime weather ended abruptly when the outside temperature unexpectedly dropped close to the freezing mark. The next morning, a dark gray sky spit frozen rain. With the memory of those balmy sixty-degree temperatures still fresh in everyone's mind, these cruel and unpleasant conditions made any time spent outside a misery.

Charles and Emily entered the Albright kitchen just before seven o'clock to find both grandmothers conspicuously occupying separate corners of the room. Although no one had yet uttered a word, it seemed to Emily that the conditions in the kitchen reflected the temperature outdoors: frosty and uncomfortable.

Charles poured Emily a cup of the black coffee before draining what was left of the pot into his own mug. After a quick taste, he asked, "What time would you like to leave, Mother?"

There was a moment where the three women looked at one another as if electing a spokesperson. Finally, Grandma Sarah turned in such a way as to show Lillian Campbell her back, and then stated matter-of-factly, "Charles, I'd like you to take me over to my house first, and then would you please drop me off at the hospital. I think your mother and grandmother have things that they need to do here."

Lillian stiffened a bit, but said nothing before walking over to the kitchen table, where she took a seat across from her daughter. From the vacant expression on her face, it was clear that Charys Albright was no longer in the same room as the rest of the family.

Gordon Albright's funeral was to be held Wednesday morning at the Cranston Funeral home. Pastor Paul Milton of Saint Paul's Lutheran Church was to preside.

In the absence of any lucid participation from his mother, it had fallen upon Charles to make all the necessary arrangements for the funeral services. But what made a tense and uncomfortable situation even worse was the constant presence of Grandmother Lillian. Although she made no effort to interject her own opinion, and would only respond to a specific question of protocol, her stern and notably glamorous presence thoroughly distracted the locals.

During their first meeting with Samuel Cranston, Charles had agreed to use Cranston's chapel for both the evening visitation on Tuesday, and then what he hoped would be a more modest and personal memorial service on Wednesday morning. By late Monday, it was clear that the number of people planning to attend his father's funeral would overwhelm the small chapel's limited seating. In what seemed to Charles a rather insensitive attitude, Samuel Cranston reluctantly relinquished his contract to hold the memorial at his facilities. It was only after a second and more pointed request that the funeral director finally agreed to provide a telephone number for the "folks at Saint Paul's who manage their schedule."

The number reached Mrs. Gloria Rickenbach, Acting-President of the Saint Paul Women's Federation. Mrs. Rickenbach did not seem especially surprised to receive Charles call; if anything, she seemed a bit put-off that Saint Paul's wasn't the "obvious first choice for Gordon's final earthly moments." The next morning in the church's vestibule, Charles, and the now ever-present Lillian Campbell, were informed "that Cranston's is fine for a smaller service, but for someone like Gordon Albright, well, there's no question that Saint Paul's is the only possible location."

Besides, as they would later learn, Pastor Milton preferred the home field advantage of working from his own pulpit.

As the large congregation took their seats after singing the service's closing hymn, *"How Great Thou Art"* (all four verses) Charles Albright was struck by two sad realities. The first was his disappointment at how utterly ordinary his father's funeral had turned out. It seemed to Charles that for someone who was anything but ordinary, Gordon Albright's "final earthly moments" had been demoted to a tragically common and impersonal service. Sadly, Charles knew that there was no one to blame for this miscarriage but himself. As he returned the hymnal to the pew in front of him, he wondered if anyone else had noticed. Would his father's friends and associates be angry for such a weak sendoff?

Earlier in the week, Charles, Charys, and, of course, Lillian Campbell had met with Pastor Milton to discuss the final funeral arrangements in the minister's handsomely appointed study. At the time, he presumed that the Albright's clergyman would know the best way to remember and honor his father. But as he helped his mother to her feet, Charles realized that not only had the bible passages been uninspired, (John 6.35-40), the mundane musical selections *("All Things Bright and Beautiful"* and *"Nearer My God to Thee"*) had made no personal connection to either his father or family.

Perhaps the most galling part of the program turned out to be Pastor Milton's performance, particularly the sermon. At their earlier meeting, Milton had carried on about his personal relationship with Gordon Albright, and had promised to "proudly wave the banner of my good friend's life and accomplishments." Except as they followed the coffin out the door, Charles tallied that there had been only five specific references to the guest of honor, while "our dear Lord and savior, Jesus Christ," had received fourteen mentions, and that was in an address that lasted less than twelve minutes.

The second of Charles' miserable realizations began as a passing awareness before eventually growing into a full-blown obsession. For some inexplicable reason he was now preoccupied with counting obscure and generally unrelated details.

It started while they were standing for the second of what turned out to be five prayers. As the sanctimonious Pastor Milton once again beseeched the Lord to, "Welcome our dear friend Gordon Albright into your celestial home." Charles realized that the wreath of red roses which lay smeared across his father's mahogany casket (the most expensive one Cranston offered, *The King's Reward*) had only nineteen of the long-stemmed flowers. He knew full well that he had ordered two dozen.

Later, while standing behind his mother at the gravesite, Charles counted forty-two cars strewn like jackstraws over the cemetery's fresh green grass; seventeen of them were Cadillacs. Back at Saint Paul's for the luncheon reception, he listened politely as twenty-three men, eighteen of which referred to themselves as "close friends of your father," informed him of how "badly he will be missed in this town." Although Charles was certain that all of these men intended their remarks as both compliment and comfort, after the first eleven recitations the intended affect began to suffer from overexposure.

At first this peculiar fascination with arithmetic was a welcome distraction from his responsibilities and grief, but before long he had branched out into even more obscure observations. There was the question of how many wheat bread versus white bread ham sandwiches the Ladies Auxiliary had provided: the answer was eighty-two white and just sixty of the wheat. Next came the question of whether there were more cups of coffee than lemonade: the answer was thirty-eight coffees and twenty-five lemonades. Which was more popular, the white or chocolate cake: in this case, it was fifteen white and twenty chocolate. How often was the expression "pillar of the community" evoked: the answer - twelve. And perhaps the most interesting computation turned out to be the number of times he'd personally overheard someone whisper, "The tall woman in the black dress? That's Lillian Campbell; Charys' mother." That happened nine times.

The last of the guests were finally making their way toward the door when Grandma Sarah cornered Charles outside the church's giant industrial kitchen to ask if he would "kindly drive me back to the hospital." In spite of his genuine concern for his grandmother's mental and physical health, after all she'd just buried a son and was now rushing back to the hospital to sit next to a comatose husband, he grudgingly obliged. The matter of returning Charys, Lillian, and Emily back to 460 West Maple was left to Gordon's longtime friend and neighbor, Howard Inglebrook.

Once he had helped Sarah upstairs to his grandfather's hospital room, he returned to the car - the Camaro. A brisk northwest wind had picked up, sending the few scattered cirrus clouds racing across the steel-blue April sky. Without thinking, Charles closed the car door and turned the key igniting the gentle rumble of the car's 350 V8. The personal autopilot in his head clicked on as he instinctively pointed the car east toward home, his childhood home.

It wasn't until the outdoor time and temperature sign on Paramour's Pharmacy caught his eye (**4:54 P.M. - 34 degrees**) that he realized he was on the same unlucky road his father and grandfather had taken just five days before. He rolled down his window and filled the car with the cold stiff wind. There was another memory there, a small unappreciated one tickling around at his consciousness.

In the fall of 1947, the six-year-old Charles Albright knew deep in his heart that he was going to be a famous baseball player, destined to follow in the footsteps of his new hero, Brooklyn Dodgers shortstop, Pee Wee Reese.

The nickname "Pee Wee" had first surfaced and stuck while Charles and his father were listening to the fifth game of the 1947 World Series between the Dodgers and New York Yankees. It was a fact that both the boy and his future hero were pee wee, and even though Charles quietly hated everything about being small, after Pee Wee Reese smashed the game-winning double to give the Dodger's a three-to-two edge over the Bronx Bombers, the boy eagerly took on both the moniker and the game. That next spring, Charles Albright reported to Pee Wee baseball practice intent on fulfilling what he had come to believe was his true destiny.

From the first day, Charles had a important advantage over many of the other boys: thanks to the many hours that he and his father had spent in the back yard, Charles could catch and throw. By the end of that first practice, the coach had already started to group the boys together by skill. Thanks to his hustle and those late afternoons in the yard, Charles easily made the first-cut. Later, when the boys were leaving the field, it was announced that the first official game was scheduled for a week from Wednesday; this meant that there would be only three practices to drill on the fundamentals and field a squad.

The Indians would not have been Charles first-choice for a team name. When it was first announced that he was playing for the Indians, and that someone else would be wearing his beloved Dodger blue, he spent the remainder of the afternoon throwing dirt clods at the garage and debating if he was even interested in playing baseball. It wasn't until his father gently reminded the boy, "We don't always get our first choice, you know," that Charles agreed to a game of catch. "Besides," Gordon added as they tossed the ball back and forth, "the Cleveland Indians have Bob Feller who's both an ace of a pitcher, and he's from Iowa."

Gordon Albright's well intentioned pep talk helped get the boy to practice, but it wasn't until later when the Indians were all seated in the dugout and the new uniforms were distributed, (a white T-shirt with the team name **Indians** printed on the front, as well as the sponsor's name - **Harper's Meats** and official number - **1** on the back) that the boy decided that maybe it wouldn't be so bad to be an Indian.

The boys arrived at the ball diamond just before 4 o'clock sporting their sharp new white shirts, the requisite blue cap, and standard-issue blue jeans. After a short warm-up, the coach gathered his team in the dugout and shouted out the day's starting line-up.

"Charley Albright, let's see, you take second base."

"This is a mistake, right," the boy wondered? "I'm a shortstop, not second base."

He looked hard at the coach knowing that he was about to announce his error; but he didn't. In fact, when he'd finished the line-up he didn't go back, he didn't even apologize. Instead, he shouted, "Okay, boys. Let's go get 'em."

This would not be Charles Albright's only disappointment that day.

In 1948, Pee Wee baseball was a five-inning game with a ten run "mercy rule." The mercy rule is an accurate description of its objective: when a team goes ahead by ten runs, the game is over and the unfortunate team with fewer runs must forfeit. It is not especially surprising that with all of his other duties and responsibilities, the Indian's coach had failed to instruct his team on this important but arcane rule.

When the Red Sox came to bat in the top of the third they were leading the Indians nine to nothing. Sadly, in those first two innings all six of the Indian batters had either gone down on strikes, or harmlessly grounded out to the infield. Should they get there, Charles would lead-off the bottom of the third.

The Red Sox lead-off hitter came to the plate and was promptly hit in the arm by the first pitch. Although more frightened than injured, it took quite a while before the terrified boy finally stopped sobbing. Even then he continued to sniffle and snivel while the umpire patiently instructed the child to "take your base." Apparently frightened by the combination of being hit by the ball and the menacing giant man in the iron mask, the Red Sox coach had to be summoned from the dugout to convince the child that he could go to first. The second batter was walked on four pitches, which required another discussion of the rules to reassure the boy on first that he could safely move to second. The third batter was a very small boy (smaller than Charles) who brought to the plate what had to have been a thirty-eight inch bat. The large stick and the small boy caused a ripple of amusement from the parents in the bleachers, but no one stepped forward to recommend a change. After hoisting the heavy lumber to his shoulder, the first pitch to the tiny boy was thrown in the dirt behind him. The Indian's catcher had been struggling all afternoon with his oversized equipment and the pitcher's shaky control. With yet another wild pitch, the lumbering fellow stumbled out from behind the plate and began to spin around wildly in a circle as he tried to locate the errant throw. Meanwhile, the fastball caromed off the backstop and rolled toward the Indian's dugout, where it finally came to rest in between the fence and the on-deck circle. The boy who was still standing on second base (the same one who had been hit by the pitch) was mindlessly rubbing his bruise when the kid from first ran toward second on the passed ball. After getting confirmation from the third-base coach that it was okay to run, the boy and his sore arm abandoned second and headed for third. The catcher's father had been standing behind home plate now hollered at his boy to "take off your mask and get the ball." When the catcher recovered the ball from among the Indian's bats, the wounded boy from second was on his way to third. This modest threat caused the eager catcher to heave the ball toward a third baseman who was daydreaming about the possibilities of going to the Dairy Queen for ice cream. The throw was both strong and accurate, but with no one paying attention the ball rolled past the Red Sox third base coach and off the field, where it finally came to rest under a parked car. Encouraged by the waving arms and enthusiastic shouts from the third base coach to, "Go home, Kenny! Go, home!" Kenny rounded third and stumbled toward the plate with his teammate right on his heels. The ball that now lay lost under a '42 Dodge never made it back onto the infield. When wounded Kenny crossed home plate, the umpire unexpectedly lifted both hands and shouted, "That's the game." This surprising statement left everyone present wondering what he meant. Both coaches were then summoned to the plate where the relevant ten-run rule was explained. With a shrug and a grin the Indians' coach returned to the dugout where he made three valiant but failed attempts to explain the situation to the boys. The game then ended happily for the Red Sox, and sadly for the Indians.

Although little was said on the way home, it was clear to Gordon that this first experience had seriously shaken the boy's confidence in his Pee Wee karma. And why not; in his first game he never touched a ball, never made a play, or was even allowed to bat. To make things worse, the young and well-intentioned coach had positioned Charles at second base, which was not his true destiny. Even though Charles was a reasonably polite and pliant kid, certainly the coach must have noticed that the boy he had put in Pee Wee Reese's position had thrown the ball over the first baseman's head - twice - and struck out without taking the bat off his shoulder.

After the game, Gordon quietly suggested to Charles "that when the right moment presents itself" he should use his "best manners" and approach the coach to ask about being repositioned to short. Taking this father's advice to heart, the boy immediately walked over to where the coach was busy talking to his pregnant wife through the wire backstop. Before the boy could get his request out, the coach reached out with a patronizing pat on the head, and a, "Good game, Charlie. We'll get 'em next time."

Driving home that afternoon they passed Paramour's Pharmacy. The warm summer air felt soft and good as it rushed over Charles' outstretched hand. By sticking his arm out of the open car window, and then lifting or lowering his palm, he could feel the warm humid air force his hand to change direction. He had forgotten about the game and was now Superman flying to the rescue.

"Can you feel it, Pee Wee?" his father asked.

Charles was confused by the question and did not answer.

"Can you feel it?" his father repeated. "Can you feel the air pushing against your hand? It's like an airplane wing. If it's shaped just right the air goes over the top faster than the bottom, and then you'll have lift. Then you'll be flying."

"Superman doesn't have wings," Charles thought to himself.

Still, he could feel the wind, and it was like his father said, the wind could take and lift his hand without even trying.

As he continued flying his airplane-hand down Eighth Avenue, Charles asked, "Can you fly an airplane?"

His father looked over at his boy and smiled.

"No. I've flown in some airplanes, but I don't know how to pilot one. That takes lots of special training."

Banking hard to the left, Charles continued, "Did you fly in an airplane when you were in the war?"

"Yes," his father replied a bit more tentatively.

"What was it like to be in a war?" the boy asked.

Without warning, Gordon Albright was transported back to a time and place - a *lucky life* - where he was known as Private Gordon Albright of the 83rd Infantry. Like a horrible movie, images, horrific images of what had once been humans now heaped in half-burnt, half-buried piles of flesh crashed into his consciousness. Then just as suddenly he was back at the stop sign on the corner of West 8th and Addams, his hands gripping the steering wheel as if he would strangle the life from the plastic.

It took another moment for Gordon to regain his balance, but the boy sat patiently staring up at his father's ashen face. Running his tongue across his dry lips, Gordon Albright carefully considered what he wanted to say.

Eventually, he offered, "War is not something that we talk about much. When you get just a little older you'll study history in school. There you'll hear all kinds of stories." Gordon paused for a moment before adding, "I suppose it's important to remember the past, maybe we can learn from it. But to the men who have fought in a war, the idea of talking about it is just not something that you do."

At first it didn't seem like his father's words were right, lots of people talked about war. His friends played war in the backyard. There were play guns and real guns everywhere. Comic books, movies, and radio shows, they all talked about war. Why would he say that men who were in a war didn't talk about war when it seemed like everybody talked about it?

"What is it, Charles?" his father asked.

The boy pulled his hand back in the window.

"Did you kill anybody in the war? Is that why you say nobody talks about it?"

They had just turned on to West Addams. With only a few blocks to go, Gordon Albright slowed the car before he turned to face his son.

ou're so very young to ask such a question, but since we never know about tomorrow, I'll tell you this... I did not kill anyone in the war, but I saw so many innocent people dead."

Gordon turned away from the boy to look out the window, but continued, "Death is all that comes from war. Don't ever forget this Charles, because someday a man is going to say to you that it's a good thing, that this war is a good thing, and it's the right thing to do. But, son, those wars, the good ones that they promise you, they're only in the dreams of those who don't have to fight them."

The warm air that had been rushing through Charles Albright's fingers suddenly turned cold and wet.

It was just after six o'clock when he pulled into the driveway to find that there were no lights on anywhere in the house. After a quick search of the kitchen, a room where every flat space was now overflowing with trays of food from the well-intentioned neighbors, Charles returned to the living room to find his grandmother descending the stairs while balancing two empty tea cups.

"Your mother and Emily are both resting," she said, as she passed him on her way to the kitchen.

After depositing the cup and saucer in the sink, she turned back to Charles who had remained in the doorway.

"Can I get you something, dear; perhaps a drink? I know that I could go for one."

"Grandmother, are you sad that you and my father were never able to get over your argument?"

Lillian did not appear especially surprised by Charles forthright question, but calmly replied, "Where does your mother keep her liquor?"

"In the living room... there's a cupboard by the fireplace, bottom shelf."

Charles dutifully trailed behind his grandmother into the dimly lit living room, what remained of the weak April sun was only just visible through the branches of an ancient burr oak that dominated the Albright's front yard. Lillian, still in her stylish black mourning dress and heels, retrieved a bottle of brandy and two glasses from the cupboard. After depositing both on the walnut coffee table, she took a seat on the sofa and poured herself a draft of the brown liquor, one larger than he would have anticipated.

Settling back on the cushion, she fixed her eyes upon her grandson at the far end of the davenport and took a healthy swallow of the brandy.

Holding both the glass and her gaze, Lillian Campbell finally replied, "Charles, your father was a good man and a fine husband to my daughter. It is terribly sad for him to die so young. Still, I've been thinking... perhaps it is somehow better, a painless instant, and then on to whatever's next."

After a second swallow of the liquor, she continued, "You need to appreciate that as a child your mother was never the rebellious type. Then against our wishes, she insisted on coming here, to Iowa of all places. Imagine our reaction when we learned of that decision? She was so determined. She thought she was in love. So against our better judgment, we allowed her to go. Four years later, Charys married your father, a dairy man's son.

The day she told us of her engagement was the day that I realized I'd lost my daughter for good. That decision ended all of our hopes and dreams. You may never understand this Charles, but Charys was not meant to live here. She could have been, should have been, someone else. And now, well, now she's a widow and a lost soul."

He could feel the blood begin to pound in his ears as she spoke.

"What did he ever do that would make you hate him so?" Charles asked.

Without hesitation Lillian Campbell calmly replied, "He stole my daughter. He stole our dreams."

Standing before the south window, his hands still tightly clenched and driven deep into his pockets, Charles Albright gazed out onto what was left of the sun as it dropped below the dreary Iowa horizon. From behind he heard her voice, softly, as if calling him back from a great distance.

"There is something that you need to do, Charles," Lillian Campbell said.

Hoping to conjure some of his father's strength, he turned to look across the sofa at the silhouette of his grandmother.

"What is that?" Charles asked.

Lillian Campbell stood, and then silently walked across the dim room to the far window and the small oil painting that hung beside it. Staring intently at the tiny canvas, she asked, "Do you know about this painting?"

"No. Not really. Only that they found it up in the attic when they moved into this house. It's been hanging there ever since."

Without looking back, she spoke as much to the painting as she did to Charles, Grandmother Lillian replied, "Neither of those statements are true."

"What are you talking about?" Charles snapped at her. "That painting has hung in that spot for as long as I can remember."

In the quiet darkness, she continued to study the picture, outwardly arrested as if it held some kind of special power. Then with precisely measured words, she replied, "Yes, dear, for as long as you can remember."

Threatened by the unexpected tone and insinuation, Charles tried desperately to recall the canvas; only the more he struggled, the more he wanted to remember, the quicker the little painting's detail seemed to evaporate. It was true that the picture had hung on that wall like a sentinel for more than twenty years. Only now, at the end of this terrible tragic day, he could not remember a single time when anyone had ever mentioned it. Like everything else in his parent's house, Charles considered the little painting an integral part of their lives and heritage. Only now why couldn't he remember anything about it?

Walking back across the room, Lillian stopped to pick up her glass before taking a seat in the wooden rocking chair beside the fireplace.

"So, I take it that neither your mother, nor father, has ever told you about the little elephant in the room?"

"I don't know what you mean," he answered defensively. "My father told me that they found the painting in the attic."

"How old were you when they moved here?" she asked.

"I'm not sure. I was going to school, second grade, maybe. I guess that would make it 1950. I was seven."

"Would you be surprised if I told you that I first saw that painting on Thanksgiving Day in 1947?"

"Are you saying that my father lied to me about something as trivial as that little painting?"

The room was mostly dark now, the only light coming from the overhead fluorescents in the nearby kitchen. Masked by deep shadows, it was impossible to identify her expressions, or where she might be looking.

When she finally spoke, Lillian asked, "Would you care to hear what your father told me that day about his trivial little painting?"

"I'm not sure. Will I like the story?"

"Not all of it," she said flatly, and then added, "but it still needs an ending."

Chapter Fifteen

Langenstein Zwieberge

"At that moment, I became intensely conscious of the fact that no dream, no matter how horrible, could be as bad as the reality of the camp which surrounded us."

Man's Search for Meaning - Viktor Frankl

"On the way to Berlin your father and a small detail of men from his battalion were ordered to secure and hold a rather notorious spot called Langenstein Zwieberge.

By the end of 1944, the Nazis had gathered so many prisoners that even with their horrible gas chambers and death marches they still needed more prison space. It was decided that a few miles north of their infamous camp at Buchenwald, a smaller one was to be built in the little town of Langenstein. The SS had chosen as the camp's commander, Paul Tschau, a truly wretched excuse for a man.

The German High Command had made the construction of the camp at Langenstein one of their highest priorities, but to meet their deadlines was going to take more energy and expense than they had first thought. You see, it wasn't just the prison space that they wanted; Langenstein was also an ideal spot for building what was to be a new and secret aircraft factory. Their plan was to excavate an enormous and impenetrable underground space from the hillside of the nearby woods. The locals called it Thekenberg. Then once finished these caves were to become a hidden factory for assembling their new jet engines. Tschau was given the job because along with being a natural sadist, he was also an expert with explosives and mining operations.

Langenstein Zwieberge provided the Germans with two valuable opportunities. There was, of course, the prison labor needed for the excavation of the caves, but it also reduced the overcrowding at Buchenwald. In a matter of just a few weeks, the camp at Langenstein had grown to more than seven thousand prisoners, all of whom were enslaved to dig those deep tunnels into the hillside. Only there was no gasoline to spare. So the prisoners were forced to remove thousands of tons of debris with just their bare hands.

The last of the Nazis were horrible…brutal to these poor people, forcing them out of the camps to labor on without food or water. I don't know how they did it, but somehow these men could turn off their feelings and ignore the thousands of innocent people who grew sick and died from starvation.

By early April of 1945, it was becoming clear to many of the Germans that the war was lost. In their anger and panic they emptied Langenstein of all the remaining prisoners, all five thousand of them, and sent them on what they called a "*todesmarsch*" - a death march to nowhere. As those pitiful ghosts struggled to walk or crawl, the German soldiers were instructed to ignore anyone who fell behind."

Completely confused and frightened, Charles asked the simple question, "Why are you telling me this?"

"Your father and his group were told to go ahead of the battalion and secure the concentration camp at Langenstein. The Army's spies had learned that both the Nazis, and their prisoners, were now gone. By the time your father arrived all that remained of the camp were two boys masquerading as soldiers, and the cold corpses of those who'd been left behind.

When the German army began to splinter and collapse, so did communications between officers and their commanders. It was this poor communication that forced Paul Tschau to leave Langenstein Zwieberge before he was actually ready. The two young boys, children really, were there that day because Tschau had sent them back to retrieve several personal items that he did not wish to have fall into the hands of the American Army."

"The picture," Charles asked?

"Yes," Lillian answered, "the picture. But there's more."

"Gordon kindly spared me the horror of what it was like when they first arrived at Langenstein Zwieberge and found only the deserted buildings and rotting corpses. But once they were established in the camp's headquarters, the lieutenant in charge directed his men into four groups of three. To be absolutely certain that no Germans were still hiding there, he sent them to search the grounds and look through all the buildings.

Your father and two comrades went to scout the eastern edge of the camp where there was a large barn. As they approached that building he must have sensed something wasn't quite right; Gordon said he'd had the feeling before and had learned to trust it. So he caught the attention of the other men and they made a plan. It was decided that before they entered the main door, your father and another man, Gibson I think was his name, would go around to the back of the building to see if there might be another way in or out.

Gordon and Gibson had just made their way around the corner of the building when they were stopped dead in their tracks by the sound of a truck engine starting inside the barn. Obviously, the third man, a Private Stanley

Kradowski, had also heard the truck, but not knowing what was happening in the building chose to remain in his hiding spot near the front door.

Then just as unexpectedly the truck motor died. It just stopped; leaving Gordon, Gibson, and Kradowski to wonder who was in the barn, and what they were doing with the truck.

Your father continued on around the building as Gibson crept up to the nearest window. There were no lights in the barn, so all he could see was a large truck, the back of which was covered with a dark green canvas. But on the backside of the building your father discovered a large double door propped wide open, apparently to allow the truck to drive out.

Gordon explained that as he stood there holding his breath and listening, he could hear the muffled sound of people talking. There was no question it was more than one, but he had no way of knowing how many. All he knew for certain was that the voices were not speaking English.

Given their tenuous circumstances it made sense that he and Gibson return to find Kradowski and then quickly inform the others that they'd discovered Germans in the barn. Your father was very clear with me on this point; he was not inclined toward some reckless attempt at storming the building. Alas, Stanley Kradowski did not share your father's point of view.

Gordon said that he was returning to where he'd left Gibson, when from inside the barn he heard Kradowski shout, "Hands in the air."

She stopped for a moment to let the drama sink in.

"Imagine how frightening that must have been for your father. So much to live for, only now one of his comrades had singlehandedly rushed an unknown number of German soldiers and was attempting to hold them at gunpoint. Apparently the very thought of this scenario had so overwhelmed Gibson with fear that he was frozen to his spot. In spite of Gordon's stern efforts to get him to retreat, he was now petrified. Grabbing the frightened soldier by his jacket, your father whispered to Gibson that he must 'Go around to the front doors and wait.' Gordon said that when he looked into his comrades terrified face he was uncertain whether Gibson would find the courage to do as he was told.

Gordon did not linger by the door, but instead crept inside and then quickly moved toward the back of the vehicle. From this new vantage point, he could see Private Kradowski facing two German soldiers, their arms high in the air, his rifle pointed directly at them.

"Albright! Gibson! Are you out there? I got two of 'em in here."

Instead of responding Gordon listened to his instincts and stayed where he was; after all, there was no way to know just how many other German soldiers were hiding nearby. So, instead of giving away his position he quietly crept to the back of the truck. Gordon's hope was that he could catch Kradowski's attention without alerting anyone else."

Grandmother Lillian paused before adding, "It's interesting to imagine all the different possibilities don't you think? So many separate ways those things could have gone. But as Gordon reached the tailgate of the truck, Gibson stumbles through the front doors of the barn shouting and brandishing his rifle. Naturally, Stanley Kradowski spins around to see who it is, and in that moment of confusion one of the Germans tries to escape by running along the other side of the truck. Private Kradowski turns to see what he presumes is a German soldier attempting to escape. He reacts by firing his rifle, hitting the fleeing boy dead-center in the back.

The fact that Private Kradowski shot the boy wasn't really a surprise to Gordon as was the startling loudness of the rifle's report. The crack of the gunshot seemed to ricochet around the hardwood enclosure of the barn, amplified by the dry dead wood. As the ringing subsided, the pungent smell of burnt gunpowder filled the air. Out of that confusion, Gordon stepped forward and leveled his rifle at the other boy. Thankfully, when the German looked up at your father, Gordon instantly realized that this person wasn't a Nazi storm trooper; this was a frightened, helpless child in a soldier's clothes.

The noise from the shot quickly brought three other GI's to the barn. Trying to make sense over all the shouting and craziness from Kradowski and Gibson, Gordon motioned for the boy to stand and place his hands on the hood of the truck. One of the soldiers was dispatched to inform the lieutenant of the situation and to bring back the medic. Sadly, by the time they arrived the German boy was dead.

Given the circumstances, it's understandable that the lieutenant and his men were now suspicious of the army's intelligence reports. The lieutenant quickly reconsidered his options, deciding the best course of action would be to lay back and regroup with the others. Before any new orders were issued he needed to know if anyone else had discovered additional evidence of the enemy. Making matters even more complicated was the fact that they were now saddled with a frightened German boy and a corpse. It was decided that someone should stay behind to guard the prisoner. Gordon and Kradowski were ordered to remain at the barn, while the rest of the men would return to join them as soon as everyone was accounted for and a new strategy set.

As you might imagine this plan did little to lessen your father's apprehensions. Sitting right there on the dirt floor of the barn was clear evidence that the Army's reports were wrong. It didn't take much imagination to believe that there were other German soldiers in the area. The shot from Kradowski's rifle could have alerted anyone nearby that they were now in the camp. If you're already anxious it's easy to imagine that you're now outnumbered and in serious trouble. Their only chance for help was going to come from the 3rd battalion, and they were still miles away.

Neither your father nor Stanley Kradowski spoke German; the boy, who Gordon thought might be thirteen or fourteen, either couldn't or wouldn't speak English.

So there they were. The boy now sitting on the dirt floor, his hands tied behind his back, petrified with fright; your father who had found an old wooden milking stool, a piece of furniture with which I would imagine he was quite familiar, was seated in front of the boy; and Private Kradowski, left alone with his thoughts, thoughts that surely would have included the unfortunate death of a weaponless boy.

The longer they were forced to wait the more agitated Kradowski got. It didn't take long before his curiosity and nerves got the best of him, and so he began, rather loudly under the circumstances, to rummage through the barn. At some point, he got around to looking in the back of the truck, where he discovered five mysterious wooden crates, mysterious because the writing on the outside of the box was in French, not German.

It turns out that those five wooden cases had nothing to do with the German war effort. They were, instead, five wooden cases filled with bottles of wine. Although neither Gordon nor Kradowski knew it at the time, this was extraordinary wine. Five cases of Chateau Latour 1928, absolutely amazing Bordeaux that likely came from Paul Tschau's own private stock."

Lillian Campbell knew a great deal about fine wine, so for the moment Charles had to allow her a detour away from his father's story.

"Bordeaux is both a kind of wine as well as a city in the south of France. In this region of Bordeaux there is a smaller village to the north called Pauillac. It is there, in Pauillac, that you can find the Latour vineyard; an extremely old and very famous house. Latour has been making exceptional and highly sought after wine for three centuries. Today, if you were lucky enough to find someone to sell you a bottle of the 1928 Chateau Latour, you might expect to pay as much as eight hundred dollars. It's not hard to understand why Tschau wanted his wine back, but it's unthinkable for him to have sent two boys after such a cargo."

Getting up from the rocking chair, Grandmother Lillian gingerly moved across the dark room to an end table near the davenport. Bending down to turn the switch on a lamp, Charles interceded, telling her, "Continue in the dark, please." She complied, but found the lighting adequate to refill her brandy glass.

"With the butt of his rifle, Kradowski lumbered ahead and foolishly broke open one of the wooden boxes. It was then that they discovered that these cases were filled with bottles of wine. Obviously, he didn't know either the vintage or its value, all he knew was that the last liquor he'd consumed had been nearly a month before in the small French town of Saint Avold. Gordon spared us the details, but it seems likely that on that particular occasion Kradowski's boorish behavior would have done little to improve international relations. So this cache of French wine must have seemed a kind of miracle, something that needed to be kept secret and guarded carefully.

Brandishing a bottle of the Latour, Kradowski jumped down from the back of the truck.

"What else is here little Kraut? What did you come for? Is there something else you don't want us to know about?" Then slapping the boy across the face, Kradowski pointed toward the corpse covered with a gray horse blanket. Shaking the bottle at the boy, the big man demanded, "Is there more of this?"

Gordon mercifully interceded and urged Kradowski to leave the boy to him. 'If these kids are here for the wine,' he reasoned, 'there may well be more.'

Private Kradowski said nothing, but turned and gave the boy another threatening look before resuming his noisy search of the barn. It turns out that in his haste to find more wine, Mr. Kradowski overlooked something far more valuable than those sixty bottles of Chateau Latour.

According to Gordon, he and the boy just sat staring at one another, I suppose wondering what would happen next, until the boy unintentionally betrayed Tschau's secret.

It must have been a little like the game we use to play at the lake house when you were a boy. Do you remember Hot and Cold? Someone hides a thimble somewhere in the room, the most difficult place that they can think of, and then when the others try to find it the person is only allowed to say either 'hot' or 'cold.'

As Kradowski prowled around all he could find were farm tools and truck parts, but twice Gordon observed the boy sneaking a quick glance toward one of the animal stalls closer to the front door. There was nothing special about the place, in fact with the floor covered in hay and manure it looked like all the rest of the stalls. In that condition it would have been easy to overlook, and that, of course, was what Paul Tschau had planned.

Gordon walked over to stand in front of the stall. Looking back at the boy, he asked, "Is there something here?"

The miserable look on the young face revealed his secret.

Your father then called for Private Kradowski to join him. Buried at the back of the stall under the hay they found another wooden crate. This one was different from the wine cases; it was more flat and squared. Unlike the others, this one had no markings of any kind.

When the boy began to protest and tried to get up from his spot on the floor, Kradowski raced over and leveled his rifle at the youngster. Frightened and distraught, the boy sank back down onto the dirt and did what children do - he began to cry.

Obviously, we could have never met, but I do think about those boys from time to time. Why, do you suppose, would Tschau send these children on such a selfish and dangerous mission? It's possible they were all that was available to him, or perhaps he believed that the children were less likely to steal his treasures. Who knows what the fates, or luck, will decide. Only Charles, you must understand something important; it wasn't Kradowski who opened that crate. Oh, no. It was your father. And inside they found three framed paintings, quite old, and clearly valuable. One of them, the Teniers, is hanging right over there on your wall."

Charles opened his eyes to a silent room that was now dark. A light was coming from the kitchen, but Grandmother Lillian was nowhere to be seen.

"How long have I been sitting here," he wondered. His last connection to reality came when the Seth Thomas clock sitting on the mantle had struck eight, or perhaps it was nine? Dazed and a bit shaky, he rose and followed the light toward what was the most inviting place in his world: his mother's kitchen.

Entering the brightly lit room he found Grandmother Lillian talking on the phone with her back to the door. He overheard her say, "I don't know for sure; certainly a day or two more. I'll have to let you know. No, I won't be able to make that. Fine, please give them my regards. I will try to call tomorrow. Good-bye."

Charles reached up and took a glass from the shelf, filling it with water from the tap. Turning to face his grandmother, he asked, "How did the picture get here?"

Lillian took a seat at the kitchen table before she replied.

"There were three paintings in the case. None of them were especially large. Two were on canvas, and the third on wood. Although I'm hardly an expert, the way Gordon described them made me believe that they might have all been done by Flemish painters. Perhaps a Rubin, maybe Van Dyck, Brouwer, who knows; the only thing we do know about this painting is that it is called *Flemish Kermess*. It was painted in the sixteen fifties by David Teniers; Teniers the Younger."

Lillian paused for a moment as if to more carefully consider her next words.

"It must have been an interesting puzzle for your father, don't you think? Here he stood, one hundred miles from Berlin but four thousand miles from home and confronted by this, well, let's call it what it is - an opportunity. He had discovered a hidden box with what appeared to be three old, perhaps valuable paintings. There are sixty bottles of a French wine, which must surely be of great value, sitting in the back of a German truck. And, of course, there's a boy who is dead, and another who is his prisoner.

The boys are the mystery. Who sent them, and why? Did they come just for the wine and the paintings? Was there something else hidden in the barn? Obviously, Kradowski and your father couldn't have known about Tschau. So how do these boys fit?

Then there's the problem of time. Gordon would have known that there was only a limited amount of time to decide what to do with their treasures. Do they share with the group? If so, how would you do that with three paintings?

What about the boy? He doesn't appear to speak English, but who knows? Would he become an ally or an informer?"

"I admire your father's solution," Lillian stated in what Charles imagined must have been one of the few compliments she'd ever offered the man.

"Under the circumstances, I don't know what else he could have done."

She waited another moment, clearly enjoying the anticipation that she'd created, and then finished the story.

"Gordon took the smallest picture, the Teniers, for himself. He then told Kradowski to choose from the other two, which he did. Gordon described it as a portrait of woman with a very dark background done on a canvas. That's all we know of the picture. Sadly, both men then smashed the ancient wooden frames and tore the pictures from their stretchers. This left the paintings completely free of their frames. Gordon took his small canvas, and after opening his shirt he carefully tucked the picture between his fatigues and undershirt. He instructed Kradowski to do the same.

The third picture was the one that had been painted on wood. Assuming the boy could not speak English, your father helped the child to his feet but left his hands tied behind his back. Using one of the few German words that he knew, he said, 'Namen, Gordon' and then touched his chest. He did this several times, until the boy showed that he understood by replying, 'Mein namen ist Gerhard.' Holding the picture in front of Gerhard, he motioned as if he was giving the painting to the boy, while saying his name, 'Gerhard.' Despite his fear and lack of trust, Gerhard seemed to understand the proposition. Gordon then returned the picture and the remnants of the two frames to the case, and then proceeded to bury it exactly where they'd found it.

Before the others returned Kradowski and your father agreed that neither would say a word about what they had just done. As for the wine, I understand that each of the men received two bottles. Apparently, there was quite a party that night, but your father managed to keep one which he later opened on May 7, the day that the German's surrendered. I suspect that it was a remarkable vintage, and occasion.

138

As for the boy, we don't know whether Gerhard ever returned to the stable to retrieve the picture. What we do know is that he was released and made a part of the local German civilians who were delegated the task of burying the dead. Let's hope that he was able to recover it and that it somehow found its way to an appropriate home.

Who knows, perhaps today it's hanging in some fine museum. That would be a *lucky life*, wouldn't it?"

"Did you like the story?" Lillian asked, confident of the response.

Charles loved the story and his father for everything. The quiet bravery, cunning, and his father's deep resolve now filled him with indescribable joy. But there were still so many unanswered, perhaps unanswerable, questions. Seated across the room, Lillian Campbell remained quiet and resolute, as if she were appraising a rival. For now everything else would need to wait until he learned the answer to the one question that had started the story. Looking over at his grandmother, he asked, "What is it that I need to do?"

Until the day she died, Lillian Campbell was a striking woman.

She was stern, certainly, and uncompromising, but unlike most people who have jobs and make money and buy homes and grow families, Lillian Campbell's life work was to perfect her own style of unequaled self-confidence and singular beauty.

It was still there in her face, the beauty - *d'une beauté envoûtante* - lined, but not faded or lost to age; expressed in a graceful, measured carriage that seemed as much feline as feminine, and always packaged in perfect timeless couture. With a power of mind and spirit so dominant that her very presence left the impression that she was wiser and larger than anyone in the room, Lillian Campbell was a living portrait of the modern American elite.

This commanding temperament, however, would come with real consequence. As you would expect, this *persona extraordinaire* took time to build, and like the pearl's smooth luxuriant layers that steadily cover the grit of sand, Lillian Campbell was now exquisitely hardened by her own meticulous diligence. There were those who saw it as purely arrogance, an egotistical display of self-righteousness for which they secretly condemned her. But by this point, now utterly impenetrable, she consumed their insignificance, making her even stronger and most certainly more alone.

Charles was surprised to find that in spite of all that the day had consumed she did not seem in any way tired or drawn out. Quite the contrary, Grandmother Lillian was remarkably energetic and focused, while he felt utterly used-up.

"How does she do it," he wondered? "After all that we've been through, what's left for her?"

Before she spoke, Lillian had pushed the kitchen chair back from the table and stood. She waited until he was looking directly into her eyes and then began in a slow and focused voice.

"I want you to give the picture to a museum. It does not belong here. This is now your mother's house. A painting like this one is far too valuable to stay here. It calls out. It wants to be seen."

I don't understand," Charles replied. "It isn't my painting, or my decision. Why don't you speak to Mother about this? Why are you asking me?"

He'd been here with her before and knew that when directly challenged her presence would only grow. So when she finally spoke the words were measured perfectly, as if she'd considered them for some time.

"I don't believe your mother will see it the same way that I do. The emotions surrounding the picture will keep Charys from doing the right thing."

"Now I'm really confused. Why would my mother feel so strongly about the painting?"

Grabbing the back of the chair with both hands, she said in an exact and calculated sentence, "This is not the first time that we have had this conversation, your mother and father and me. I believe the first time I mentioned giving the painting to a museum was that first Thanksgiving Day in 1947. Your father was disinclined to that proposal."

"Is this what the two of you have been fighting about, this little painting?" Charles asked.

Lillian drew herself to her full majestic height as she looked down on Charles.

"Gordon and I have disagreed about many things, but this painting, this 'little' picture as you called it, has always been a focus for things larger and unspoken. Your father felt that the picture belonged to him, and I certainly appreciate that point-of-view. After all he'd gone through, I imagine he saw it as a kind of reward; compensation perhaps for the horrors of war.

But all of that has changed. This painting should not be hanging in a widow's home in Cedar Rapids, Iowa, hidden away from the world. Quite the contrary, it should be shared. The best way, the only way, is to donate it to an institution worthy of its important place in history."

She turned and walked toward the kitchen door. Just before leaving the room, she looked back at Charles and added, "You must persuade your mother to let me find an appropriate home for the painting."

Chapter Sixteen

Mazel Tov

"My life is nothing but room for you."
Mother Night - Kurt Vonnegut

A second full week had passed since his father's death. In order to discuss the future of his employment, Charles needed to return to Chicago and meet with his boss.

It was the Sunday after Gordon's funeral and he had driven Emily back to the city so that she could return to work at WGN the next day. Just before they left Cedar Rapids, Grandpa Bill's doctors had hinted at some good news, including an announcement for a possible surgical procedure. After a quick meeting with his boss on Monday morning, one where he was granted both a second week of vacation and some well-intended condolences, Charles climbed back into the Camaro and made a hasty return to the hospital. He arrived just in time to consult with the doctors at four o'clock.

"The good news is that during the last twenty-four hours Mr. Albright has shown some very positive signs. We believe he may be moving toward regaining consciousness," announced Dr. Tomasello. "This is particularly timely because we were considering a procedure that would reduce the intracranial pressure that is the cause of some of his problems. Given the little signs that both your grandmother and I have seen, it would be best to hold off for a day or two and monitor his condition."

It was the tone and context of that last remarkable sentence that helped Charles identify what he hoped was a change in fortunes. Granted, at that moment Grandpa Bill had done nothing more than flutter his eyelids, but it was from that tiny episode that the possibility for some kind of recovery was now marked and measured. Forty-eight hours later, Bill Albright opened his eyes for the first time in more than two weeks.

In the coming days, Grandpa Bill took real but nearly imperceptible steps back toward the light. Slowly, maddeningly slow, he began to find his precious mobility while suffering the frustration of dysarthria and an inability to articulate speech. But there was hope now, life-affirming hope, a condition that had been absent for too long.

Kenny Cernik, the boy who crashed into Gordon Albright's Cadillac, survived the collision, suffering massive internal injuries and two broken bones in his neck. Kenny not only missed his senior prom, but would never graduate from high school. There was almost no one who cared.

After seven weeks as an ungrateful guest and sponge of Mercy Hospital, Kenny was unceremoniously released into the care of his mother, Arlene Cernik. Arlene, and her freshly divorced husband, Jack Cernik operated a small and infamous tavern near the Hawkeye Downs dirt track called the Blue Light. Known by both the authorities and their resentful neighbors as a biker bar, the Blue Light was the bane of local law enforcement. If there was trouble west of Wilson Avenue, it likely involved patrons of the Blue Light. If there was an after-hours altercation in the parking lot of the nearby Whitewash Pancake House, it likely included the clientele of the Blue Light. If someone was looking to relieve themselves of some especially good product, the best place in town to do so was, without question, the Blue Light.

After thoroughly overstaying their welcome at Mercy, and with nowhere else for her invalid son to go, Arlene was forced to roll young Kenny's wheel chair into the Blue Light every morning just before the lunch crowd from the Quaker Oats plant began to congregate. Kenny's convalescence and therapy consisted mainly of busing tables, emptying ashtrays, and stealing drinks. All of which he did with little enthusiasm or a hint of kindness.

Sadly, Bobbie Vesley's parents would never appreciate the potential of their bright little girl. They would instead remain angry and frustrated by their lifetime sentence as the parents of "the little girl who died."

In this version of her *lucky life,* Bobbie was the third of the four Vesley children. Given the child's birth order and quiet disposition, it should come as no surprise that she would always see herself as the one who was unappreciated and overlooked - because she was. Her two older sisters, Cindy (twenty-two) and Kathy (twenty) had both graduated from Washington High School with little fanfare and no special acclaim. They then met all expectations by assuming quiet careers as a receptionist for a local dentist (Kathy) and a tax "specialist" at H & R Block (Cindy).

It was Bobbie's younger brother, Allan, who held the strongest claim to his parents' affections, principally for his growing notoriety as a defensive football player. Like his father Vernon, Allan Vesley was a large boy with an attitude. Since he and his "old man" were the only Y-chromosomes in a house full of X, Vernon made certain "his boy" was rigorously trained to be aggressive, hard, and utterly uncompromising. By winning a starting position as a linebacker for the Washington High Warriors in his sophomore year, he had not only gained great favor with his father, but was also getting serious looks from the athletic departments at both the University of Iowa and Illinois.

Bobbie's modest funeral was a sad but accurate reminder of her status within the Vesley family. If the famous scientist is right, a different version of Bobbie Vesley's *lucky life* will see her potential better fulfilled.

The most troubling of Charles' present realities was how to help his mother cope with her new emotional baggage.

Just days after her husband's funeral, Charys Albright began accompanying her mother-in-law to Mercy Hospital where they would dutifully ride the shiny antiseptic elevator up to the sixth floor - room 612. It was there in that tiny confining space that the two women spent their days; one desperately hoping for the smallest flicker of consciousness from a comatose husband, the other deliberately fleeing her future and the choking memory of a dead one.

There was never much in the way of conversation, but once they had arrived and gotten the updates on Bill's condition each woman would assume their own familiar schedule.

For Sarah the morning began by dutifully checking the water level in the many "get-well" flowers that now filled every available nook and cranny in the tiny hospital room. Once satisfied that each would live to go home with Bill, she then found the remote control and turned-on (but muted) the television in anticipation of her soaps. From her purse she retrieved the morning's Cedar Rapids Gazette and laid it on the nightstand, folded and ready in case her husband would suddenly wake and wish to know the news of the world. With everything now in its place, Sarah Albright would then drag the hospital's standard-issue plastic chair up next to the bed, where she would courageously take hold of her husband's unresponsive hand.

Unlike her mother-in-law, Charys had no specific responsibilities. Once Sarah was settled she would quietly reposition the room's other piece of furniture (a tired leather recliner) so that she might have a clear view out of the window. As silent as Sarah's muted television, Charys Albright would spend her day vacantly watching the hospital's monotonous traffic patterns and the continuous ebb and flow of each new, grim-faced visitor.

Grandma Sarah recognized the deepening depression and urged Charys to find alternative ways to spend her time, but the widow politely ignored her advice; there was, after all, nowhere else for her to go. Charys Albright was now trapped between her own unremitting remorse and a smothering antipathy toward the future. Without purpose or resolve the guilt festered into a sickening agar of regret, relentlessly growing into the misery of a life with no prospects, no opportunities, and no hope.

Throughout the summer of 1967, (the "Summer of Love") Charles and Emily spent their weekends traveling back and forth between Chicago and Cedar Rapids, watching as the two (Charys and Bill) inexorably changed places. As Grandpa Bill slowly, hopefully, began to work his way back, first with simple movement, guttural sounds, and finally a glint in his eye, Charys miserably resisted food, lost interest in her appearance, and refused to make plans of any kind, especially those that might include someone from outside of the family.

It was the innocent June Steffens who struck upon a possible alternative to Charys Albright's morbidity. With their wedding temporarily on hold so that they might deal with Charles' family needs, Emily had chosen to remain with June in the old Wilson Avenue apartment until after the wedding. Then one night over a late dinner, it was June who suggested, "You know, it might make your Mom feel better if you guys would set a date for your wedding and let her get involved. Maybe you should consider having the ceremony in Cedar Rapids?"

At first, Charys was pleasant but utterly disinterested in taking a role in their wedding plans, even if it was going to be held in Cedar Rapids.

"Why," she asked one night over a take-out pizza dinner, "would you ever want to get married here?"

With each week's visit, Emily cheerfully brought her mother-in-law more questions and small opportunities to help. Finally, with the ceremony less than two months off, Charys capitulated and offered to meet with the florist and hotel catering staff.

The decision to move the wedding two hundred-fifty miles west brought with it several interesting problems. For instance, after Pastor Milton's uninspired performance at his father's funeral, it was impossible for Charles to seriously consider holding their wedding at Saint Paul's Methodist. Another stick in the spokes came when they discovered that they could not use their friend, Judge Jonah Rothstein, to officiate the ceremony. The Iowa Code is emphatic that the "presiding official must be from Iowa," something Steiner clearly was not, neither by birth nor residence.

Fortunately for Emily and Charles, there were alternatives.

Grandma Sarah knew that the very thought of a using a different church for her grandson's wedding would cause a substantial rumble from within the inner circles of the Saint Paul Women's Auxiliary; an august group with which she had dutifully served for more than forty years. Only Sarah Albright (the "little Dane" as she was now dismissively referred to by Gloria Rickenbach and some of the more churchy old women of Saint Paul's) now saw herself in a different place, one where the old social standings and conformities had lost their meaning. Although she had never mentioned it to anyone before the accident, Sarah also found Pastor Paul Milton something of a stuffed shirt, and saw no reason to further accommodate Cedar Rapids convention by insisting that her grandson's wedding be held at his church.

Her alternative was Grace Presbyterian. Half the size of the newer and showy Saint Paul's, Grace was much more like its name: a warm and welcoming building with a devoted congregation. To add a bit of spice to the mix and a tweak to the ladies of the Auxiliary, there was the latest local "development" at Grace that Grandma Sarah felt certain would influence her modern grandson and his fiancée. As it happened, Grace Presbyterian had recently lost their minister to the larger parish of Chanhassen, Minnesota. In a decision that startled many of the locals, including those conservative older members of the neighboring Saint Paul's, the Church Board at Grace Presbyterian selected as their new spiritual leader an attractive and untested thirty-two year-old woman.

Margaret Anne Summersweet was born on April 2, 1935 in the small western Illinois town of Pekin. A serious and bookish young woman, Margaret was the oldest of the three Summersweet children; the identical twin brothers (Michael and Daniel) were just eighteen months younger.

During Margaret's formative years her father, Arthur Summersweet, was unavoidably unavailable. Seven thousand miles away, Arthur served the war effort in the South Pacific as a member of the infamous 37th Infantry Division. What made the "infamous 37th" infamous was their exceptional courage and determination in securing the final liberation of the Philippines.

In February of 1945 (Margaret would have been ten-years-old) General Walter Krueger and his boys were given the harsh challenge of taking Manila back from twenty-thousand angry Japanese soldiers. What made the twenty-thousand Japanese angry - especially angry - was that they had been left stranded by their Emperor with only the cynical instructions to, "fight or die." After thirty days of combat, (thirty horrific days where a thousand Americans soldiers, fifteen thousand Japanese, and a quarter of a million Philippine civilians died) Arthur and his comrades would tear down the Japanese flag that had flown over Fort Santiago, thereby bringing an end to one of the fiercest and most destructive battles in the Pacific theater.

Once safely back home, Arthur took the first available job he could find, which turned out to be as a typesetter and part-time reporter for the Pekin News. Thanks to his strong work ethic and punchy prose style, he soon landed a spot on the city desk at the Dubuque Telegraph Herald.

It would be Margaret's mother, Anita, who suggested the possibility that their clever daughter attend the University of Dubuque Theological Seminary.

The Summersweet's hometown of Pekin was hardly a hotbed for the women's liberation movement, but back at the turn of the century, Anita's mother had been something of a Chicago suffragette. With the cause as a permanent part of her psyche, Anita carefully picked her battles, eventually convincing her husband that their daughter had both the mind and disposition to take on such a timely challenge. Anita could see in her first-born the talents of a confident orator, an uncanny memory for faces, and a deep vein of common sense; all qualities she considered critical to the clergy.

After leaving the seminary, Margaret spent her next seven years as a free agent for the UPCUSA, making brief stops in Peoria, Sioux Falls, and Council Bluffs before finally landing the top job at Grace Presbyterian in Cedar Rapids. She anxiously reported to work on Monday, March 6, just two days short of her thirty-second birthday.

Though no one ever publicly described the Board's decision to hire Margaret Summersweet as "radical," there were several other more colorful adjectives that got tossed around the local coffee shops. Even though it was 1967, it was still uncommon to find a woman (especially a young, attractive single woman) as the minister of a conservative Midwestern congregation.

Curiously, the greatest trepidation for young Pastor Summersweet's appointment did not come from the membership of her future congregation, but rather from the conservative old men at the neighboring Saint Paul's Methodist. Although it was hardly any of their concern, these old poops eagerly took their uneducated potshots at the woman's capabilities before they'd even had the chance to meet her. One of the common coffee shop themes was the smug comparison between Pastor Summersweet's gender and the perpetrator of the "original fall."

Of course, none of them ever said a word outside their own condescending little clutch, but what worried those old boys the most, right down to their sagging support stockings, was not a matter of Revelations, but one of elevations. It was a fact that on Sunday mornings this new young female minister was going to be perched high on the pulpit, looking straight down on those Presbyterians. From this superior location, Pastor Margaret would be preaching God's words and ministering to their spiritual life; which, by the way, begged the question, "How much life had Pastor Margaret Summersweet lived, anyway?" This elevated status implied she was now God's right hand... woman, meting out His sacraments, and officiating at all the familiar events. With such an unhealthy break in tradition, how much longer would these Methodists be able to hold out before the women of Saint Paul's started demanding equal billing?

Margaret Summersweet knew better than to share any personal philosophies from the pulpit. But for some her role as Grace Presbyterian's new, young female minister linked her to every liberal point-of-view and freethinking position under the sun. It shouldn't have made a difference that she was a woman. It shouldn't have made a difference that she was young. Yet, there were those for who it did make a great deal of difference. Before she'd unpacked her bags, Margaret Summersweet was labeled and convicted of being anti-war, anti-government, pro-abortion, and pro-women's liberation. Cedar Rapid's buzzed with comments and conclusions all created and endorsed by God-fearing Christians who had never heard a word that the woman minister had to say.

Sarah Albright was quite aware of this situation, and still happily recommended both Grace Presbyterian and Pastor Margaret Summersweet to her grandson and his future wife.

"Pastor Summersweet?" Charles asked, although he needn't. It was clear from the description that Grandma Sarah had provided that this woman was the person he and Emily hoped would marry them in less than sixty days.

Margaret Summersweet was noticeably taller than Emily and Charles, and carried an athletic build that made some of the local's wonder if she hadn't once played basketball. She had lovely fair skin and sharp chiseled features. Her face was surrounded by short brown hair that was fashionably cut. She looked smart but comfortable in black trousers and a long-sleeved white shirt. A large crucifix on a thin golden chain rested comfortably around her neck. On this occasion she did not wear the minister's white collar.

The three shook hands and were politely invited to adjourn to the Minister's study where coffee was poured and pleasantries exchanged. Pastor Summersweet's casual management of the conversation felt like the room, which was both warm and welcoming.

Soon enough, "Pastor Margaret," as she told them she preferred to be addressed, said, "I understand from your grandmother that the two of you would like to be married here at Grace. Is that right?"

"Well, yes," Charles began. "I suspect Grandma mentioned some of the circumstances around the need to change our plans. Originally, we were going to be married last May in Chicago, but my father died in a car accident which also injured my grandfather. The timing was wrong, so we're making new plans. We also wanted my mother and grandmother to be able to help with the arrangements, so we thought it best to move the wedding here to Cedar Rapids."

Pastor Margaret nodded, and then added, "Please accept my condolences on the loss of your father." She paused for a moment to study the couple, and then asked, "If you don't mind me asking, why not go to your family's church? Saint Paul's, right?"

"Saint Paul's isn't my church," Charles replied with perhaps a bit more enthusiasm than was necessary. "My parents and grandparents go to Saint Paul's, but Emily and I have no real connection there."

"Forgive my questions, but wasn't your father's funeral at Saint Paul's?" Then she hastily added, "Don't misunderstand, I'd just like to know what's motivating your choices. As you've probably heard, I'm new to the area and, well, there are professional considerations we need to keep in mind. Pastor Milton is a colleague of mine…" She left the sentence purposefully dangling, awaiting Charles and Emily's reply.

"We're not trying to put you in a bad place, "Emily offered. "We, I mean Charles and I, have no affiliation to a church or pastor here in Cedar Rapids. We were told by our family about your church, and from what I can see its closer to what we had in mind than Saint Paul's."

"Thank you," Pastor Margaret replied "but are we talking about preferences of furnishings, or is it something else?"

Charles looked across the coffee table to where Pastor Margaret sat confidently straight-backed in her armchair. He forced down his first defensive reaction, and then after a couple of deep breaths, offered, "I appreciate your situation here, and I don't think we want to cause some kind of professional problem between you and Pastor Milton, but, frankly, the man did not do a good job at my father's funeral. I can't imagine him doing our wedding. He's probably a good minister, but we're looking for something else; something that is a little more about us and a little less about, well… God." He quickly added, "No offense."

"None taken," was the instant reply.

"You seem like nice people," Pastor Margaret continued, "and I'd be happy to marry you here at Grace Presbyterian, but there are certain traditions at our church that need to be considered. First, a Presbyterian wedding requires that the couple meet with the minister two or three times before the ceremony, so that we can visit about the challenges of being and staying married. There are the spiritual questions as well. That would require quite a commute and commitment from the two of you. Second, we'd need to make sure that appropriate dates and times are available, and we can do that before you leave. But most important, I must insist that before anything else you inform Pastor Milton and receive his blessings."

Charles was just about to begin his protest with the phrase, "I don't really think that it's any of Pastor Milton's concern," when Emily announced, "We'll be glad to meet with him, and I look forward to our visits with you."

The couple's appointment with Pastor Paul Milton was little more than perfunctory. Although Charles had worked himself up over what he believed would be a contentious debate on why he preferred a young woman minister and a Presbyterian church over the man who had just presided at his father's funeral, it never happened. Instead, the five-minute exchange was mostly focused on the well-being of his mother and grandmother, and how they were "getting along."

As the couple left the preacher's well-appointed offices, Charles emotions were split between his relief of now being shed of the sanctimonious Pastor Paul Milton (the minister), and his own annoying cynicism for Dr. Paul Milton (the business man), a person whose obvious self-interests were focused on keeping what was left of the Albright family within the fold.

In the coming weeks, Charles was surprised by just how informative and ultimately supportive Pastor Margaret's counseling sessions turned out to be; this, in spite of the obvious detail that the woman had no firsthand knowledge of the topic. Yet, she gently opened those little packages of emotion and concern that couples seem to naturally hide. In her role as guide, Pastor Margaret rarely took a position, but would instead facilitate intelligent and meaningful dialog about sensitive topics and behaviors that Charles would have been ill-at-ease to discuss elsewhere. More than once, he was surprised to find a theme that they'd considered during their Saturday morning sessions had worked its way back into the couple's daily conversation in a way that offered an informed point of departure.

The decision to move the ceremony to Cedar Rapids, Iowa made the couple's original plans for a small intimate event even smaller. When the wedding was planned for Chicago the couple had a considerable number of friends that they hoped would attend, but once it was moved five hours west to Cedar Rapids it seemed both unfair to ask and unlikely that their local friends would attend. For their final count the couple sent eighteen invitations to their friends, eight replied in the affirmative.

The other side of the family would present their own unique concerns. The one and only time that Charles had visited Freeland was back in February when he officially asked Emily's mother for permission to marry. Strenuously warned, but still surprised, Charles would later describe his future mother-in-law's reaction to the happy news as "polite indifference." As for the handful of other Krist's that he met at a local coffee shop, their lack of enthusiasm had left him feeling about as welcome as a wet pair of shoes.

The only relative that Emily believed would have any regard for her happiness was Grandma Saffii. Sadly, her health had become such an inconvenience to her family (a double whammy of severe arthritis and type-one diabetes) that her son's spouses were now openly demanding her relocation to what they snidely nicknamed the "Old" Oaks Retirement Center.

It was on the first Sunday in February when she stoically agreed to leave her home of forty-seven years and move into the nursing home. Saffii had just finished five hours of hard labor to feed and cleanup after her family, a chore she did on her own so that the others might attend worship services at Saint John's. She had just put away the last of the dinner dishes when son Thomas and wife Barbara gave her the "good news" that there would soon be an opening at Old Oaks.

She accepted their uninvited arrangement under the condition that they promise to look in on her husband Alder every day, just to "make sure he's taking his meals and medicines."

The sentencing didn't take long. Within a month, Stephen and Barbara had made the arrangements and closed the deal. Crossing the Oaks' threshold, Saffii understood that no one, especially Barbara, ever expected her to walk out of there again.

"This is where they've brought me to die," she decided, as the bubbly Old Oaks director offered to show them to Saffii's room.

As far as guests from the Albright side, both Charys and Sarah had pooled their names and ended up mailing around forty invitations. They focused on those friends who they knew would remember Charles, as well those who could restrain themselves from making any emotional outbursts regarding the Albright's still-recent tragedy.

After a lengthy discussion, and a bit of bending, the couple elected Emily to contact Grandmother Lillian regarding any invitations that she would care to make. They both anticipated that she would again offer to host a reception at her home, which she did. This time, Emily graciously accepted, hoping that their compliance here might make for a happier and more pleasant ceremony there.

On Saturday, October 28, 1967, eighteen months and nine days after meeting outside the Goodwin Theater, Emily Krist and Charles Albright celebrated their love and commitment by marrying one other at the Grace Presbyterian Church in Cedar Rapids, Iowa.

Far from a lavish or extravagant affair, Emily and Charles wedding was instead a reflection of the couple's personal interests and affections. Largely because the two of them were assuming the costs, there were certain trappings and traditions (like flowers, photographs, and an elaborate wedding dress) where the scale was significantly reduced. There were other places, however, where the couple's careful budget was generously ignored. One of those blessed expenditures was the outlay for music.

Alice Wandstadt and Erica Rahlson, two of Emily's closest friends from the Goodman School, were hired and brought to Cedar Rapids to provide music for both the ceremony and reception. It turned out to be money well spent. Erica was engaged to play the piano and guitar, Alice the vocal accompaniment.

Alice Wandstadt was originally from Green Bay, Wisconsin where she grew up in a large and musical family; her father and mother were both on the faculty at the University of Wisconsin-Green Bay where he taught voice and she piano. Along with their tenured teaching positions, the Wandstadts also hosted a popular syndicated Sunday morning radio show, *Worship with the Wandstadts*. Thanks to their charming and talented children, the long-running, ninety minute broadcast had built a substantial following throughout the upper-Midwest. At its peak, *Worship with the Wandstadts* was considered a blessing and a ritual for both their loyal listeners and the satisfied station managers of those twenty-eight AM radio stations that carried the popular program. After Alice left to attend the Goodman School in Chicago, it would take nearly eighteen months before the local affiliates stopped getting calls and letters inquiring after Alice and when they might expect her return to the fold.

Not only was Erica Rahlson a talented actor (she had just finished a wonderful six-week summer run as understudy to Carrie Snodgrass in the Goodman's version of *Oh! What a Wonderful War*), but she was also a highly accomplished pianist who made her living as a rehearsal accompanist with the Lyric Opera of Chicago. In their second year at the Goodman Academy, Erica and Emily had co-starred in a student production of *She Stoops to Conquer* where Emily played Miss Constance Neville, and Erica the conniving, willful Kate Hardcastle. Their deep and lasting friendship began by surviving both the emotional tribulations of a young insecure director, and the very real challenges of interpreting a dated play.

The couple had enthusiastically turned over the roles of musical director and performer to Alice and Erica, encouraging them to use their considerable talents to the highest end. Emily simply instructed the girls, "Imagine it's your wedding. What would you want to have played?"

The girls happily accepted their friend's challenge and produced a remarkable and thoroughly memorable program. For the prelude, Erica dedicated a superb recital of both Schumann's *Traumerei* and the *Waltz in C-Sharp Minor* by Chopin. Alice sang twice during the ceremony, performing *Du Bist Die Rue* by Schubert, and later Bach's masterpiece, *Bist Due Bei* to an astonished and appreciative congregation.

Unlike so many larger and more complicated ceremonies, in this *lucky life* Emily and Charles' service went off without a hitch. People arrived promptly at three o'clock, there were no complications with any of the logistics, and the weather provided a picture perfect afternoon. For this example, much can be said about the value of simplicity.

June Steffens joyfully assumed the role of Emily's maid-of-honor, while Judge Johan Rothstein served as the best man. Standing on opposite sides of the aisle awaiting the entrance of the bride, June had been transformed by a stunning deep phthalo-blue dress that featured a bateau neckline and a dramatic gathered skirt, all handmade by her mother, Ingrid.

As the familiar call of *Treulich Geführt* wrapped the guests in anticipation, a radiant Emily Krist slowly, gently, confidently made her way down the aisle to her waiting intended.

"Today," announced, Pastor Margaret Summersweet, "we are here to celebrate the love and marriage of Emily Krist and Charles Albright.

The act, the commitment to marriage, is certainly one of the most joyous and significant traditions we humans know. Right now, all around the world, people of every nationality, culture, and religion are performing a similar ritual because they share something with Emily and Charles, they are in love.

In one sense marriage is an agreement, a contract between two people who are in love. Later, the five of us here will consummate the contract with our signatures. But for the next few moments, let's consider the less secular and more ethereal side of love.

Now, love is a special word, in fact, it is without question one of the most powerful and important words anywhere. Whether it's in Italian, which is pronounced *amore*, or Russian *ljubovj*, or the Japanese who say *Ai*, at a Hebrew wedding you'd hear the Rabi talk about *ahava*, or if you were from Iceland you'd pledge your undying *ast*. Love, in any language, is sought after, needed, wanted, desired, but impossible to buy.

Love is many things. Goethe thought, 'love is an ideal thing,' while marriage, he believed, 'was a real thing.' You can see that Mr. Goethe was a man of few words, but big ideas. Still, the word 'love' has been around far longer than his simple sentence. As a part of our language, love has been in the English lexicon for more than eight hundred years. The fact that we feel love, well, that's been around a lot longer.

The word is spelled, L-O-V-E; just two simple little vowels and two happy consonants. It can be either a noun or a verb... but then so can help, hope, and humor.

For such an important word it can be curiously assigned a lesser role, as in something we fancy, like a new car that we would just... love? Or, maybe something that we could go for, perhaps an ice cream cone. To show you how we undervalue love, it only offers the modest reward of seven points in Scrabble. Two weeks ago in the Sunday crossword, "love" was the poetic answer to the nine-across clue, 'makes the world go round.' Then there's tennis where a score of love will never let you win.

In our Christian tradition, devotion, and its partner marriage, requires a commitment to act lovingly, which means without reward. During our time together your love was the focus of our discussions. Where did this love come from? What makes it real? Is it strong enough to survive all that life offers? Charles and Emily, you two have been blessed with a strength and friendship that revealed your love, but makes no promise to sustain it. The need to nourish our love is why we marry, and why the tradition can be found in virtually every culture and people on God's great earth.

Through your marriage love becomes a virtue represented by your kindness and affection for one another. Love is real. God is love. Amen."

"Could I have everyone's attention, please?"

Jonah Rothstein was standing and lightly tapping on his wine glass as everyone turned toward the front table where the wedding party was seated.

"I understand that as Charles' best man it is my responsibility to offer a toast to the newly married couple. I've also been told that sometimes the best man uses this opportunity to tell embarrassing stories about the couple, mostly the groom. Though I'd be happy to tell you an embarrassing story about Charles, I unfortunately don't know any. Here's hoping that doesn't make this a poor toast.

What I do know about my friends Charles and Emily is how blessed they are as a couple. You see, they are truly in love, and that folks doesn't happen every day.

Charles and I met in college, and I am the lucky one for it. Back in those days, Charles was a very serious young man. I guess it was one of the qualities that I first admired about him. Clearly, Charles Albright was well raised here in Cedar Rapids, Iowa.

I am from Brooklyn, New York, and as you might guess with a name like Jonah Rothstein, I was born and raised in the Jewish faith. We do things a little different at Jewish weddings, but the goal is the same; that is, to celebrate. To celebrate the love and happiness that Emily and Charles have discovered.

As I was reminded this afternoon, my favorite parts of a Jewish wedding ceremony are a lot like your Christian service. There are rings and vows that are exchanged. There's some wine that gets drunk along the way, which is nice, but there's a phrase that the bride offers when she gives her new husband his ring that I think is especially appropriate. She'll say, *'Ani l'dodi v'dodi li'* which means, 'I am my lover; my lover is mine.' And that feels about right, doesn't it?

Ladies and gentlemen, I'd like to teach you a Yiddish phrase that fits the moment; Mazel tov. You should shout this out because it's what we all wish for you Emily and Charles, and that is, good luck. So everyone raise your glass and... *Mazel tov*!"

The Roosevelt Hotel is located in the heart of downtown Cedar Rapids, Iowa. A little tired after forty-seven years, but still quite capable of showing her past glory; it was here at the Roosevelt where the Albright's wedding reception would be held.

On this happy occasion, the once impressive hotel offered the couples' guests two contrasting perspectives. To those visiting from out-of-town, the agreeable accommodations provided their friends with a taste of local history and a relaxing quality of nostalgia. Not so much for those folks from Freeland, especially the Krist family. Throughout the service and reception the in-laws proclaimed the Roosevelt Hotel a worrisome inconvenience, complaining loudly about its high prices, even though they had purchased nothing, and the unreasonable challenges of navigating their way through what they considered, "the big city."

Despite the chilly reception he had received from the Krist family during his first visit to Freeland, Charles was amused by just how many of their kin had accepted the invitation to travel to Cedar Rapids and join the wedding celebration. Although he never bothered to count, Charles was certain that there were at least a dozen new faces happily making their third trip through the buffet line. His one financial consolation was that to a person the Krist's were teetotalers.

Not so, however, for those who had married into the family. Johanna Krist discovered her enthusiasm for wine about the same time that she realized there was never going to be another man in her life. It seems likely that these two discoveries had a common source of origin, which could be traced to her longtime friend, and June's mother, Ingrid Steffens.

It wasn't until late in the summer of 1958 that Ingrid Steffens finally reconciled herself to the fact that her husband David preferred to be anywhere but where she was. This had been a gradual awakening; the Steffens had been married for nearly twenty-two years before she accepted the fact that her husband was not only gone more than he was home, but that he clearly preferred it that way. This utterly depressing news should not have come as surprise, after all, Ingrid had done very little - that is if you don't include raising the children and managing the household - to encourage her estranged spouse to stay at home. Her personal lack of interest in the man, his body, or his work had left David feeling that his presence was neither needed nor missed. It was the perfect recipe for divorce.

Given Ingrid's indifference, one might imagine that David's life on the road was lonely and singular, perhaps even sad. This would not have been the case. When asked, he would speak lovingly of his two children, and genuinely appeared to enjoy seeing them in properly scheduled doses. As for those unscheduled solicitations that a life on the road will offer, he never once left his feet to show any interest in the company of another woman.

That's not to say that David Steffens was without passion. Quite the contrary, he was an enthusiastic golfer that played to a four handicap. Thanks to an upbeat attitude, his frequent visits to the links, and the good habit of generous tipping, David Steffens was affectionately welcomed by every pro shop manager and greens keeper in Southwest Iowa. After all those years as a golf widow, Ingrid Steffens finally understood that her husband got more pleasure from a well-struck three-iron than he did an evening with the woman he married.

154

Once June and Emily had abandoned Freeland for Chicago, the only constant in Ingrid's life was Johanna Krist. The two women discovered that they generally agreed on most things, especially their grinding distaste for men. But in those four years since the children's departure, it seemed as if Johanna had become even angrier and more temperamental. Her moods were so severe that Ingrid often left her friend's company more depressed and miserable than if she'd stayed home.

So it came as a mixed blessing when they discovered that one way to calm Johanna's anger was to apply a healthy dose of German Kabinett.

These crisp white wines became Johanna's favorite, and she bought them by the case. Not in Freeland, of course, but by driving forty miles to those invisible liquor stores in Council Bluffs, she could buy her remedy without the anxiety of any local encumbrances. She would drink a Riesling if there was food involved; occasionally a decent rose, but it had to be highly chilled; or in a pinch, if there was absolutely nothing else available, she would make the best out of a sweet syrupy Liebfraumilch. At this point, it was not unusual for her to wake up of a morning with a drumming headache, a thick sour taste in her mouth, and two empty green bottles on the kitchen counter.

Along with her growing habit for the grape came the rationalizations. Thanks to the Kabinett there was the one where she was now a more sophisticated person, one with considered opinions about her preferences and point-of-view. With a long-stem glass in her hand, Johanna could swirl the sweet amber liquor and imagine that she was enjoying the tasty libation while lounging on the deck of a private yacht, merrily engaged in a remarkable conversation with her fine and fascinating new friends as they secretly made their way toward a hidden Aegean rendezvous with Jack and Jackie. Graciously tipping the green bottle to refill her friend's empty glass, Johanna Krist was transformed into the generous hostess: warm, charming, and all too happy to receive her welcome good company.

Except her dreams would fly in the face of her reality; the truth was that in this version of her *lucky life,* Johanna Krist was an unhappy woman with too much time on her hands, a constant nagging inner voice, and the need for a daily escape.

For Johanna and Ingrid to be able to enjoy the wedding reception without the fear of embarrassing themselves in front of the sober self-righteous Krist's, the two had to direct a deception. Johanna understood and wisely feared the kind of backbiting gossip that Barbara Krist would relish spreading around Freeland should she find the mother-of-the-bride imbibing in, heaven forbid, alcohol. So after their first small glass of rose, one that would naturally be recognized as celebratory by everyone, including the nosy Krist's, Johanna and Ingrid's plan was to take turns slipping out the side door of the banquet room. Once free of the crowd they could then secretly cross the lobby to the Roosevelt's cocktail lounge. With the help of the Gas Lamp bartender, they would then replenish their drinks in what they imagined were inconspicuous coffee cups. If all went well the two mothers could enjoy the spirits of the occasion under the ruse of heavy caffeine consumption.

"Good evening, again," Lillian Campbell announced as she approached the corner table where Johanna and Ingrid had quietly concealed themselves. "A charming party don't you think, Johanna? Emily is a lovely bride."

Like her daughter, Johanna Krist was also deeply anxious about Lillian Campbell. On this occasion it took only that single innocent sentence from the lean woman in the fabulously expensive dress to trigger all the warning bells inside her head. Despite her mildly numbed sensibilities, it was still obvious that this woman reeked of inherited wealth and unforgivable vanity.

In an uninvited flashback, Johanna suddenly remembered those first childhood lessons, the ones that her father had painfully taught to the tune of a hickory stick.

"Oh, how he would have despised this arrogant woman. He would have seen for what she truly is, a disgrace to God's will and the Commandments; a peacock, and servant to Satan."

"Still," she thought, "there is something lucky about the woman. Oh, it's probably wrong, clearly wrong, but who wouldn't want some of that money? Timothy was right about money as the 'root of all evil', but surely he wouldn't begrudge an old woman just a little, would he?"

But then there was the *other* voice, the one that came from deep down inside her own tired and terrible soul. It was the one that got loud and angry. The one that was difficult to satisfy. The one that didn't give a damn what Father had said, or how much his stick had hurt her. Now thanks to Lillian Campbell and all that show and filthy money, the dark conniving voice had returned, this time using an especially condescending tone to remind Johanna of just how little she'd accomplished with her own life.

"She's looking down on you," the *other* whispered. "Look. There she is, the Queen of your daughter's new family. And here you sit, Johanna Krist, the mother-of-the-bride, so belittled and forgotten that you've been reduced to sneaking into a hotel bar just to refill your chipped coffee cup with cheap wine."

Johanna Krist shuddered, and then replied, "Thank you, Lillian. It is a lovely evening. Would you care to join us?"

The round table sat eight. Johanna and Ingrid were seated with their backs to the wall facing the front of the room, while Lillian took the chair directly across from them. A small vase of cheerful yellow daisies blocked their view of one another. Once seated, however, Lillian immediately reached across the table and moved the distracting vase to the side. After taking a small sip from her glass of white wine, she set it down and smiled affably at the two women.

"Are you two still drinking coffee?" Lillian Campbell asked. "I'd be awake all night," she added, peering down into the nearly empty cups.

No one said anything for some time. Instead the three listened politely as Erica Rahlson executed a lovely hand-roll flourish to finish what had been a delightful version of Erroll Garner's gem, *Misty*.

As Erica acknowledged the applause, Lillian began again, "It's wonderful that so many of the Krist's could join us tonight, don't you think?"

"Is that an insult," the *other voice* wondered?

Johanna chose her words carefully, and then replied in a deliberate pace.

"Well, they don't get out that often, and this is a very special occasion for my late husband's family."

"It is unfortunate about your husband," Lillian said without guile or reservation. "Emily told me that he died four years ago from a heart attack; very sad. It would have been so nice to have him here to walk her down the aisle. It's such a proud moment for a father. It certainly was for my husband on the day that Charys married Charles' father."

A second loud alarm bell went off in Johanna's head. She and Ingrid had been strenuously warned by their children that the topic of Gordon Albright's death was considered off-limits and should be avoided.

Only the *other* had spotted an opportunity.

Johanna took the last sip of wine from her coffee cup, and then with false enthusiasm remarked, "Charys has done a wonderful job."

Ingrid stiffened beside her, recognizing that Johanna had just served-up a testing forehand and was now anxiously awaiting the return.

"I presume you're referring to the reception," Lillian replied in that frighteningly emotionless voice. "Actually, this beautiful party was almost entirely your daughter's good work. I should know, I offered on more than one occasion to provide her assistance, but clearly Emily is a very capable young woman."

Smash - a backhand volley to Johanna's weak side. There was no mistaking that Johanna Krist had met an equal.

"It's not too late to let it go, leave with a draw," she thought. "After all, it is my daughter's wedding. This is hardly the place and time..."

Except now there was the wine and the *other* voice, the persistent angry one that was always so hard to satisfy. So far, Johanna and Ingrid had made only three trips to the Gas Lamp lounge to refresh their coffee mugs; on a typical evening, Johanna would need to drink twice that amount before the *other* would be placated enough to stay quiet.

"Yes, well, Emily's never been afraid of hard work." Ingrid unexpectedly interrupted.

Surprised by the outsiders sudden intrusion into their rally, both Johanna and Lillian turned toward Ingrid as Alice Wandstadt began an enchanting version of the Carmichael and Mercer tune, *Skylark*.

> " *Skylark, have you anything to say to me,*
> *won't you tell me where my love can be?*
> *Is there a meadow in the mist*
> *where someone's waiting to be kissed?* "

"Now what are you two doing back here in the corner, hiding?"

Barbara Krist was a large, (not heavy) handsome woman best known within the limited social circles of Freeland for her massive head of honey-colored hair (as thick as a brush), a harsh piercing voice (possibly capable of cutting steel cable), and a deep, lifelong hatred for the mother of the bride.

Only six weeks after graduating from Freeland High School, Barbra Ann Toft would contentedly marry a mild and gangly farm boy named, Stephen Krist. Everyone thought they were a perfect match, after all it said so over and over again on the hastily scribbled farewells and silly innuendo in the back of Barbara's 1938 Freeland High School yearbook.

Barbara and Stephen were both farm kids and firstborns. With that kind of heritage and birth order there was never any question about their future. They were expected to maintain tradition by finishing high school, and then instantly settle down to work the families' farms. Both had experienced the same childhood, one built upon hard work and deep religious conviction; they assumed the same of their children. Their unwavering commitment to Saint John's Lutheran Church demanded three things: bear children, honor your parents, and praise God above all things. In return there was the promise of a planned and reliable future; one that came with an ironclad guarantee to life's most challenging questions and, of course, eternal rest in a place where the streets are paved with gold.

Without a warning she was there, standing beside the table with both hands on her wide hips, looking down upon the three women. As Lillian turned to see who had interrupted them, Barbara Krist held out her large paw and said, "We met earlier. I'm Emily's aunt Barbara, Barbara Krist. My husband Stephen is that tall bald man hovering over there by the door."

Lillian nodded her head indicating that she remembered their encounter, but said nothing.

The *other* playfully tested the water, asking, "You aren't leaving are you, Barbara?"

While keeping direct eye contact with Mrs. Lillian Campbell, Barbara Krist replied, "Stephen is certainly ready to go, but I think we might stay a bit longer. So, Mrs. Campbell, I understand that you live in Chicago, too."

Before Lillian could answer the big woman extracted one of the small folding chairs from under the table. After a quick inspection to confirm that its structural integrity was suitable to manage the load, Barbara Krist lowered her considerable self onto the plastic seat right between Lillian and Ingrid; her gigantic blue purse landed on the floor beside her with a thud.

Delicately placing both of her massive mitts on the table, Barbara Krist smiled agreeably at the thin woman from Chicago. Displaying prudent caution, she then carefully repositioned her bulk into the suffering folding chair.

She was just about to open her mouth to speak when a wide and unattractive scowl unexpectedly spread across the woman's broad face. It seems the location of the innocent vase of daisies - a distraction that was apparently equal to a pile of excrement on the clean white table cloth - was causing Barbara's consternation; her unpleasant expression seemed to beg the question, "Why are these flowers here?"

Picking up the tiny glass vase as if it had cooties, Barbara hastily returned the innocent bouquet to the center of the table. With Johanna's view once again blocked by the flowers, the *other* slyly peered around the centerpiece to offer Lillian Campbell a peculiar smile; an apparent acknowledgment of Barbara Krist's unwanted interruption.

Taken aback by both Barbara's unexpected interruption and Johanna's bizarre new behavior, Lillian Campbell turned her attentions back to the intruder before politely replying, "Yes. I've lived in Chicago my entire life."

"That's interesting," Barbara pushed back. "What was it exactly that your husband did before he passed?"

There was a moment of cool assessment before Lillian Campbell replied, "He was a lawyer."

Remarkably out of sync, Barbara Krist reached down into her blue suitcase to retrieve a Brownie Starflash camera, and then announced, "Well, a city like that is just too big for me. Take your picture?"

Lillian seemed baffled by whether the last sentence had been intended as a question or declarative statement. A second later the flash ignited, momentarily blinding her victim. Without breaking stride, Barbara continued, "I get worried with Stephen trying to drive here in Cedar Rapids. I can't imagine him in a big city like Chicago. And there's all that violence and crime. I guess I'm just a small town girl at heart."

As their conversation stalled, Johanna sat back and reveled in the knowledge that her nemesis, even with her impressive size and sour disposition, was no match for the likes of Lillian Campbell. What a welcome diversion. This unexpected feeling of satisfaction had done wonders, and had even persuaded the *other* to temporarily step down and relax. It was with a contented smile that Johanna absentmindedly reached out and picked up her coffee cup to enjoy a sip of the rose, only to discover that it was now empty.

This was the opportunity that Barbara Krist had been hoping for. Like a stalking predator lying in wait, she had watched suspiciously as both Ingrid and Johanna left the party with empty coffee cups, only to return cautiously carrying two that had been refilled. Weren't there waiters patrolling the room carrying coffee urns? Obviously, the "wino widow" was sneaking out to get her liquor, her fix, and at her own daughter's wedding no less.

"Here Johanna, let me take care of that for you. Ingrid, would you and Johanna both care for another cup?" Barbara asked in a loud voice brimming with intense satisfaction.

Ingrid quickly replied, "No, thank you, Barbara. I don't care for any more."

"How about you, Johanna, care for another drink?"

In less than three hundred milliseconds, Johanna Krist's blood pressure spiked forty-seven points. Deep inside her wounded brainstem the amygdale released an overdose of adrenaline and cortisol, effectively shutting down her brain's logic centers. Mentally all hell had broken loose. Under these affected conditions, (pupils now fully dilated, face flushed crimson, normal breathing stopped, and a heart that was pounding like a hammer) Johanna Krist's fully constricted brain could only issue an emotional response to the primeval question of fight or flight.

Taking full advantage of the impaired logic center, the *other* was preparing to recklessly spit out the most venomous comeback her broken brain could concoct, when from out of the blue, Lillian Campbell calmly interrupted, "That is so very kind of you, Barbara, but before you joined us I was just collecting the ladies to come and have a final picture taken before the bride and groom leave us. Bring your things ladies, we won't be coming back."

It took Johanna a second to realize what had just happened. As she stood, still glaring at her archenemy and not exactly sure that she wouldn't prefer to stay and have it out, Ingrid was suddenly there next to her, pushing a purse and the empty coffee cup into her tightly clenched fists.

Lillian smiled politely at Barbara Krist, and then said, "Come along, Johanna. Ingrid. This is such a special night for our beautiful children."

It was closing in on ten o'clock.

The Krist's had all gone home with little fanfare and very few thanks. June and their Chicago friends were off in the corner, all laughs and sighs as

160

they happily polished off the last of the champagne. Jonah Rothstein was nowhere to be found, but had earlier been spotted chatting-up Charles' cousin, Annette Albright.

Annette was the youngest and most gregarious of Thomas Albright's four children. She had graduated from the University of Iowa in 1964 with a degree in anthropology, a distinction that would leave her father staring at his check book and shaking his head. After a botched marriage to what could generously be described as a failed beatnik, she moved back from Portland to Iowa City to take up the more practical study of Jurisprudence. She had yet to pass the bar, but the family was hopeful that the third time would be the charm.

Once it was certain that the Krist's were all safely on their way back to Freeland, Lillian Campbell quietly excused herself from the group just long enough to make a special visit to the Tap Room. She returned from the bar with a young man in tow who nervously carried an oversized silver tray covered with glasses and two bottles of wine. Politely dismissing the waiter, Lillian counted: Charles, Emily, Charys, Johanna, Ingrid, June, and one for herself. She then carefully poured the decanted wine into seven long stem glasses.

"June. Will you join us, please," Lillian asked, although it was hardly in the form of question.

Surprised by the invitation, June excused herself from her friends to come stand beside her mother.

With all the glasses now filled and distributed to the wedding party, Lillian offered a brief toast.

"Dear Emily and Charles, congratulations on this your special day; all of us here, your family, wish for you the happiness and good fortune you deserve. You have made us proud, and we love you for it. This wine, this special wine, is what I believe your father would have insisted upon, Charles. We drink to love, to happiness, and to family. So, as Mr. Rothstein so eloquently put it, *'Mozel tov'.*"

The glasses collided with a pleasing clink. Around the room beaming smiles and tears of happiness greeted one another as the stoic Lillian Campbell reached out to embrace her new granddaughter-in-law.

Charles had never tasted anything quite so perfect, but he did not need to look at the label to identify the wine they were drinking; there would be only three people who could possibly know the significance of pouring a 1928 Chateau Latour. To the rest of the group the wine was delicious and certainly special, but for Charys, Charles, and Lillian this moment, and this wine, acknowledged the missing fourth in a way that each could savor in their own way.

"May I have this dance?"

Charys Albright looked up and smiled to see her newlywed son extending his hand in an invitation to join him on the dance floor.

"I would be delighted," she replied in a voice that reminded him of time when his father was still alive.

Charles gently took his mother's hand and then escorted her to the small empty dance floor. With a smile and a nod to Erica and Alice, the musicians began Gershwin's extraordinary, *Someone to Watch over Me.*

Left standing between her mother and new grandmother-in-law, Emily Albright watched contentedly as her husband purposefully guided his mother around the dance floor. It had indeed been a wondrous day, one of the few days that she could remember where she'd felt utterly confident in herself and her future.

"Is it possible to be this person every day?" she wondered, even though all her hyper-charged emotions were now traveling faster and in orbits that felt impossible to reproduce. "Isn't there some way that I can save just a little piece of this for tomorrow, and next week, and next year?"

"Emily is a beautiful girl, Charles. I'm so happy for you." Charys smiled and continued, "It's been such a long time since I've been dancing. Thank you for asking me."

In a day that had been filled with deep permanent emotion, Charles Albright looked into his mother's soft blue eyes and contentedly replied, "Of course, Mother. Thank you."

"Have you and Emily been practicing," she asked? You're marvelous."

"Well, not really. We did practice a little, but…"

A moment passed before Charles offered, "Mother, I want you to know how grateful Emily and I are for all the help you gave us. It's been a wonderful day and we sincerely appreciate it."

As Alice stepped back and allowed Erica a moment with just the melody and chords, Charys face suddenly turned serious. "Charles, while we have this time let me just say that we'll be all right, Sarah and I. Your grandfather will always need us, and that's its own blessing, to be needed, I mean. I don't want you to think that we expect you to come here every week. Now is your special time with your new wife."

"Fine, Mother. I can still call, can't I?" he laughed.

Alice had returned to the lyric,

> " *Won't you tell him, please to put on some speed,*
> *follow my lead, oh, how I need,*
> *someone to watch over me.* "

The music had stopped, but moving now to their own special rhythm mother and son were oblivious to the rest of the world. Following a short heartfelt embrace, the couple was walking back toward the group when Charys gently pulled on her son's hand to slow him down. When he turned to look back, she had just reached up with her free hand to wipe away a tear.

"Charles," she said, "you to do what you want with the painting. Listen to Lillian if you wish, but the Teniers' is yours. That was always your father's intention. It was for you."

She could see the confusion in his face, and as if anticipating his need for an answer, she added, "Just remember, dear, if you decide to give her the picture you may never see it again. It will certainly be well received by the museum. And who knows, it's probably very important and something they need to fill out one of their collections."

Charys paused to glance over at her mother before adding, "Then there's your grandmother. Heaven knows, she'll enjoy her moment. Only Charles, that will also end our portion of the story, your father's story."

Fearing she'd said too much, she offered, "Do as you wish, dear, but not on my account… and certainly not for your grandmother."

For the next sixty-one days the painting did what paintings do, it hung in its private place on the wall in Charys Albright's living room, right between the bookcase and the window, in the exact same place that it had been for the past eighteen years. It remained suspended in that spot, the only spot it had known since it was smuggled out of Germany inside a soldier's shirt. If it could it would tell a long and fantastic story of the many owners and different places that it had been. In the three hundred and fifteen years since Teniers put brush to canvas the little picture had been exhibited in salons, displayed in the homes of the rich, hidden in hovels, and ignored in castles. It had been bought, gifted, and stolen. Along with being viewed and admired by thousands, it could also rightly claim one thing that many cannot: it had been respected.

There were moments where Charys thought she would take it down and put it away, but she didn't. Instead, she began purposefully ignoring it, sometimes even avoiding the living room just so she wouldn't be confronted by its silent presence. Then after the third time of going the long way around through the kitchen to get to the stairs, she became so angry that for a moment she considered doing something rash and wicked.

"I am making this painting into something it is not," she admitted to no one. "It has no feelings. It is inanimate, a thing. Stop acting so silly and emotional about it. After all, it's no longer yours. It's just a matter of time and they'll return and it will be gone, just like Gordon."

Charles and Emily spent their honeymoon in Paris.

Once they returned it seemed like there were a million and one things that needed their attention, so it wasn't until after the New Year that they finally returned to Cedar Rapids for a short two day visit. During that time nothing was said about the Teniers, but as Charles was taking their bags out to the car he discovered what he assumed was the painting wrapped in a khaki Army blanket and left beside the front door.

Lightly touching her grandson on the shoulder, Lillian Campbell exclaimed, "These photos are charming. Would you please make a copy of this one of you and Emily in front of the *Sainte-Chapelle*? It reminds me of when your grandfather and I would visit Paris. We loved that church, and would visit it every time we were there. *"L'intérieur de l'église était très belle."*

Charles nodded that he would oblige her request, and then smiled contentedly at his new wife. It was good to be home.

Besides *le charme romantique de Paris*, Charles personal history with the great city made it the perfect place to take his new bride on their honeymoon. Back when he was still an undergraduate at Northwestern, his mother and grandmother had taken him on a European summer vacation that included five days in Paris. As a seasoned visitor to *La Ville-Lumière*, Lillian Campbell enthusiastically assumed the role of tour guide and historian, happily sharing her intimate knowledge of the city's important tourist destinations, as well as those more remarkable details that you could never find in the guidebooks. His vivid memories from that first trip, along with several weeks of clandestine planning, had provided enough working knowledge of the city that it seemed to Emily her new husband truly was the *sophistiqué*. Along with the famous museums, humbling architecture, and fabulous restaurants, Charles also took his new bride shopping; shopping in a way she had never imagined with clothes, shoes, perfume, and jewelry all *fantastique*. Except her favorite shopping, in fact her favorite experience of the entire trip, was the two afternoons spent exploring the small galleries and salons near the *Rive Gauche*.

It was in one of the small galleries that Charles decided the fate of the Teniers.

"Grandmother, there's something that Emily and I would like to talk with you about."

With a sharp feline turn of the head, Lillian Campbell graciously smiled and asked, "Yes, Charles. What is it?"

"Well, we'd like to talk with you about father's painting."

Lillian Campbell set down her glass of the 1968 Villamont - Pouilly Fuisse, the one that the newlyweds brought back from their trip, and then offered them her full and unemotional attention.

Taking a deep breath, Charles began, "I know that you remember our conversation about the Teniers. We've been thinking about it, too. On the way back we made a decision, and I hope you'll understand.

You and Dad had an impossible relationship. Eleven years without talking to one another. As difficult as that might have been for the two of you, and maybe it wasn't, maybe it was just inconvenient, you had to have known how hard it was on Mother and me. Although no one was ever allowed to speak about your quarrel, it was obvious that nothing was going to be done to change your point-of-view.

While we were in Paris, I thought a lot about how different it might have been if Dad had lived to see Emily and I married. Perhaps as part of the celebration there would have been some kind of reconciliation. Who knows? But the night that you told me his story, I was so angry and sad it was difficult for me to understand how he came to have the *Kermess*. I mean, it's amazing and frightening, and unbelievably sad. At the same time, it is such an important part of his history. What hurts so much is that he never felt he could share it with me. I truly want to believe that someday he was going to tell me, that there was going to be this great day when he'd finally open up, but, I guess we'll never know that either.

Grandmother, I'm not sure that I understand all the reasons why you want me to give the painting away, and maybe that's not what's important. I only know what's important to me, and that's that we're together, as a family. I want to always remember my father and that amazing heroic decision to save the Teniers. But I think the best way to do that is not by hanging it in our home."

Charles Albright smiled at his wife before turning to his grandmother and saying, "Emily and I are asking for your help, Grandmother. I want us to honor Gordon Albright, together; you, me, Emily, and Mother. With your help we can make sure that both stories are told, the story of the *Flemish Kermess*, and the one about the remarkable man who saved it."

PART TWO

Chapter One

Bad Blood and Blue Hair

"…a sense of the fundamental decencies is parceled out unequally at birth."
The Great Gatsby - F. Scott Fitzgerald

When the phone rang she looked up at the digital clock next to the bed where her suitcases lay open but still only half-filled. It was already eleven-forty in the morning on December 23, 1970.

As the phone continued its bothersome noise, Emily Albright noticed that the disgusting smell coming from the backed-up kitchen sink had made its way across the living room and was now silently encroaching upon the bedroom, where, until just the moment before, she'd been on her hands and knees scrubbing the cat vomit out of their beautiful new Persian rug, the one that she had splurged on only last month. Amplifying her rising anxiety was the prospect that at any moment her husband Charles would come bursting through the door with the expectation that she was prepared for an instant departure. She could anticipate his mood; before leaving for work that morning he had explained to her that if they left before noon they could collect his grandmother at her apartment, beat the westbound rush hour traffic, and be in Cedar Rapids before dark. There was a split second where the heavily pregnant Emily Albright considered letting it go to the answering machine, but having now hauled herself up from the floor, she went ahead and lifted the receiver from its cradle only to hear the one voice on the planet that could make matters even tenser.

"Hello, dear; I trust all is well and everything is on schedule?"

Emily paused to carefully consider her reply.

Her first instinct was to deliver the most direct answer possible, perhaps flavoring it with a mild hint of distress. It was safe to assume that Lillian Campbell understood the notion of empathy; it was, however, far less likely that she appreciated delays in scheduling.

"Well, a little behind I'm afraid," she offered with a bit more timidity than desired. "Charles just phoned to say that he was leaving the office and should be home shortly, and then we'll be right over to pick you up. I'm certainly looking forward to spending time with you and the family," she added with an obvious and overplayed tone of hopefulness.

"Yes," the voice replied a little colder than before. "Actually, Emily, I called for another reason. It's a bit peculiar, but just a moment ago your aunt Barbara called. She said that she needed to speak with you right away, something about your mother. Apparently, she doesn't have your telephone number at the new apartment. How she found mine I can't guess, but be that as it may, I thought I should alert you. I gave her the number. I trust that was the thing to do."

Emily felt a wave of dizziness and automatically reached out to grab the night stand next to the bed; inside her distended stomach a baby boy eager to test his strength pushed hard against her right kidney. All that stood between her rolling pitiful stomach and another mess on the new Persian rug was seven months of constant practice. Swallowing the tiny hiccup of bile that now burned the back of her throat, Emily lofted a pitiful prayer that she was suffering a temporary loss of hearing. The alternative was unthinkable; nothing good could possibly come from a conversation with her aunt Barbara Krist, especially not today.

"Are you still there, dear?"

"Yes. Yes, I'm sorry. I'm still here," Emily replied as she lurched across the little table to grab at the half-filled glass of tepid water leftover from the night before. After taking a long swallow that polished off what remained, she gasped, "Did she say what she wanted?"

"I'm afraid not. The only thing she mentioned was that she wished to speak to you about your mother. I sensed some urgency on her part, so I gave her the number. I do hope that everything is all right with Johanna."

"Yes, well, thank you. I'll call her right away, and then we'll come pick you up. I guess we'll see you in a few minutes. Thanks for letting me know. I appreciate it. Goodbye for now."

"You will call me before you leave, won't you? So I can alert the doorman."

"Certainly," Emily replied, her thoughts now five hundred and fifty miles west from where she currently sat in her apartment at 819 West Deming Place.

The fact that Barbara Krist did not have her niece's phone number was not an oversight. Formerly Emily Krist, now happily Emily Albright, she had never offered it because she had neither reason nor desire for her aunt to call. The notion that Barbara would ever contact her mother to request the number was absurd, so deep and passionate was their hatred that it had long ago rendered any form of interpersonal communication impossible.

Their loathing for one another was now legendary throughout Nishna County. Long before Johanna's husband Jacob had died from a heart attack at the ridiculous age of thirty-eight, the two women had drawn swords and sides. Out of respect for her lost son, Grandma Saffii continued to invite her

168

daughter-in-law to the Krist family gatherings, but Johanna always declined; none of the other Krist's objected. But now that Saffii was interned at the Oaks Retirement Center there was no longer any need for the façade of pleasantries between the two women - ever.

Certainly, Emily and Charles were aware of the bad blood; their infrequent mother-daughter telephone conversations generally included at least one scornful attack upon her sister-in-law, or the joyful retelling of some recent misfortune. The enthusiasm with which Johanna delivered these stories raised the couples concerns about the possibility of her personal involvement. Although they were still unaware of Johanna's enthusiasm for the grape, or the growing strength and devious encouragement coming from her *other* voice, it was becoming clear that at some point soon, Emily would need to confront her mother. A minute before leaving for Christmas with her in-laws was hardly the time she had in mind.

The phone was answered on the third ring by her uncle, Stephen Krist. Stephen was her father's brother, and the eldest of Saffii and Alder Krist's three sons.

"Hello, Uncle Stephen. Merry Christmas! This is Emily Albright calling."

"Well, Emily. Good to hear from you and Merry Christmas right back at you."

"Uncle Stephen, is Barbara around? She called earlier and I wanted to get back to her before we left town."

There was a short pause, and then, "She sure is, honey. Give me a minute and I'll put her on the line." Then before setting down the receiver, he added, "Tell Charles and his family Merry Christmas for me."

"Yes, sir," Emily offered, but by then there was no one on the line.

Only a few tense seconds passed before Emily could hear the sound of hard-soled shoes walking quickly across a wooden floor. Then the receiver was picked up from a table and her aunt's unpleasant voice growled, "Hello, Emily. Thank you for calling me. I'll get right to the point; something must be done with your mother."

What followed was a dead and ominous silence which Emily presumed was for effect. After several more uncomfortable moments, she asked, "I'm not sure I know what you mean, Barbara. What must be done with my mother? Has something happened to her?"

"Not yet. But unless you get that woman under control, I will be forced to call the sheriff and have her arrested."

Although Emily had steeled herself for the worst, even in her wildest dreams she could never have anticipated anything quite as obstinate or quarrelsome as this threat. It was one thing to watch from a distance as her mother feuded with a relative as tiresome as Barbara Krist, but it was quite

169

another to be boldly threatened with her mother's incarceration minutes before she was to leave town for her first Christmas with Lillian Campbell. Sitting there on the edge of the bed, her hand kneading the silk maternity nightgown which lay on top of the half-packed suitcase, she wondered if this was the worst that Aunt Barbara had to offer, or was it possible that she was holding back for just the right moment to drop the really big one.

"Are you there, Emily?" the loud and unpleasant voice complained. "I'm sorry to say this, we're family after all, but this time your mother has gone too far. I know it's the holidays, but this is the last straw. She has broken my camel's back."

"What has she done?" was all that Emily could think to say.

"What has she done?" Barbara repeated in a mocking tone. "I'll tell you what she's done... everything. She sits up there in her little house, day and night, plotting ways to make my life miserable. That's what she's done."

"I'm sorry, Aunt Barbara, but could you be a little more specific? I know that you and Mom don't see eye-to-eye, but what exactly has she done to make you so angry?"

The explosion from the other end of the line was so shrill that it forced Emily to hold the phone at arm's length.

"My hair is blue!" Barbara Krist screamed into the receiver.

Shocked by the hilarious notion of her large loud aunt with blue hair, it was all that Emily could do to keep from laughing out loud.

"I'm sorry, Barbara. Did you say that your hair is blue?"

"Yes!" she bellowed. "This is your mother's doing. I could kill her."

A thousand reasonable questions overwhelmed Emily's concentration.

"Barbara, I do want to help you. But I don't understand how my mother could have caused you to have blue hair?"

There was a deep and pregnant pause before Barbara Krist's strained voice returned.

"I don't know how she did it. I just know that she did it," Barbara hissed, followed instantly by the more petulant, "I was in the Pamida last week and she was there. Somehow she must have added something to my, well, to my hair-coloring package. Anyway, this is just the last in what has been a long line of tricks that I've had to suffer from your mother. Heaven knows Pastor Frederickson has tried to help me to forgive these... these assaults, but Emily, I am at the end of all earthly patience."

There was a moment of silence followed by the now pious voice of Barbara Krist saying, 'to me belongeth vengeance and recompense; their foot shall slide in due time: for the day of their calamity is at hand.' That's Deuteronomy 32:35."

Fighting back her growing sense of desperation, Emily countered with, "Well, Barbara, right now I'm getting ready to leave town to visit my in-

170

laws for Christmas. I was hoping to come out to Freeland and see Mom, but it kind of depends on how I'm feeling. I'm eight months pregnant you know."

Emily paused hoping that by playing her pregnancy card it would trigger a moment of sympathy. But the receiver remained silent.

"Anyway," she continued. "Could I call her, and then get back to…"

"No!" Barbara defiantly interjected. "No. That is unacceptable. She has ruined my holidays and I demand satisfaction."

"What kind of satisfaction do you want?"

"What I want is for your mother to move far, far away. But, in the spirit of the holidays, if she apologizes to me, in person, and before Christmas day, I will consider not pressing charges against her."

Emily's head was spinning. "How can this be happening? Is this crazy woman serious?"

A moment later, she heard herself say, "Okay, Barbara. I'll see what I can do. I'm sorry your hair is blue. It's certainly not a good color for Christmas."

As soon as it came out of her mouth Emily knew she'd regret the comment about Christmas.

Sensing that she now had the upper-hand, Barbra Krist lowered her voice to add a final thought.

"You know, Emily. I expect that those of us who still live out her in Iowa must seem pretty small and far away to someone like you, but let me assure you, either you get your mother under control, or it will be a Christmas the two of you never forget. Good-bye."

Emily moved to lay the receiver back in its cradle; the buzzing dial tone added the perfect accompaniment to her aunt's harsh closing.

Charles, who had been waiting impatiently in the living room, appeared in the bedroom doorway. Obviously anxious about getting on the road, he was quite unprepared when Emily looked up and asked him, "I wonder how she managed to turn her hair blue?"

They were still thirty minutes east of Des Moines, and another full hour away from Freeland, when Emily noticed that Charles did not look well. The couple had been traveling west from Chicago on Interstate 80 the entire afternoon, pausing just long enough to deposit Grandmother Lillian in Cedar Rapids before hastily pushing on for Freeland.

It was nearly eight o'clock, moonless, bitter cold, and dark as pitch. The modest traffic meant fewer headlights to spoil what was otherwise a beautiful deep-black Iowa winter sky, rich with hundreds of brilliant stars. Inside the Camaro, however, the dim light from the dashboard was adding a sickly green tint to Charles already pasty complexion.

"Charles, are you feeling okay?" Emily asked.

He looked over at her as if it hurt to move. His eyelids were heavy, his brow damp with sweat.

"I don't think so. It's so hot in here. Em, we're still a long way from Freeland, but do you think you could drive a while?"

They pulled over to trade places at a deserted filling station near Newton. Forcing the car door open against the bitter winter wind, the mother-to-be managed to struggle to her feet. Then after cautiously making her way around the front of the car, Emily reached inside to help her fading spouse out of the Camaro's deep bucket seats. Once safely back inside the expectant mother managed to twist herself around and then rummage the backseat looking for Charles overcoat, which she then used as a blanket. He was asleep before they got back on the highway.

After the confrontation with her aunt, Emily knew that she really had no choice but to call her mother.

The phone rang and rang until Johanna Krist finally picked up the receiver. With a leaden voice, she asked, "Who is it?"

After the brief small talk, Emily quickly got to the point.

"Mother, I just spoke with Barbara and she says that you've been... well, how did she put it, she said you've been 'plotting to make her miserable.' I know it sounds crazy, but she claims you turned her hair blue. You didn't, did you?"

"I can't imagine what that woman is talking about," Johanna responded with an obvious tone of amusement. "She told you that I turned her hair blue? Really, Emily, how is that possible?"

Her tone and attitude seemed to confirm that she knew a way.

"Well, she says that unless you apologize, and you have to do it before Christmas, she's going to call the sheriff."

"Do you really believe she would do that?" Johanna asked with an obvious lack of concern. "The woman is insane. No one takes her seriously."

"Mother, does she have blue hair?"

"I think she might," Johanna replied. "I was visiting with Ingrid just yesterday, and she told me that she and June were having lunch at the Drop Inn Diner. She said she'd overheard a couple of the ladies in the booth behind her say that Barbara was having some kind of trouble with her hair. Of course, I haven't spoken to her majesty in some time so I can't really say for sure..."

"Well," Emily interrupted, "you may believe that no one takes Barbara Krist seriously, but if she walks into the Sheriff's office with a head full of blue hair, well, they're going to have some questions. Of course this is going to completely ruin our Christmas plans, but I've spoken to Charles and he agrees that we should come home to Freeland tonight. Perhaps tomorrow we can figure out a way to keep Barbara from having you arrested."

The protracted pause on the other end of the line left Emily hopeful that her mother was considering a possible truce. Then Johanna returned, and this time with a curiously different voice, one that for a lack of a better word seemed darker.

"Drive careful then," it said. "I'm looking forward to seeing that blue hair."

It was nearly ten o'clock when they finally crested the last of the four great hills (Freeland's easternmost landmark) and began the decent into town. In stark contrast to most of the other little houses all merrily decked-out in their colorful Christmas glory, the tiny Krist house was dark, cold, and entirely unfriendly.

Charles had slept hard for the last ninety minutes but awoke with a start when Emily turned off the engine.

"We're here," Emily offered with a smile that she hoped looked optimistic.

As they entered the weathered front door, Emily cried out, "Hello? Mom, we're here."

No one replied, but from somewhere in the dark Bing Crosby's warm baritone was softly crooning *White Christma*s.

"Mother, where are you?"

Following the music back toward the kitchen, Emily snapped on the light as they entered the room. Sitting passively at the table, her back against the wall and both hands in her lap, Johanna turned slowly toward the door and offered her daughter an oddly distant smile. In front of her sat an empty coffee cup and an open box of chocolate covered cherries.

"Merry Christmas," Johanna said in a distracted welcome.

"What are you doing here in the dark?" Emily demanded.

Johanna considered her daughter for a moment, and then weaving ever so slightly, replied, "Just listening to some Christmas carols and waiting for you to arrive."

She smiled, and added, "And now you're here."

"Well, Mother, Charles isn't feeling well. He needs to lie down. So, I guess we'll use my old bedroom? Is that okay?"

"Certainly, it's still at the top of the stairs."

Emily managed to help her sick husband up the narrow wooden stairs and into the single bed before returning to fetch the luggage from the Camaro. Once she'd lugged their bags upstairs and got Charles dressed for bed, Emily realized that not only did her back ache but she too was feeling nauseous and lightheaded. Rummaging through the bottom of her purse, she discovered three aspirins and half a Rolaids tablet. Forcing down the last bite of the dry bitter medicine, she hoped that her discomfort was only indigestion from the fast food hamburger she'd eaten earlier, and not from something that should be waiting for another four weeks.

By the time Emily got herself back down the steep stairs, Johanna had moved from the kitchen into the tiny living room, where she now sat passively on the sofa next to a pile of ancient quilts and a gray pillow. The old woman had turned on a small lamp that sat on the dusty end-table next to the couch.

Glancing around the dim and tired space, Emily instantly recognized the shape of a deeply scarred, straight-backed wooden chair; one with a familiar well-worn red cushion and a harsh personal history. She knew the miserable thing as the "Devil's chair," so branded by her mother, and forever linked to the place where little girls who misbehaved were sent to perform their penance. Tonight, in spite of Satan's eternal claim on the furniture, Emily chose the hard bone-breaker hoping that its uncompromising rigidity would feel good on her road-weary back. Sinking into the useless cushion, she allowed herself a moment of peace before the first salvos were fired.

"Emily," her mother said quietly. "I don't want to sound ungrateful, but why are you here?"

Completely taken aback by the question, Emily peered across the poorly lit room at her mother. Wasn't it just a few hours before that they'd spoken on the phone about Aunt Barbara's threats? Had she already forgotten the blue hair? Was it possible that her mother's memory was fading that badly?

"Don't you remember?" she began wearily. "We talked about Barbara, and how she'd called me. She said she was going to contact the police if you didn't…"

"My memory is fine," Johanna interrupted sharply, "but I'm still not sure why you're here."

Emily closed her eyes before lightly laying both hands on her distended stomach. Throughout her last trimester this simple act (a gentle caress to the unborn child) had given her an unanticipated sense of satisfaction, and some much needed fortitude. Looking down on her swollen belly, Emily was reminded that it would only be a few more weeks before she too would become a mother

"Is it me?" Emily asked. "Why is this house so cold?"

Johanna didn't appear to notice and didn't bother to reply. In spite of the chill, the old woman wore only a light house dress, a shabby blue cardigan sweater, and a pair of tired slippers.

For Emily, this frosty temperature only amplified her suspicions that a dark and tangible melancholy now owned the place. The absence of

174

anything warm or welcoming confirmed that whatever was left of her childhood was now lost to something darker and unknown.

From deep inside Emily's anterior cingulate a synapse unexpectedly fired, delivering a surprising thought to her conscience; a kind of Christmas miracle.

"Why are you acting so selfishly?" she asked herself. "Why wouldn't you want to share the happiness that this baby will bring with her?"

The hippocampus instinctively responded with a flood of harsh and unpleasant childhood memories, followed by the obvious question, "Why would you offer something so beautiful to someone so difficult; someone just as likely to ignore your kindness?"

The frontal lobe added its unemotional perspective, declaring that it was both she and her mother who had created this history; it took two to build such an uncompromising barrier, a wall each had purposefully erected to keep the other away. There was no denying that their wall had been built by four, not two hands.

"You could at least try" the frontal cortex demanded, "It's Christmas."

"I know what day it is," the hippocampus pushed back. "Besides, since when has it become your job to seek peace with her?"

A split second later, Emily refocused to find herself back on the hard and uncompromising chair.

"I'm sorry, Mother," she offered. "I'm tired. Why don't we get some rest and tomorrow we can work on what we'll say to Barbara?"

Johanna behaved as if her daughter had said nothing.

"The reason I asked why you're here is that I don't want you, or Charles, involved in my... situation with that woman."

In spite of her mother's harsh words and her own bone-weary fatigue, Emily forced herself to concentrate.

"Something's definitely different now. What is it," she wondered? "It feels weird; wrong, more wrong."

Was she mistaken? No. Even though it seemed like the words were coming from her mother, there was something different; a quality in her voice. It was like the one she'd heard before, it sounded like the one on the phone.

"That's it, that's what's different; the voice, darker and angrier."

From her spot on the Devil's chair, Emily looked across the room to try to catch her mother's eye. Except Johanna's gaze had shifted and was no longer on her daughter; it was beyond her. Johanna Krist was now somewhere beyond her daughter, somewhere ahead of reason. While her expression maintained its steady unemotional countenance, the *other* continued, "Tomorrow, or the next day, or the next, it means nothing, really. I have no intentions of ever apologizing to that woman. You must go home Emily. A girl in your condition should be at home."

Then before her weary daughter could respond the *other* pushed it over the edge.

"And I don't want you here."

Instantly, Emily felt as if she'd been transported to the top of a high mountain. Not only was it cold, but the air seemed thin and insufficient; there was no oxygen left in the room. She was afraid to take a breath for fear that it would be her last.

The hippocampus immediately responded, "See what I mean? Such a hateful remark, too."

Under the circumstances there were only two possible alternatives.

Emily pushed herself up out of the horrible chair and walked forward to where her mother sat on the sofa. After looking down upon the old woman, a person who had demanded so much but given so little, Emily Krist Albright reached out and beckoned her mother to stand.

Slowly, Johanna reached up and timidly grasped her only child's hands. With a small tug, Emily encouraged her forward off the cushion.

Standing now, facing each other, the daughter gently placed the mother's hands upon her stomach and the child. The baby, unaware of the moment, mercifully chose to kick and roll to his right.

Grandmother Johanna felt the life inside her daughter.

"Oh, Emily, what's to become of me?"

The *other* hated empathy. Sympathy was anathema. Compassion and kindness were qualities of the weak. It was solitude that it wanted; a silent place where the two of them would be left alone.

"Isn't it always so much better when we're alone?"

So, as it had done many times before, it quietly retreated to let the old woman return. The *other* withdrew confident that she'd soon be back, welcomed back; needed when she lacked the courage.

"There's not one reason to be in a hurry," it thought. "There's plenty of time. Let them have their moment."

There was very little sleep for Emily that Christmas Eve morning.

To begin with there were Charles frequent noisy trips to the upstairs bathroom; the house had but the one. Then there was the muffled Christmas music coming from the radio in her mother's bedroom; Johanna had insisted on taking the transistor radio to bed saying it was the only way that she could fall asleep. Along with these noisy distractions there was the steadily growing assortment of family complications. There was her mother's bizarre behavior, made even more real by the need to come up with a plan that would placate the angry aunt without losing what little ground she'd just regained. Then adding only insult to injury was the unsuccessful exercise to locate a comfortable spot on the sofa's miserable rollout mattress. But the last straw *(la coupe est pleine)* came at two-forty in the morning when her unborn child decided that it was a good time to dance.

To try and calm her mind, Emily fell back on something she'd done with some success as a child. Back in school, she would imagine all the different problems that were confronting her as a part of a play - her play. It had been some time since she'd written anything more than a few quick thoughts to her journal, but her skills for plot and dialog were still quite capable of storyboarding all the pieces to this complex production.

By dawn she had the first act completely staged. Act Two would rely heavily on her aunt's vanity, her mother's desire to see her future grandson, and the respect everyone owed to an eighty-one year-old woman.

Half-an-hour later, Emily heard the first stirrings from her mother's bedroom. By seven o'clock, Johanna had made her way to the kitchen, still wearing the same house dress and cardigan. Passing the kitchen sink, she withdrew last night's coffee cup, splashed some water to rinse it out, and then resumed both her seat and weary pose.

"I have a suggestion I'd like you to consider," Emily began as she poured her mother a cup of the freshly brewed Maxwell House. "When was the last time you spoke with Grandma Saffii?"

Chapter Two

Saffii Moeller

"May you live every day of your life."
Jonathan Swift

As Emily and Johanna climbed out of the '64 Ford station wagon (the same vehicle that five years before had taken her to the bus stop and a new life in Chicago) the overcast skies began to spit a fine mist of ice. It is this weather that Iowan's fear most. Should the two conditions of ground temperature and ambient air collide at the freezing mark the roads will take on the qualities of an ice skating rink; travel is not advised.

There was a moment when Emily looked up into the miserable gray sky and considered returning to the safety of the tiny house on Locust Street. The beads of ice that stung her face were quickly covering the parking lot pavement; the roads would soon get very slick and provide the perfect excuse to abandon ship.

"Perhaps it's too dangerous to stay," she thought. "Besides, would Barbara really call the sheriff on Christmas? It's possible she's bluffing. It would be just like her to try and drag some kind of stupid apology out of Mother. But what if she really did something that turned her hair blue? Obviously, blue hair is no good, funny, but not good. So really, what would happen if we just turned around and went home? Nothing, probably, only we'd be surrendering and giving Barbara an early Christmas gift."

That last thought was enough. A brave and hopeful Emily Albright hooked her mother by the arm and pushed ahead toward the front doors of the Oaks Retirement Center.

In spite of the unexpected contextual change that the foreboding weather had forced upon the scene, Act II appeared to be running smoothly with the entire cast delivering their lines on cue and hitting all of their marks. There was a moment of concern when Barbara Krist went off-script to question the setting for her mother's apology, but wisely the playwright had anticipated such a possibility and had written an alternative ending to the scene.

"Mother thinks that Grandma Saffii will take her side," she falsely confided to Barbara over the phone. "We both know that won't happen, but perhaps she can help talk some sense into her."

Emily's subservient and conciliatory tone was perfectly played. Barbara quickly agreed to the meeting location.

"Oh, Grandma, it's so good to see you," Emily exclaimed, as she bent over to gently hug the old woman in the wheel chair.

Saffii Krist reached out to hold her granddaughter's face in her trembling hands.

"What a wonderful Christmas present you are," she whispered in a voice nearly invisible.

Saffii Krist, originally Saffii Moeller, was born in 1889 on a productive eighty-two acres of farm and forest that hugged the windy eastern shores of the Mississippi River just north of La Crosse, Wisconsin. Saffii's story begins six years before her birth when her mother, Arja Gammelgaard-Bjerre, was compelled by circumstances mostly outside of her own control to flee Denmark for the States.

A lean young woman with sharp pointed features and haunting gray-green eyes, Arja Gammelgaard was the second and least favored of Ampiel and Anna Gammelgaard's three daughters. Other than the DNA that Ampiel had donated to shape her handsome face, Arja would receive very little else from her cold and dispassionate father. A teacher of mathematics and physics at the *Schwarzwald Akademie für Jungen*, Gammelgaard had spent the past fourteen years in mind-numbing complacency, a kind of self-induced stupor that comes from trying to teach disinterested teenage boys the fundamental physical laws of nature.

There had been a moment once - a seminal opportunity - where in a different version of his *lucky life* Ampiel Gammelgaard could have been a part of something more important than himself. Except in a myopic fit of anger, Ampiel broke away from his colleague and childhood friend, a brilliant passionate scientist named Heinrich Hertz, over the most common of academic quarrels - top billing. When the injured party (Hertz) moved on from Schwarzwald to the University of Kiel, Ampiel Gammelgaard remained in southern Denmark with his wife and new babies. By building on their earlier work, Heinrich Hertz went on to make the first of his three great discoveries, confirming James Maxwell's groundbreaking prediction of electromagnetic radiation. Ampiel Gammelgaard's name would not appear anywhere on the manuscript.

With each passing term, Ampiel promised to seek out his lost colleague and find a way to mend the damage, but like the sad drunkard who forever promises to overcome his addiction he never did. Instead, poor Heinrich Hertz would conclude his *lucky life* dead from blood poisoning before his thirty-sixth birthday, permanently ending any chance for reconciliation.

Arja Gammelgaard was never known for her patience, or planning; she would, however, become as passionate as her father was indifferent, as ambitious as he was arrogant, and as motivated as he was mediocre.

In her formative years, Arja watched as the hated Germans marched into her homeland of southern Denmark, well-armed and with a bully's intention to seize control over the region's prosperous farms and contented families. For those like the Gammelgaard's who lived along the border, the governing authority was constantly shifting back and forth between the legitimate Danes in the North and the invading Germans to the South. It was this combination of political schizophrenia and her father's maddening indifference that eventually ignited the child's passion.

By her sixteenth birthday it would have been difficult to find two more disconnected souls; two people still living under the same roof, but headed in opposite directions. That is until a rainy spring day in April when the teacher of physics finally ran out of excuses and reluctantly agreed to help officiate at the *Akademie's* annual spring track meet.

A *lucky life* has no consciousness of its own, no metaphysical capability to influence the outcome of our actions. *Lucky life* is the construct of our time filled with nothing and everything; out on the edges lives the memorable, the paradoxical, along with our so-called logic and irony. There may be, for example, a measurable level of irony in a *lucky life* where a teacher of numbers and angles, vectors and velocity, a teacher who also suffers from a severe case of myopia, commits a serious miscalculation of both distance and trajectory from a javelin thrown by one of his own students. In this particular example, Ampiel Gammelgaard will never see the instrument of his own death; his daughter Arja will. Seven days later, and only hours after her father's funeral, Arja Gammelgaard will leave her home and family with a secret.

Still reeling from the horror of her husband's unexpected and ghastly death, Arja's mother saw her daughter's hasty midnight departure as an impetuous and hateful reaction to the family's pointed misfortune. But unbeknownst to everyone - especially her mother - two days after her father's impalement, Arja secretly married the special boy that she had been seeing; a boy who shared her passion for a free Slesvig, a boy with heart and courage, a boy - in this case Haldor Bjerre - who had been both Ampiel Gammelgaard's prize student and the ironic source of the misdirected javelin that had killed him.

The spring of the errant javelin and hasty nuptials would also coincide with one of the frequent German re-occupations of the Slesvig-Holsten region. After abandoning Flensburg in the dead of night, Arja and new husband Haldor would walk and hitchhike the sixty kilometers to the larger university town of Kiel. It was there that they hoped to join the revolution.

Travel turned out to be more complicated than they had imagined. Along the way Haldor - the now infamous Slesvig Dane with the good arm and bad aim - was recognized and confronted by many of the locals with an easily anticipated set of questions. Apparently, killing someone with a javelin was more newsworthy than the couple anticipated.

Still, they were young and committed, eventually finding refuge with seven other likeminded and equally impoverished patriots in a miserable hovel near the university. It was over stolen eggs and surströmming that the innocent brotherhood earnestly hatched their first plan. Everyone agreed that what was needed was a scheme that would recruit a bold new army of impassioned locals, the start of a homegrown militia that would one day launch a counterattack on the evil German invaders.

A secret late night meeting intended to recruit local supporters was to be held at a nearby tavern. The *Fede Svin* (*Fat Hog*) was the perfect location; a seemingly innocuous tavern that was frequented by many of the local university students and absolutely guaranteed to be safe. Because of their passion and "firsthand knowledge of German tyranny," the mutineers unanimously elected their newest and most naïve soldiers as the revolution's spokesmen. The newlyweds were humbled by their colleague's confidence and proudly dedicated themselves to the plan.

Unfortunately, as often happens with this sort of thing, word of the secret meeting leaked out. The only people the couple found in the bar that night were an aged innkeeper, his portly deaf wife, and five of von Bismarck's youngest and most ill-tempered soldiers. Their leader was a twenty-two year-old thug and malcontent from the industrial ghetto of Moabit named Uwe Richter. When the tavern door slammed shut, the stunned and outnumbered newlywed's made no effort to resist the screaming German boy-officer and his shiny sword.

In what was to be a clear case of overstated expectation, Richter and the boys had been told to expect anything, including a murderous gang of marauding rebels. As they lay in wait for the Danes, these overzealous young soldiers had gotten themselves so worked-up that they actually believed they were about to enter into mortal combat with a renegade band of merciless killers. Imagine their surprise when all that they found to fight was an unarmed and cowering couple from the sticks.

In a desperate ploy to bolster his shaky leadership, young Uwe loudly demanded that his cohorts bind the frightened Bjerre's hands behind their backs before forcing the captives to kneel on the floor before him. After verbally assaulting the young couple for nearly an hour, Richter finally dispatched two of his infantry men to return to the headquarter offices on the outskirts of the city. Since he was unable to read or write Uwe instructed his boys to inform the Captain that they had, "successfully captured two of the resistance ringleaders, and would hold them at any cost until further orders."

Two hours later, no word had come back from the headquarter offices.

Feeling cut off from his superiors, and therefore empowered to manage the situation himself, the little German turned on the frightened innkeeper demanding food and akavit.

It didn't take long before the powerful drink did its job, inebriating the staggering children and shattering any shared sense of decency. While the small company stumbled wildly around the captives, their shiny swords and long guns waving in the candlelight, the German boy-soldiers kept up a steady stream of pointless vulgar slurs at the innocent Danes. Meanwhile, back in the shadows, Richter, his red eyes glaring lasciviously at the foolish young woman, was considering a far different and more personal enterprise.

Once the drink had gained full control the soldier's shouts turned physical with hard merciless punches for the boy and childish fondling of the girl. In his first protest since their capture, Haldor struggled to his feet pleading for Arja's release. From out of the dark, Ewe Richter - a drunken ridiculous boy only a year older than the Dane, his eyes now devil-red from smoke and drink - fell upon Haldor Bjerre and senselessly skewered him with his sword. The pitiful protester bled to death watching as Richter and his boy soldiers stole from Arja the one gift she had yet to give her new husband.

Two years later, after immigrating to Wisconsin to join her sister-in-law's family, the widow Arja Bjerre reluctantly attended a spring Sunday social hosted by the North La Crosse Baptist church. It was there that she met her second husband - and Saffii's future father - Mikkel Moeller. Before the harvest began that fall, the twenty-four year-old Arja would marry Mikkel and take up the hard life of farming his eighty-two acres of land; eighty-two acres made possible by the largess of the La Crosse and Milwaukee Railroad, the United States government, and this version of Saffii's *lucky life*.

Along with their livestock, the row crops, and an impressive orchard, Arja and Mikkel also managed a small lumber operation. In those days, the rich black pine forests of western Wisconsin had attracted a sizable number of transient men in need of work. These were tough hard men capable of cutting and transporting the huge pines from the Moeller's forest to the nearby river. One of those roughnecks was a very young Alder Krist, the future husband of Saffii Moeller.

In Emily's eyes her grandmother Saffii Moeller-Krist had no equal.

Like most of her generation, the small woman from Wisconsin had lived through a time of extremes, an era recognized for both its unequaled human growth and wasteful folly. In her eighty-one years, Saffii would experience two world wars; devastating global battles that took the lives of more than eighty-million people. And as if that wasn't enough bloodshed, between nineteen forty-five and the end of the twentieth century this unrelenting chain of human conflicts mercilessly stole another forty-five million lives. Line up the corpses end-to-end and they would stretch most of the way to the moon.

On the other side of the ledger, an industrial revolution transformed Saffii's generation with unprecedented advances in medicine, education, and human understanding. New technologies expanded the amount of earth that humans could cultivate, and made possible the remarkable shift from a single family farm to market-driven agriculture. More food fueled a massive population explosion, and with it the unprecedented challenges of accommodating a new cultural and ethnic awakening. Technological breakthroughs like radio, television, telephones, even rockets to the moon made instant communication of fact and propaganda available to everyone. The physical Earth was still the same size, but as people became more connected they paradoxically grew further and further apart.

Saffii Krist was good at what she did; regrettably, those efforts were seldom recognized by anyone other than the occasional offhand "thank you" for a well-cooked meal. Her opportunities to receive a formal education had been limited to five years in a country school house. After that, life lessons came from her kin; her classroom was the family farm where school began before sunrise, and ended long after the dishes from the evening meal were put away. Electric lights came to her home in 1958, indoor plumbing in '64. Until Christmas of 1966, she made delicious, prize-winning meals four times a day in a wood-burning stove. She would survive polio and measles epidemics, typhus, rubella, and influenza. She lived through the Great Depression, Prohibition, two separate runs on the local bank, an uncle who stole, another who drank, and the senseless death of her older brother, Frej.

Painting Saffii Krist's life with such a broad brush makes it feel remarkable and important - and it was. But there were millions of others who lived through their own version of these extraordinary circumstances; their own *lucky life*. What makes Saffii Krist's different, perhaps heroic, was not so much when she lived, but how she lived.

Arja and Mikkel Moeller's first baby (Frej) died of pneumonia when he was only four. When he passed Saffii was a six-month old newborn, and even though she would never know him, her sad mother made certain that she would never forget him.

As a bereaved mother unable to manage her own grief, Arja Moeller insisted, despite all evidence to the contrary, that her beautiful blond boy had never left them. For the rest of her days this sad and misguided point-of-view took on its own weird life, one that manifested itself in the most maudlin of ways.

A good example was at meals and evening prayers. Without fail, Arja always laid out a perfect place setting right next to hers, as if she somehow expected the dead boy to request a second helping. Whenever neighbors would congregate to enjoy the small talk of the day, Mother Arja constantly spoke of her children in the plural present tense. A small family portrait - a tintype that had been taken shortly after Saffii was born - featured mother and father, baby Saffii, and Frej, anxiously clutching at his mother's skirt. This small picture was the only earthly image of the boy and had been lovingly hung in the Moeller's tiny parlor, right next to the family's large wooden crucifix. On more than one occasion, Mikkell had unexpectedly returned to the house to find his cheerless wife staring longingly into the photo of a distant past.

Along with this stifling sadness, Mother Arja also carried the heavy burden of guilt; guilt for two deaths that were entirely out of her control. This sorrow and endless remorse gave her no peace and left her anxious and angry with those who were still alive. Saffii's deepest and most lasting memory of her mother was that of a harsh woman, "quick in temper and sad of heart."

Everyone was surprised - not all were pleased - when six years later another boy - a special boy - was born on Christmas Eve.

"This one is special. This boy will do great things," Mikkel Moeller proudly announced to the congregation.

Forever conscious of Frej's sad fate, Mikkel and Arja insisted that this baby should also have the Lord's guarantee of a permanent place in his celestial home. In order to meet their end of the heavenly bargain, the Moeller's brought their newborn son before the congregation to be baptized just ten days after his birth. Joyfully displaying the tiny mewling child to the twenty-six delighted Danes, Mikkel proclaimed, "His name will be Poul Moeller. Mark this day! It is the beginning of his life in the service of Christ and his fellow man."

The cheering members of the newly formed Free Evangelical Church enthusiastically welcomed baby Poul into their midst with a rousing rendition of *Jesus, Hail, Enthroned in Glory*. Unfortunately, Poul Moeller never heard a note; in fact he would never hear a note, a song, or any sound made by man or nature. The boy - the special boy - had been born stone-deaf.

After only a few weeks with their newborn, the Moeller's began to grow concerned by what they considered the baby's peculiar behavior. Frej and Saffii had both been active and inquisitive babies; Saffii claims that she never bothered with crawling, and after only eleven months went straight to walking. In contrast, Poul seemed timid and skittish, often distressed by even the gentlest embrace.

It was with great trepidation that on his first birthday they took the baby Poul to the doctor, the closest being seven miles south in La Crosse. As for selecting a physician in La Crosse, the options were severely limited, there were only two. The Moeller's choice was Doctor Emile Hirsch.

Doctor Hirsch was a young, lanky German immigrant who had arrived in the United States by way of Milwaukee. Stepping off the boat, his plan was to continue westward by rail across Wisconsin, Iowa, and Nebraska, all the way to Denver where he planned to put out his shingle in the cool mountain air.

He didn't get that far. After three days of being stranded by a freakish April snowstorm, Dr. Hirsch abandoned his plans for Colorado to remain in La Crosse. It was over dinner that first night at Mrs. Addie Stager's boarding house that he learned the small but clearly burgeoning community had only the one doctor - Doctor Poldi Sprekles. The pragmatic German recognized opportunity.

The Moeller's choice of Doctor Hirsch over Doctor Sprekles was awkward, but understandable. Most folks in the region knew old Poldi Sprekles as a good and caring physician, a compassionate man who had helped most of them through life's most difficult problems. Yet in the bottom of Arja's wardrobe, covered by a bolt of embroidered Irish linen, was a polished wooden box. Hidden inside this chest were two of Arja's most precious mementos: the bloody white shirt that Haldor Bjerre had worn on the night of his murder, and Frej Moeller's death certificate - the one signed by Doctor Poldi Sprekles.

Arja deposited baby Poul in the doctor's steady hands and then stepped back anticipating the worst possible news. To the Moeller's surprise it took only a few minutes of poking and prodding for Doctor Hirsch to diagnose Poul's problem.

"This infant is deaf," he stated matter-of-factly, while handing the baby back to its startled mother.

Unlike the good Doctor Sprekles, most of Doctor Hirsch's patients acknowledged that the young physician's bedside manner lacked both polish and sympathy; which it did. However, from a purely academic perspective, Hirsch was clearly a better trained physician, and a thoroughly modern man-of-science; someone significantly ahead of his time. His superior skills as a doctor and surgeon were deeply influenced by his enthusiasm for the new discipline of evolutionary biology; that is, the study of early human adaptations on modern people and culture. The result of blending these disciplines can be observed in his diagnosis of Poul Moeller.

In a heavy German accent, one that reminded Arja Gammelgaard-Moeller of another time and other suspicious young Germans, Doctor Hirsch tried to explain to the Moeller's, "Because he has been robbed of one of his most important senses, the boy is anxious and frightened. Any animal

185

without the biological advantage of being able to hear approaching danger will, naturally, be afraid. He constantly anticipates the worst, fearing that at any moment something unknown and dangerous will present itself. I suppose there is some consolation, however, if we lived on the plains of the Serengeti he would soon be someone's dinner."

Arja and Mikkel looked at one another bewildered by what dinner on the Serengeti had to do with making their little boy well.

It would go unspoken by both the family and the hired workers, but the Moeller farm was a dangerous place to live and work - especially the lumber mill. Depending upon which version of *lucky life* you were living, the potential number of natural or man-made calamities was incalculable. As an evolutionary biologist, Doctor Hirsch might suggest that one reason these "dangers" mostly went unspoken was, "When confronted with the capacity for catastrophe, a person will learn to ignore these inherent dangers by allowing them to go unspoken. Constantly worrying over such things will render a person cuckoo."

For the young Poul Moeller just looking out the front window could produce a highly conflicted reaction. On the one hand, all the new and exciting activities going on around him were naturally compelling, while the reality of his personal captivity left him deeply frustrated and sad. For his parents, Poul standing at the window was just another unhappy reminder of what they saw as their little boy's lifetime of limitations. In spite of Doctor Hirsch's pragmatic advice and positive approaches to helping the child, it was commonly believed by the Moeller's family and friends that the helpless deaf boy was not only incapable of comprehending the simplest ideas, but that he would always be incapable of comprehending the simplest ideas. For the miserable Mother Arja, Poul's silent presence at the window only confirmed her worst fears: that is, beyond the glass lay certain and inescapable peril, dangers that she must shield him from forever.

Of course, forever proved to be an awfully long time, and one's *lucky life* does go on. Thankfully, with the boy's maturation and the steady passage of time, the notion that the child was to stay forever a prisoner of the house became too heartbreaking and inconvenient for even sad Mother Arja. When the stars finally aligned, Poul Moeller was permitted to sit outside in the grass beside the house. This privilege, this risky adventure, was allowed only under Mother Arja's strictest direction: "The baby must always be in the company of another!" So from the cool shade of an old oak, Poul was permitted a closer more personal view of his little portion of the world. Naturally, he found the nearby lumber mill the most fascinating and compelling place of all.

By July of his fourth summer, Poul had studied, search, and inspected everything alive or dead within his small circle of Indian grass. It was originally called "Mother Arja's circle" and it both defined and limited the boy's sphere of exploration; however, it would be his sister Saffii's version that gave it joy and hope. Originally, Mother Arja had produced a length of twine fifty feet long which she laid out on the grass in the shape of a circle. The boy was placed in the middle of the ring with the specific permanent instructions that he never set foot beyond its arc.

It was while sitting with her brother and watching the busy world around them that Saffii first recognized the paradox in a circle of twine. On the one hand, the brown string had temporarily freed her brother from the cruel familiarity of the house, while simultaneously imprisoning him from the larger beautiful beckoning world. It was from that sad insight that the notion of attaching those twenty-four pieces of colored ribbon to the circle of twine first manifest itself. By carefully laying the cord and bright ribbons on the grass, Saffii had created what was henceforth known as "Poul's little star."

Unlike her daughter's successful efforts to reach Poul, Mother Arja's attempts to teach the little deaf boy even the simplest lessons would leave her at best exasperated, or worst, gnashing her teeth. Programmed with only a limited degree of patience, Arja's efforts to train him to stay inside the circle were done exclusively by corporal intimidation. Whenever young Poul would stray beyond the colorful cutoff, he was summarily wrapped on the palm with a heavy wooden spoon. Given the boy's propensity to drift, it would take a significant number of the painful blows before the child finally recognized this simple association.

For sister Saffii this harsh treatment seemed contrary to her personal experiences. If she wanted their German shepherd Skiver to mind, she offered him kindness and tempted him with treats. The idea of striking the dog, or a cat, or any animal for not doing her bidding seemed wrong. But then she was only ten, and the people in her world rarely listened to what she had to say; they were far too busy telling her what to do to pay any attention to what she thought. Saffii's quiet and pleasant disposition made her easy to overlook, at least until it was time for chores, and there was never a day when the Moeller's did not have plenty of chores.

In the Psalms young King David demands of the Israelites, *"You will eat the fruit of your labor."*
Mikkel Moeller agreed.
It had taken four long years of breaking earth and their backs before the farm was well enough established that they could begin the lumber business. That spring, Mikkell and his brother-in-law Luca Fleisher hired the first group of transient lumbermen to cut and transport more than one hundred

giant pines to the nearby river, where they were then floated downstream and sold in La Crosse. From those profits, Mikkell and Luca were able to expand the operation and establish their own mill, a steam-driven lumber operation dedicated to providing fine hardwoods for the area's growing furniture industry.

From the beginning, the operation found a fair profit in cutting the larger hardwood's, mostly oak and maple, which were then dragged by horse-drawn sled back to the mill. The foundation for the boiler and engine were placed on two massive slabs of sandstone; enormous pieces of flat rock that had to be carted in from the Sauk County mine nearly fifty miles to the East. The power to run the operation came from a sixty-horsepower, Hill-Curtis steam engine, manufactured in Kalamazoo, Michigan. On any given day, the Moeller's lumber mill could cut eighteen hundred board feet of the most beautiful maple timber you would find anywhere.

The mill was a forty foot long rectangular building, open on the east and west ends, and covered with a tarpaper roof. It was located only two hundred feet west of the house, and one hundred-fifty feet south of the barn. Just inside the entrance was a carriage where the rough timber would be fixed with sawdogs before it was pushed forward into the screaming circular blade. To operate the impressive machinery required at least six men: the sawyer, the carriage rider, two frontmen to position the timber and tie the dogs, and two backmen to off-load the finished boards.

Because a saw mill is both dangerous and loud, finding and keeping experienced men to work the long hard hours was often a challenge. When a perfectly hammered sixty-inch blade attacks a forty-five-inch maple hardwood at six hundred revolutions per-minute, the sound and pitch will exceed one hundred-twenty decibels; a scream so piercing and painful that it forces the newcomer to stuff rags, paper, or cotton into his ears. The severe friction on the blade will soon cause the blistering metal to warp and shift. Smoke and sawdust will cloud the air making it hard to see and difficult to breathe. The triple-boiler that provides the superheated steam steadily discharges both an unstable gas and an extremely hot liquid; contact with either is seriously hazardous.

Saturday was the busiest day of the week at the mill - delivery day. To meet the growing number of orders placed by the finish carpenters and artisans of western Wisconsin, an entire complement of workers was needed to safely operate the machinery.

The mill workers would appear just before sunrise. On most mornings there would be six or seven of them, silently walking down the Moeller's rutted two-lane road toward the mill and a payday. Behind the men, like a pack of hounds prowling and sniffing after a warm trail, came the boys. These were the youngest boys, the nonessential ones; too old to stay behind with their mothers and the infants, but too young to work in the mill. They came with hat in hand, dutifully waiting behind their fathers or uncles (or whoever they were attached to) hoping that today Mikkell Moeller might have something for them. It might be the garden that needed weeding, horse stalls that wanted for a cleaning, pruning in the orchard, or hay that needed to be put up; anything safely away from the blade that might pay them a few pennies.

As an employer, Mikkell Moeller had no official rule about when a boy was old enough to work in the mill, he would just know. His decision was based partly on what he called "smarts" and, of course, how hard a fellow could work. But mostly it was the smarts. Despite everyone's best intentions there were plenty of accidents, some of them terrible. Along with the kickbacks that could send shards of splintered wood flying like bullets, a distracted worker would sometimes lose his fingers to the merciless blade. The white-hot steam from the boiler could deliver an agonizing scalding to even the most vigilant. Given the chances that a worker could be hurt - or worse - it made good sense for Mikkell Moeller to keep the men and his equipment under close watch. After all, a man that was hurt was a man that could not work.

"Who are all these people?" Saffii wondered as she and Poul peered out the front window. "Where do they come from?"

It seemed to Saffii a straightforward question, but as she was learning, adults rarely provided simple answers to her simple questions.

"Tramps and vagabonds, people with no homes," was Mother Arja's short disparaging assessment of the mill workers.

Saffii's father provided a more business like perspective. "They work for us here at the mill," he told her. "We pay them fifty cents a day, lunch, and a dozen eggs on Saturday."

It was rare for Saffii and Poul to ever meet any of the farm help. In the case of the hired hands, there was no reason they would be anywhere but the forest, the fields, or the mill. As for Saffii, she was strictly forbidden to go anywhere near the mill. On the Moeller farm people had their jobs and their places, and they were expected to stick to them.

There was, however, one exception: Sine Fleisher.

Mother Arja's first husband, Harold Bjerre (the murdered Dane) had an older sister, Ulla. It was Ulla's husband, Luca Fleisher, who had generously made it possible for his widowed sister-in-law, Arja to immigrate to the United States. It was also Luca's financial support and tireless work that had made the current success of the mill possible.

Direct and hardheaded men, Mikkell Moeller and Luca Fleisher embraced the Ecclesiastes' message that *"two are better than one, because they have a good reward for their toil. For if they fall, one will lift up his fellow."* Only the Bible can be tricky and often presents conflicting perspectives. For instance, Romans, 8:13 demands that we *"owe no man anything, except to love one another."*

Given all that the Fleisher's had done for them, it was only natural that Arja and Mikkell would feel beholding to their in-laws. Along with sponsoring Arja's immigration to the States, it would be the Fleisher's who introduced her to Mikkell at that first Baptist Social. Then, of course, there was the money and all the hard work that both Luca and Ulla had put into starting the mill. So as family, friends, and business associates, Mikkell and Arja's gratitude was generously extended to all the Fleisher children, with the possible exception of the most challenging of their four daughters, Sine.

Sine Fleisher was thirteen and the youngest of the four girls. She was a handful. A self-absorbed and unpredictable youngster, she delighted in taking full advantage of her birth order and the lenient treatment she had received from her weary parents. She did what she wanted when she wanted, worked only when berated, and then only until the adults were out of sight. Worse still, she was a deceiving and conniving sort who took a perverted pleasure in arranging elaborate conspiracies, the kind of play where a well-placed suggestion would result in a quarrel between two innocents.

Sine grew up in an environment completely foreign to Saffii Moeller. While Saffii spent the better part of her day laboring to help her family feed, clothe, and shelter themselves, Sine spent the bulk of her time observing her older sisters in their principle occupation: scheming about boys. Even at the tender age of thirteen, Sine Fleisher had already developed a haughty and conceited manner that drew the attention of both foolish school boys, and their prudish mothers.

"I can't believe I have to stay out here on this awful place all afternoon. There's absolutely nothing to do."

Saffii regarded her cousin carefully, she knew from her history with Sine that it was unlikely the girl would humble herself by joining them in their play. Even so, it was still best to be wary of the older girl; when there was no one around she loved to pinch Saffii's arms or pull her hair. With one eye on her now mobile younger brother, and the other on her spiteful cousin, Saffii knew to say as little as possible. If they were lucky, she might find their company so boring that she would wander off on her own.

Only there was the matter of nature's call.

"I'm sorry. It must be boring for you," Saffii chanced, hoping that the pleasantries might soften her cold-hearted cousin long enough to ask.

Stooping to mindlessly pick a small white flower from a large splash of clover, Sine absently replied, "Yes, it is."

Saffii quickly plunged forward.

"Sine, would you please watch Poul for just a minute. I need to, well, I need to go and…"

The question must have seemed so tedious that all Sine would do was wave her hand in Saffii's direction.

"He mustn't go outside of the circle," Saffii yelled at the girl's back.

Running full speed toward the outhouse, she knew that she had only a few precious minutes to finish her business and return. Even a short delay would provide her cousin the opportunity to abuse Poul.

"Who are all those people?" Sine asked the boy as she pointed toward the mill. Then laughing at herself, she added, "I don't know why anyone would bother to speak to you. You're such a little fool."

Even though he couldn't hear her, Poul had noticed that the taller girl was now speaking at him. He chose to ignore her. As far as he was concerned this one was just another in that gaggle of mean girls who would often appear for Sunday meals, or on holidays. The tall sisters rarely paid any attention to him, but when they did it mostly took the form of a wicked pinch or nasty kick. After all, the boy couldn't speak, so who was he going to tell?

He happily returned his attentions to the small calico cat that was now creeping alongside the giant lumber sled just outside the door to the mill. Then as the cat arched its back and sprang forward toward its prey, Poul Moeller stood up and began to run full-speed toward the mill. His cousin, meanwhile, had carelessly turned her back on the now vacant circle and was aimlessly wandering toward a nearby patch of honeysuckle and sweet William that had caught her attention.

Not two minutes had passed before Saffii returned to find that neither her deaf brother nor indifferent cousin were anywhere to be found.

"Mother," Saffii screamed, as she began to run toward the mill.

At first Poul was surprised that no one was picking him up and putting him back in the circle. His past efforts to venture outside his "star" had always resulted in a swift return, often with a stinging slap to his hand. That unpleasant thought passed quickly because the calico cat had missed its mark and was now quickly moving away from the shady spot next to the lumber sled. By the time Poul crossed the two hundred feet between the house and the front door to the mill, the cat had scampered past a large pile of sawdust and down a steep ravine into a dried-up creek bed. Beyond the dusty channel, now filled with masses of bluestem grass and pokeberry, was the Moeller's orchard. Further west of the fruit trees was the pine forest, and eventually the river.

Because the slope of the ravine was steeper than any terrain the boy had ever experienced on his own, by the time he got to the bottom of the gully Poul was running, stumbling out-of-control, and into the tall grasses. Thanks to an especially dry summer, the little stream that generally ran freely along the west side of the mill was now gone; all that remained was the new vegetation and the many sharp rocks that littered the bottom of the withered brook. It was one of those larger pieces of granite that caused Poul to trip and fall into a substantial patch of bluegrass. This perfectly timed fall will produce the first of what turns out to be several missed opportunities to find the lost boy.

Mother Arja heard her daughter's cry and instantly set down the tin of sugar. Rushing through the back door still holding her wooden spoon, she could see both the empty "star" and Saffii's back as the girl ran toward the front door of the mill. A fierce panic rose in Arja's throat as she too sprinted toward the building and the familiar dangers that lay inside.

As Saffii Moeller approached the front entrance on the east side of the mill, Alder Krist walked out of the back door on the west side. Just that day, Alder, now age twelve, had been given his first opportunity to work with his father in the mill. Normally, the judicious Mikkell Moeller did not allow younger boys anywhere near the dangerous machinery, especially the blade. On this occasion, Alder's unexpected presence was the result of a shortage in trained labor, the large number of orders that needed to be filled, and this particular confluence in his *lucky life*.

All morning, Mikkell and his men had been busy cutting larger logs into twelve foot strips of hickory for the Braydon brothers of La Crosse. As the heavy, wobbly, one-by-six boards came out of the saw, Alder and his father Timo would grab them, and then lug the flexing strip of wood outside to be stacked in the back of a wagon. It took all of the boy's strength to boost his portion of the load, but Alder's desire to make good, and the fifty-cent wage, turned out to be sufficient incentive.

The sawyer, old Dante Price had just finished with the last of the "one-by's" when Mikkell Moeller called for a break. The white-hot blade was slowly winding down as the men and Alder stepped away from the carriage and then outside into the clear morning air. It was at that precise moment that Alder would have been in the right place to spot Poul had the boy not just stumbled and fallen into the bluestem. Oblivious to any of the unfolding events, Alder turned and followed the other men as they gathered at the well for a drink of water and plug of tobacco.

After calling a halt to the work, Mikkell Moeller and Luca Fleisher were now standing in the eastern doorway considering the lumber orders that remained to be filled. The two were confounded by the scene developing in front of them.

First, there was young Saffii running pell-mell toward them screaming something which couldn't be heard over the descending howl from the slowing saw blade. Then there was Mother Arja, some distance behind Saffii, but also running at top speed while shaking what looked like a large wooden spoon. Finally, and furthest from them, was Sine Fleisher who was standing by the South edge of the house apparently collecting a bouquet of flowers?

When all the parties had gathered (*sans* Sine) Saffii breathlessly explained the situation. Despite her confusion in sorting out the pronouns, (I, me, she, he…) the message of the missing boy was clear enough to produce several reactions, Mother Arja's being the most dramatic and least helpful. When Saffii uttered the words "Poul" and "missing", Arja was so overcome that she fell face first into her husband's arms screaming the little boy's name while madly beating upon his broad shoulders. Trying to look over his wife's head and flailing arms, Mikkell did his best to encourage Saffii to share more information about what direction the boy might have gone; a futile effort drowned out by the pathetic wailing from Mother Arja.

Fortunately, Luca Fleisher understood the situation well enough to reassemble all the men into a posse. This proved to be a fairly easy chore since most of the workers were already curious about the commotion and had begun to wander back toward the mill. In his directions to the men, Luca went on in some detail to make sure that the agitated crowd was aware of the boy's special affliction. Still, as the group frantically ran off in every direction to search for the little lost deaf boy, Luca Fleisher could be seen hands on hips and shaking his head in wonder as the well-intentioned workman shouted the child's name.

Young Poul was not hiding from anyone, but because of the fantastic series of missed opportunities in this *lucky life,* every time the child should have been found something intervened.

After the boy got up from his first fall in the grass, his attentions were drawn to a pair of black swallowtail butterflies who were lazily making their way toward the garden and the corn patch. From the corn patch, Poul idly wandered toward the stable, conveniently shielded from view by the wooden fences and the Moeller's two prize Konik draft horses. After his cheerful visit with the horses, he gave chase to a gray tabby that had been peering at him from behind a large oak tree next to the barn. From the oak to the orchard, from the orchard back across the creek, and from the creek it was up the ravine and under the very wagon Alder and Timo Krist had just loaded with hickory. There Poul and the calico lay watching as a dozen adults and two children ran frantically around the place, apparently chasing their own tails.

Meanwhile, the first wave of urgency that had filled the men of the posse was quickly being replaced by anxiety and a growing sense of dread.

The worker's systematic searches of the mill, the barn, and the surrounding livestock pens had left them all empty handed and scratching their heads. Where could the little boy be?

Forcing himself to fight back his own feelings of helplessness, Mikkell Moeller called everyone back together. Before expanding the search Mikkell paired the men together and sent them back through the buildings one last time to make sure that nothing had been overlooked. Alder Krist and his father were told to look around the outside of the mill, an area that had been methodically searched by at least half the men, and the frantic Mother Arja.

Walking along the south wall the two moved anything not nailed down, but, of course, found nothing. This was because Poul Moeller had just wandered across the creek and back up the ravine toward the mill where he had joined the calico in the shade under the wagon.

Incredibly, Timo Krist was leaning against that very same lumber wagon when he removed a red handkerchief from his back pocket to mop his brow.

"Wherever that little fella is, I hope he's found some shade," Timo said to his son.

It would be his father's words that provided the epiphany for Alder Krist. Squatting down next to his father, Alder peered under the wagon and into the cool shadows where a small smiling boy sat holding a contented calico cat.

"Father," Alder said quietly. "I found that little boy."

It had been a remarkable first day on the job for Alder Krist. To begin with, it was his first day; although he'd tried to get on several times before, today he was actually hired to work in the Moeller's lumber mill, right there beside the other men, men who were three times his age and twice his size (including his father, especially his father) to do the same job for the same pay. Then to tip it in, he'd been the one who found the little lost deaf boy. That distinction brought plenty of back-thumping praise from the men and an extra fifty cents from Mr. Moeller himself.

When Alder first held out his hand to Poul Moeller, the younger boy looked up quizzically as if to ask, "Who are you?" Offering both a gentle smile and an open palm, Poul reluctantly freed the calico and then reached out to accept the older boy's invitation. Flanked by Alder and Timo, young Poul was guided around the North side of the mill and back to where the Moeller's and Luca Fleisher were still standing as they considered where to expand the search.

Mother Arja's scream brought the men running.

For a brief moment everyone shared in that wonderful feeling of relief. The little boy was back safe in the loving arms of his mother, who was now happily smothering him with kisses. It was a tender and beautiful sight that left even the hardened lumbermen feeling warm and familial.

That is until Mother Arja finished with her kisses and began the beating. In front of God and the lumbermen, Mother Arja's emotions suddenly twisted from loving relief to a cruel attack. Furiously seizing Poul's arm with one hand, she began dragging the little boy back toward the house, all the time mercilessly beating him with the wooden spoon she still carried. This was not just a single swat - a perfectly reasonable punishment for the fright that he'd given everyone - this was a ruthless assault, so harsh that many of the workmen were forced to turn away. More than one of the men looked to the boy's father anticipating, hoping, he'd intervene on his son's behalf. Instead, Mikkell Moeller grimly turned his back upon his manic spouse and walked on toward the East door of the mill.

Mother Arja's screech had effectively announced the safe return of the boy. Saffii, who had been frantically searching along the ditches of the old dirt road, heard the alarm and quickly came running from beyond the South side of the house. Overjoyed to see Poul safely back in Mother Arja's arms, Saffii rushed to join their celebration. But before she could cross the yard, Poul's horrible bawling stopped her in her tracks. Her moment of joy was lost to surprise, and then fear, as her own mother began to violently beat the young boy.

"How can she do this? He's safe!"

Another horrible blow to his back followed by more screaming from Poul.

Saffii had heard her brother cry before. All children cry, even deaf ones, but Poul Moeller's was different. For most children you can hear the familiar sounds of fear and pain in their cry; for someone like Poul there was also a deeper layer that resonated with anger and humiliation. It was a personal anger for what he could not understand, and his own private humiliation for what he did. Saffii had heard it before, and she understood. She understood it because it was the same way she felt when her mother would beat her.

As Mother Arja approached where Saffii now stood waiting in the dirt drive, her reaction to her daughter's presence was to lambaste the boy again, even harder if that was possible.

"This is your fault, sister," she screamed.

Arja's eyes were wild and her chest pumped liked a bellows. The tight bun that always imprisoned her dark gray hair was now mostly loose; long strands had fallen around her face and across her heaving shoulders.

Saffii, small Saffii, daughter Saffii, stunned her mother when she boldly reached out to hold back the woman's arm. In her rage, Arja easily pushed the girl backwards, and followed it with a stinging whack to the side of her child's face. The blinding pain screamed like the saw blade, leaving a cut on her cheek and tears in her eyes.

Lumbering on toward the house, Arja pushed past the girl as she raised the weapon for another blow. Quickly regaining her balance, both feet beneath her, young Saffii leaped forward to grab at the wooden spoon just as Mother Arja brought it down upon the wailing boy.

Suddenly, (surprisingly) the weapon (the spoon) was in the girl's hand.

Spinning madly to her left, Mother Arja dropped the boy to the ground while grabbing for the daughter. This time Saffii was faster and quickly jumped back out of reach.

"Give it to me," hissed her mother.

What can you do when you realize that you have completely crossed over the line; when you know that it is impossible to ever go back to the place you were just seconds before? How does that feel when you're only ten years-old? Ten years-old and you know that you will never receive or give love to your mother again?

As Arja advanced, her open hand now demanding the spoon, Saffii resolutely retreated, step for step, until they were both standing on the grass right next to Poul's colorful star. The wooden spoon was childishly hidden behind Saffi's back.

"Give me the spoon," Arja insisted, her teeth still clenched.

"You mustn't hit him. He's safe now," Saffii said, trying not to cry.

Arja barked back, "Do as you are told."

"No."

The line was now indelibly drawn.

"No," she repeated, "you will not hit him again."

The two realized the presence of the third at the same moment; standing beside them was Sine Fleisher, ridiculously holding a bouquet of flowers.

Without a word, Sine reached behind Saffii's back and calmly removed the spoon from her cousin's grasp. Then turning to face her crazed aunt, the girl suddenly cracked the spoon over her thigh, easily breaking it into two separate pieces of wood. Handing the broken spoon to a stunned Mother Arja, Sine then walked over to where Poul was sitting alone on the dirt road. She reached out her hand to help the boy to his feet, and then coolly handed him the flowers. Looking back on her cousin and aunt with utter contempt, Sine Fleisher then turned and walked off toward the mill, the orchard, and eventually the river beyond.

Chapter Three

Bob Barker Visits Old Oaks

"As we grow old the beauty steals inward."
Ralph Waldo Emerson

"So, don't you have something to say to me?"

The pleasantries were over. Seated across from Johanna and Emily on the opposite side of a long wooden dining table was Barbara Krist and her middle daughter, Elaine Christensen. From her spot, Emily could look past them and through one of the nursing home's large picture windows on to what could only be described as rapidly deteriorating weather. This unexpected development was adding a healthy dose of drama to what was already an edgy situation.

For whatever reason - perhaps spite, she did favor her mother in both size and disposition - Cousin Elaine had brought along her newborn, an unhappy three-week-old boy named Scooter, or Scamper, or perhaps, Scottie. Emily hadn't been clear on the introduction because at the time she'd been focused on Aunt Barbara's mood; this new notion of accommodating a mewling baby into the production was not especially welcome.

A second unforeseen distraction sat on the opposite side of the room. Hunkered down in their worn recliners and wooden rocking chairs, half a dozen Old Oak residents were all keenly studying a hazy black-and-white picture on an ancient Sylvania television. It was hard to tell from where she sat, but given the group's reaction, which was mostly shouting suggestions or loud random complaints, it appeared that they were watching a game show called, *The Price is Right*.

Apparently anticipating a failed mission and the need for a hasty departure, neither Barbara nor Elaine had bothered to take off their winter coats; Barbara had, however, carefully removed the wet plastic rain cap she'd worn from the car to the building, and was now daintily holding the little plastic package in her large fingers. Her hair, Emily noted, was still cut the same length, and with the identical color that she'd always worn. The one difference, if you could call it a difference, was that her hair was perfect, perhaps a bit stiff, but still perfect; not one hair was out of place. Under the circumstances, Emily thought that her aunt looked quite nice and sincerely hoped she wasn't wearing a wig.

At the head of the table, Grandmother Saffii was slumped down in her wheel chair in what Emily imagined to be a terribly uncomfortable position. A raggedy afghan covered with stains had been thrown across the old woman's lap. Sadly, her osteoporosis was now so advanced that it was a labor for her to keep her chin elevated enough so that she could look at whoever was speaking. Along with her diabetes and painful arthritis, there was a growing concern among the Old Oaks nursing staff that Saffii might also be suffering from some kind of oncoming dementia.

"How," her morning nurse Margret Thiele would ask, "can an eighty-four year-old woman with all those problems ever have a reason to smile?"

This comment revealed as much about Margret Thiele as it did Grandmother Saffii.

"I said, don't you have something you wish to say to me, Johanna?" Barbara was asking again.

Emily prayed that her mother would stick to the script and capitulate. Three words, "I am sorry" was all that was needed to be said and the nightmare could be over in time for Christmas.

"Well, yes, now that you mention it," Johanna answered.

Emily held her breath.

Barbara looked down her nose at the two of them.

Elaine dabbed a gob of milky spit from Scooter's mouth.

Saffii closed her eyes as if she'd just nodded off.

Then Johanna Krist smiled a wicked smile, and announced, "I just love what you've done with your hair."

And it was on.

Without warning Scooter, or Scottie, or Scamper let out an ear-piercing scream that ignited a freeform improvisation. All the main characters had gone completely off-script, adlibbing both their blocking and dialog. Separated by only the dining room table, the two antagonists were now on their feet shouting angry threats and mad curses. Emily's well-drawn play was collapsing around her like an elementary school musical.

In what seemed a misguided effort to quiet baby Scooter, Elaine began to vigorously bounce the tiny newborn up-and-down, apparently thinking that she could calm the terrified infant by inducing vertigo. Remarkably, it worked. After only a few vigorous tosses the little guy began to gurgle and coo, which allowed Elaine a split-second to reach into the nearby bag of baby supplies and locate a bottle of formula. With remarkable precision, Elaine then stabbed the rubber nipple into the baby's pliable mouth, temporarily ending one of the scene's many distractions.

As the adult voices grew from shouts to screams, three of the morning nurses and two of the cleaning crew appeared in the kitchen doorway; no one entered the room. Instead, the staff all nervously peered around the corner as if fearing that their presence might bring the fight to a premature conclusion.

Order was temporarily restored when one of the Old Oaks residents, Mrs. Gretchen Wilson (Emily's first-grade teacher) leaned out from her worn recliner and shouted in a remarkably loud clear voice, "Quiet down! We're watching our program here."

Johanna, Barbara, and the Oak's staff all stared dumbly at the old woman, but no one said a word. For that brief moment the only intelligent sound in the room came from Bob Barker when he roared to someone in his audience named Anna Belle Wonders to "Come on down!"

From somewhere beneath all the confusion and anger, Grandmother Saffii began to mumble, incomprehensibly at first, but then, "I want to think about my baby Jesus." she whispered.

After a short pause to regain her strength, Saffii forced her chin off her chest so that she might look directly at the two adversaries. Neither sat, but both lowered their fingers and their eyes.

Saffii continued, "I loved baby Jesus, but he's dead now. He was my baby Jesus, and I loved him so. He was a beautiful boy, so full of life. But he died. He died because I forgot to take care of him. I forgot that he needed me. So he went to a place where no one else could go, he went there in his own mind, and he stayed there. I forgot just how much he needed me, because no one else would bother. So, he died."

Saffii's head had rolled over onto her left shoulder in a way that looked painful, but she somehow managed to continue.

"My mother had no patience for us, for Poul and me. Then she got sick and she left. She left one day and we never saw her again. Papa said she was going to a better place, but it was only better for her. After that, Poul and I were all alone. Papa wasn't able to help. He was too sad. He was too sad for himself.

So they all died. Papa, Mother, and Poul all died.

That's how it is. We die. My time's coming, soon, and you two will be after me, and then you two. That's how it is."

No one spoke. In the corner of the room, the television roared a crazy cartoon commercial about dirty showers and magic scrubbing bubbles, but by this point everyone had turned to look at the one person in the room who seemed to have an intelligent thing to say.

"You two, you two married my boys. Selfish women, you've hated each other since the first day you met. Now you're here on my baby Jesus birthday, and look what you've done. You made this baby cry. You worry your children. And you got my friends all stirred up so they can't watch their program. What's wrong with you?"

The ominous sound of sleet against the large picture window drew Emily's attention away from this remarkable new version of the play. The wind had picked up considerably. The ice that was now pelting the side of the building sounded like someone was throwing handfuls of sand against the glass. The weather had turned into what Iowan's fear most.

"Mother," Emily turned back to the table, "it looks like the weather is getting bad. Why don't we make our apologies and let Barbara and Elaine get the baby home before the roads get any worse?"

Both women were still standing and facing each other across the wooden dining room table. A smug look of satisfaction had appeared on Barbara Krist's face. She was anticipating what she'd come for, to finally humble her nemesis, Johanna Krist.

"You need to listen to me," croaked the tired voice of Saffii Krist, "I don't have much time left for you. So start by sitting down, please."

The two women did as they were told.

"What is it that you want, Barbara?" Johanna asked in a weary voice, darker and with a notably slower cadence than before.

Emily recognized the change in tone right away. It was the *other voice*; the one she'd heard on the phone, the one from last night. It was true then, this *voice* was coming from her mother.

Barbara sensed something too and appeared to be studying Johanna carefully before answering.

She began, cautiously, as if she was talking to a child.

"I want you to apologize to me."

Then with growing confidence, the large woman added, "I want you to say you're sorry for all the tricks and the games. For all those magazine subscriptions I never wanted, especially that filthy Playboy. I want you to confess to writing those nasty letters to the newspaper, and then signing my name. And I want you to promise, in front of Saffii and your daughter, that you will stop forever and leave me alone."

There it was, right out in the open. All Johanna had to do was pick it up and hand it back to her with those three words.

"Please, Mother," Emily whispered.

A noticeable shudder twisted Johanna's head and shoulders. Her eyes were closed, her head held low. It was clear that some kind of internal battle was taking place.

Then Johanna Krist spoke.

"I apologize, Barbara," she said in what seemed a sincere but defeated voice. "I hope you can forgive a lonely old woman."

Barbara Krist looked at Johanna with an odd mixture of satisfaction and bewilderment. She had extracted her pound of flesh. She had finally won her victory. Now after that apology she should feel vindicated and triumphant, only was this really the same person who'd played all those awful tricks on her? Was this the woman who had somehow made her hair blue?

200

"Johanna?" Barbara Krist asked. "Are you all right?"

"Yes," she replied. "Tired, I think. Emily's right, we should all go home before the weather gets any worse."

As Johanna turned to gather her coat and pocketbook, Barbara Krist also stood and said, "Merry Christmas, Saffii. If the weather doesn't get too bad, Stephen and I will be by tomorrow after lunch."

"I'll be here," was Saffii's happy reply.

Elaine busily gathered the last of the baby's things as Barbara Krist turned to look back at Emily and Johanna.

"Merry Christmas, Emily," she said. "We'll look forward to hearing how you and the baby are getting on." Then with a questioning look at Johanna, she added, "Don't be a stranger, Emily. I'm sure your mother will be glad to have you and the baby."

Touching Saffii's shoulder, Barbara Krist turned to her daughter and announced, "Let's go before this gets any worse."

There was a pregnant pause before she declared with extraordinary self-righteousness, "I accept your apology, Johanna."

She had dreamt of this day, even imagined it as a newspaper headline: **Arch Enemy Johanna Krist Humbled**. It was to be the *coup de grace,* (the blow that kills) the final finishing touch that would proclaim victory over her greatest adversary. Only something was wrong. Johanna said nothing as she raised her tired eyes. Along with a confusing Mona Lisa smile, there was a puzzling expression that could easily be masking her true feelings. Was Johanna there? Who had apologized? Was it a sincere act of contrition, or a ruse?

Sensing that her victory was somehow tarnished, Barbara huffed and marched out into the misery of the ice storm.

Emily watched through the frosted picture window as Barbara, Elaine, and baby Scooter struggled against the fierce wind and blowing sleet to cross the icy parking lot. While Elaine fussed with securing the baby into the car seat, Barbara gamely attempted to scrape the hard-crusted ice from the frozen windshield of her new Chevy Impala. After only a minute or two, the big woman gave up trying to clear the glass and hurriedly climbed back into the driver's seat, leaving only a tiny eight-inch periscope-hole to peer through. In spite of this ridiculous view, Barbara Krist refused to wait until her car had warmed-up enough to melt more of the ice. Instead, she spun-out of the frozen drive, fishtailing her way down the lane toward Cherry Street.

Inside the toasty warm Oaks Retirement Home, Emily pulled a chair up next to Grandma Saffii's wheelchair and was happily holding the old woman's knurled and arthritic hands.

Struggling to lift her head, Saffii viewed her granddaughter's smiling face, and then whispered, "You look beautiful, my dear. I'm so very happy. Will you promise to bring the baby and show me?"

"Of course we will, Grandma. I'm sorry that Charles couldn't have been here, but the poor boy is home sick with the flu."

Then turning to her mother, Emily added, "And we should probably be getting home to him."

As she stood up, Emily said, "Thank you, Grandma. I love you."

"You're welcome. Look after your mother, dear."

There was a fleeting exchange between Johanna Krist and her mother-in-law, one that might have gone unnoticed if you weren't watching closely. It took the form of a knowing smile and an imperceptible nod of acknowledgement. Emily saw it, perhaps she was meant to, but the effect seemed to leave Johanna brighter and not so heavy.

"Merry Christmas, Saffii."

The old woman struggled to lift her head, smiled, and replied, "Back in business, boys,"

Chapter Four

Always Turn Into a Skid

"I am not an angel, I asserted; and I will not be one till I die: I will be myself."
Jane Eyre - Charlotte Brontë

It took nearly twenty minutes before the old Ford's defroster had warmed the glass enough so that Johanna could attempt to scrape the ice from the station wagon's windshield. In the meantime, the two women sat huddled inside the car, their teeth chattering as the wiper blades uselessly dragged back and forth across the frosted glass. It was too cold to talk, besides once they got back to the house there would be plenty of time to discuss the result of their summit. Clearly, Emily and Charles were not going anywhere in this weather.

Pleased with herself for thinking more like a mother, Emily had purposefully sought out the restroom before leaving Old Oaks. But between the shivering efforts to stay warm, and the active baby that was now tap dancing on her bladder, Emily was aware of a rising need to return to the facilities. Since it was only a five minute drive back to her mother's house, she wisely chose the relative warmth of the station wagon over the treacherous trip back across the icy parking lot.

The Oaks Retirement Home sits on top of the first of four hills that mark the eastern city limits of Freeland, Iowa. From its elevated location, the residents enjoy a remarkable westerly view back across the valley and down on to the small burg. It is this view, particularly at sunset, which the Oak's administrators like to show their prospective clients.

Cherry Street is normally a benign stretch of blacktop that leisurely winds down the hill and empties onto the well-travelled Iowa Highway 6. During the past few years several of Freeland's nicer new homes had been built along the meandering lane, and with them came improved roads, gravel shoulders, and wooden guard rails on the turns. As part of the neighborhood's covenant, all the residents agreed to take "appropriate measures" to decorate their fine homes with multicolored lights and flashy, non-denominational displays. The neighbor's collective enthusiasm had made Cherry Street the destination for those locals wishing to view holiday lights. Sadly, the dangerous road conditions meant that on this Christmas Eve no one was likely to enjoy their efforts.

By the time Johanna was finally ready to risk the roads they were as slick as a skating rink; slowing down was difficult, stopping almost impossible. As a widower with no one to drive for her, Johanna Krist had become reasonably skilled at getting around during inclement weather. Her experience had taught her the three keys to navigating on ice and snow: keep your speed down, pump your brakes when trying to stop, and the counterintuitive maneuver to always steer into a skid.

The station wagon crept out of the parking lot and down the short lane to the Cherry Street intersection. Johanna cautiously turned left and began the descent down the shallow grade toward the first curve, never allowing the car to go much faster than a person could walk. No one spoke. The only sounds came from the car's loud defroster fan, the sleet pelting against the windows, and the crunch of tires on the glassy road.

Emily was doing her best to ignore the growing need for the facilities, but between the tense driving conditions and relentless rush of hot air blowing out of the car's defroster, her resolve was rapidly fading. As a hopeful distraction, she took up a kind of mantra, repeating the phrase, "Bottom of the hill, two more blocks. Bottom of the hill, two more blocks."

It was less than five hundred feet from the corner to the first of the three Cherry Street curves. This first bend was really only a minor jog in the road and was there to accommodate a beautiful century oak tree that grew along the West side of the street. To protect this extraordinary landmark, the city's maintenance crew had built a substantial wooden guardrail between the road and the tree, but long before mother and daughter reached the barrier it was clear that the barricade had been smashed to pieces and Barbara Krist's new Impala was now planted headfirst into the trunk of the oak.

"Mother," shouted Emily.

"I see it," Johann replied, while gently tapping the station wagon's brakes.

Despite her light and calculated touches, the back end of the long car began to slide to the right, drifting sideways down the road and straight for the back of Barbara Krist's Impala. Stifling a scream, Emily prepared herself for the broadside collision as Johanna sharply spun the wheel to the right, steering into the skid, and miraculously correcting the car's trajectory. Still tap, tap, tapping on the brakes, the Ford slowly slid by the smashed guardrail, finally coming to a stop on the gravel shoulder of the road fifty feet below Barbara's car.

"Are you okay?" Johanna whispered to her daughter.

"Yes, I think so," Emily replied. "What do we do?"

Johanna stepped down hard to lock the emergency brake.

Although the pavement wasn't especially steep, the station wagon had come to rest parallel with the side of the road. Peering out of the frosted window, Emily could see that if she were to open the passenger-side door, she'd be stepping down three or four feet into a shallow drainage ditch.

"I can't see anyone in the car," Johanna said, "but one thing's for sure, it's not running."

Emily knew little about automobiles, but it was obvious that the frozen car had collided headfirst into the oak, crushing the front bumper, and pushing the radiator back into the engine. Impaled upon the giant tree, the car was clearly terminal.

"I guess I better go and see if they're still in the car," Johanna said as she struggled to open her door against the howling wind.

"Wait a minute, Mother. What if someone's already picked them up, or maybe they walked down the hill to one of the houses? After all, it's been at least twenty minutes since they left the Oaks."

"Let's hope you're right," Johanna said as she wrapped her wool scarf over her head. "Except no one left while we were waiting for the car to warm-up, and getting up this hill would take a miracle."

Johanna glanced back over her shoulder, and said, "I'll be right back. You stay here and leave the car running. It's a shame there's no such thing as a portable phone."

Just trying to stand on the shallow icy slope required Johanna to hold on to the side of the car for support. She had no more than gotten her feet safely beneath her when the fierce wind caught the open door and slammed it shut, leaving Emily to watch from inside as her mother inched her way along the station wagon's flank. When she finally reached the taillights, Johanna cautiously crept to the side of the road where the gravel offered better footing.

Emily rolled down her window and stuck her head out.

"Be careful, Mom," she yelled at Johanna's back.

"Oh, my god," Johanna shouted into the frozen wind. "She's in the damn ditch. Emily, Barbara's fallen. Damn. Damn. Damn."

Working her way back up the hill toward the dead Impala, Johanna began to shout, "Barbara! Are you all right? Barbara... say something. Damn. Damn. Damn."

It was hard to hear over the howling wind, but from down in the ditch Johanna could just make out Barbara Krist's faint whisper as she pleaded, "Help me."

"What is it Mom?" Emily yelled out the window.

"Barbara's fallen by the car. She's hurt. I'm going to try to climb down this ditch and..."

The rest of her words were lost to the wind.

Getting down on her hands and knees, Johanna Krist crawled backwards down into the ravine where her archenemy and hated sister-in-law now lay whimpering in the snow.

Everything about Barbara Krist's situation was wrong.

To begin with she had attempted to pilot her large, rear-wheel drive vehicle at normal driving speeds in an ice storm without proper visibility. After turning onto Cherry Street and accelerating to the ridiculous speed of twenty miles-an-hour, she quickly realized that it was going to be impossible to steer, or stop. In this case, it was the wooden guard rail and century oak that managed to arrest her velocity.

The crash sent the radiator into the engine and passengers into the dash. Neither of the women was wearing their seatbelt. When metal struck wood, the top of Elaine's head hit and splintered the windshield, momentarily rendering her unconscious. The impact threw Barbara into the steering wheel, cracking her eleventh and twelfth ribs, and bloodying her lower lip. The only person unaffected by the impact was baby Scooter who lay sleeping warm and cozy in the back seat.

When she had regained her composure, Barbara realized two things: First, her left side hurt, badly. Second, her middle-daughter Elaine was unconscious and bleeding from her forehead. Barbara's rash and unreasoned reaction to the predicament was to get out of her car and go for assistance.

Just stepping out of the vehicle made her side ache. The harsh northwestern wind blew stinging sleet into her eyes and frigid gusts of cold air up her skirt. Closing the car door and taking a step forward, Barbara's slick leather sole shoes betrayed her balance and put her on the ground. The heavy fall finished the business by fracturing the *costae fluitante,* rendering the big woman momentarily unconscious. By the time Emily and Johanna arrived she had regained consciousness, but hypothermia was setting in. Barbara Krist was in serious trouble.

"Barbara, can you hear me?" Johanna shouted, as she crawled toward her sister-in-law. "Can you hear me, damn it?"

"Johanna? Is that you?"

"Yes. Where are you hurt?"

After forcing open the car door, Emily realized that in her condition the drop into the ravine would be too steep to manage without a fall. Remembering all the trouble that Johanna had just experienced, she wisely chose to slide across the seat and exit through the driver's door.

"You must not fall," became the expectant mother's new mantra.

As Emily made her way to the rear of the station wagon, she could see her mother on the ground beside Barbara Krist, who now lay partially turned on her side and apparently trying to speak.

"Where's Elaine?" Emily screamed into the storm.

Johanna and Barbara looked back down the hill at Emily.

"Stay in the car," Johanna pleaded.

"Where is Elaine?"

Kneeling there beside her archenemy, the merciless northwest wind pelting her face with biting sleet, Johanna understood she couldn't manage Barbra alone. Clearly, the woman could not get up, nor could she last much longer laying on the frozen ground. There was no other choice but to accept Emily's help and hope that neither fell.

"Can you stand?" Johanna asked Barbara.

"I don't know, maybe. Get Elaine and the baby."

"We will, but we've got to get you to the car or you'll die. I sure as hell don't want that on my conscience."

Barbara Krist eyed Johanna suspiciously, but recognized that her only hope would have to come from this woman, this hateful ridiculous woman and her pregnant daughter.

Emily had miraculously made it down to where the other two women were still lying on the ground.

"Come on, Emily. Help me get her to her feet. She may be broken up inside."

First to her knees, and then struggling to her feet, Barbara gritted her teeth and stumbled forward, propped-up by Emily and Johanna. Balancing against one another, the three women managed to stagger out of the ravine and down the hill toward the station wagon.

Once they'd gotten the big woman into the back seat, Emily assured her aunt, "It's going to be all right, Barbara. We'll go for the baby and Elaine."

It was up the hill, and then back down the ravine to the passenger side of the Impala. Johanna knocked on the frost-covered window, but there was no reply. Prying open the frozen door, they found Elaine conscious but staggered by the blow to her head. The baby was still contentedly asleep, covered by blankets and oblivious to the cold.

"Emily, get the baby, and I'll help Elaine," Johanna commanded.

As she reached into the backseat to unbuckle the car seat, Scooter drowsily opened his eyes expecting to see the familiar face of his mother. A gust of frigid air blew into the cold car startling the baby and setting off his crying.

"It'll be okay, Scooter," Emily said, lifting the child out of the car seat. "You'll be just fine."

Johanna had managed to pull Elaine out of the car and then propped her up so that her niece's left arm was draped over her shoulder. They were carefully shuffling their way down the hill and were almost to the car when Elaine inexplicably turned to look back toward Emily and Scooter. The unexpected move caused both women to lose their balance and fall hard on the gravel. Johanna was on the bottom with Elaine landing full force on her rescuer's right side.

"Mother," Emily shouted shuffling her feet a bit faster to reach her.

Elaine slowly rolled off of Johanna, but lay splayed-out on the cold road vacantly staring up into the dark gray sky.

With the blanketed baby still in her arms, Emily knelt beside her mother.

"Mother! Please, Mother. I need your help. We all need you. Don't be hurt."

Johanna managed to turn on her left side and look up at her daughter. "Stupid girl," she muttered. "Look what she's done to me. Emily, I can't move. I don't think I can walk. You need to get the baby and Elaine in the car. Then come help me."

Emily reached out and touched her mother's icy cheek.

"I'll be right back."

Johanna nodded and offered her daughter a weak smile.

Thankfully the station wagon was still running and the cabin was warm and dry. Emily handed the baby to Barbara who was now lying in the backseat, her back propped against the passenger side door.

"Where are Elaine and Johanna?" Barbara demanded.

"They fell coming down the hill. I've got to go back."

Elaine was still lying on her back but conscious, frightened, and confused. As Emily knelt beside her cousin, Elaine begged, "Where's the baby?"

"In the car. He's okay. Come on, you've got to get up."

Emily reached out to help Elaine get to her feet when she noticed that the right side of her cousin's wool stocking cap was now smeared red by blood.

"Okay, Elaine. Here we go."

Pulling the heavy girl to her feet, Emily slowly shuffled her down the remaining few steps to the driver's door, then pushed her into the front seat and helped her slide over to the passenger side.

By the time she returned for her mother, Johanna had gotten to her knees; the pain on her face revealed how badly she was injured.

"Let's get you in the car," Emily demanded.

Sliding the last few feet to the tailgate, Emily and Johanna hugged one another until they could finally open the back door. From the grimace on her face, it was clear that any weight she put on her right side caused excruciating pain.

Climbing in the driver's door and looking around at the condition of her family, Emily was staggered by the scene: sitting next to her was her cousin, Elaine Christensen, clearly in shock and still bleeding from a large gash to her forehead; in the backseat, propped uncomfortably against the passenger side door, her aunt Barbara lay collapsed in pain, a frightened three-week old baby held tight to her chest; and sharing the available space, also in desperate pain from what could be either a broken hip or fractured ribs, was her mother.

To try to calm her nerves before releasing the emergency brake, Emily gulped down a deep breath of the hot dry air that was still blasting from the station wagon's defroster. Then clutching the wheel with both hands, she forced herself to focus on the challenge at hand: to successfully navigate a giant car full of seriously injured people down a frozen hill in a raging ice storm.

Unlike her mother, Emily had only limited experience driving a car, and no history on icy streets.

The day after her sixteenth birthday, Emily did successfully drive for her license, but after passing the test she would not get behind the wheel for another six years. While still in high school the actual need for her to drive anywhere was limited; Freeland is, after all, a very small town, and she lived only two blocks from school. Then just a month after getting a license her father would die. Given the tense and adversarial quality of their relationship, the idea of asking her mother to take the family car out for a drive was not something she'd ever seriously considered. Once they had moved to Chicago, Emily and June found the Chicago Transit Authority a trustworthy and affordable means of transportation. So, it wasn't until Charles finally pushed her to get behind the wheel that she gained any practical experience as a driver.

Sadly, no amount of training or previous experience could have prepared her for this predicament.

As she pulled the lever into drive, Johanna whispered from the backseat, "You can do this Emily. Go as slow as you can. Only tap the brakes."

With one last look at her broken family, Emily gingerly took her foot off the brake. As the car began to creep forward, the anxious driver unexpectedly hammered back down on the brake causing the car to lurch forward and shift its pathetic load. A disconcerting moan came from her aunt in the backseat.

"Come on, Emily," her cousin Elaine offered. "Go for it."

Now strangling the steering wheel with both hands, Emily tried again. Slowly, the station wagon moved ahead, one wheel on the road and the other on the gravel.

The first of the three curves was the most gentle and emptied out onto a short straightaway of about a thousand feet. Next came Ekland's Curve, the steepest and most severe of the three. Once around the sharp bend the road opened into the steepest portion of the hill, a shallow but straight-line drop of about two hundred feet, before a final small turn and a long straightaway out to the highway.

After successfully navigating the first shallow bend, the makeshift ambulance was headed toward Ekland's curve. By constantly tapping the brake pedal, Emily had been able to keep the car's speed down to a crawl, but as they exited the broad sweeping turn she must have applied too much brake, sending the back-end of the wagon sliding sideways.

From behind her, Johanna insisted, "Turn into the skid."

While still tapping the brakes, Emily wrenched the steering wheel to the right, paradoxically reversing the problem and forcing the backend of the station wagon to the left. Correcting, and then overcorrecting, she courageously fought the long car all the way down the steepest portion of the hill and into the final curve. Thankfully, the car was parallel with the road when it came out of the turn and into the last long line of straight road.

When they finally reached the stop sign at the highway, Emily relaxed her death grip on the wheel and took what she was certain was her first breath since the ordeal began at the top of the hill.

No one in the car said anything.

The Freeland Community Hospital is only two blocks north of Main Street on the corner of Second and Elm. Fortunately for the extended Krist family, the little bit of State Highway 6 that Emily needed to navigate had been heavily salted. Travel was still hazardous, but not insane.

As soon as she pulled under the red-and-white striped canopy that protruded beyond the hospital's emergency entrance, Emily began vigorously honking the station wagon's horn. Her expectation was that a squad of fully equipped medical personnel would rush out of the door to render aid and comfort to her battered people.

Surprisingly, no one came.

Again, she laid on the horn, but still no one appeared at the door.

"Where are these people," Emily wondered out loud.

"It's Christmas Eve," her aunt mumbled. "There won't be many people on duty. You should go in."

"Go in," she thought to herself? "I've got a car full dying people and I need to go into the hospital to find someone that will help us?"

It was at the moment when she reached for the car door that she recognized there was a damp and unexpected sensation in her lap. Pulling open her coat, the pregnant woman looked down past the steering wheel to find her trousers, underwear, and the car seat drenched in amniotic fluid.

"Oh, my god… Mother, my water just broke."

Carolyn Benson was the "nurse on duty" that afternoon. A car horn sounding outside the Emergency Room would have normally received all of her attention, but in this version of her *lucky life,* Nurse Benson had left the front desk to visit the restroom. Since the hospital had only a handful of patients, and it was, after all, Christmas Eve, the administrative staff had assigned only a skeleton crew to the dayshift. At that particular moment, those staff members who would have normally been available to deal with such an emergency were occupied elsewhere; this left no one in the receiving station of the Freeland Community Hospital Emergency Room when a station wagon full of very needy people arrived.

Looking down into her wet lap, Emily hoped that somehow she was dreaming all of this craziness. Any minute now she was going to wake-up back in her own bed, her husband Charles snoring peacefully beside her, and the cat contentedly curled-up on her feet. Once she was awake all of this madness would make for a remarkable story, one that she would enjoy telling him over breakfast.

Only she really was soaking wet. Unless she'd peed herself, and she hadn't done that since she was four, then all of these injured people, this insane weather, and deserted hospital was no dream - a nightmare for sure - but no dream.

Emily Krist struggled to pull herself out of the car before shuffling uncomfortably toward the entrance of the hospital's emergency room. The sensor in the rubber map signaled for the double-doors to open. A breath of warm moist air and bright welcoming light beckoned her to enter.

As the pregnant woman approached the vacant reception desk, Carolyn Benson returned from the lavatory.

"Can I help you?" she asked.

"Yes," Emily replied in a curt and noticeably anxious tone, "we need all the help you can find."

Emily knew as soon it came out of her mouth that her blunt response to Nurse Benson's reasonable question came off a bit snide, maybe even hostile; after all, she was a stranger to the nurse, and by all appearances someone who had just wandered in off of the street.

It wasn't until Carolyn opened the driver's door to the station wagon that she understood the accuracy of the anxious pregnant woman's request.

"Yes," Nurse Benson replied, "I think you will need all the help we've got... maybe more."

Chapter Five

A Child is Born - Business Booms

"A flower can't choose the place where it blooms,
and a child can't choose the parents they're born to."
Fairy Tale - Hiro Mashima

Dallas Gordon Albright was born at 10:43 P.M. on Christmas Eve, 1969. On December 27, the Freeland Tribune ran the following birth announcement:

> Freeland, Iowa – Mrs. Emily Albright - formerly Emily Krist of Freeland - and Mr. Charles Albright of Chicago, Illinois are parents of a son, Dallas Gordon Albright, born December 24, 1969, at the Freeland Community Hospital. At birth, Dallas weighed four pounds, two ounces. Grandparents are Mrs. Johanna Krist of Freeland, and Mrs. Charys Albright of Cedar Rapids. Both mother and child are doing well. (See story: "Christmas Eve Rescue" page one, 12-26-69.)

It was the birth announcement's last sentence, and its reference to the Tribune's front page story about the Cherry Street accident, (**"Christmas Eve Rescue: Krist Saves Krist's"**) that distracted many readers from the happy news of Dallas Albright's safe arrival.

Because it happened so infrequently, many of the locals were surprised when both the Omaha World Herald (**"Daring Rescue Saves Family"**) and the Des Moines Register (**"Pregnant Woman Saves Kin"**) picked up on the drama and printed feature stories of their own. Remarkably, all three told consistent versions of the same event.

By five o'clock the afternoon's icy precipitation had turned to a light airy snow; Santa's annual visit was saved. Christmas morning saw a high pressure system move in, and with it came clear azure skies and a dazzling holiday sun; temperatures climbed back above the freezing mark making the streets and sidewalks of Freeland once more safe for pedestrians and cars. During that same stretch of time, Elaine Christensen received two pints of blood along with twelve stitches to her forehead, Barbara Krist was treated for two fractured ribs and frostbite to her fingers and toes, while Johanna Krist was immobilized, sedated, and placed in the surgical cue to repair a broken right hip.

While all of that was going on, Dallas Gordon Albright was born. Among the noteworthy that share his date of birth (but none of his DNA) include: General George "Blood and Guts" Patton, multimillionaire and notable recluse, Howard Hughes, the drug-addled bass player for Motörhead, Lemmy Kilmister (aka, Ian Fraser), and, of course, the proclaimed son of God, Jesus Christ.

Thanks in part to the Cherry Street accident, the baby arrived eighteen days before his due date. The doctor on duty was Dr. Raymond Peterson.

An osteopath and intense stickler for detail, Dr. Peterson would write in his hospital report, "Technically, the Albright delivery cannot be considered premature. Mrs. Albright was in the thirty-eighth week of the pregnancy." His personal notes go on with lengthy and gratuitous praise for the hospital staff, the nurses, the mother, and the baby in what he defined as a "textbook delivery. All parties performed exactly as expected." These professional commendations mark one of the few times that such a statement will ever be made about Dallas Albright.

Because people seem to need to do it - and it is, after all, the season for stories - every Christmas/birthday Dallas Albright will be forced to endure the enthusiastic retelling of his own birth story. From the point of pure drama he's got a good one, except every year when the story arrives - and it arrives every year - the narrators fail to consider how their annual recitation of the Cherry Street adventure might affect Dallas' long-term perspective. In hindsight, it might have been unfair that his kin assumed his first Christmas was always going to be his most important.

After the obligatory four days, Emily and her small healthy baby were discharged from the Freeland Community Hospital. Emily's mother, Johanna was not so lucky.

The accident on Cherry Street where Elaine Christensen had slipped and fallen on Johanna resulted in a Type Two (complete, but not displaced) fracture of the femoral neck; in lay terms, a broken hip. From a forensic perspective, the damage to the head of Johanna's femur could not specifically be attributed to her fall. Although the icy pavement was certainly hard enough, and Johanna was demonstrating the first signs of osteoporosis, it was more likely that the direct application of Elaine's velocity and weight to the vulnerable bone caused the injury. After an unpleasant bit of surgery, followed by a regiment of mind-numbing and highly addictive drugs, Johanna Krist would require three months of bed rest and serious physical rehabilitation before she would recover her mobility.

The elephant in the room was, of course, the *other* voice. Before the summit with Barbara Krist and the Cherry Street accident, whatever was happening to Johanna's mind seemed to Emily conveniently far away. The combination of infrequent telephone conversations, and the fact that they were five hundred miles apart, had allowed Emily to rationalize her mother's peculiar behavior. If she thought about it, Johanna's moods seemed more confusing than concerning. But that convenience had changed now that Emily had experienced the *other*, and personally witnessed its effect on her mother. For this version of her *lucky life,* Emily Krist Albright was about to suffer a serious reorganization of plans.

Anxious to make arrangements for maternity leave, Emily had met with her boss at WGN television in early November, almost two full months before Dallas was born. At the time, she imagined those first six weeks to be joyfully spent in their new Chicago apartment attending to the new baby's needs. If it worked out like she had scripted, after the first forty-five days Charles would obviously see that the baby needed a full-time, stay-at-home mother, and would insist that she give up her job for the child. Only now, thanks to the Cherry Street accident, there were all these unexpected and worrisome changes to the plan. Instead of a happy mommy-life in the suburbs, Emily Albright was now confronted with a long list of bleak questions starting with her role in her mother's convalescence.

On the other hand, Charles had no qualms about extending his time away from the Bear Sterns' offices. He'd had an especially good year and left Chicago for the Christmas holiday in the good graces of both his boss and the partners.

For the big boys at Bear Sterns, Charles Albright had finally arrived, and it was about damn time. In those eighteen months since his father's passing, the Northwestern preppie had moved up a class. No longer just a suit with an advanced degree, thanks to his hard work and personal commitment, Charles had become one of their best closers.

Of course, he had his own elephant in the room - his grandmother. Everyone from the partners to the janitors understood that his best asset - better than his good looks and personal charm - was his grandmother, Lillian Campbell. Now thanks to the generosity of Otto Campbell's widow, a new and especially lucrative list of prospects was being made available to her fortunate grandson.

Naturally, the bosses and the big boys had been accommodating. They recognized that these things take time, and that a certain level of trust had to be reached before a young man could be expected to fully exploit a resource as substantial as Lillian Campbell. People in the corner offices were all smiles whenever Grandmother Lillian would unexpectedly pop in for a visit; she was, after all, still one of the city's best-known and most influential socialites. It remained mostly unspoken, but everyone was expecting great things from Charles Albright - especially Lillian Campbell.

There had been a confusing and uncomfortable moment at the office Christmas party when his highly inebriated boss (Stephen Chance Arlington) had stumbled into him just outside the men's room. With one arm draped heavily across Charles' shoulders, the staggering drunk somehow managed to reach into his coat pocket without spilling his Dewar's.

"Keep it up, Albright," he mumbled before shoving a very serious bonus check into Charles' breast pocket.

When the thick fool unexpectedly embraced him, Charles thought he could feel the world around him constrict.

"So," he wondered, "this is what success is supposed to feel like?"

Later, while sitting in Emily's hospital room on that first Christmas morning, anxiously holding his newborn son and looking straight into the face of the future, he turned back to reconsider the question: "Is this the best I can do?"

The first time this surprising indecision surfaced was in the early days of Emily's pregnancy. On that occasion, he dismissed it as just the normal nerves of an expectant father. Only they persisted. In the next few weeks, there seemed to be even more of these aggravating moments, flashes where his normally disciplined mind would unexpectedly wander off-center. It wasn't just the annoying lack of focus that troubled him, it was the emerging sense that he needed to defend his own life's choices.

To keep his balance he started building rationalizations.

"There's nothing to worry about, really. After all," he told himself, "I designed this course myself. This is my plan, and damn it thanks to all of my hard work it's about to pay off. It won't be long before there'll be enough so that I can do for my family what my father did for his.

Of course there are heavy expectations, but that's the price everyone pays, right?"

By December 1969, things were changing fast. The passion that had fueled the decade's cultural overload had become as diluted as its good intentions; inertia was all that kept the great social experiment stumbling forward. Everything was still shifting, and just as unpredictably, but now it was without the benefit of a recognizable enemy. The summer's relentless procession of death (Kent State, Brian Jones, Tate-LaBianca...) had perfectly presaged the end of the century. The very thing people had come to trust was no longer trustworthy. Dylan was headlining in Vegas. Nixon was a clown on Laugh-In. And Woodstock, well, Woodstock begat Altamont didn't it.

For those elite who ran ahead of the curve there was no question it was time to move on, to find something different, simpler, more pure. Things had gotten so bad that wherever there were people there were hassles. The air was gray, and the rivers were catching fire. The search was on for the next place guaranteed to set your soul free. It turned out it that it was *Up on Cripple*, and if you hurried, there was still time to get back to the land.

In contrast to those hipsters who were now raising their own, Charles's colleagues at Sterns were closing off, barring the windows, and padding their accounts. They'd replaced their tie-dye for Brooks Brothers, grass with Stolichnaya, and free love with a second wife and a balloon mortgage. To the hustlers at Bears, "Trust no one over 30" was as corny as it was sentimental. The new executive notion of ethos had shifted from the inside out, to buttress a modern and warped version of the American work ethic. For the brethren, the cliché of "hard work" was now code for "ruthless" and conveniently replaced the childish assumption that integrity was a virtue.

Charles worried, "did I miscalculate somewhere? I wonder who you can trust with that kind of question."

There was his family, of course, the long line of success where each in their own way had signed on to the contract. As far as Charles could see they all appeared to be the better for it.

But on that Christmas morning, sitting there on that hard, straight-backed hospital chair and looking down on his own child's utterly dependent face, Charles Albright made a decision, a kind of pledge. In his own sweet naiveté, Charles decided he would never lay that kind of expectation on such a beautiful face. That's what he said that day, and he knew he meant it, but in this version of his *lucky life* there will be many situations that will help him - compel him - to forget that promise.

Chapter Six

Jonas Weber Makes an Offer

"You have not known what you are —
you have slumber'd upon yourself all your life."
Leaves of Grass – Walt Whitman

The day after Christmas, June and Ingrid offered their personal gift to the Albright's.

"Under the circumstances," June began, "we'd like to have the three of you come and stay with us. We've got plenty of room. You can stay as long as you need, and we won't take no for an answer."

The "circumstances" to which June so politely alluded was Johanna's convalescence. Mumbling through the Demerol, Johanna had made it clear that she did not intend to become "Grandma Saffii's roommate." Confronted with that harsh ultimatum, Charles began considering options, particularly the condition of the little house on Locust Street. If she was to return there would need to be serious structural changes to accommodate both her physical and mental convalescence.

"This is no small job, Em," Charles told his wife. "It's going to require professional carpenters, plumbers, and electricians. Not to mention a boatload of money."

Once again the solution to another of Emily's life-challenges was provided by a surprising source.

June Steffens moved back to Freeland soon after Emily and Charles were married. Her unexpected decision came as a surprise to the newlyweds, but as June explained, her father had grown weary of the life of a traveling insurance salesman and was planning to open his own agency in the nearby town of Greenfield. He was hoping that his daughter would return to manage the office.

There was a great deal of speculation among the local busybodies about why David Steffens chose to open an insurance office in Greenfield rather than his own hometown of Freeland. The gossip's reasoning was simple: the more time he spent in Greenfield the less time he would be spending with Ingrid. According to these nosy parkers, if he permanently moved back to provincial little Freeland there would be an expectation that he either divorce his wife of twenty-six years, or live with her. For David neither of these were compelling options. In his mind divorce was the same as failure, something he equated with Arnold Palmer's disastrous back nine at the Olympic G & C, or Sam Sneed's triple bogey on the Spring Mill 18th. By extending this reasoning, Ingrid was and always would be his wife; he just didn't love her, or want to live with her. Such a self-serving point of view satisfied David's needs to a tee, while reaffirming Ingrid's conviction that men were a plague. Regrettably, their ongoing marital conflict kept sweet June trapped in the middle.

David Steffens' insurance office was a success from the day he opened the front door. This was due largely to his long and successful history in the insurance business, a thorough knowledge of the products, and his remarkably convivial nature. Other than the testy relationship he maintained with Ingrid, everyone else found David Steffens a charming and pleasant man. Within weeks of his arrival in Greenfield the insurance man had become an active and enthusiastic community volunteer, happy to serve on any local board or committee that would take him. With David Steffens around town celebrations and parades never lacked for a chairman. He was so generous with his time that he even took on those jobs that no one else wanted, including dressing up as Santa for the Chamber's annual *Toys for Tots* giveaway.

So how could this apparently kindhearted man have such a miserable relationship with the only woman he had ever loved? What made this couple so bitter that they could find no patience for one another?

It certainly wasn't their children; by this point, both were grown and on their own. Although hardly wealthy, the Steffens didn't want for much, despite the doubly expensive life of separate cars and homes. Both were reasonably healthy, their parents were still alive, and each had a cadre of friends that seemed to fill the gaps left by their testy marriage.

So how was it that in this version of their *lucky life* the one person with whom they had the most in common was also the one person that they dread being around. A remarkable waste, but because a *lucky life* assumes an infinite number of permutations, you can assume that in at least one of them David and Ingrid Steffens will find a happier and healthier relationship; just not this one.

June agreed to move back to Freeland and into the old green house with the stipulation that Ingrid never complain about her work, or her father. Every morning at seven o'clock she would dutifully pilot her beige '62 Chevy Nova the fifteen miles to Greenfield, stopping along the way at Dally's Bakery to pick up two dozen doughnuts and a sack of ginger snap cookies. By eight she had unlocked the door and flipped over the cardboard "We're Open" sign.

It didn't take long before the locals began to wander in for a cup of coffee and the local gossip. Fully cognizant of the power in a jelly doughnut, David Steffens had strategically made the lobby of his office the home for Greenfield's new early morning coffee clutch. By nine o'clock, the enterprising Mr. Steffens had secured more business than he would see the remainder of the day.

Business boomed and with it came the opportunity to expand. After just six months on the job, June decided to get her insurance licenses and was soon writing protection for life's inevitable calamities. Like her father, June was both a quick study and utterly likable; so likable that most of their new business was by referral. There will be one particular referral that is critical to this version of Emily, Charles, and Dallas Albright's *lucky life*.

Keith Traugott - the giant boy who had taken June to the junior-senior prom - learned from a classmate that she had recently moved back to the area. It was a fact that Keith did not go to the Steffen's insurance office specifically for insurance; it did, however, take nearly a month for the big man to screw-up enough courage to call on her, June being the one and only girl he had ever asked on a date.

After four long tough years, Keith was still living with his parents on their cattle farm north of Freeland. No one could say that he hadn't done his best to get along with his ornery father, Ottman Traugott, but the emotional distance between the son's natural passivity and the father's explosive temper ultimately forced Keith out of the livestock business and into one better suited to his skills and temperament: carpentry.

It was obvious that in both heart and hands Keith Traugott had inherited his maternal grandfather's quiet temperament and skill at woodworking. While in high school, Keith earnestly studied all the practical class work that they offered. Still, it took another four tiresome years before his *lucky life* provided him a welcome apprenticeship with a local German craftsman, Jonas Weber. It was welcome because a steady job in a trade that he loved finally allowed him to escape his father's home and harsh treatment. An unexpected bonus was that Jonas Weber's temperament was the antithesis of what Keith had experienced at home. Deliberate, precise, and affable are three good qualities for a finish carpenter.

It was late on Friday afternoon. June was rushing to fill out the three new contracts she'd signed just that day. If she hurried she could still get them in the day's mail before the long Labor Day weekend started.

"Excuse me, June?" said a familiar voice.

"Be right with you," she replied, her back to the front door.

"That's okay. Take your time."

June stopped licking the final stamp and then turned to face the customer. Keith offered a meek smile before ducking his head.

"Keith?"

"Hi, June," he mumbled into his giant chest. "How are you?"
It was all he could think to say, but it was enough.

"When do you think you could start?"

Keith Traugott ran a giant hand along the door frame that separated the Krist's small living room from an even tinier enclosed porch.

Without looking at Charles, he replied, "Well, it isn't up to me. But I guess I can talk to Mr. Weber and see what he thinks. With Christmas and everything, we're kinda in between jobs."

Keith then looked over at June, Emily, and the baby who were observing from the kitchen door. There was a lovely moment - an invisible connection between June and Keith - and then he added, "But I could do a drawing of what you want, and then maybe put some numbers down, at least so you could get an idea of what it'll cost. It won't be a bid or anything, but it would be in the ballpark. Just so you've got an idea of what it'll cost, I mean."

Emily reached down to take June's hand, and then offered, "That would be great, Keith. We really appreciate this. Mom will get released from the hospital sometime next week, and Ingrid's been so sweet to let us stay at her house until we decide what we're going to do with this room. So you can see it's kind of important to get going right away. You know my mother; she's made it clear that she doesn't want to go up to Old Oaks."

Charles looked up at Keith (who was nearly a foot taller) and added, "You know, Keith. I'm going be here for at least another week, maybe I could help somehow? I mean I don't know much about carpentry, but I could help with the demolition."

"That might be okay," Keith replied. "If you want, once we get the plan approved and an okay from Mr. Weber, then you and I could seal the porch and get on with taking out this wall. It'll be cold work outside, but we could do the inside at night."

Like everyone in Freeland, Jonas Weber had heard about the Cherry Street accident and wanted to help. After a short meeting where he looked at Keith's drawings and the numbers, he agreed to take on the project. The next afternoon, Keith and Charles began sealing the exterior windows and preparing the interior space. The little bit of furniture that Emily planned to keep was moved out of the room and stored in the green tool shed, the very one where she'd lost part of her pinkie.

For the next week, Charles did his best to help Keith as they began the job of converting the long neglected rooms into a livable space. By New Year's Eve, the old living room had been gutted in preparation for expanding out onto the porch.

Although no one could have known it at the time, the couple's decision to bring in the New Year in Johanna Krist's barren living room was especially prophetic. The lawn chairs brought over from Ingrid's garage, the pizza on paper plates, the radio playing the wonderful eclectic hits of the past year, (*Bridge Over Troubled Water, Close to You, American Woman, Let it Be, I'll Be There, Spill the Wine, Fire and Rain, Evil Ways...*) and, of course, the pass-around, six-day old baby Dallas, provided everyone a brief sense of optimism. The cheap champagne helped, but just being together felt good and right, like something that should last. No one made it to midnight, but the make-believe countdown and kisses at ten o'clock were just as real and heartfelt as anyone experienced on Times Square. Tomorrow was a new day, a new year, and a new decade. At that moment, it all seemed so shiny and wonderful.

"Emily, I'd like to ask you to think about something, but don't answer right away, okay?"

It was nearly ten-thirty when she finished giving Dallas his late night bottle. She laid the newborn baby in the crib and then turned to face her husband who was sitting on the edge of the bed holding one boot, the other still on his foot. Both June and Ingrid had retired. The house was dark and quiet.

"Okay," she answered with an obvious tone of skepticism, her arms tightly folded across her chest.

"Not a particularly open pose," he thought before he spoke.

"Well, here's the thing. The last two weeks have been a real eye-opener for me. I can't tell you how much I've enjoyed working with Keith and Mr. Weber and the guys. You know I've never worked with my hands like this, but there's something really satisfying about it. I can't exactly put my finger on it, but at the end of the day you can see what you've accomplished. There's something gratifying about that. You know?"

Emily smiled and nodded. At this point she was not altogether surprised by her husband's remarks, it was apparent that Charles had thrown himself into the job and was making his usual energetic effort to be both helpful and encouraging. After a day or two, the workmen had grown accustom to having the extra hands around, and found jobs where he could help, even if meant just pushing a broom. When there wasn't something specific to do, Charles would observe from a respectful distance and then follow-up during a break with technical questions about what they'd just done. Both Keith and Mr. Weber were also conscious of his interest and had begun taking extra time to show Charles some of the more technical aspects of the work, particularly those things that had to do with money and time.

By the end of the second week, the crew had finished the rough carpentry and had moved back to the cabinet shop to make room for the plumbers and electricians. Charles remained on the job site and observed as two new trades were introduced. A week later, Keith and Mr. Weber returned to finish the job.

"Well, anyway," Charles said while unlacing the other boot, "this afternoon I had an interesting talk with Mr. Weber. Keith had run down to the lumberyard to pick up the rest of the quarter round and some paint, so it was just the two of us."

Emily sat down on the opposite side of the bed.

"He confided in me, I guess. First, he asked what I thought of Keith. So, I told him we thought he was a great guy, and that we were happy about how he and June were getting on. He agreed and said he was happy about it, too. But then he asked whether I thought Keith could manage a business. It was so out of the blue, but I was honest with him and said that I didn't really know. It seemed like he was good at the carpentry, but maybe not so good at the business. No knock on Keith, but, I mean, he's not really trained to manage a business, and I'm not sure he's even interested."

The baby moved in the crib and momentarily distracted Emily from the story. "Go on," she said as she stood and peered down into the crib at the sleeping child.

"Anyway, here's the strange part," Charles continued. "Mr. Weber and I were sitting there in the kitchen having a cup of coffee and waiting for Keith when he asked me how I liked the carpentry business. He said it looked like I was enjoying myself and getting along pretty well. I told him that I did enjoy the work, but asked what he had in mind. So he came out with it. He asked if I'd like to buy his business. He said he was ready to retire, but he wanted to take care of Keith and the other fellows. He told me that even though the guys were good carpenters, none of them could make the business decisions. I guess after getting to know me a little, he thought maybe I'd be interested in a change. Can you imagine that?"

Emily kept her promise and didn't say anything, but instead undressed and put on her pajamas. She climbed into the bed, plumped the pillows, and then leaned back against the wooden headboard.

"It sounds like you're interested in this."

"I don't know, maybe," Charles replied as he pulled on his pajama shirt and then slid into bed.

With a last look into his wife's face, he reached over to switch off the overhead light, and then lay his head on the pillow. For a moment, they remained silent in the dark room.

"I know this is so crazy," Charles began, "but I've been thinking a lot about the future, and now out of the blue this thing presents itself. It's crazy, right? But it may be something that's worth thinking about. What do you think? Could you live here in Freeland and be this close to your mother?"

Emily lay down and rolled over to face her husband. She could see through the frosted bedroom window beyond their feet to the colored holiday lights on the house across the street. In the crib beside her, the Christmas baby, wrapped in his heavy blanket, slept peacefully. The rest of the house was still.

The last thing Emily offered, at least until she would wake again for the two A.M. feeding, was this thought, "I'm not sure about my mother, but have you considered what you'd say to Lillian?"

The next week Charles returned to Chicago by himself.

The work on Johanna's house was finished and the new furniture had been delivered. Pushing her wheelchair through the door and into the bright new space delivered one of the most intensely satisfying moments that Charles Albright had ever experienced. It wasn't just Johanna or Emily's appreciation for all the hard work and money that he'd spent. What he was feeling was the kind of intense satisfaction one gets from something that has been done well. He'd certainly known that feeling, but not from something quite so personal. He could look anywhere in the room and see his mark, a place where he had labored. It was special, and he wanted more.

Charles boss at Bear Sterns (the Christmas drunk) was utterly flabbergasted by his letter of resignation. Chance, as he insisted people call him (although everyone who knew him preferred Steve) offered only this encouraging farewell, "You are an absolute idiot."

His plan was to begin at Sterns, and then once irrevocably committed move on to the far more intimidating prospect of meeting with his grandmother. After some thoughtful deliberation, Charles chose the neutral ground of the Coq d'Or in the Drake Hotel, a place that was both familiar to his grandmother, and particularly public.

"Oh, Charles, it is wonderful to see you," Lillian Campbell exclaimed as she breezed into the hotel's bar.

"Thank you, George," she said handing the barman her fur coat without bothering to look at him. "Would you be so kind and bring me a champagne cocktail, please?"

George acknowledged her request and had begun to walk away when Lillian spoke over her shoulder, "Oh, George, I've changed my mind. After all, we're celebrating. Bring the whole bottle and a glass for my grandson." With a beaming smile, she then turned her full attention back to embrace her grandson, and asked, "Now, tell me, how is that baby?

Holding his grandmother's chair as she sat down, Charles considered the question carefully, after all, the last three weeks had arguably been three of the most dramatic in his life. Where should he begin? There was the baby, the accident, Johanna's health, or perhaps the real reason he'd come to Chicago, which was to tell her that he was moving his family - her family - five hundred miles west to a tiny rural community in Southwest Iowa?

"Dallas is good, Grandmother. Emily did a wonderful job. He's healthy and happy and beautiful. We're so fortunate. I mean, under the circumstances, with the accident and everything. Emily was amazing."

Charles was prepared to carry on about "amazing" Emily's experience on Cherry Street, except George had returned with the champagne and was now hovering over his grandmother. Lillian turned to consider the label on the green bottle before absently waving her hand in an unspoken approval. After an elaborate procedure clearly staged to please Mrs. Campbell, George silently dislodged the cork into his white towel. The lanky waiter then majestically poured the tiniest sample for Grandmother Lillian to taste. "Fine," was all she said, and then held out her glass for the barman. After filling her glass, and then pouring one for Charles, George carefully packed the bottle into the nearby ice bucket. In a rather haughty and overplayed whisper, he then asked, "Will there be anything else, Mrs. Campbell?"

"Not right now. Thank you, George. I want to hear all about my new great-grandson."

Charles chose the high road and began his story with the delivery of the baby; only it wouldn't have mattered, the moment that the story lingered on any of the other topics great grandmother Lillian Campbell would interject a question that forced Charles to return to the baby Dallas. They were on their second glass of champagne before he'd even gotten to the renovation of Johanna's house.

"So, Charles, you haven't said anything about when Dallas and Emily will be returning. I can't tell you how anxious I am to see that baby."

Recognizing his moment of truth, Charles set down the empty champagne flute and screwed-up his courage.

"Well, actually, Grandmother, they won't be back for a while. See as I started to tell you, I remodeled Johanna's house so that she could get around better while her hip is mending. Anyway, we've decided that Emily and Dallas will stay in Freeland and help with her convalescence."

Grandmother Lillian stiffened in her seat, but her expression remained affectedly neutral.

"What about Emily's position at the station?"

"Yes, her job. You see both Emily and I have resigned our jobs. We've decided to make a change, Grandmother. An opportunity has come along, and both of us think that it would be the right thing for the family to move to Freeland, I mean."

He studied her restrained features and tried to imagine what was going through her mind. A rumble of anxiety rippled in his stomach that made him wish he'd consumed something more than the champagne.

"It seems that there is more to celebrate than I had anticipated," she offered, in a remarkably upbeat tone.

Now silent and attentive, Grandmother Lillian listened as Charles re-engaged his scripted story starting with the Cherry Street accident, Dallas' birth, June and Keith's rekindled relationship, the remodeling of Johanna's house, and then closing with an upbeat retelling of Mr. Weber's offer to buy his business.

"I'm as surprised as anyone, but I believe that I've found something I want to do with my life. This work gives me a real sense of accomplishment and satisfaction. It's something that I really need. So, we're going to move to Freeland, Iowa and start a whole new adventure."

"Oh, Charles, it will all go by so quickly."

Fanned out in front of them were the four photos that Charles had brought of Emily and the baby.

"You try to hold on to it, try everything you can to keep it from slipping away, but before you know it all those memories become hazy until all you're left with are flashes, little short movies of your life."

With a smile she picked up the photo, the one that featured Emily and baby Dallas sitting in the wooden rocking chair that he'd just bought from Jonas Weber.

"Keep them close, dear boy. When you reach my age you'll be glad that you did."

This was the first time he'd ever heard his grandmother date herself with regret. Her unexpected confession felt odd and out of place; after all, it was other people who suffered and complained about getting old, Lillian Campbell lived above it all. In Charles estimation his grandmother was utterly unique and vital, truly invincible. "Who knows," he thought, "she just might live forever."

"I know you deserve the chance to make something for yourself," Lillian offered. "You've earned it. Few young people have worked as hard as you. I just wanted it to be here. It's selfish, I suppose, but here in Chicago I can help you."

The champagne was gone; all that was left were two empty glasses. The bar was beginning to fill with hotel guests; beautiful people, some in evening clothes, who laughed and carried on as if they were the only ones in the room, and in that version of their *lucky life* they were.

"So much has changed since your grandfather and I were your age. I often dream about what it would have been like if he had lived. I imagine we would have stayed in politics, but it would have been hard for him, he didn't care much for television. He thought it was too personal, too close. And now, well, it just overwhelms us, doesn't it. Can you imagine your grandfather on a television advertisement?"

"I loved his career, and all that we achieved together," she added wistfully. "He was a fine man, Charles; honest and driven like you. But these days a life in politics will dirty even the cleanest soul."

Eventually the conversation turned back on itself.

"It looks as if I will need to rethink my plans. I was hoping that at some point you'd be taking my place, after all someone's going to have to manage the Campbell resources, and believe me there are several out there just waiting for the chance. It makes me so resentful and tired. It's not like I haven't given my share. But I must confess I've lost some of my enthusiasm. I can't help them as much as before, and I simply refuse to be seen as just another old woman with money."

"Oh, Grandmother, you'll never be seen as 'just' anything."

If he'd seen it on someone else's face, that small smile, he might have interpreted it as demure, perhaps even shy. Then she quickly added with a confident nod, "In our day, Charles, we moved mountains."

A moment passed before Charles asked, "Are you disappointed in me?"

"Oh, dear, how could I be?"

She reached across the table and took her grandson's hand in her own.

"I don't like to admit this, but Charles, you are very much like your father."

Then lightly squeezing his hand, she added, "I'm not sure that this is a virtue, but Gordon Albright was completely comfortable in his own skin."

Then she chuckled, and added, "I may have resented that the most."

Chapter Seven

Dallas Albright – Beautiful Boy

"Atoms are not things, they are only tendencies."
Werner Heisenberg

Dallas Albright - the beautiful boy - lived his life like water, always seeking the simplest way, the lower ground; drifting indifferent to his own promise and potential; indefensibly confident that whatever path he was on was the path meant to be.

Once at a parent-teacher conference, Dallas' second-grade teacher had boldly confessed to his mother that there were times when she would look at the boy and be reminded of "the shimmer on a tranquil stream. You know, beautiful, gentle, and effortless." Not especially surprised or offended by the observation, Emily Albright smiled, politely, and then encouraged the now blushing and uncomfortable teacher to proceed with her more academic assessments. Only later, after she'd learned of Dallas' apathy for his schoolwork and subsequent poor marks, would she regret not asking whether the teacher's curious observation was intended as a compliment or a warning.

In *Ode to a Grecian Urn*, Keats confidently proclaims that, *"Beauty is truth, truth beauty, that is all ye know on earth, and all ye need to know."* Given the dated language and hyperbole, it's no surprise that his poem rarely makes an appearance anywhere outside the high school classroom. Still, Mr. Keats is right about one thing: Physical beauty is its own advantage. The beautiful boy would come to understand and enjoy this advantage at a very tender age.

This notion of mistaking beauty for truth is not an especially new one. Back in 1886, Doctor Emile Hirsch (the doctor and evolutionary biologist who cared for Saffii Moeller and the good people of La Crosse) would craft a remarkably practical hypothesis about why we treat pretty people the way we do.

"There is something appealing and enticing about a beautiful face," he proclaimed. "Over time, Nature has left us predisposed to trust beautiful people. The more beautiful, the more we assign them traits of kindness, integrity, even intelligence; whether they are earned or not."

In those first five years, the beautiful boy enjoyed a predictably normal life. From the start there appeared to be an especially quick mind and the absence of any major medical problems. Along with the customary overindulgent affection provided a first-born, his parents also bestowed upon him a heavy dose of their own genetic code. The result was a person roughly three-quarters the size of his peers.

For some children this smaller stature might have seemed a hindrance or obstacle, but in the case of Dallas Albright it only seemed to amplify his physical beauty and personal charm. Unlike other children, the beautiful boy carried himself with such an unexpected level of detached confidence that it confused his peers, and gave adults the impression he was looking down on them. This supercharged ego left him standing on the outside looking in, contentedly alone in a friendless lonely place that people hope to avoid. It was this uncommon trait of utter self-assurance that left the good people of Freeland confused, and mostly cold.

In the early '70's, Freeland, Iowa was a safe and reasonable place to raise children. There were, however, notable shortcomings.

For one thing, the community lacked any kind of racial diversity. The significance of such a statement is revealed in this remarkable fact: In spite of being born in 1970, Dallas Albright will not meet a person of color until he is sixteen-years-old. This important experience will occur in the confines of the Anamosa Juvenile Detention Center.

As far as some folks were concerned this deficit of diversity was not specifically a problem. For them the problem was color: the browns, the yellows, and the blacks. Among this vocal minority, the colors and their tribulations were viewed as a phenomenon exclusive to larger cities, and those misguided souls who lived in the South. It was because of these color's problems that this subset of sanctimonious Freelander's lived exactly where they lived.

For this noisy group, teachers - especially high school teachers - were another population that required close scrutiny. Until their intentions and politics were made clear, and this assessment often took many years, the locals viewed new instructors with either skepticism or outright distrust. Highly personal matters such as a teacher's appearance, their religious affiliation, or even their choice of friends were dissected and analyzed by the local busybodies before being blessed or indicted. So tenacious was their sleuthing, so obvious was their method, that many of the new faculty felt ostracized upon arrival; snubbed by the very community that had hired them to teach their children. Naturally, the newcomer's reaction to this intense surveillance was to avoid those that made them feel out of favor. Instead of trying to become a part of the community, it was safer to seek comfort among their peers and spouses. To those intolerant citizens who saw no value in an outsider's perspective, this kind of meek behavior provided all the validation they needed to condemn them as an interloper.

Ignorance and economics only made the problem worse; it was a particularly bitter pill when even the youngest and most inexperienced teacher made more money than they. The length of their summer vacation, a paid summer vacation at that, only added to the suspicion that teachers and their damnable unions were somehow holding the local tax payers hostage. Their mistrust was confirmed when most new teachers would stay in Freeland only as long as it took to find a higher paying job somewhere else.

Culture and the arts, especially modern art, ("My three-year old could paint better than that") were held suspect, or more often ignored altogether. Access to a theater or museum meant traveling sixty miles to Omaha, which was something most folks generally did but once. Craftwork and artwork were interchangeable words. In this case, a colorful handmade quilt that had won a blue ribbon at the fair would be considered as valuable and artful as any classical painting. For the good people of Freeland, art was obviously in the eye of the beholder.

Restaurants were few and fell into four categories: roadhouses, diners, buffets, or the sort where you were expected to roll down the window and shout your request at a metal box. The notion of fine dining not only embraced the quality of the fare, but also took into consideration quantity and price.

The hospital and the medical community endeavored to keep abreast, but without the latest procedures and access to expensive equipment, they were professionally obliged to send more and more of their patients to the larger nearby cities. Once this practice began there was no going back for anyone.

At first, people felt guilty about traveling those few extra miles to the nearby larger communities, but it was there they could find the range of goods and services that the smaller local businessman couldn't afford to maintain. Just a few miles down the road were the larger towns where there were enough people to support, even grow, a stable economy. Thanks to the presence of doctors and dentists, lawyers, and a whole new assembly of professional people, mid-sized communities were attracting those first big box stores - the Wal-Marts, the K-Marts, and the Woolcos. Without dependable local support, the businesses in those smaller towns - towns like Freeland - were undercut and then slowly, torturously bled to death. The inevitable decline in America's heartland was the result of corporate decisions made by invisible people thousands of miles away.

Even though Emily Krist-Albright had been born and raised in Freeland she was not one of them. It was common knowledge that she had moved away, far away, and to the city of Chicago. Then while she was gone she married a "city husband." A nice enough fellow, for sure, but still someone new, someone that had seen more of the world, experienced more than they, someone whose intentions were unclear; an outsider who was not one of them.

From Charles Albright's perspective there was no question that the move to Freeland had been an enormous risk to both his finances and personal relationships. But with his usual determined energy and serious business savvy, Charles was soon able to take the old Weber Construction and turn it into a profitable venture. Thanks to the growth spurt that was happening in the larger nearby communities - the same communities that were enjoying their economic success at the expense of the local Freeland businessman - a small construction boom allowed Charles to expand Weber's original five-man crew to twelve. Within eighteen months, two additional crews were kept busy doing finish work for the new homes they were building on spec, while an additional five men had to be brought in to keep up with cabinet and furniture orders.

This remarkable success did not go unnoticed by the natives. Even though the majority of locals - the silent, stable majority - were glad for the commerce, there were also those whose deep prejudice and jealousy for anything - or anybody - from the outside required that they stay aloof and distant from the innocent Albright's.

But as much as Charles Albright brought to the table there was no question that the success of Weber Construction was the product of a partnership. Along with the initial venture capital, Charles understood the complex business of banking, investments, labor, insurance, and, most important, how to accurately bid their work. But all of that acumen, education, and energy was worthless without Keith Traugott. It would be Keith's lifelong residency and family reputation that opened those first doors and made Weber Construction possible. It was Keith who taught Charles the trade, the value of quality craftsmanship, and the secret inside workings of their little town. Without Keith Traugott, Weber Construction would have failed before it began, and Charles Albright knew it.

Chapter Eight

A Kiss is Just a Kiss

"Who in the world am I?
Ah, that's the great puzzle."
Alice in Wonderland – Lewis Carroll

Dallas Albright's first day of school had little in common with his mother's same experience. Where Emily was panic stricken, Dallas was indifferent. On that first day, Emily had but the one friend - June Steffens - while her son knew a handful of the nearby neighborhood children. Her kindergarten classroom was in a tired ancient building constructed in 1935; her son was part of the first kindergarten class in a brand-new modern facility. Emily walked two blocks, Dallas rode a school bus. Emily was an only child who lived in a tiny little house just east of downtown Freeland. Dallas, and his younger brother Andy, had just moved into a lovely and spacious new home, one that his father's construction company had recently built on the South side of town, the prosperous side of town.

It would be an exaggeration to suggest that a child's character could be defined by a single event, but on Dallas Albright's first day of school he will meet two boys - Will Samuelson and Douglas Capernick - who play essential roles in this version of his *lucky life*. Like Dallas, Will and Douglas were also the first children born into their families, and though physically and intellectually quite dissimilar this common quality of being first-born guarantees that the boys will share a common perspective; one based on a raging sense of guilt for those things both done and undone.

Will Samuelson's father, Eddie was also first-born. A quiet affable fellow, Eddie had cheerfully worked for the city's Public Works Department for the past twelve years. He labored on in the tiny two-person department, not necessarily because he wanted to, but because of his father and wife.

Eddie's father, Corporal Russell Samuelson returned from his European tour of duty in the fall of 1946 partially deaf and mostly crazy after a German land mine detonated under the jeep he was driving. As harsh as that sounds, it seems Russell's *lucky life* dealt him a better hand than the General he was transporting back from the front; the unexpected explosion shattered the jeep's windshield and neatly decapitated the innocent officer, while leaving Corporal Samuelson shell shocked and with a perpetual buzzing in his ears.

Once back in Iowa, Russell inherited the family farm. Coming from a long line of the strict and traditional, Russell expected that his son Eddie would also want to farm those two-hundred-and-twenty acres before bestowing it upon his children. Only in this version of his *lucky life,* Eddie's heart just wasn't in it. After struggling for a year studying soils and farm management at Iowa State University, he eventually crapped-out and returned home with his tail between his legs, defeated and directionless. With nowhere to go, and no real training for anything but the farm, Eddie Samuelson seemed doomed to a life he could neither escape, nor enjoy.

Opportunity presented itself when he unexpectedly discovered his courage and proposed marriage to a former classmate, Marie Tillton; a girl he had secretly loved since the second grade, but had never bothered to tell. Remarkably, she accepted his proposal on two conditions: First, no matter what anyone else wanted, Marie insisted that they always live in their hometown of Freeland; that was fine with Eddie. Second, despite his father Russell's wishes, they could never live on his family's farm but must instead dwell in town. These two reasonable mandates were the result of Marie's powerful familial need to live near her kin (a very large and extended clan that included sixteen first-cousins) and the sad-but-true reality that she suffered horribly from asthma. There was no question that the endless cloud of Iowa farm dust would have made her life a misery.

So instead of the eldest son fulfilling his father's dream of managing the Samuelson family farm, Eddie contentedly took a job with the city of Freeland. There, according to his disgruntled father, he "frittered away the better part of the day standing on the end of a shovel."

Douglas Capernick's father - Stanley P. Capernick - was the President of Freeland's only bank, the Freeland Trust. Thanks to his father's prestigious and profitable position, Douglas and his three younger brothers would grow up in one of the city's few landmarks - the Ehrmann Estate. The ostentatious home, which the jealous locals referred to as "Capernick's cottage," had been built in 1914 by Arnold Ehrmann, the first-born son of the city's founding father, Arvine Ehrmann. In spite of its showy status and ridiculous heating bills, the fourteen-room monster is still proudly described in the National Registry of Historic Places as a "celebrated example of fine 19th century Victorian architecture."

Every Christmas, the Capernick's would hold an open house where Stanley P generously invited the bank's largest depositors to "stop by and share a glass of holiday cheer." The much-anticipated occasion provided the city's worst blabbermouths a free invitation to come and swill Stanley Capernick's liquor, while openly prowling through the closets and cupboards of the beautiful old house. Mrs. Capernick, of course, hated the annual intrusion. Her most recent and misguided attempt at crowd control was to station Freeland High School students throughout the house. This did little good; the students were either intimidated by the belligerent drunks, or complicit in the skullduggery. It is an unfair truth, but most people are fascinated by what lies behind the closed doors of the rich.

On that first day of school, Dallas Albright had not yet met either Will Samuelson or Douglas Capernick. This was not because Freeland was such a large or expansive community (at the time it boasted 4,307 residents) but was rather the result of the standoffish nature of its people. In the short five years that the Albright's had lived in Freeland they had made only a handful of new friends, most of who were in some way connected to the Weber Construction Company. This meant that Dallas and his brother Andy played with the children in their south-side neighborhood. As for Douglas, the Capernick cottage was located in the older established center of town, across the street from Christ's Congregational Church. The Samuelson's humble two-bedroom house sat next to the Evergreen Cemetery on the far northeast side of town. Until that first day of school, proximity and a whiff of prejudice would keep the young boys isolated in their own separate versions of Freeland.

When Dallas and his mother arrived at Kindergarten Classroom B, they found a brand new facility crazy with children and their anxious mothers. Taped to the front of each shiny new desk was a clean white piece of paper bearing a child's name written with impressive clinical precision. Although he couldn't read any of the other names, Dallas did spot his own and anxiously began tugging on Emily's sleeve, pulling her toward his personal place among the chaos.

It didn't take long before the novelty of this first day of school began to wear thin. The night before, Emily had read to Dallas the teacher's letter describing, **"What to expect on your first day of school."** So far, Mrs. Friese had met most of the goals, including: learning the teacher's name, identifying which bathroom was for boys and which was for the girls, the location of the student's cubby, a lengthy and pointed warning never to pull the red-handled fire alarm, and how to sit quietly while others were talking. As vital as this information is to the smooth operation of the classroom, her lengthy remarks were now straining the patience of the eighteen five-year-olds in Classroom B. It was a blessing for both student and teacher when the ten o'clock bell rang for recess, signaling that Dallas and his classmates could finally abandon their desks and the day's assignment of drawing a picture of their family.

A seasoned veteran with twelve years in the trenches, Mrs. Friese had tactically stationed herself by the door and was now waiting patiently for her charges to become quiet before releasing them onto the playground. Dallas, whose desk was in the second to the last row, found himself near the back of the line and therefore one of the last children outside. By the time he finally broke out into the sunshine and then sprinted across the playground, all the swings had been taken, the monkey bars were a tangle of flailing arms and legs, and the merry-go-round was spinning madly on its axis with no sign of ever stopping to take on new customers.

Frustrated, and feeling a bit ignored, Dallas wandered aimlessly back up the hill toward the school building where a group of children, children he did not know, were loudly engaged. To the vigilant Mrs. Friese - who had now assumed a position outside her classroom door - he must have looked especially forlorn.

"Well, Dallas, what do you like to do?" she asked.

At first the boy took Mrs. Friese' question at face-value and had started to construct a reply that highlighted his enthusiasm for watching cartoons, when it dawned on him that she was probably not interested in Bugs Bunny, but was more likely referring to the nearby playground equipment.

He politely regarded his teacher, and then lacking a definitive position offered the fallback kid-reply, "I don't know."

It was at that moment in Dallas' *lucky life* that the two boys who had been playing tetherball on the equipment right next to where the teacher and Dallas were standing stopped their game just long enough for Mrs. Friese to interrupt.

"Boys, do you have a spot for a third player?" The tone of her request suggested that if they did not currently have a place they should find one.

Dallas recognized the taller, dark-haired boy from Kindergarten Classroom B; he sat two rows to his right and one desk ahead. This was Douglas Capernick. The other boy, the smaller sandy-haired kid with the face full of freckles, was a complete stranger. This was Will Samuelson.

In spite of Mrs. Friese's kind effort to include Dallas in the boy's game, tetherball is not a sport that can be played by three. The simple object of the game is to whack the ball in a way that it winds around the pole. You win when the entire rope is strangling the stick. The ball will only go around the pole in one of two directions: clockwise, or counterclockwise. Since the game must be played within our four known dimensions, (length, width, height and time) there isn't much a third party can offer, other than to disrupt and frustrate the efforts of the other two competitors.

"Hey, kid. Stop hitting the ball!" yelled Will.

"Sorry," Dallas replied, but he really wasn't. He didn't like the game, and he wasn't sure he liked these two new boys.

Stepping back to allow them to continue on without him, Dallas looked around the playground eager to spot someone that he knew. The tetherball was now whipping quickly around the post, faster and faster, as the rope got shorter. Douglas, who had clearly played the game before, had his opponent

234

wildly hopping up and down as he tried in vain to keep the yellow ball from touching the pole.

"I win! I win, you loser," Douglas Capernick shouted.

Seemingly unaffected by his defeat, Will grabbed the ball and threw it in the opposite direction apparently hoping for a rematch. The victor, however, had already turned his back on the tether ball to face the new boy in hopes of playing a different kind of game.

"What's your name, kid?"

"It's Dallas. What's yours?

"That's Will, and I'm Douglas. I'm in your class, but he's not. He's got old lady Milton.

After delivering this keen insight with notable confidence, Douglas turned back to yell at Will.

"Loser," he shouted a second time, but got no rise from the other boy. Apparently lost in his own world, Will Samuelson contentedly smacked the tetherball as Douglas' disparaging remark bounced off his back.

With his last attack going untested, Douglas shifted direction.

"You're short, Shorty," he said, slightly amused by what he considered a clever manipulation of adjective and noun.

"So what," Dallas replied in a remarkably calm unaffected voice.

Douglas Capernick considered the beautiful boy for a moment before stating the obvious, "Babies are short."

Dallas remembered what his father had told him about bigger and louder boys and courageously maintained his eye contact.

"Babies aren't shorter," he spit back. "They're smaller, doofus."

Although neither of them understood it at the time, but Dallas bold use of the word "doofus" had drawn an invisible line in the sand. Such an aggressive and unexpected comeback from the smaller boy demanded that the attacker either up the stakes, or fold; physical threats were generally the next level in the jousting, but at five, Douglas Capernick was not yet familiar with this particular protocol and unintentionally overlooked his obligation to corporal intimidation. He instead proceeded straight to what he considered his most formidable attack.

"I'll bet you can't make that girl cry, Shorty."

With a surprisingly evil grin - one that reminded Dallas of Popeye's archenemy, Bluto - Douglas Capernick pointed to a nearby covey of Classroom B girls who were playing an enthusiastic but amateurish game of Four Square.

Dallas turned around to look toward the group as Douglas continued, "The one there in the blue dress. Bet you can't make her cry."

From over Douglas' shoulder, Will chimed in, "Do it, Shorty."

This was certainly not on the list of the kindergarten activities his mother had read to him the night before.

As he considered the two new boys, now standing side-by-side with their hands shoved deep down into the pockets of their shiny new Levi's, Dallas reviewed his options. Although he wasn't especially opposed to making the little girl in the blue dress cry, he couldn't understand why these boys thought that this was something he should do. It was easy to imagine what his mother would think of this kind of behavior, but still there was something niggling inside him that said it would be okay to go ahead and do this little thing just once.

"Maybe," he wondered, as he looked back at the girl, "making new friends isn't always about doing what you're supposed to?"

While Dallas Albright was certain that he had never seen the little girl in the blue dress, this was not true for either Douglas Capernick or the congregation of the Freeland Methodist Church. All of these people would have instantly recognized Debbie Dorsett because her father was their minister and spiritual leader.

In the fall of 1975, Freeland, Iowa boasted seven unique religious denominations, including: Saint Mary's Catholic Church, Saint John's Lutheran Church, the Freeland Methodist Church, the Central Church of Christ, Bible Baptist, the First Church of Christ Scientist, and the Berra Gospel Assembly. Dallas Albright did not know Debbie Dorsett because his family attended the Lutheran church. The Capernick's, however, were Methodist - rather infrequent Methodist - still, Douglas knew both Debbie Dorsett and her parentage. Though it would be years before the tall, black-haired boy would understand irony as a rhetorical device, on this occasion he still thoroughly enjoyed the wicked-pleasure of selecting Debbie Dorsett as a target.

Unlike the three boys, Debbie Dorsett was not the first born in her family; she was third, right in the easily ignorable middle. In the case of the Dorsett's, Debbie and her sibling's birth order was notably balanced: the older two children went girl then boy, while the younger went boy then girl. Contentedly sandwiched between adoring brothers, Debbie Dorsett had no enemies in the world; in fact, she lived such a cloistered life that no one had ever raised their voice to her, let alone their hand.

As he stood considering his victim, Dallas Albright either ignored or chose to overlook two obvious but important details: Debbie Dorsett was also small and also beautiful.

"C'mon, Shorty, we're waiting," Douglas demanded.

"Okay, doofus. Watch this."

The beautiful boy nodded fiercely at the two antagonists, and then marched straight off toward the girls. As he approached the group, Debbie

236

Dorsett was standing with her back to him unaware that anything out of the ordinary was taking place. The other three girls, however, watched with considerable interest as a small determined boy proceeded straight for them. His stern look and mysterious intent was so distracting that the ball they were playing with got away from them and rolled off toward the door to Kindergarten Classroom B. As she silently waited for one of the girls to go and retrieve the ball, Debbie Dorsett was utterly oblivious to the fact that Dallas Albright was now standing directly behind her.

"Go ahead, Shorty. Do it," shouted Will.

Debbie Dorsett heard Will Samuelson's directive at the same moment that she sensed Dallas' presence. She spun around to find that a strange boy, a small and beautiful boy just her size, was now standing right in front of her.

Dallas Albright did not say a word to Debbie Dorsett.

Instead, he smiled pleasantly at the pretty girl. Then quickly leaning forward he kissed her, openly, brazenly, right on the mouth.

It was not an especially long kiss, but everyone present was stunned by this sudden and startling act.

Debbie's first reaction was to push herself away from the beautiful boy, but remain standing in the same spot. She was not crying.

The other three girls simultaneously responded in the only way five-year-old girls respond, they went, "Ewwwww."

Still, Debbie Dorsett did not cry.

Dumbfounded by the kiss, Douglas Capernick managed to ask, "Why'd you do that?" This made the girls go, "Ewwwww," again.

And still, Debbie did not cry.

After twelve years, Mrs. Friese was not only a seasoned veteran of the classroom, but of recess duty as well. This rich experience taught her that it was important to always be on the lookout for odd or incongruent gatherings of students. This assembly certainly qualified.

"Is there a problem here?" she asked.

This made the girls go, "Ewwwww" and Debbie Dorsett cry.

The note that Dallas brought home from school that afternoon was short on detail, but pointed in its expectation.

> Dear Mrs. Albright:
> While at recess this morning, Dallas kissed one of his classmates. We view this behavior as both inappropriate and disruptive. Please instruct your son on proper comportment and manners while at school. This incident has been

reported to Principal Hockney, but is unlikely to go on his permanent record.

Regards,
Harriet Friese

Dallas learned three things from kissing Debbie Dorsett. First, kissing a girl does not always make them cry. Second, a group of girls is called a "giggle." During his private discussion with the bemused Mrs. Friese, she repeatedly used this descriptive synonym in reference to the group of girls playing Four Square. And third, his two new friends did not then, nor will they in the future, always have his best interests in mind.

Chapter Nine

Johanna Krist

"A painter should begin every canvas with a wash of black
because all things in Nature are dark except where exposed by the light."
Leonardo da Vinci

After the fall back on Cherry Street, Johanna Krist's ability to manage her own life was effectively reduced to choosing between the television or the radio, whether the Meals on Wheels should be delivered at five or five-thirty, or if she should pretend to be asleep when her daughter stopped by for a visit. There was always that brief moment of guilt before she hobbled into her bedroom, but it didn't last long. Besides, a moment of guilt was a lot easier to deal with than the *other's* incessant complaining.

It had taken nearly ten weeks of painful rehabilitation before Johanna no longer needed the walker to help her get from the coffee pot back to the kitchen table. The anatomical reduction (realignment) and internal fixation (use of rod and screws) had made it possible for her to walk again, but she was never the same. The slightest chill in the air would send shooting pain from her pelvis throughout her thin frame, sometimes so intense that it would take her breath away.

Even though Johanna did occasionally hide at the sound of her daughter's car, she understood that she should at least act grateful for all that Emily and her husband had done for her. It mostly went unspoken, but the decision to leave their life in Chicago and move to Freeland, not to mention remodeling the old house and all the additional financial help they would provide, had spared her from a premature incarceration at the Old Oaks Retirement Home.

Back in the day, Johanna and Jacob had never considered saving money for a retirement largely because his job as the town's blacksmith brought home only enough to make ends meet. Then there was Pastor Fredrickson's expectation that all the Saint John's families contribute to what he sanctimoniously called their "tender tieth"; an ecumenical euphemism for the usual ten-percent, plus a special private "gift from the heart." Living that close to the bone left little for the future; besides, who could have imagined that the giant man would blow-up his heart and die at the tender age of thirty-eight? The little dab of life insurance Jacob carried, along with a small inheritance that she had received on her mother's death, left Johanna with just enough to get by, but little more.

As for the *other*, it never forgot, nor forgave. From the moment they awoke after surgery there had been a steady stream of carping and criticism about the decision to help Barbara and Elaine back on Cherry Street.

"You wouldn't do what I told you. You just had to go back."

"I couldn't very well leave her in the ditch, could I?" Johanna meekly replied.

"Why not? It's that kind of weak thinking that's left us crippled."

As the months passed their arguments only got louder and more frequent. By the time the beautiful boy was old enough to go to school there were only two ways that Johanna could quiet the quarreling: the first was to take two Pethidine with half a glass of Kabinett, the second was to entertain her grandsons.

"Where is that woman?" Emily wondered as she hung up the phone.

The kitchen windows were open to let in some of the beautiful morning, a light summer breeze stirred the curtains to flutter. Off in the corner of the backyard, Dallas and the ever-present two - Will and Douglas - were digging a remarkably large hole near the spot where only the week before she'd planted a lilac bush. What they planned on doing with or in the hole was unclear; all Emily knew was that this was the third time that morning she'd tried to contact her mother without an answer. Something was not right. After all, it was Johanna who had unexpectedly phoned the night before, insisting that Emily be sure to call her before eight so she wouldn't oversleep and miss her hair appointment.

"Dallas, will you come here, please," Emily shouted through the open window.

The boy looked up from his digging. With no effort to hide an obvious frown, he crawled out of the hole handing the shovel to the smaller of the two boys before slowly ("Too slowly," Emily thought.) ambling back to the house.

While still a good distance away, he shouted at the window, "What do you want?"

Forcing down her impatience from yet another of the boy's endless challenges, Emily replied, "I asked you to come here, please."

"Yeah?" he muttered, as he approached the window. "What do you want?"

"I need you to do something for me. Would you stop what you're doing for a minute and ride your bike over to Grandma's house? I want to know if she's still home?"

Pressing his nose up against the window screen contorted his face into a grotesque expression.

"Why don't you call her?" he asked.

Emily released an exasperated breath.

"I've tried, dear. She doesn't answer. Please, just hop on your bike and go see what's wrong with her phone. It won't take you ten minutes. The hole isn't going anywhere."

The beautiful boy shrugged his shoulders and then turned to shout back at the others, "Hey, come on. We gotta go over to Grandma Jo's and see if she's still alive."

Emily rolled her eyes at the callous remark, but quickly added through the screen, "I want you to go, Dallas; alone. I don't want the other boys to bother your grandmother."

Dallas turned as if he intended to continue the debate, but Emily had already disappeared back into the house.

"Grandma!" the boy shouted, as he pushed open the backdoor and stepped into the little mudroom off the kitchen. "Hey, Grandma Jo, where are you?"

No one answered. The only sound came from the television in the front room.

"Are you sleeping?"

Anxiously peering around the kitchen corner into the living room, he was surprised when he didn't find her dozing in the oversized recliner. Other than the soft drone from the soap opera playing on the television, the room was empty and still.

Stepping cautiously into the familiar space, Dallas noticed that the door to his grandmother's bedroom was almost closed. Through the thin sliver he could just see inside the dark room to where the shades had been drawn and the curtains pulled tight.

Creeping up to the door, he whispered through the crack, "Grandma? Are you awake?"

Nothing stirred; the room remained still as sleep.

Boldly pushing open the door caused a shaft of the morning sunlight to stab across the bed, revealing the boy's shadow over the unmistakable shape of a body.

"Hey, old lady, Mom says you gotta get up. Come on," he shouted as he walked over to the foot of the bed. "Get up!"

His eyes had adjusted to the dim gray light, but the figure in the bed had still not moved. Familiar shapes were emerging from out of the shadows. Next to the door was her old-timey dressing table; its fractured mirror showed a thin black line that ran as straight as a string from corner to corner. A great polished cedar chest, still rich with its sweet sultry aroma, was left at the foot of the bed. Next to the head, up where the boy would not look, sat a dusty nightstand; an ancient transistor radio softly spilt Andy Williams into the background. The photos on the wall, the ones of he and his brother, and especially the larger one of his unknown grandfather, were all staring down at him, apparently curious what he would do next.

Turning to face the lump on the bed, he whispered, "Grandma?"

The boy was surprised and mildly annoyed when he realized that his guts were churning. Both hands were trembling so badly that he forced himself to sit down on the corner of the familiar cedar chest, his back to the silent unresponsive shape on the bed. The touch of the polished wood and the sweet permanent smell of the cedar box instantly reminded him of its contents.

"Holy shit," the eleven-year-old boy said out loud. "I gotta get the stuff out of here."

What Dallas Albright experienced next was that thrilling instant between unhinged panic and calm self-confidence. During the past few months, the beautiful boy had been taught to manage these super-charged emotions by deliberately corralling them, and then taking full advantage of their power. Despite his tender physical age, the boy had already been through enough to know how to quiet a shaky resolve with his intellect and a laser-focused attention to detail.

"I'm not lookin' at you. I'm not," he repeated, inching his way forward toward the head of the bed.

Although this situation was considerably different from anything he'd ever experienced, still he knew exactly what had to happen, exactly where the key to the cedar chest was hidden; he just hated the whole idea of retrieving it.

The bent and aged body of his grandmother lay on her left-side facing away from the door. With the shades and curtains drawn, the room seemed especially close and warm. Her only blanket was a tired comforter that covered her naked feet. On the nightstand next to the bed were several bottles of pills and a mostly empty wine glass. Bent at the elbow, her bony white arm lay impassively on the gray pillow case, a gnarled arthritic hand tucked peacefully beneath her cheek.

The boy moved quickly and without remorse. His hand shot out to grab the thin golden necklace that hung around his grandmother's throat. With a sharp quick motion, he jerked it free from her still body.

Knowing he had only a few minutes to act, he pulled the frayed blanket off of the feet. Ignoring the white-blue ankles and dirty soles, Dallas fit the key into the lock and opened the lid to the cedar chest. Carefully spreading the comforter on the floor, he began to empty the contents of the box onto the blanket: A tall silver chalice that had once proudly sat on the altar at Saint John's Lutheran Church - their first job; there was an ornate and tarnished saber once used by some local patriot during the Civil War, and then proudly hung in the local VFW hall - their trusting nature and unlocked doors made it the simplest of all the jobs; a cracked and tarnished trophy celebrating the 1945 Girl's State basketball championship - why they couldn't have taken a boys trophy always made him cross and resentful; four large gold coins commissioned by the Freeland City Council to commemorate the town's sesquicentennial - these had been boldly lifted from under the nose of the old sourpuss librarian; and the best of all, his personal triumph, a .38 caliber, snub-nosed police revolver that he'd pinched one afternoon from the front seat of the unlocked Sheriff's cruiser.

There was a moment as he pulled together the four corners of the blanket when he considered putting everything back the way it was.

"I could leave it all and let her take the blame. Why not, she's dead. What difference could it make to her?

"Besides," he thought, "we don't really need any of this junk. Maybe the gun, but if we get caught with Sheriff Brayton's gun, well, that's gonna be bad. All this other stuff was her idea. She did all the planning and told us everything to do. Yeah, it was a kill to get away with it, especially fooling all those stupid adults, but none of this junk means anything. Maybe if they find the stuff in this chest they'll blame her? After all, everybody knows she's crazy."

The .38 felt heavy in his hand, heavier than he remembered. He absentmindedly spun the chamber and watched the bullets go around until they stopped and fell into place, a live weapon. Standing to face himself in the cracked mirror, the beautiful boy pointed the revolver at the dim and fractured reflection. If he looked just the right way it seemed like he had two guns and two arms, kind of like being in the funhouse at the fair, except he wasn't, not even close.

Without warning the telephone rang sending a furious jolt of electricity up his spine. By the second ring he knew who was calling.

"Dallas? Is everything all right?" his mother asked.

The beautiful boy paused long enough to work himself into a magnificent frenzy.

"I think she's dead," he shrieked into the receiver. "She's not moving. Mommy, I'm so scared."

Before the ambulance arrived, before his mother, his father, and the Sheriff came, Dallas Albright returned to his grandmother's bedroom.

Dallas made the decision. He made it all by himself because that's the way it had always been. Douglas was the muscle. Will was the lookout. Dallas was the brains. That's how she saw it anyway, and that's how it worked. So when he gathered up the blanket filled with their crimes and cleverness there was no hesitation to consider what the others might want. This was up to the brains.

Slipping out the back door, he quickly lugged the cumbersome package to the tool shed, the very tool shed where his mother had lost her pinkie many years before. There among the tools and ancient trash, Dallas

Albright purposefully hid each item, even the Sheriff's revolver. When he was sure that only he could find them, the beautiful boy grabbed the blanket, and then just before running back to the house he peeked out the door, looking sharply in all directions to be certain no one was watching. Back in the creepy bedroom, he carefully spread the comforter over the dead woman's feet. Without looking back the beautiful boy closed the door and quickly left the house. He wanted to be discovered outside and in tears.

Chapter Ten

A Blue Frisbee

"In a world of thieves the only final sin is stupidity."
*Fear and Loathing in Las Vega*s – Hunter S. Thompson

It took nearly ten days before the three of them could finally dispose of the loot, but even after they'd agreed to throw the stuff down old man Rooney's well there were still serious problems.

The first week was consumed with getting the old woman buried. Since it was his first funeral and everyone's expectation, Dallas forced himself to look sad and weepy, even though he felt nothing. The old woman had made sure he understood how important it was to give people exactly what they wanted.

"You watch 'em, Dallas," she once told him. "People will tell you in their face exactly what they want from you."

So he gave his parents and the few well-wishers that showed-up - which did not include a single Krist - just what they expected: a sad little boy who had lost his grandmother.

After that there was a weird time when his mother either wanted him near her, or was pushing him away; she was as confused as any adult he'd ever known. His father was no better; any effort he made to comfort her would either send her off to the bedroom on yet another crying jag, or straighten her back in anger. To avoid this manic depression, both Dallas and his younger brother Andy would abandon the house as soon as they could get away and not return until supper time.

Dallas was resting quietly in bed, anxious for the light in his parent's bedroom to go off. It had become a nightly habit for the beautiful boy to watch and wait until they retired. Then after he was confident they were asleep, he would quietly slip out of bed and turn on the small portable television that sat on the desk across the room. With the sound carefully muted, he'd quickly jump back into bed and watch as the small screen steadily spread its blue light around the familiar space.

Even though he'd been going through this routine for weeks, there wasn't a favorite program or anything special he wanted to watch; in fact, there wasn't anything on those eighty-nine channels that he imagined was worth his time. What Dallas Albright sought from the steady haze of television flicker was not entertainment, but a way to turn off the day; a method to shut down the infernal noise in his head. The box's monotonous sputter of disconnected colors and shapes had become the only way for the eleven-year-old boy to fall asleep.

It was after eleven o'clock and the light from his parent's bedroom was still on when the door unexpectedly opened. As his father turned back to respond to something that his wife had said, Dallas tapped the television remote control to shut down the box. A moment later, Charles Albright thumped across the hallway and appeared in the boy's half-open doorway. The nightlight that was plugged into the floor outlet next to the desk covered his father's bare feet in soft yellow light, but left his face in the shadows.

"You doin' okay, Champ?"

Dallas rolled over on his right side to face his father. The subdued lighting was making it especially difficult to read his mood. After discreetly sliding the television's remote control under the covers, the boy replied, "Yeah, I guess so."

Apparently hoping for more, Charles entered the room and sat down on the bed beside his son.

"Well, your mother asked me to look in on you. She's worried that maybe you're... well, you know, not doing so well."

"Why doesn't she ask me?"

"I don't know. Maybe she's not doing so well herself."

The boy lay in the darkness thinking about the possibilities in that last sentence, all the while hoping that his father would be satisfied with his answer and go back to bed.

But he didn't. Instead, Charles continued, "Anyway, buddy, we all need to try to keep movin' on. I know you're probably tired of hearing it, but if you ever want to just talk we're here for you."

Hoping that if he didn't reply it might signal an end to the conversation, the beautiful boy rolled over with his back to his father.

"Listen, Dallas," his father asked, "while I'm thinking about it, you know that morning when you were in Grandma Jo's house? You didn't touch anything, or maybe move anything, did you?"

Dallas could feel his throat tighten.

"What do you mean?"

"Well, you know," Charles added, "did you pick something up and maybe set it down in a different place?"

"What's this all about?" he wondered, rolling on his back. Like rewinding a tape recording, he quickly replayed as much of the scene as he could remember. Other than the blanket on the old woman's feet, and the stuff in the cedar chest, he couldn't remember touching anything.

"I don't remember too much," he began. "It was kinda scary, you know? But I don't think so."

"That's okay. No big deal. If you think of something let me know."

Then he was there, bending down over the boy and lightly kissing him on the forehead.

"Good night, Dallas. I love you, son."

On his way out, Charles paused for just a second to glance back at the boy. Offering a weary smile and a nearly imperceptible nod, he pulled the door mostly closed behind him. The light under the doorway went out leaving only the constant yellow glow of the nightlight. The house was still. The only things still running were the clock on the mantle and Dallas Albright's anxiety.

Ehrmann Park is located on the far west side of Freeland. On its best day it is a small decaying city park with few amenities and no charm; its singular point of interest would be a crumbling wooden footbridge that spans Frog Creek, a small and brackish stream that aimlessly meanders through the sparse woods and pitiful picnic grounds. On a hot Wednesday morning in late July, no one who would have thought twice about the three boys sitting at a picnic table near this meager stream.

"Musta been kinda creepy finding Grandma Jo like that?" Will asked. "Did she have her eyes open?"

Without a word or warning, Douglas Capernick mercilessly turned on the smaller boy and slugged him hard in the shoulder.

"Shut up and forget that junk. We got work to do."

The bigger boy quickly turned back to direct his question at Dallas.

"You think it's safe to go get the stuff out of the shed?"

Dallas Albright was sitting across the table with his back to both the boys and the slow-moving water. Looking up from where he'd been mindlessly whittling away on the corner of the table with his red-handled Swiss Army knife, he thought out loud, "No. Not yet; there's still a whole lot of people around the house, you know, digging through her stuff and boo-hoo'n all over the place. It's so bogus. Nobody liked her when she was alive, but now that she's gone..."

He left the thought hanging and went back to defacing the table.

"Well then it won't be too long before somebody else goes out and looks in the shed, will it?" Douglas asked, impressed with his own deep reasoning.

Dallas had been thinking about that, too.

"Who knows," the big kid added, "maybe they've already been out there."

Still nursing his sore shoulder, Will piped up, "Why don't we just go over there tonight and grab the stuff? Nobody'll be watching."

Douglas Capernick turned as if we were going to hit Will again, but the threat of another blow had already sent the smaller boy cowering toward the bank of the stream.

"Shut up," Douglas shouted at the retreating boy, "we need to think. Why don't you go keep a lookout or something?"

Dallas stopped his carving long enough to watch Will Samuelson stumble over to the edge of the dirty water. Even though he never looked back, Dallas knew from experience that the small freckled-face kid was hurt; maybe not so much from being slugged, that happened all the time, no, this was from the words.

Except that was the way it worked; Douglas never had a kind word for anyone, especially Will. Will was such a puppy. He had no other friends, so he was always there, hanging out, waiting for one or the other of them to get done with whatever it was they were doing without him. He wasn't exactly a sad kid, at least you couldn't tell it from looking at him, still nothing he said was ever really appreciated or even welcomed.

Since that first day on the kindergarten playground six years ago, Will Samuelson had stayed pretty much the same. Sure, he'd grown a couple of inches and put on a few pounds, he could even read a little and knew his multiplication tables to times six, but that was pretty much it.

Every Friday morning they made him get on the small bus that traveled over to the "special school" in Alton. As far as Dallas could tell this approach didn't seem to be helping Will in any obvious way; it did, however, provide perfect ammunition for a guy like Douglas Capernick.

"How you getting' along with the head-cases?" he'd laugh. "Anybody get lost today?"

As hard as he tried to hurt Will the kid never once complained, and he never went away. Even when Douglas would lay into him, calling him a "retard" or a "dumb-ass," little Will would only hang his head and shuffle his feet until the bigger boy grew tired and moved on.

Truth be told, Will Samuelson was easily distracted and a lousy lookout.

Douglas Capernick was now standing on top of the wobbly picnic table, his size-10 tennis shoes were inches from where Dallas sat mindlessly carving on the table.

"Come on, man. We need to go and get our stuff before somebody finds it."

Of the three of them, Douglas had physically changed the most. He was a big kid, almost as big as a man, with jet-black hair and cold dark eyes. He liked to fight, and was known to pick them. He generally won. As for school, he was smart enough but never did anything more than what was asked. His father's position as President of the Freeland Trust insured that everyone in town knew him on sight. But that kind of notoriety also required that he keep certain family rules and manners. Any reported departure from the old man's protocols usually meant bad times and bruises for the oldest son.

The odd perspective of looking up at the tall boy against the bright blue morning sky made it seem as if Douglas Capernick had suddenly become a giant.

So, what do you say to a giant?

"Okay," Dallas ceded. "Let's do what Will said and go tonight. He's probably right. No one will be watching, especially the backyard."

Hearing his name, Will perked up. He absently threw the stick he'd been using to dig at the mud out into the stream and then jogged back to join the others.

"What'd I say, Shorty?"

"Shut up, moron," Douglas said, as he jumped down from the table. Then shoving Will in the chest and back out of the conversation, he asked, "What time? Sunset? Dark? Shit, we could go right now. Nobody cares, man."

Dallas knew that wasn't true. There were plenty of people who cared. He cared. In fact, there was nothing he wanted more than to be rid of the stuff. From that first night at the church, he recognized that the things they'd stolen had no real value, they never could. Besides, he'd seen enough movies to know that keeping it around was a sure way to get caught. Even before Grandma Jo kicked, he'd had this nagging feeling that the junk was growing like a chain around his ankles, constantly pulling and dragging on him. His best hope was that by getting free of it he might also shake the grinding feeling that something really bad was about to happen.

"I guess it wouldn't hurt to ride over by the house and scope it out," Dallas offered.

They had climbed on their bikes and were just getting ready to leave when the Douglas unexpectedly reached out and grabbed the handlebars on Dallas' Schwinn.

"Where are we gonna hide the stuff?" Douglas asked.

"What do you mean?" Dallas asked. "It's like we said before, we're going to throw it down old man Rooney's well. Nothing's changed. It's just junk, man. Once we get rid of it nobody can accuse us of stealing anything. We're all free and clear."

Keeping his tight hold on the handlebars, Douglas Capernick looked hard into Dallas' eyes before he replied, "Okay. We can dump the other junk, but I want the gun."

From the fierce look in those cold black eyes, Dallas knew that the big kid was expecting an argument; he also understood that if Douglas wanted the gun there was going to be very little he could do to keep him from taking it. But of all the stuff that they'd boosted, the one sure thing that had to go was the revolver. Stealing a silver cup from a church was one thing, but it was a whole different day to rip-off a cop's gun. Besides, there were bullets in that gun, real bullets.

"Why do you want the gun?"

"I don't know," Douglas laughed. "Maybe I'll shoot you."

From down near the paved street, the one that ran back into town, Will yelled, "Come on, guys. Let's go."

Douglas paused another second before letting go of the handlebars.

"Tell the retard to shut up," he said with a look that Dallas found easy to understand.

Will was right about one thing: at ten forty-five on a Wednesday morning in Freeland, Iowa nobody paid any attention to three boys on bicycles.

Johanna Krist's quiet eastside neighborhood was one of the oldest and most humble in town. The unassuming houses were small and pleasantly ordinary with their patched roofs, hand-painted flower pots, and crumbling sidewalks. These were the homes of working people struggling to make the mortgage; folks who'd just retired, their shiny campers now parked under the portico alongside the house; and the seriously aged, too well or too poor to take up residence somewhere else.

A typical August morning in Iowa, by eleven o'clock the thermometer had already reached a stifling eighty-eight degrees with a forecast that predicted afternoon temperatures in the mid-ninety's. All the windows were closed down tight, while the little window air conditioners valiantly buzzed and throbbed. Other than an occasional disinterested motorist, the only other creature that could be seen was a prostrate cocker spaniel that was lying immobile in the shade of Maddie Walhart's front porch.

"Come on," Douglas demanded, wheeling his bike up the driveway and straight through the backyard toward the little shack.

As he stepped forward to unhook the shed's latch an entirely unexpected and worrisome thought stopped Dallas Albright cold.

"What if the stuff's not here," he wondered? "Maybe that's what Dad was talking about? What if he came in here and found something, like the gun, maybe?"

From behind him he could hear the other two as they got off their bicycles.

"Come on, let's get going'," Douglas complained.

Dallas Albright considered his options before deciding, "Probably best not to mention it. Better to be surprised together."

With a sigh and a swift yank, Dallas pulled open the door and stepped inside the little building; the tiny space felt like a dusty oven. A quick appraisal gave no indication that anyone had been there before them. Under the workbench was the large plastic box filled with toys that he and his brother would play with when they would come over to visit Grandma Jo. As he expected, a blue Frisbee was still lying on the top of the heap.

"Here," he said to Douglas Capernick, "take this. In case somebody comes we can act like we're playin' catch."

The taller boy eyed him suspiciously, but handed back the toy.

"Good idea, Shorty. Only we won't be here that long. Get the stuff and let's go."

Hanging on the wall next to the infamous push mower were three empty burlap sacks. Dallas pulled one down from the rusty nail and held it out for Douglas.

"Here," he said, "hold the bag open."

Dallas remembered exactly where he'd hidden each of the items and moved quickly to retrieve the cup, the trophy, the wooden box, its gold coins, and the key to the cedar chest. Without any feelings of remorse, the beautiful boy callously dumped the swag into the burlap sack.

The sword, however, posed an unanticipated problem; it was too long to fit in the bag without the ornate handle and its golden tassel conspicuously sticking out of the top. The boys all realized the difficulty at the same moment, but Douglas lack of patience temporarily resolved the dilemma when he handed the sack to Will, and stated flatly, "You figure it out. Where's the gun, Shorty?"

The big kid held out his hand, a wicked grin of triumph on his face.

There was no question that sooner or later he would give the kid the gun, and the longer they stood there in that hot dirty box the more likely it was that someone was going to see them, someone who would wonder why they were there, someone who'd call his parents to inquire about what they were doing, because, after all, it's what people do in a small town. With only the two possible choices, the beautiful boy pushed past Douglas Capernick.

In a dark corner of the shed, Dallas knelt in front of a sizable stack of ancient newspapers tied with twine. Hanging like the proverbial Sword of Damocles on the wall above his head was his grandfather's push lawnmower. Back in that crazy moment when the old lady lay dead in her bed and the rest of the world was about to crash down around him, Dallas had stood there on that thin line between panic and calm and cleverly tucked the .38 deep into the mass of old news. Now fishing around in the tight dusty bundle his hand touched the only thing in the entire shed that could be cold.

"Give me the gun. We gotta get out of here."

He pulled his hand out of the papers and slowly stood.

For the first time since his Grandma Jo had set him on this path, he was afraid. Dallas Albright knew in his heart that when he handed this crazy kid the gun he was going to shoot him. In that clear awful moment, the beautiful boy imagined himself lying on the dirt floor, blood seeping out of his chest to mix with the blood from his mother's severed finger.

He was about to die.

With his head down and eyes closed, resolved to his fate, Dallas Albright held out the silver revolver.

"Okay, let's go."

The beautiful boy opened his right eye and looked down on his white T-shirt. Incredibly, it was still white. Another second went by before he realized that Douglas hadn't killed him. His heart was beating. Air was going in and out of his lungs. He could see, he could think. He wasn't dead.

The door to the shed was still open, and in that bright glistening light of day the beautiful boy could see the others standing beside their bikes. Douglas was now busy closing the metal buckle on his shiny black saddlebag, while Will stood scratching his head as he labored over how he would ride his bicycle while holding the burlap sack with its frustrating oversized cargo.

Dallas Albright staggered out into the light overwhelmed with the possibilities of being alive.

"Hey! What are you kids doin'?"

From around the corner of the house a tall bald man with a brightly sunburned head was walking straight for them.

"I said, what are you guys doin' here?"

"Don't move," Douglas whispered loud enough so that Will could hear him.

"Hey, Mr. Arnold, how's it going'?"

Douglas Capernick rolled his bike confidently straight toward the man, but stopped a good twenty feet away.

The man - Mr. Harvey Arnold - suspiciously cocked his head to one side. Then with a surprised reaction of recognition, he countered with, "Oh, it's you, Douglas. You had me kinda worried at first. I didn't know who was back here."

"No problem," Douglas offered, "it's just us."

Both holding their ground, Mr. Arnold carefully studied Douglas Capernick before he spoke. "Yeah, so, what are you doin?"

"Well, we were just…"

Before the kid could finish the sentence, Dallas stepped out of the shed and said, "We were looking for this Frisbee. I left it over here in the shed. See?"

Holding up the blue disk for Mr. Arnold to see, Dallas walked over to where Douglas was still standing beside his bicycle.

Obviously confused, Harvey Arnold put his hands on his hips and looked hard at the three boys.

"Are you the Albright boy?"

"Yes, sir. This is my grandma's house. We had some toys and stuff in the shed that I wanted to get."

"Yeah, okay. Who are you?" Harvey Arnold asked pointing at Will.

Will had done precisely what Douglas had demanded, he hadn't moved. Still standing next to his bicycle, the burlap sack in hand with its handle and tassel clearly visible, the small boy turned to look at Douglas as if asking for permission to speak.

"Oh, that's my friend, Will," Douglas intervened. "You know Eddie Samuelson, right? That's his boy."

The three watched as the adult struggled to process the information. When it seemed to take longer than Douglas Capernick thought necessary, he pressed the man, "so, what are you doin' here, Mr. Arnold?"

Apparently glad he no longer needed to make sense out the situation; Harvey Arnold pointed back toward the house, and said, "Well, I'm working with the bank to try to sell this house. I just came out to put a "For Sale" sign in the front yard and thought I'd check the doors when I spotted you guys out back here."

The expression on his face made it seem like he was expecting something more from the boys, only when he didn't get it he clapped his hands together and shouted at Dallas, "Hey, toss that baby over here."

Taking a couple steps toward Harvey Arnold, Dallas confidently flipped the blue disk toward the man. The boy's experience and skill sent the Frisbee gliding across the lawn in a perfect trajectory. As the blue disk gently sailed toward its target, Harvey began hopping up and down like a ridiculous clumsy kid; none of the boys were surprised when he fumbled the catch.

"No problems," he yelled, bending over to pick up the Frisbee. "Go long, Doug. I'll hit you with a pass."

Dallas could see Douglas Capernick roll his eyes at the thought of running after a Frisbee tossed by Harvey Arnold, but the tall boy grudgingly handed over his bike to Dallas, ducked his head, and began to lope back toward the house.

"Right, all right," shouted Harvey, "let the old master show you how it's done."

It was clear "the old master" was not.

Harvey Arnold stepped into his throw with far too much enthusiasm and no ability. The blue Frisbee fluttered high over Douglas head, sailing well past the intended target, until it finally landed on the roof of the house with an exasperating whack. The three boys turned to stare at Harvey Arnold with the same look of contempt that they would have given one another had one of them thrown the Frisbee on the roof.

"Oh, oh," was Harvey's clever response. "Yeah… okay. Well, I'll get it down when it's not so hot. Sorry, kid."

Harvey Arnold shrugged his wimpy shoulders then turned to walk away. The boys said nothing.

Dallas looked up at the blue Frisbee, which now rested peacefully on the roof, and smiled. Thanks to the foolishness of this utterly inept adult, he had just received his own personal **GET OUT OF JAIL FREE** card. Even if Harvey were to tell his father that he'd found them in Grandma Jo's backyard, he now had a perfect excuse – the Frisbee. And even better, since the doofus had so skillfully thrown the thing on the roof, it was a lot more likely he'd just keep the whole thing to himself. If there was one thing that Dallas knew for sure it was that adult's hated to embarrass themselves, especially in front of other adults.

For the moment he was golden. What remained was getting out to Rooney's and dumping the bag before they were seen by someone else. If his luck held out he'd be home before lunch with a whole lot lighter load, that is, unless Douglas Capernick had other plans for his new toy.

Chapter Eleven

The Decision of Complicity

"You become responsible, forever, for what you have tamed."
The Little Prince - Antoine de Saint-Exupéry

Old Man Rooney's real name was Aldo Phillip Rooney.

For as long as anyone could remember, Aldo Rooney had lived alone on a small farm on the edge of town just north of the new elementary school. The unique appeal of Mr. Rooney's farm was the large and productive apple orchard that lay just over the fence from the school's playground. By mid-September most every kid in town would have found their way over that fence to secretly enjoy the fruits of Mr. Rooney's labors.

To those locals who knew him, Aldo Rooney was considered a reclusive and reliably angry man. Earlier that spring, after a long and painful struggle, Mr. Rooney succumbed to tuberculosis. With only an aged sister in Des Moines and a distant cousin in Council Bluffs, Old Man Rooney was otherwise all alone. In fact, other than an empty chair at the monthly Knights of Pythias meetings, and the occasional late afternoon sightings at Dutch's Tavern, hardly a soul would have noted a change in Freeland's demographics. That is until the rumors started circulating that the old man's spirit had returned to haunt his dilapidated farmhouse. Such a tempting creepy possibility had made the abandoned property a popular place for kids taking a dare, or young lovers looking for a spot to be alone. Dallas, Douglas, and Will were among the many that had gingerly tiptoed up to the broken-down old house with the high hopes of catching a glimpse of the phantom Rooney. It was on such an occasion that Will Samuelson discovered what would become the final resting place for their crimes.

As a way to properly kickoff of their summer vacation, the boys had accepted their rivals challenge to visit old man Rooney's place. That evening, as the last scarlet seconds of the sunset were turning the sky dark blue and purple, the three boys cautiously crept through the overgrown orchard on their way toward the house. With the former owner now away seeking his celestial reward, those left holding the earthly mortgage saw no reason to spend any additional money illuminating the forsaken farm. This austerity left the place especially dark and foreboding.

To keep from tripping over the mounds of debris that the absentminded old bachelor had left strewn around the yard, it was necessary for the boys to move with care. In just the few steps between the machine shed and the barn, they'd already come across a rusted-out lid from a milk can now buried deep in the tall grass, a cracked rake handle still sticking out of a mangled wooden crate, a sizable stack of half-burnt rubber tires, along with heaps of worn-out and unrecognizable farm equipment. Without proper light these ominous shapes presented themselves as weird and dangerous bumps; mysterious outlines that seemed capable of reaching out to grab any anxious trespasser.

"Quiet! Listen," Douglas whispered. "Did you hear that?"

Even though no one had spoken for minutes, Dallas and Will remained silent.

"I think it came from the house. Come on."

Before either boy could react, Douglas was gone into the shadows.

"What do we do?" squeaked Will.

"I don't know," Dallas replied. "Maybe we just stay here and wait for him to come back."

"Okay with me," whispered Will.

The two boys stood mute and motionless for what must have seemed like a very long time. Then from somewhere near the corner of the house a cat shrieked, immediately followed by a long low moan and the crash of metal against metal.

"What was that?" Will said grabbing Dallas by the arm.

With the world quickly coming unglued, Dallas tried his best to remember what Grandma Jo had taught them about fear.

"Being afraid is for fools and people who get caught," she once said. "You boys stay sharp and quiet. Let the rest of the world run right by you. Believe me, if you keep your cool while everyone else is crazy, you'll own this world."

With a banshee's howl it came out of the darkness rushing like a runaway train. A great black shape suddenly appeared from the left, bowling over Will and sending the little guy ass over teacups into the darkness.

"Oh, no, no, no," Will whimpered.

A familiar voice came from out of the darkness. "Ooooooh," it cackled. "I am the ghost of Old Man Rooney come to scare the shit out of you. Ooooooh."

"No. No," the frightened boy cried. "Leave me alone."

Although he couldn't see him, Dallas knew from his cries that Will had gotten to his feet and was now running back through the debris in the general direction that they'd just come. After only a couple of steps there was a thick ugly thud, followed by a groan... and then silence.

Out of the dark, Douglas Capernick asked, "Do you think he's hurt?"

"Probably," Dallas replied, hoping that the catch in his voice didn't betray him. "We better go see."

From over near the west corner of the machine shed, the two could hear Will Samuelson quietly crying. Approaching what they hoped wasn't a broken boy, Douglas inexplicably tripped over something massive and immovable, sending him hard to the ground.

"Damn it," barked the boy. "What is that?"

From a spot in the deep grass, Will sniffled, "I don't know. It got me, too."

Limited mostly to his sense of touch, Dallas gently kicked with the toe of his tennis shoe at the spot where he thought the others had fallen. After only two attempts his foot connected with a solid metallic object.

"It's some kind of grate made out of metal bars," Dallas told the others. "I can feel a bunch of holes here, like it's been welded."

Then cupping his hands together, he whispered down in to the void, "Hello." A long moment later came the echo.

"I think it must be pretty deep," Dallas suggested.

By then Douglas and Will were on their feet and peering down into blackness.

"Wait a minute," Douglas offered, "I'll be right back."

Without an explanation Douglas turned and ran around the corner of the shed. A second later he had returned.

"I'll bet this was Rooney's well," Douglas suggested. "Somebody must've covered it with the bars so you couldn't fall down in there. It's gotta be deep. Listen."

Holding up a sizable stone, he bent over the grate and then dropped the rock.

"One thousand and one… One thousand and two… One thousand…"

A splash of water could be heard from deep down in the hole.

"I bet it's more than a hundred feet to the bottom; sounds like there's some water down there, too. Man, what a perfect place to dump a body. Got anybody you wanna get rid of?"

It was cooler in the shade of old man Rooney's apple trees, even pleasant if Dallas didn't stop and think too hard about why they were there. To avoid being spotted, the boys had travelled every possible side street and alleyway between Johanna Krist's backyard and old man Rooney's apple orchard before finally ditching their bikes in the tall grass near the fence.

"Let me throw it down," Will pleaded.

No one objected. By this point the junk in the burlap sack had become so unimportant that neither Dallas nor Douglas had any interest in its final disposal. What did remain, however, was the very serious question of Douglas Capernick's intentions for the contents of his saddlebag.

The echo of a splash from deep down in the hole was followed by Will's giddy reaction, "Did you hear it? That was the cup."

"Who cares? Throw the whole sack down there and let's get going," Douglas demanded.

The tall boy had turned away from the well, but was now glaring back at Dallas - anticipating.

Douglas Capernick's black eyes and hard uncompromising stare reminded the beautiful boy of a time in his own backyard when he'd surprised a giant bull snake that was innocently sunning itself in the grass. As the two suspiciously studied one another, the big snake steadily lifted his head as if considering a confrontation. Its black eyes never left the intruder as it remained coiled - also anticipating.

It was only later, after he'd mercilessly hacked the five foot reptile into tiny bits with a hoe, that he considered the consequences of the act. Staring down on the bloody parts, he wondered whether the snake had been the victim, or a fool; after all, the bull snake had done nothing but startle him, and yet there it lay. One moment it was sentient and alive, the next a bloody corpse.

Then to make matters worse, instead of praising his bravery and courage, his father had scolded him for killing what he called, "the defenseless creature."

"That snake eats mice, Dallas. It's an important part of the chain." His father's rant, however, did not bother to explain why the innocent mouse was a less important part of the chain than the bull snake.

As Will struggled to shove the burlap sack through the metal grate, Dallas wondered which was worse, stealing all of those things only to throw them down Old Man Rooney's well, or, letting Douglas Capernick keep the gun. He certainly had no regrets for taking the stuff; it had been a kick and was all for laughs. As for those other words like thief, robber, or crook, well, those were just words. In his mind, it was all about being smarter than the adults. And they were. Every plan had worked perfectly, even if they did have to carry along the extra baggage of Will Samuelson. Thanks to Grandma Jo's plans, the three of them were able to sneak into all of those places filled with old people doing their jobs, and then right under their noses walk off with their prized possessions.

That was a true smile.

But the gun, well, that was another matter.

As far as Dallas was concerned there was one giant problem with Douglas keeping the gun: unlike the other junk that was now safely at the bottom of the well, when somebody found the gun - and they will find it - there were going to be a thousand and one questions. Sure, the big kid was tough, but sooner or later he was going to crack, and when he did all hell was going to break loose.

"What are you lookin' at?"

"Nothing," Dallas lied.

"Okay, then let's get going," Douglas said. "I'm hungry. You guys want to eat at my place? My old lady's gone to Alton for the day, so there's nobody home. We can eat whatever we want."

A soft splash came from the well.

Will Samuelson stood up and naively asked, "Aren't you gonna throw the gun in?"

Douglas maintained his steady gaze on Dallas, but replied, "Not today. I'm keeping it for a while. I may need it. Okay by you?"

Will appeared surprised by the question, or perhaps it was that he'd been asked.

"Sure, why not?"

"You got anything to say?" Douglas asked.

Dallas had plenty to say. Keeping the gun was a bad idea, a dangerous idea guaranteed to cause real problems, maybe even get somebody killed. Only Douglas Capernick was not about to throw the revolver down the well. Clearly, he'd made up his mind. Any kind of pushback from Dallas was liable to set off a confrontation that could never end well.

"You got any peanut butter at your place?" Dallas asked.

A week later, just before lunchtime, two men who worked as carpenters for Weber Construction pulled into the Albright driveway in one of the company's trucks. In the back of the pickup were two large cardboard boxes and a cedar chest. After conferring with Emily, the door to the garage was opened and the men carried all three down to the basement storeroom.

Dallas discovered the chest later that afternoon when he went into the room hoping to find some of his missing comic books and Mad magazines. He hated it when his mother would clean his room, especially when she'd pick things up from the floor. By this point, he'd complained enough that she'd stopped throwing his stuff away, and instead left his treasures in a box in the storeroom.

His first reaction to the cedar chest was that he'd seen a ghost.

"What's the stuff in the storeroom?" he asked his mother, hoping that the question sounded innocent and spontaneous.

Emily looked up from the stack of bills that lay spread across the desk in front of her.

"They're things of mine," she replied, "from Grandma Jo's house, pictures and things from when I was a girl. We're planning to have an auction soon, but those are things I want to save."

She studied her son's face as he contemplated the news.

"What's in the chest?" he asked.

"I'm not sure anymore," Emily replied.

"I think it's locked."

He realized the mistake as soon as the words came out of his mouth. From the curious look in her eyes, it seemed like she was surprised by both his comment and the idea that he'd already tried to open the chest.

She pushed her chair back from the table, and began, "One Christmas when I was six, my father made that chest as a present for mother and me. He gave both of us our own key, which he put on a golden chain. Where he got the money for the chain, I'll never know. But we would keep all our most prized possessions and secrets in there, half for Mom and half for me. It was very special."

She gave him a tightlipped smile before adding, "The only problem is that there's no longer a key. I've misplaced mine, and even though I've looked through most of Mom's things, there's just no key. I can't get in."

She pushed around some of the papers on the desk, and then, just before she started to cry, added, "I guess we'll have to get your father to open it. Won't we?"

As far as Dallas knew the cedar chest was never opened. Even after he'd left the house for good, it sat silently alone in the corner of the storeroom. Over the years, boxes and all sorts of unused or unwanted household debris ended up burying the trunk, but not the rich and unforgettable smell. The storeroom became one of those places that Dallas Albright would avoid.

Chapter Twelve

The Super Sport

"Life is life, and kind is kind."
On the Road – Jack Kerouac

What will become of a young man who imagines that he is superior to everyone he meets, someone who lives indifferent to the challenges and hardships of life, an egotist who considers himself untouchable, unassailable, and indestructible?

Dallas Albright will pass through the next five years of his life in a self-induced state of apathy. Along with his caring, indulgent family there will also be those generous souls who try to teach him; adults that willingly share both their patience and kindness. Except in this version of his *lucky life*, these well-meaning folks will all be viewed as flat and two-dimensional, assigned no more or less value than any other. For this boy facts were irrelevant, emotions extraneous, nuance ignored. Disinterested with history and indifferent to the future, Dallas Albright's adolescent years are spent in the cold dispassion of his own massive ego.

The beautiful boy becomes a handsome young man. Still small, always small, he comes to understand that the face he sees in the mirror is split: admired by some, and disliked by many others. But like all of his gifts, this one is also deemed unimportant and ignored.

Those that cared, and there would be fewer and fewer of them every year, had generously tried to provide the young man with opportunities. There kindness had provided chances to explore and experiment, but to no avail. With only their good intentions, Dallas was cajoled into participating in the traditional rituals of small town Iowa: music, scouting, sports, and church. The piano meant practice – obviously, that was out. Scouting assumed fraternity and recognizing authority – not a chance. Team sports demanded dedication and desire – just forget about it. Religion required a concern for your own mortality and a commitment to strengthening your soul – definitely out.

By the time Dallas Albright turned sixteen, he had become a parent's greatest fear: a child with no interests, no apparent friends, and no desire to communicate.

The Albright's argued for weeks about giving him the car.

Emily maintained that not only did the boy lack the maturity to manage such an important and dangerous gift, she was certain that this particular car would offer the kind of temptation he could not manage. There was no question in her mind that if they gave the boy the car, she would be awakened one night by the police informing her that her oldest son had just been killed in a fiery crash.

"That is not a boy's first car," she argued late one evening as the two prepared for bed. "Besides, what does he need a car for anyway? We'll take him if he has to go somewhere."

To try to soften her concerns, Charles argued that they could strictly enforce a combination of rules and a non-negotiable agreement that the boy would work weekends and summers for Weber Construction. She might be surprised; the responsibilities of a car could reinforce good mature habits, maybe even greater dependability. Who knows, it might even bring them closer as a family.

Charles Albright was a smart man. Pasting on his "trust me" smile, he hoped that she didn't see through his weak rhetoric for what it truly was - subterfuge; subterfuge in a desperate maneuver to reconnect with his son in some real and meaningful way. Back in his days at Bearn Sterns, he'd learned that desperation was the absolute worst place from which to negotiate, or make a tough decision; especially a decision like giving the boy a car - his car, his pride and joy, his '68 Super Sport Camaro.

"This is the worst idea you've ever had," Emily capitulated, confident that the gift of a 325-horsepower machine would prove her right.

It was Christmas Eve, 1986.

Charles had agreed to be home by five, only the drinks had started early. Scattered around the Weber Construction offices was a loud and happy crowd of mostly men, all holding drinks and overflowing paper plates filled with food. This year he had promised himself that the "boss" was going to take a few extra minutes to visit with each of his guys, just to say thanks for all their good work. After all, it was their skill and effort that had built those houses, not his. They were the ones who were out there every morning at seven, regardless of the weather. They were the ones who actually did the work, and without them there would be no Weber Construction, no nice home on the south side, no Country Club membership, or college fund. Before pushing that thin envelope into each one's expectant hand, the least he could do was make sure that they knew he knew.

This had not been the best year that Weber Construction had seen, in fact, Charles knew it was mostly luck that kept them from laying-off half of the third crew. All that had saved those men's jobs was a judicious reallocation of the company's rainy day funds, and a long awaited settlement from the bank's foreclosure on a foolish young couple who'd bought more house than they could afford – happy Christmas.

Charles set the empty can of beer down on the corner of his desk right next to the framed photograph he'd taken last Christmas of Emily and the boys at Epcot Center. Out in the shop the party had shifted gears and was now noticeably louder; shots of Jack Daniels and heavy metal music had replaced the sober eggnog and well-intentioned Christmas carols. By now most of the older family men were wisely making their way out the door, what remained was a handful of the rowdy younger fellows determined to swill what was left of the bosses' Christmas cheer. Trying his best to apply a little of the season's spirit to the occasion, Charles hoped that these noisy drunks would call it a night before the Deputy Sheriff showed up. No need for that tonight, not tonight. Tonight was special. Tonight was the night.

There was a gentle knock on the half-open door before the giant head of Keith Traugott peered around the corner.

"I'm getting' ready to hit the road and wanted to say merry Christmas before I left."

Charles returned to the moment and waved for him to come in.

"Yeah, I'm going too. Things are starting to get a little loud for me. Besides, tonight's the night that Em and I are going to give Dallas the Camaro; can't be late for that."

The big man smiled and nodded his head without showing much emotion. Back in November, Charles had enthusiastically shared with his friend their plans to give the boy the car, and even though he never said a word about the intelligence of that decision, Charles sensed he didn't approve. It took a lot to get Keith Traugott to push back any opinion that might differ from his, but this time his silence suggested that his true feelings might dampen Charles enthusiasm.

"Anyway," Charles added, extending his hand, "Merry Christmas to you and June, and to baby Carl's first Christmas. I hope it's great."

Keith quietly accepted his friend's handshake, as he replied, "Same to you. And thanks for getting us through these last couple of months. I know it was kinda shaky there for a while, but you did it again, for all of us, I mean."

From the look on his face it was clear that he was honestly grateful, which instantly produced in Charles a sharp internal twinge of guilt. Since the beginning, Charles Albright had done his best to ignore those feelings; after all, it was his business savvy that had made both of them a handsome living - his being especially more handsome. Besides, they'd always been good friends. They socialized together. Their wives were constantly planning and playing together. For heaven sakes, he was the godfather to his friend's new baby boy.

Yet, in moments like this one, he couldn't deny that there was also plenty of guilt; a nagging reminder that maybe he owed Keith Traugott more.

For the past fifteen years, Weber Construction was a sole proprietorship owned outright by Charles Albright. After the first few years of safe steady growth, Charles' forecasts were projecting even greater opportunities than he'd first imagined. With a strong push from Emily, Charles went against his first instincts and offered June and Keith Traugott an opportunity to buy a portion of the company. It had been a weird and one-sided conversation. After explaining both the projections and possibilities, Keith still turned him down flat, saying that he was satisfied with his salary and uncomfortable owning any portion of what he still saw as the Albright's business. "After all," he added, "Mister Weber never offered the company to me. I 'spose he figured I didn't have the money or brains to make it work." He ended his refusal by saying, "Sorry, Charles, but it just doesn't feel right to me."

That night on his way home from work, Charles secretly cheered Keith's foolish refusal to buy even the little ten percent he was offering. His ignorance, or lack of backbone, meant the Albright's would maintain their control and, of course, more of the revenues. Sure there was more risk staying a sole proprietorship, but not nearly as much as there was potential for profit. Since then Charles had been happy to never mention it again.

"Well," Charles offered, "we were lucky. Besides those last two contracts you helped me to sign were really the difference. Here's hoping that we get the bid on the Turner's apartment complex over in Greenfield."

Charles reached down and rapped his knuckles on the desk top for good luck, then hoisted the empty can of Budweiser as a salute. Looking past the can into his friends face he could see that this time there was more.

"What is it?" Charles asked. "Something's bothering you. What?"

Keith Traugott hung his head like a kid who'd been caught at something he knew he shouldn't have been doing.

"Well, I probably shouldn't be saying anything. I mean, it really isn't any of my business, and I know that you're looking forward to Christmas and giving Dallas that car."

There was another pause before Charles anxiously pushed his friend, "What?"

Keith took a giant breath, and then began, "I knew a boy back in high school. A nice enough kid, he went to my church. Anyway, he was real good with cars and loved to work on 'em. And he had a pretty fancy one that he'd spent hours and hours on. He rebuilt the engine all by himself. So it was fast, the fastest car in the county.

Well, he use to run it awful hard, then one night he was coming back from Adair where some kids had gone bowling. They said he was making about ninety when he dropped the front wheel off the shoulder and into the gravel. When the back-end started sliding, he jerked the car back up on the highway and across the lane right into the side of another car. Lucky the

264

kids were okay, but the old man driving the other car lost control and crashed into the ditch. He and his wife died the next day."

"Why are you telling me this?" Charles asked, knowing the answer.

"Well, like I said, it isn't really my place, but I know you want what's best for the boy, and we do too. So, anyway, cars like that Camaro can be a real temptation. My Christmas wish for you and Emily is that Dallas will understand that."

The big man dropped his head and shuffled his feet hoping that his heartfelt message had been received in the spirit in which it was intended.

Charles had picked up a pencil from his desk and was tapping it nervously in his open palm before he asked, "Who were the old people who died in the car accident?"

"They were my grandparents," Keith replied. "Good people who were just headed home from a card party at the neighbors. Shame they didn't stay for one more hand."

Steppenwolf's anthem *Born to be Wild* suddenly thundered out of the shop's speakers next door.

> *"Get your motor runnin', head out on the highway...*
> *Lookin' for adventure, in whatever comes our way.*
> *Born to be wild!"*

"Yeah, that is a shame," Charles thought out loud.

Peering through the viewfinder of her Pentax, Emily Albright announced, "Happy Birthday, Dallas" as she clicked off yet another picture of the beautiful boy slouched indifferently on the sofa in front of his stack of gifts. Despite her attempt at enthusiasm, she knew the boy hated having his picture taken; a glance through any of their family scrapbooks revealed dozens of similar photographs confirming this point-of-view.

"How about if I get one of all three of my men sitting in front of the fireplace," Emily bargained, hoping that by involving father and brother the three might eventually surrender to her wishes.

When no one moved, Emily resolved herself to the fact that the two pictures were all that she was likely to get without a full-on fight. Trying to avoid any appearance of disappointment, she quickly turned to pick up her empty wine glass from the coffee table.

"Santa, would you mind?" she asked, gently shaking the glass.

Nodding dutifully, Charles took the wine glass from his wife's lovely left hand. He smiled to himself when she instinctively returned the hand to her lap in an automatic effort to hide her missing digit; a lifetime of unconscious anxiety over something that had happened more than thirty-five years ago.

When he returned from the kitchen with the slightly overfilled glass of chardonnay his oldest son was opening another of his birthday gifts: a handsome but predictably black sweater.

"Smile, dear," Emily pleaded as the boy wadded-up the garment and reached out for another box. Turning as little as possible, he regarded his mother's camera with the familiar mix of disdain and boredom. As he planned, the photo captured his apathy perfectly.

"Here, Dallas. I got you something, too."

Andy Albright would turn fourteen in May. In spite of the two year gap in their age, Andy was already four inches taller and ten pounds heavier than his older brother. Where Dallas was closed off and sullen, Andy was outgoing and enthusiastic. Unlike his older brother who did as little as he could, Andy's button was pushed; he was constantly moving. It was Andy who craved the company of others, while Dallas preferred to be left alone. It seemed as if their only common qualities were their inescapable heritage and a street address.

"Thanks, brother," Dallas replied while accepting the amateurishly wrapped shoe box. "Well, whatever it is, it's heavy."

After an enthusiastic shake of the box, the older brother began tearing away the red and green paper revealing a Florsheim shoe box liberally taped on the sides. Wrapped in what must have been a full roll of paper towels was a large, black industrial flashlight. Automatically pressing the rubber switch on the back ignited the powerful beam which Dallas happily turned on his younger brother's smiling face.

"Nice. Thanks, Andy," Dallas offered, as he placed the flashlight under his chin to create a shadowed and macabre view of his handsome face.

For that moment, that silly precious moment, Emily thought she recognized in herself a lost sense of peace. Her brain split; one part wanted to analyze the dynamics in the hopes of repeating it, while the other half urged her to just let go and allow the moment to last as long as it would.

Before it could be resolved, Charles intervened.

"Happy sixteenth birthday, son," he began. "This is what I'd call a special birthday. One that will hopefully stand out and be one you always remember. So, to help with that, your mother and I decided to give you something special."

Emily straightened in the chair. Absently reaching forward to place her wine glass on the coffee table, Emily inadvertently spilled most of the chardonnay onto the dark wood and magazines that were lying there.

"Oh, sorry," she exclaimed. "Sorry. Sorry. Andy will you get a paper towel, or something."

With his planned speech now interrupted, Charles gritted his teeth and turned to walk back into the kitchen. Digging around under the sink, he discovered both a fresh roll of towels and a small steady leak coming from the seal around the garbage disposal. Cursing under his breath, he began tearing the plastic wrapper off the package just as Andy shouted from the living room, "Never mind, Dad. There's a bunch of towels already out here in the box with the flashlight."

While Emily and Andy mopped up the spilt wine, Charles motioned for Dallas to join him.

"Come on, everybody. We've got one more gift, but this one's out in the garage."

With a sigh and a forced smile, Emily answered, "We'll be right with you."

"Where are we going?" she repeated for the third time.

Even though they'd been married almost a whole year, Charles could never resist the temptation to surprise his new bride. This one, however, was exposed the minute they pulled into the Strassenberg GM dealership.

"Charles, what's this all about?" Emily asked, knowing full-well that the tall man in the obnoxious plaid sports coat was about to sell her husband a new automobile.

"Good morning, Mrs. Albright. It's a pleasure to meet you. My name is Carl, Carl Polanski. Welcome to Strassenberg Motors. Can I get you something to drink? A cup of coffee? How about a soda?"

Charles just smiled.

"Dallas, your mother and I would like to wish you happy birthday with what we hope you will think is a very special present."

Charles put his arm around their oldest boy and walked him toward the far corner of the immaculate garage to where a vehicle draped with a gray canvas waited. Emily stayed back watching intently for any sign of enthusiasm.

With a slightly overplayed flourish, Charles pulled the cover off the car and extended his hand. Dangling from his fingers was the keys to the jet-black 1968 Super Sport Camaro.

Realizing she'd forgotten the camera, but afraid to miss the moment, Emily walked over and stood next to her beaming husband who had just launched into an animated description of the car's qualities and features.

"I bought this car as soon as it came off the assembly line. It was just something I had to have, and, thankfully, your mother liked it too. Well, not so much when she was pregnant, but before that, man, we had some great times in this car."

Dallas face must have shown his confusion by the repetition of this well-known piece of family history, forcing Charles to quickly added, "But now it's yours. We, your mother and me, we want you to have it."

Emily smiled, but her heart was heavy.

"Did we do the right thing giving this machine to the boy? How will we take it back when he fails?"

Charles enthusiastically explained, "I got the big block in it when I ordered the 396."

"And there he goes again with the numbers," she thought. "He always thinks that people know what he's talking about, but all I ever knew was that the thing was fast. And I just gave it to my first-born child."

"Yeah, yeah," Charles enthusiastically replied to a question from his son, "it's got the Holley four-barrel."

Running her hand over the cold, black metal hood, Emily remembered that this was her first car, too. Despite the smarmy salesman and his cheesy sports coat, that day had been fun and still held a special memory for her. She remembered how Charles had made such a big deal out of looking at other cars (even a hideous gray-green family station wagon), but she knew that it was the Camaro that he had his heart set on. Impractical and expensive were her first thoughts, but as far as she knew it was the only self-serving thing the man had ever done in his life. She remembered thinking that this practical man, the financial genius, her loving and caring man, deserved a car that his father would have called frivolous, maybe even foolish.

As he bent over and unhooked the latch to the hood, Charles went on, "The man that sold it to us confessed that even though they weren't supposed to talk about it, this car is virtually race ready. I know that sounds like a sales pitch, but he wasn't lying."

The second it came out of his mouth, Charles knew he'd overplayed his hand. Looking up at the boy's mother only reinforced that his approach was emphasizing everything problematic about this powerful machine. Except how could he explain why this car meant so much more than muscle? This finely tuned vehicle had been his way to balance all the hard work and seriousness with the kind of confidence that comes from having something special. It was a winning edge; a considerable car for people who appreciated power and potential. He could count the number of times on two hands where he'd let those 325 horses loose. Still, no matter the occasion or season, whenever he turned the key, and that L35-V8 rumbled to life, he knew that it would always be available. It was always ready.

Over the years, he'd come to know every bolt from fender to fender, but never once had he considered the hours spent maintaining the machine an inconvenience or a drudgery; greasy hands and scarred knuckles were an important balance to the long hours spent pouring over printouts and stock reports. It was important to know that the car looked good and would still turn heads, but it was what was under the surface, under the hood, that gave him the real buzz. Eighteen years later, the Camaro was as clean and strong as the day he'd bought it.

As Dallas Albright, the beautiful boy, slipped behind the steering wheel and then gently ran a hand across the dash, Charles smiled hoping that his son might discover the same joy, the same confidence that this car had offered him.

Chapter Thirteen

So Unexpected – So Weird

"That's the thing about girls. Every time they do something pretty, even if they're not much to look at, or even if they're sort of stupid, you fall in love with them, and then you never know where the hell you are. Girls. Jesus Christ. They can drive you crazy. They really can."
Catcher in the Rye - J.D. Salinger

Dallas Albright did not drive his new car for more than thirty days.

Winter slammed the Midwest after Christmas, relentlessly hammering Freeland with a miserable mixture of snow and ice storms that lasted the better part of January. It wasn't until February 2nd that the boy was finally able to persuade his mother to chauffeur him to Alton so that he could drive for his license. On this occasion they did not take the Super Sport; instead, he was relegated to the family's staid Caprice Classic, a vehicle Dallas hoped to never be seen driving again.

Even though the weather would keep him off the streets of Freeland, Dallas still spent most of his free time either sitting behind the wheel, or with his head under the hood of his black car. The oil had been changed, the spark plugs replaced and gapped, and the interior detailed - twice. Charles was as happy as he could remember, even if it meant lying on the cold concrete floor to show his boy the beautiful intricacy of the Camaro's front-end linkage. It was true that there were now moments of real conversation at the dinner table - albeit car-talk - but those promises he'd once ignored were now mostly being kept. Despite what appeared as positive changes, Emily was constantly reminding herself to remain firm to their bargain; his well-established history of disappointment demanded that they not get too far ahead of themselves; after all, everything was riding on a boy who had never been reliable.

Dallas, of course, felt nothing new or different about the way he looked at the world. All he knew was that there was a powerful black car in his garage just waiting for him to set it free. The delays only heightened the anticipation, but he understood that if he was ever going get the green light to drive the car he had to play the game, which meant pleasantries and habits he mostly found stupid and useless.

The buzz around school that morning was that something horrible had happened to the Space Shuttle. Then just before third period, Principal Greenway came on the PA system.

"Students and teachers, can I have your attention, please. The television news has just confirmed that earlier this morning the Space Shuttle Challenger exploded during take-off from Cape Kennedy. It appears that all seven crew members, including Christa McAuliffe, the teacher in space, have died. I would ask that we all observe a moment of silence in honor of the astronauts and their families."

Dallas watched as all around him the heads of his classmates bowed in a collective reverential response to the principal's order, that is, all but one. Of course this kind of communal nonsense meant nothing to the beautiful boy, but of all the people to be ignoring such a spiritual directive, especially one that insisted that they pray, why was the Methodist minister's daughter now looking right at him?

Then Debbie Dorsett smiled.

This was not the kind of smile people offered when they were having their picture taken, in fact, this smile - this look - was utterly unfamiliar to the boy. No girl had ever looked at him this way, which only amplified the terror.

Like a switch had suddenly been thrown, the classroom nosily re-engaged, ending the humble tribute to the seven roasted astronauts. Picking up from where he'd been interrupted, Mr. Carling pleaded, "Students, please. Chaucer's *Canterbury Tales* are still relevant." His position was highly debatable.

For the next twenty-two minutes, Dallas Albright faded in and out of an aimless and unenthused discussion of the *Knight's Tale*. Struggling for a possible explanation to Debbie Dorsett's peculiar behavior, he occasionally glanced over in her direction, and, remarkably, every time he did she was still staring at him; studying him with the same intimidating smile that left him feeling a little like he might be prey. By the time the bell rang signaling the end of English and the beginning of his lunch period, Dallas Albright was consumed by man's greatest challenge: the need to understand the meaning behind a woman's smile.

Standing in the long and noisy lunch line, Dallas tried to stop thinking about Debbie Dorsett's curious expression by instead focusing his attentions on the normalcy of tuna casserole and cling peaches. Most days, Douglas Capernick and his new pal, the menacing Gordon "Goon" Gordonski, would already be seated and holding court in the back corner of the lunchroom. Now as Dallas made his way toward their usual corner spot, he could see that Debbie Dorsett and three of her friends had already beaten them there. It seemed weird, but Debbie's girlfriends were all beside themselves with giggles and whispers, while she, the preacher's daughter, sat stoically in the corner wearing her Mona Lisa smile.

Desperate not to appear confused - or worse - he looked around to find an open spot before this girl's incessant laser beam stare drew attention from the other kids.

From behind him came the familiar voice of Douglas Capernick.

"What's she lookin' at?"

"Good question," he thought, but said nothing and shrugged his shoulders.

Fifth period was P.E.

Like most days, Mr. Curt Bethranger stuck his head into the locker room where the boys were changing into their gym clothes, and announced, "You're playin' dodge ball, fellas. Don't nobody get hurt. I'll be right back."

No one was surprised by Mr. Bethranger's announcement that he would be "right back." As most of Freeland now knew, Curt Bethranger was suffering from an advanced addiction to nicotine, exacerbated by his pending divorce from his wife, fifth-grade teacher, Jill Curry-Bethranger. At this point in the thirty-three year-old physical education teacher's life, his addiction had become so demanding that he was forced to retreat to the teacher's lounge for a smoke and a cup of black coffee at least once an hour. His peers found him to be both a pity and a disruption, which meant that they mostly ignored his problems.

It was unclear to the students and faculty of Freeland High School whether Curt Bethranger's marital tribulations were the cause or result of his depression. As his relationship imploded, so did his personal habits. Despite his academic training as a physical education teacher, Curt Bethranger had become the poster child for how not to treat your body. Since that fateful night when his wife announced her intentions to divorce, he'd gained seventeen pounds, developed an uncontrollable tick in his left eye, and had taken up reading and reciting verses from the Old Testament; he was especially fond of the Psalms. To make matters worse, once Jill moved out of their apartment, Curt Bethranger was left to manage his own housework and laundry. His lack of interest in personal hygiene, mixed with the heavy nicotine consumption, left his clothes reeking of cigarettes and body odor. It was hard to be around Curt Bethranger.

The only thing Dallas Albright hated more than P.E. was dodge ball.

An infamous and utterly ridiculous game, dodge ball pits a group of boys positioned on one side of the gymnasium against another of equal number on the opposite side in a mad, free-for-all battle. The object: to throw and hit an opposing team's player with one of several balls, usually volleyballs, as hard as you possibly can. When hit, you are both "out" of the game, and the witless recipient of a substantial welt. The value of the game is suspect. It provides students no stimulating exercise, requires little athletic talent, and imparts no lifelong skills, that is, unless you consider deep cruelty or the desire to mercilessly attack someone smaller than yourself as a lifelong skill.

It is noteworthy that even in this age of liberation the ludicrous game of dodge ball is almost never played by young women. This intelligent divergence in curriculum may either be an example of the gender's good judgment, or the last vestige of customs applied during a more chivalrous time. Either way, Dallas Albright believed that dodge ball clearly demonstrated why the X-chromosome had climbed to a more highly evolved limb in the tree of life.

"Same teams as last time," Douglas Capernick announced as he entered the gymnasium. "We'll be on this side. You losers can park it over there."

Douglas Capernick was good at games, especially games where he could take advantage of his physical size and an aptitude for intimidation. Earlier that fall, his skill at confrontation had been used to its fullest advantage on the football field.

Even though it had been just another in a long string of mediocre seasons for the Freeland Tigers, (this year's win-loss record was a middling 3 and 5) it was Douglas hard-nosed play as a defensive linebacker that stood out and gained him significant notoriety in important places. Thanks to his violent and uncompromising approach to the game, he was selected First-Team All-Conference, as well as an "Honorable Mention" on the Des Moines Register's "All Iowa Team." There were many of the local Saturday morning quarterbacks who confidently believed that one day soon Douglas Capernick would be playing in Kinnick Stadium for the great Hayden Fry. This was especially true of his father, Stanley P. Capernick - University of Iowa Class of 1960.

"Stand there, Shorty," Goon Gordonski demanded of Dallas. "We'll use you as bait."

Now that Douglas had befriended this new thug, Dallas and Will had become the go-to targets for the Goon's frequent and painful abuse. In spite of the trio's longstanding history of larceny and well-guarded secrets, this established fraternity guaranteed neither favor nor support from Douglas Capernick. On more than one occasion, Dallas could remember his so-called friend standing by as kids larger and older cruelly administered what they considered an upper classman's prerogative; that is, painful hazing in the guise of beatings and bruises.

Once between classes, Goon, and another of the vapid football jocks ("Crip" Pilton) cornered Dallas outside the locker room and were about to draw a black mustache on his face with a permanent Magic Marker when Douglas finally intervened.

"What's goin' on?"

"Nothin'. Just havin' some fun with Shorty, here," Goon laughed.

"Okay," Douglas casually replied.

Then turning to walk away, he added, "You know he might look better with a goatee?"

This surprising suggestion apparently signaled to the assailants both an unspoken approval and the green light. Two days later people were still laughing and pointing at the poorly drawn marks on Dallas chin. Later, when confronted about his apparent lack of support, Douglas reaction was notably apathetic.

"Maybe you should thank me," he suggested. "If I hadn't said something you'd be walking around with a lousy mustache instead of that little dab of black on your jaw."

Douglas Capernick's team easily won the first two skirmishes without losing a man. Dallas had ignored Goon's suggestion that he act as "bait," and instead retreated to his preferred location in the back of the room. From this inferior position he had successfully avoided both being hit by the ball, and being called upon to "storm the barricades," a Capernick euphemism for ignoring the rules and crossing the center line to invade the enemy's territory. Once over the border, the larger boys would seek out the smallest and most helpless, and then mercilessly bombard them into submission.

Normally, Dallas stayed as close to the back wall as possible, venturing out only to retrieve an errant throw or when chastised by Douglas Capernick. As Douglas, Goon, and the others mounted their third and most reckless offensive - the cruel pummeling of a younger feebler freshman who had strayed too close to the line - a random loose ball rolled near Dallas' feet. In a remarkably uncharacteristic move, Dallas picked up the ball and raced toward the border in the hope of adding further insult to the whimpering boy's injury. Sprinting through the mayhem, he spotted the underclassman near the bleachers, curled in a fetal position with his hands spastically jerking in a pitiful effort to cover his head. Taking aim and setting himself to launch his bomb, Dallas reared back to throw just as he spotted an incoming guided missile. Before he had time to take evasive action, the volleyball hit him full on and hard in the side of the head. In that brief moment, the microsecond before the ball rebounded away from his cranium, it felt as if the surface of the smooth sphere had completely wrapped itself around his head and exploded, producing the classic opposite and equal reaction.

Staggered by the force of the blow, Dallas Albright twisted to his right just as two more missiles found their mark; a low blow to the groin, immediately followed by another strike to the back of his head.

Somewhere a whistle sounded, and then the distant echo of a voice shouted, "Okay, everybody line up for calisthenics. Off the floor, Albright. Let's go, fellas."

Mr. Bethranger had returned but brought with him no mercy.

Left with a maddening ringing in his ears and slightly blurred vision, Dallas made his way through the crowded hallways and up the stairs to his sixth period class. It was here, in the fifty minutes of tedium known as American History, where he hoped to find solace and time to recover. Sadly, in this version of his *lucky life* the teacher of the tedium - Ms. Jessica Aldonetru - a tiny painted blond with a screech for a voice and the political leanings of Benjamin Fine had decided that her students' apparent disinterest and rowdy behavior were grounds to administer a surprise quiz. For this occasion, the punishment would be a review of Chapter 18, *"The United States 1945-50: Post World War II,"* a period which Ms. Aldonetru enthusiastically referred to as "the creeping age of capitalism."

Thanks mostly to his scrambled faculties it took nearly half the allotted time before Dallas' vision would clear enough so that he could decipher Ms. Aldonetru's lengthy, erudite questions. When the bell rang signaling the end of the suffering, Dallas had answered only six of the eighteen questions.

On the positive side, he had forgotten about Debbie Dorsett's smile.

The Drop-Inn Diner is a dubious landmark on the Main Street of Freeland, Iowa.

For nearly forty years, the Drop-Inn has been owned and operated by lifetime Freeland natives, Edna and Ken Weatherwax. Along with their longevity in the restaurant business, Ken Weatherwax had also earned some small local notoriety for the remarkable claim that he was the cousin of Charlie Weatherwax, owner and trainer of the famous television star, Lassie. This bold statement, one that relied solely on the proprietor's questionable veracity, and a small unframed 8 X 10 photo of the famous collie that had been thumb-tacked above the restaurant's tiny window into the kitchen, was finally confirmed in the spring of 1964. It was on a beautiful day in late April when Charlie and the current iteration of Lassie (Lassie #4) paid a visit to Freeland. Along with a triumphant tour of the local elementary school, Lassie was also offered the ceremonial key to the city along with a 50-pound bag of dog food from the Farmer's Cooperative.

Best known for Edna's delicious homemade pies and cobbler, ("It's the lard," she liked to say) the Drop-Inn had always been a popular spot among the locals, particularly the breakfast and lunch crowd. However, by 3:15, the

Drop, as it was affectionately known to its largest client-base, was flooded with famished Freeland High students. Since the late 50's, the Drop had been the only place to go after a long day of school; presuming, of course, that you were old enough.

In Freeland there are specific unwritten rules governing the behavior of its young people. One of the longest standing and most respected of these rules states that only juniors and seniors are allowed to enter into the inner sanctum of the Drop-Inn Diner. Any male underclassman foolish enough to ignore this longstanding edict was likely to suffer deep humiliation and severe corporal punishment at the hands of the Posse.

Like the Drop-Inn Diner, the Posse first appeared in the late 50's. Its sole resolute purpose was to guarantee that Freeland High School's social structure and time-honored traditions were strictly and steadfastly enforced.

In those first years, the Posse's *raison d'etre* grew out of the basic human need for kinship, a common sense of identity, and the desire for power. Reborn every spring with a new membership of elite senior boys, it was the Posse's own rich history and prestige that made the society self-sustaining. There had been five senior members in the first class; there would be five senior members for the class of 1986. From day one there had been no by-laws, no internal structure, and certainly no written history. Like the phoenix, every spring the Posse would rise from the ashes of its own appeal.

There were many who hoped to be a part of the Posse; in fact, there were those Freeland fathers who had once been members themselves who now expected that their boy would win one of the coveted spots. But there could only be five. In an organization solely committed to upholding tradition, there were only five because there could be only five. Without a formal hierarchy or elected leadership, the Posse succeeded because of the inherent equality among its members. If there was a dispute about selecting someone for membership, it was resolved in the same time-honored way that it had always been resolved - with skin. Just knowing that you had to fight your way in provided a harsh but practical approach to such a rigorously self-selected membership.

Its current members - the class of 1986 - were completely and contentedly ignorant about the organization's particulars. By word and deed this infamous five had proudly demonstrated that they were one of the most notorious and unforgiving in the Posse's long history. The malevolent quintets' hazing had been so severe and merciless that all of Freeland's male freshmen lived in abject terror of being caught alone on the streets. Their harsh legacy was going to be hard to live down or improve upon.

As the two boys slid down the four blocks of icy sidewalks from school to Main Street and the Drop-In Diner, Dallas said nothing to Will Samuelson about his peculiar experience with the minister's daughter.

Football had been over for nearly three months, and even though it was "technically" prohibited for high school students to practice out-of-season this unenforceable edict did not keep zealots like Douglas Capernick and his new friends in the "Goon Squad" from their harsh and uncompromising workouts in the weight room. Thanks to the hours and hours of monotonous bench presses, curls, and flies the Freeland boys had undergone an astounding physical transformation. There were whispers that their impressive new bulk might have benefited from chemical assistance, but since no one was eager to confront their success with any kind of negative remarks, the boys continued on with whatever it was they were doing and grew even larger. As in politics, the hopes for a winning football season will permit people to overlook highly questionable behavior.

Opening the door to the Drop-Inn allowed the acrid smell of stale coffee and hamburger grease to escape like foul steam from an aged radiator. As usual the little room was packed with noisy happy kids, plates of greasy food, and rock n' roll music played at a thunderous volume.

There were several qualities that made the Drop-Inn popular among the local young people, the most attractive of which was that after two-thirty in the afternoon the only adult ever visible in the greasy spoon was the proprietor, a scowling fat man who could be found perched on his stool near the kitchen door, silently aloof like the Buddha. The severe look on his face gave the impression that he was perpetually angry and unhappy, but that was mostly for effect because in the next ninety minutes Mr. Weatherwax's establishment would take-in twice as much money as it did throughout the rest of the day. Ken Weatherwax didn't much care for kids, but he had learned to love their money.

Along with decent food at small-town prices, (a half-order of fries sold for twenty-five cents) the management had always maintained a well-stocked jukebox filled with the popular tunes of the day. Times change, and so did the selections, but over the years old Ken Weatherwax had learned to make the most out of the symbiotic relationship between kids and popular music. Despite his personal feelings, he had learned that to insure his patron's enjoyment of their music it was essential that the volume of the jukebox always be kept at painfully high decibel levels. It followed that if they were sonically satisfied more of the minor's money would soon be feeding his machine.

Looking around the busy cafe, Dallas finally located an open table in the back near the jukebox, one that was still covered with the previous patron's dirty dishes and a thirty-five cent tip. As they went to take a seat,

Wendy Biggerstaff, one of the two waitresses working that afternoon, rushed by with a plate full of onion rings and shouted, "Hey, guys. I'll be right back to get those things."

The two sat in silence as an especially weak Bryan Adams tune (*Run to You)* blasted out of the nearby box.

"Kinda crowded," Will said mostly to himself. Dallas nodded in agreement, but said nothing as he slid the expensive black ski jacket off his shoulders and onto the back of the chair.

Over the years, Will had learned that it was best to say as little as possible, especially if Douglas Capernick was around. Perpetually desperate for any kind of companionship, the small kid now spent his mornings with the other "special" students in the South wing of the building, mostly bored and afraid of his teachers. Then after lunch he was forced to rejoin the others for the obligatory Business Math, and his only elective: two blocks of auto mechanics.

Although no one knew it, Will Samuelson did not care for auto mechanics. Back in the fall, a well-intentioned but particularly lazy guidance counselor had convinced his parents, "Will, should be taking the kind of courses that can help him find work once he graduates."

The boy's unspoken objection to spending his afternoons in the auto shop was not so much about working on cars, but more about his relationship with the other students. At best, he was dismissed, ignored, or rejected by the very kids that he had grown up with. At the worst, he was bullied and beaten by the same thugs who were themselves ostracized by their peers. The closest thing to kindness that Will Samuelson ever experienced was the indifferent tolerance he received from Dallas Albright.

Their fries and Cokes came and went as did the steady stream of Freeland High students. Dallas was preparing to pay the bill when a group of girls who'd been occupying the large booth on the other side of the room got up to leave. The last person to slide out of the high-backed booth was Debbie Dorsett.

When she looked at him it felt as if his esophagus had swollen shut.

For the more myopic people of Freeland, Debbie Dorsett's defining feature was that she was the third of Stephen and Lecia Dorsett's five progeny. Because she was the Methodist minister's daughter, people automatically pigeonholed her into that exclusive caste of the devout, a classification that was certainly true on its surface, but when exaggerated left the very real possibility of stealing whatever individuality she hoped to enjoy.

278

At a time when most young girls were consumed with the ridiculous flamboyant styles of the day, one's deliberately fashioned and merchandized to a generation awestruck by MTV, Debbie Dorsett chose the path less conspicuous. Her amber hair was usually pulled back to emphasize a thin and finely chiseled face, one accentuated by high attractive cheekbones. Unlike the painted idols that her classmates so eagerly plagiarized, Debbie's beautiful unblemished skin and quiet gray eyes went unpainted and mostly unnoticed. There was the occasional nod to fashion, but as a rule she would downplay her curves by wearing slacks or jeans and loose fitting tops.

As for her friends, they were satisfied not to compete among Freeland's "popular crowd." The girls she enjoyed played in the band, volunteered to make the yearbook, and generally kept good grades; fashions, fitting-in, and boys were generally not their first concern.

Moving like a small covey of quail flushed from cover, the other girls instinctively split away from Debbie Dorsett when she approached the table where Dallas and Will were still sitting.

"Hey, Dallas, I got thirty cents. You want some money? You know, for the food," Will asked, apparently oblivious to the approaching girl.

"What?" Dallas asked. "What? No, that's okay," he fumbled, never taking his eyes from hers.

Then she was there, right beside him.

"Hi, Dallas," was all she said as she slid a small yellow piece of paper across the table.

Debbie Dorsett did not stop or turn to look back, but walked straight toward the front door and her waiting friends.

Once the door had closed and all of them were gone, Dallas Albright looked down on the table where the yellow piece of paper lay next to a plate stained bright red with ketchup. He was aware that his heart had started beating again, but he needed to breathe.

An annoying buzz interrupted his thoughts. It was Will Samuelson.

"What's it say?" Will asked.

Dallas had no idea what the note might say, or meant, but he was certain that he did not want to learn the answer while sitting in the Drop-In Diner with Will Samuelson and the thirty other nitwits; all of who were anxiously staring at him.

He opened his hand and allowed the now sweaty money that he'd been holding to fall on the table. Standing, a little shaky, he looked down at Will whose empty blue eyes reflected a common question, "What do we do now?" Sliding his coat over his shoulders, Dallas offered, "I gotta go." Picking up the mysterious slip of paper, the beautiful boy grabbed his jacket and hastily walked out of the door.

"Call me, please. 329-4111 - Debbie."

It was nearly nine o'clock.

For the past two hours, the beautiful boy had been locked in his bedroom where he fretfully considered the possible meaning of the yellow piece of paper and its twenty-nine characters.

Why was this girl asking him to call her? What could she want? And what was with all the drama of a note? With only this limited data available it would be impossible to form any kind of reasoned conclusions. Still, there was something in the way that she had looked at him, something about her friends' behavior, something that said she was interested in him; but why?

There was, of course, only one way to find out.

A woman's voice came on the line.

"Hello. Yes, um… hello. I mean, this is Dallas Albright. I'd like to speak with Debbie, please."

"Yes, Dallas," the voice replied. "Wait one moment, won't you?"

Several years seemed to pass before the voice of Debbie Dorsett came on the line.

"Hi, Dallas; thanks for calling. I'm sorry about the note, but anyway, thanks for calling."

Dallas wasn't sure if it was his turn to say something, or if he should stay silent and let her continue; his steadily intensifying anxiety insured the latter as the default option.

"I suppose you're wondering about why I wanted you to call me. Well, you know the Valentine's Dance is coming up next Saturday and I'm one of the girls, there's like six of us, who've been nominated for the Queen contest. I won't win or anything, I mean they never let a junior win, but I really need an attendant, you know, a guy who will walk with me down the aisle and go through the ceremony. It's not a very long thing, but that's kinda the way it works."

She paused for a moment to catch her breath.

"Well, I was trying to think of someone and my friend Celia, you know, Celia Obermann, she sits next to us in English, she thought maybe you'd be a good person. So, I wanted to ask you if you'd be my escort to the dance."

Dallas was flabbergasted and struck mute.

A very, very long ten-second passed before anyone spoke.

Then Debbie came back on the line, "I mean it's no big deal. If you're already going, or don't want to… I mean, I understand."

Somehow, Dallas uttered the incredible sentence, "No… I mean, yes… I mean, well, no, I'm not going, but, yes, I would like to go with you. Yes."

280

There was a brief pause on the other end of the line, followed by the slightly confused but clearly cheerful reply, "That's great. Maybe tomorrow we can talk at school, or at the Drop, and I can tell you what we have to do. It's no big deal, but my mom's pretty hyper about me doing this, so, anyway, how about tomorrow after school? I can meet you at the Drop-Inn. Does that work?"

"Sure."

"Okay. Thanks. See you then. Bye."

The receiver went dead as Dallas head exploded.

It had been an extraordinary day.

Although he and Debbie had only the two classes together, it seemed like everywhere he went she was there, surrounded by a gaggle of girlfriends, smiling calmly, and always making eye contact. Why had he never noticed her before?

Then there was the unexpected moment in Mr. Carlings' third period English literature class when their eyes met just as Karen Kloppenburg began to read aloud from Christopher Marlowe's play, *Doctor Faustus*; the one that begins,

"Was this the face that launched a thousand ships
And burnt the topless towers of Ilium?
Sweet Helen, make me immortal with a kiss."

For some reason he neither understood nor anticipated, the beautiful confusing words produced a rush of awkward embarrassment that shot up his spine and then through his brain like an electrical shock, forcing him to look away from Debbie and down on his text book.

For lunch he was back at his old table with the Goon Squad, enduring another twenty minutes of their stupid jokes and verbal assaults on any unfortunate fool who passed too close. Even though he knew how dangerous it was, he couldn't help himself from occasionally sneaking a cautious glance across the room to where Debbie and her friends were sitting. Had any of the knuckleheads around the table even suspected such an interest, it would have unleashed an intolerable explosion of stupid remarks and physical hazing. He knew it, he hated it, but that was the price he paid to the people with whom he associated.

By the time the last bell rang, Dallas Albright was electric with anticipation.

To avoid the complications of explaining to Will why he must go the diner alone, Dallas raced out of the building without stopping at his locker to dump his books or retrieve his winter parka. Halfway down the hill there was a brief moment of regret that he'd not confronted Will directly. This reaction wasn't so much about feeling bad for ignoring the guy, but more because he was concerned that the kid would just show up and expect to join them. The countermove was for Dallas to get to the Drop ahead of the others and secure a table with only two chairs.

Thankfully, wonderfully, Debbie Dorsett came alone.

The conversation began tentatively with Debbie doing most of the talking. She cheerfully explained how the coronation ceremony was to work and the things Dallas needed to consider: like wearing a suit, buying her a corsage, and providing the transportation. The later would be no problem; he was already imagining her reaction to the Super Sport.

What came as a complete surprise was that after only a few minutes together this remarkable girl, a person with whom he'd gone to school for more than ten years but of who he knew almost nothing, seemed attentive, even interested in the dumb little ideas he would offer. Before long he heard himself telling her things that he would have never shared with anyone: feelings about school, his so-called friends, and even his challenging relationship with his parents. She listened to it all, nodding her head, and even agreeing about how difficult it was to talk with her own folks. Time was meaningless, and if there were other people in the diner Dallas was unaware of them. Across the table was a singular beautiful face looking back and smiling at just him.

"Can I get you guys anything else?"

Debbie Dorsett turned to the waitress and spoke first. "No thanks, Wendy. I need to be going."

Wendy nodded as she tore the bill out of her pad before judiciously dropping it in the middle of the table.

Dallas quickly grabbed for the piece of paper while reaching for his wallet.

"Let me pay mine, okay?" Debbie offered.

"No. It's okay. I want to…"

Dallas knew she was about to stand up and leave, but he selfishly did not want to stop looking at this face. How many times had she passed by while he contentedly ignored the world? Had she been right there next to him as he stood oblivious to everyone and everything? Was it possible that she had always been there, but until this moment he'd never seen her? It was incredible, impossible, and unbelievable. Was this happiness? Better question: Does it go away?

The need to buy Debbie Dorsett a corsage, a word he recognized but with which he had no personal history, forced Dallas to finally break down and share the unexpected change in his social status with his mother. She was, of course, delighted, giddy delighted, which only amplified his already heightened anxieties. With predictable uninvited enthusiasm, Emily took it upon herself to call Debbie's mother under the guise of inquiring about the color of her dress, "a courtesy," she explained, so that they might buy a flower of an appropriate complementary color. The fact that she was taking such excessive pleasure in this new and highly personal experience stole only a small portion of his own enthusiasm.

Standing in front of the mirror and looking at himself in his blue suit made him feel stupid. The last and only time he'd ever worn the thing, which he swore would be the last time he'd wear the thing, had been the previous summer for his church confirmation from Saint John's Lutheran. He was mildly put-off by the fact that it still fit. Thankfully, his father interceded after the third photo and rescued his son with the line, "Look at the time, Em. This fellow needs to be on his way."

Even though he'd been given the keys to the Super Sport back on Christmas Eve, they'd mostly hung on the hook by the refrigerator alongside the keys to the family Caprice and his father's pickup. After he finally got his license, he'd been allowed to drive the car a total of four times; all during the day, and always by himself. On each occasion, his father would mercilessly drill him on the importance of safety, their one-sided, non-negotiable agreement about passengers - there weren't to be any until the end of March - and the need to set a good example for his younger brother by being a "responsible driver." So far, he'd lived up to his side of the bargain.

In spite of all of his anticipation about taking out the Super Sport, the act itself came with serious reservations, ones that took the form of deep bucket seats. Like his father, Dallas was short. At five-foot-five, he could see over the steering wheel well enough to drive safely, but if you were to see him through the driver's-side window all that appeared was the top of his head. From this perspective he looked like a kid driving a powerful muscle car, which is exactly what he was but did not wish to be.

To elevate his profile, Dallas tested a dark blue cushion which perfectly matched the car's upholstery. This boost offered some vertical improvement, but the thought of using it to cruise the streets of Freeland with Douglas Capernick at his side was out of the question.

Stepping out into their large and immaculate garage, ("A place for everything, and everything in its place," his father would demand) Dallas Albright pushed the glowing yellow button to open the double-sized garage door on a cold and windy February night. A swirl of biting wind around his ankles confirmed the evening's weather forecast, the one that had called for a combination of clear high pressure skies and frigid temperatures; temps cold enough to cut through even a heavy overcoat.

For the past twenty-four hours, he'd been making a meticulous set of mental notes to insure that he didn't overlook even the smallest of detail.

The cassette mix-tape of music he hoped Debbie would like was loaded in the car's tape deck, the corsage (a twelve dollar lavender cymbidium orchid) was pinned inside its clear plastic box and was now sitting on the passenger seat beside him, he had twenty-five dollars in cash in the high hopes that after the dance she might want to stop for something to eat, and tucked secretly into his jacket pocket was a small box of Tic Tac breath mints.

As he slipped the car into reverse and gingerly let out the clutch, the Super Sport glided out of the garage and down the driveway toward a strange new world.

The Dorsett family lived next door to the Methodist Church in a small and unassuming clapboard house provided by the members of the parish. In order to make sure that there would be no slip-ups in getting there, Dallas had secretly made a practice run by the place earlier in the afternoon. As he slowly drove his powerful black car past the church parking lot next to the house, he tried to imagine how five children and two adults could manage in such a tiny place? After all, the house that he lived in was twice this size but only needed to accommodate four.

This important question was temporarily tabled as the beautiful boy physically forced the car door open against the blustering wind. With the clear plastic box firmly wedged under his left arm, Dallas noted the tremble in his right hand as he reached up to knock on the Dorsett's weathered front door.

Before he could lay skin to wood, the porch light flashed on and the door opened a crack to reveal a pair of bright blue eyes. This, he decided, must be Debbie's youngest sibling, Judith.

"Hello," Dallas said to the eyes. "Is your sister ready?"

The girl said nothing but closed the door, leaving the anxious boy to wonder and shiver in the cold glare of a 60-watt light bulb.

A moment later the door reopened; the small blue eyes were replaced by Debbie's older brother, John.

John Dorsett was a year older and a senior at Freeland High School. A slim, sandy-haired boy only slightly taller but much thinner than Dallas, he too was wearing a blue suit, although in his case it showed considerably more wear. As far as Dallas knew, John Dorsett had been invisible his entire life; he played no sports, took part in no extra activities at school, and was meaningless to anything, or anyone, that Dallas had ever met. As the two stood and stared at one another, the beautiful boy was reminded that even though they lived in the same small town and went to the same little school, he knew absolutely nothing about this person.

"Sorry," the taller kid finally offered, "it looks like Jude didn't do a very good job of greeting you. Come on in. I think Debbie's about ready."

The house was warm and smelled of sausage and cooked cabbage, making it all seem even closer and smaller than it looked from the outside. From an adjoining room, Pastor Stephen Dorsett suddenly appeared, wiping his hands on a white towel that had been wrapped around his thin waste. Smiling broadly while extending his hand, he approached Dallas in three long strides.

"Hello, I'm Debbie's father. You must be Dallas."

"Yes, Sir. It's a pleasure to meet you." Dallas replied, while offering what he hoped was a firm confident handshake, a greeting that he'd been practicing in the mirror for three days.

"Yes," the minister countered with a confident honest smile, "it's good to meet you, too. Things have been a little crazy around here with Debbie's nomination, and her mother's, well, let's say enthusiasm."

Dallas wasn't exactly sure what he meant by "enthusiasm," but before he was forced to reply another Dorsett (Debbie's younger brother, Aaron) appeared at the bottom of the nearby stairs. In a loud and melodramatic voice, he announced, "Ladies and gentlemen, I present to you the Queen of the Freeland Valentine's Dance, her highness, Queen Debra."

"How corny," Dallas thought, but then Debra Dorsett appeared on the narrow stairwell.

She was a dream, shimmering in a long-sleeved dress of pale blue, a thin silver necklace with its pendant cross draped elegantly around her long graceful neck. Her hair was still pulled back, but now it was braided and impeccably tied. If she wore make-up, and certainly she did, it had been applied so perfectly that it was invisible.

Striking a regal pose, the beautiful queen majestically stretched out her gloved hand to lightly touch the younger brother on his shoulder.

"Arise, young man,' she laughed while looking over at Dallas and stopping his heart. "Be quick about it. My carriage is waiting."

What followed was as unfamiliar to the beautiful boy as the landscape of the moon. The family, all five of them, willingly, happily, enthusiastically gathered together for pictures. Mrs. Dorsett, who had just rushed down the stairs, fluttered for a moment over Debbie to adjust some microscopic hair that was out of place, and then after offering to take his coat began to arrange the queen and her "escort" into a series of different poses and locations. There were three photos of Dallas presenting Debbie with the corsage, five photos of Dallas gamely trying - unsuccessfully - to pin the flower onto the shoulder of her dress, two more of her mother adjusting the flower, eight pictures of the two of them standing first side by side, then arm in arm, and then again back side by side, six of just Debbie, four of the queen and her father, six with her mother, and three that Dallas snapped of the whole family. The only reason that the photo session stopped was that they finally ran out of film; the three rolls in Mrs. Dorsett's purse had to be "saved for the processional."

When the couple finally escaped the stifling heat of the little house and stepped away from the shelter of the Dorsett's front porch, a stiff northwest wind mercilessly whipped at their backs. Thin wisps of high stratocumulus clouds raced across a moonless, ink-black sky, occasionally allowing the brighter stars to blink on, and then disappear. In his best impression of a gentleman, Dallas shuffled a step or two ahead of his date to politely hold open the passenger door to the Super Sport; an act of chivalry that he had never performed before in his life.

After sliding into the driver's seat he glanced over at Debbie who now sat serenely beside him. Smiling at him - only him - she offered, "Thanks again for being such a good sport about all of this. My mother is being just so weird." Although he wasn't exactly sure what she meant by "weird," he was delighted to find that in the Camaro's deep bucket seat she was the same height as he. Across the console that divided them, the pale-green iridescent glow of the dashboard lights illuminated a calm lovely face that smiled back at only him. Her long, elegant hair was pulled around to lie on her shoulder, while the gloved hands rested quietly in her lap. He knew he could sit there in that spot all night, say absolutely nothing and still be perfectly happy.

Except she'd asked him a question, hadn't she? It was something about her mother, maybe?

Peter Gabriel answered for him.

"Sledgehammer."

The cassette player in the Camaro had been pre-loaded with a mix-tape, one that had been prepared with the same level of precision and attention to detail as a professional defusing a bomb. Before getting out of the car to walk up to the Dorsett's front door, Dallas had with both purpose and forethought shoved the plastic cassette into the tape deck so that it would begin playing with the start of the engine. Anticipating the likelihood of his own anxiety and its certain negative impact on conversation, he settled on an up-tempo tune that would last just long enough to get them from her house to school. *Sledgehammer* (by the English singer, Peter Gabriel) was the perfect combination of hip, but not too hip; snappy, but still something you could talk over.

As Peter Gabriel recommended, *"All you do is call me, I'll be anything you need."* Dallas unconsciously put the car into first gear and released the clutch. The black Camaro rolled forward, lurched once, and then tragically died. His poor work with the clutch had killed the engine on the very first moment of his very first date.

The crush of embarrassment left him inert. He looked down at the steering wheel as if to ask, "How could you do this to me?" and then anxiously turned to look over at Debbie Dorsett to assess the damage.

"I didn't know you had a car, Dallas. This is very nice. When did you get it?"

Snapped back into reality by her wonderful face-saving questions, questions that meant she either didn't notice or didn't care that he'd just foolishly killed his own car right there in the church parking lot, Dallas quickly reached down and restarted the waiting machine. As he slipped the Hurst T-shifter into reverse, applied a slightly higher rpm, and then anxiously released the clutch, he replied, "Thanks. This was my parent's car when they first got married. They gave it to me for Christmas."

She smiled and turned to look out the window, nodding her head in time to the music.

"God damn," he thought. "Where have I been?"

It was a remarkable night for the beautiful boy, but then he had nothing with which to compare it.

Debbie's consuming smile and confident ease around the other candidates made the actual coronation ceremony considerably more laid-back than Dallas had imagined. There was a mildly shaky stretch that lasted about five minutes when he had to escort his candidate down a long aisle of paper streamers and endless flashing cameras - including those of his own mother - while Whitney Houston droned on and on about *the greatest love of all.*" But after they'd gotten up on the stage and Debbie was just about to sit down, she gently pinched his arm and smiled in a way that he hoped said more than "thanks."

Debbie was right in her prediction that a senior girl would win. On this night a popular cheerleader named Samantha English was named Queen of the Freeland High School Valentine's Day Dance. She and her friends all seemed very happy about it. Debbie Dorsett and Dallas Albright were equally pleased, but for entirely different reasons.

Like most boys his age, Dallas Albright did not know how to dance. Perhaps if he had understood Shaw's perspective that "dance is the vertical expression of a horizontal desire" he might have been more enthusiastic about the experience. However, in his defense - and, sadly, there is little that can be said in Dallas Albright's defense - this was not an activity that Debbie Dorsett had mentioned as one of his responsibilities.

"Alright ladies and gents, it's time for the Queen's first dance. Can I get our Queen and her court out on the dance floor?"

The DJ dropped the needle on Lionel Richie's tiresome *Say You, Say Me,* and in those silent seconds before the music started Dallas Albright will discover one of Mother Nature's more powerful truths: When Debbie

Dorsett smiled at him in that way, (that, "I know you don't want to, but I want you to." kind of way) he knew he was going to follow her out on the dance floor and do whatever she asked. The clear, sharp, smart part of his brain yelled its warning that he was being manipulated, that she was using her feminine charms to control his thoughts and behavior. But he welcomed it. Putting his arm around her waist nearly buckled his knees. It was being this close, so close he could see the dark flecks in her gray eyes, hear her short crisp breathing, and smell the intoxicating combination of perfume and perspiration that ended this version of his life, this *lucky life,* and opened his cold selfish heart to a new possibility.

"Didn't know you could dance, Shorty?"

The menacing voice of Douglas Capernick came as an unwelcome surprise.

With the gymnasium's main overhead lights off, and only a handful of colored spotlights left to illuminate the dance floor, it was difficult to immediately locate the voice. Shielding his eyes against the glare, Dallas discovered that Douglas was not alone; standing beside him was Goon Gordonski and, surprisingly, Will Samuelson. In their raggedy blue jeans and thin white T-shirts, all three were seriously underdressed for both the occasion and the climate. Each wore their own version of a dull smirking grin, the kind that made him feel like he'd been caught doing something stupid and laughable.

With Debbie now shielded behind him, and his so-called friends lurking portentously in the dark, it appeared that he'd made a serious miscalculation by not informing them of his date. But between his growing infatuation for the girl, and his own personal need to remain private and disconnected from them, he'd purposefully chosen to remain silent, hoping to at least get through this first date without their interference. If something good came of it, then fine, he'd face that with more confidence; if not, he could dismiss it as a stupid lapse in judgment and take his lumps.

Over in his corner of the gymnasium, the DJ suddenly screamed, "What's ailin' you people, anyway? Well, you know Mr. Electric's got the cure! Let's jump!"

Mr. Electric's silly challenge was immediately followed by the scratch of needle on vinyl and the well-known synthesizer opening to Van Halen's massive MTV hit, *Jump.*

From somewhere back in the darkness, Will Samuelson giggled, "Yeah, Shorty, those are some pretty good moves." A split second later the ugly sound of a hard, bone-crunching punch could be heard as Goon Gordonski turned upon the smaller boy.

"Yeah, I'm a fantastic dancer," Dallas muttered mostly to himself.

Stepping out of the bright lights, he quickly surveyed the situation with a particular interest in potential exit strategies; under the circumstances, this was no place for Debbie Dorsett.

Douglas continued to eye him suspiciously, but added, "Nice suit. Hi, Debbie. It's pretty cool that you were one of the Queen candidates. Sorry you didn't win. You know I voted for you."

"Thank you, Douglas. Did you bring a date?" she asked, already knowing the answer.

Still keeping a steady gaze on the beautiful boy, Douglas replied, "No, not tonight. We just heard that our boy Dallas was going to be here, so we thought we'd stop by."

"How'd you hear that?" Dallas asked.

"Well, I called your house to see if you wanted to hang out with us, and your mom told me you were here. She was kind of funny, you know? She said you had a date. Well, I thought how could that be, I mean, you didn't say anything to me. Did he say anything to you, Gordon?"

Forcing his visibly trembling hands down into the pockets of his jeans, the giant goon sneered back, "Nope."

"How about you Will? Did your buddy here say anything about escorting this beautiful girl to the Valentine's Dance?"

Before the smaller boy could reply, Douglas turned and glared at him in a way that made it clear he would be wise not to make a sound.

"I guess it must've just slipped your mind." Douglas concluded, as he turned back to inspect the couple.

"Yeah, I guess so. It happened sort of fast," Dallas offered, hoping to let it drop.

A smile that could never be confused with anything happy spread across Douglas Capernick's face, just before he turned on Debbie and abruptly pulled her out onto the dance floor.

"Come on, let's dance," he shouted over the music.

A moment later the two were out under the colored lights.

Van Halen's powerhouse *Jump* is a loud immense tune that does not offer a common danceable groove. For Debbie, who now found herself on the dance floor with a boy whose motives were both masked and utterly suspicious, this uncomfortable situation had suddenly shifted her *lucky life* light-years from the familiar. Fiercely planted in the center of the dance floor's kaleidoscope, Douglas began by offering his anxious dance partner an impudent smile of encouragement, all the while steadily tapping only the right toe of his shiny, snakeskin Tony Lama boot. Apparently aware of her shrinking options, Debbie Dorsett responded cautiously, first by moving her arms and shoulders in time with the backbeat, before tentatively circling the striking young man like a gypsy around the campfire.

A wave of surprise and then recognition swept across the floor as the other dancers realized that something unusual and potentially explosive was happening. Those still left on the floor began to slowly drift off into the shadows in order that they might better study this unlikely couple.

Dallas did not like what he saw, or felt; a new and inexplicable emotion was causing his blood pressure to soar and the bile to rise in his throat.

"This is so wrong," he thought. "Why is this guy, who's supposed to be my friend, acting this way? What's the point of his coming here anyway; to make me look stupid, to ruin my night with Debbie?"

From behind him came a small voice whispering something in his ear.

"Careful with these guys," Will warned him. "We've been into the medicine, if you know what I mean."

Dallas did not know what he meant. This was a new and confusing phrase.

"Medicine, what kind of medicine," he wondered? "Booze? Pot? Something else, maybe?"

While Eddie Van Halen's screaming guitar solo jet propelled the song into an even higher orbit, it appeared as if Douglas Capernick was still in control. With mostly attitude and very little movement, the handsome confident kid effortlessly dominated both the space and his dance partner.

The same could not be said for Goon Gordonski. Straddling the line between the dark and the light, the giant kid was now hyper-fixated on the only couple left on the dance floor. Swaying like a drunk while manically chewing his lower lip, it was clear that whatever "medicine" he'd taken had pushed him very close to the edge. His trembling hands and spastic efforts to find the rhythm left no doubt that the monster had been wound too tight.

Then Mr. Electric was screaming at them again.

"Hey, hey, hey, there friends, Mr. Electric's got a request to play this one by Robert Palmer. I know I'm *Addicted to Love!*"

The sudden shift from the synth-powered Van Halen to crushing chainsaw guitars and the steady crack of a four-beat had left the room in mild confusion. As those observing from the edges watched to see if this new and unlikely couple were going to continue to dance, Debbie Dorsett cleverly resolved the matter by first offering a bemused smile and short curtsy before spritely walking back toward the dark place where she had left Dallas and Will. With a triumphant grin, Douglas Capernick melodramatically bowed to the other invisible dancers while waving to his imaginary ovation.

From out of the dim, Goon Gordonski unexpectedly lurched forward at the innocent girl, cruelly grabbing her slender naked wrist and dragging her back toward the center of the floor.

"Come on, Queenie. Dance," Gordonski shouted at the terrified girl. A gob of white spittle flew from his mouth and landed on the hem of her blue gown. "I wanna dance, too."

Without any sense of rhythm or style the giant began spastically flailing his muscular arms above his head in a freakish exercise that was both out of sync and step. Alone again in that spot of green light, Debbie Dorsett now stood unmoving and inert; panic screamed from her eyes. The only other person still on the dance floor was Douglas Capernick who remained off to the side, still smiling, but detached and disconnected, his arms tightly folded across his chest.

Although the situation defied all reason, for Dallas Albright this *lucky life* was now frozen in space and time. In those first precious seconds, the beautiful boy had already considered three different options for what he would do next, including pulling the fire alarm. Through those pointless years of attending public school, the worthless weekends he'd wasted at Saint John's, the unwanted enthusiasm of the scouts, the open hostility of his guidance counselors, the busybody teachers and, of course, his own tragic family, it had been the strange apprenticeship with Grandma Johanna that now proved valuable. Of all the people who had tried to dominate him, to remake him into some version of themselves, it was his crazy grandmother who had provided a useful education. It was Grandma Jo who made sure that in those unexpected moments where everyone else had gone mad, he could still think clearly. Experience had taught him that a nightmare like this had little to do with size; it was all about being faster, smarter, and absolutely fearless. He knew what to do.

"I said dance, bitch," the Goon bellowed down on the petrified girl. "Come on. Let's dance."

Dallas Albright was deliberately moving along the dark edge of the shadows, when from behind him the small swift Will Samuelson suddenly appeared. In an instant, he zipped past the mad giant to gently take the terrified girl by the hand. Then neatly spinning her away from the brute, Will shouted back over his shoulder, "Come on, Debbie. Let's you and me dance."

"Your lights are on, but you're not home," shrieked Robert Palmer, just before the huge boy crashed forward and mercilessly cold-cocked little Will Samuelson in the side of the head, sending him to the floor in a heap at Debbie's feet.

Mr. Electric glanced up from his stack of records just in time to see the small boy's head bounce off the hardwood of the gymnasium floor. The shock and complete brutality of the scene caused the startled DJ to spastically lurch forward over the turntable and onto his equipment. The phonograph needle ripped across the vinyl producing a horrible shredding sound that instantly silenced both Robert Palmer and the crowd of stunned witnesses. In the split second of pristine silence that followed, Goon Gordonski would be forever left standing over the cataleptic Will Samuelson, his giant right paw still balled in a fist.

Dallas was there now on his knees in between the broken boy on the floor and the frozen girl in the green spotlight, a motionless brute towered over them. From back in the shadows, the dull murmur of voices was getting louder and louder; the voyeurs and vultures were rapidly descending on the scene. Debbie's brother, John unexpectedly appeared. Without a word or a glance at either Dallas or the monster, the older boy put his protective arm around his catatonic sister and swiftly led her back into the darkness.

"Hey, big fella. Maybe we better get going."

Douglas Capernick warily pulled on the back of the thug's sweat-soaked T-shirt. "Will's gonna be all right, but maybe we should…"

A spastic twitch of Goon Gordonski's enormous head spun it sideways to consider Douglas Capernick.

"Whoa, no worries. Be cool. We can hook up with Will later, but we better get going."

"Will," Dallas whispered, as he pulled the boy upright against his chest. "Can you hear me?"

A trickle of blood oozed from his right ear and ran part way down his neck onto the collar of his T-shirt. Dallas looked up at Douglas Capernick with the hope that before any adults showed up he would personally drag the diseased animal out the back door and kill it.

"You should go now," Dallas said, then abruptly turned his back as a shield.

Looking down on Will's innocent face, he could hear his grandmother's voice reminding him to, "Stop with the emotion and stay clear."

Still, it remained an indisputable fact that there was no place on earth for someone as cruel and warped as Goon Gordonski. What more evidence did anyone need than the smashed pathetic boy that now lay unconscious on the gymnasium floor? The perfect permanent solution was for this freak to be culled from the tribe; tied and drug out by his heels before being painfully, publicly destroyed. Goon Gordonski did not need medicine; he needed to be executed in the most humiliating way possible. Only a truly brutal and bloody death would communicate the message of "hands off" to all those other assholes who behaved just like him. It was time that little mindless boys should be free from fear, free from thugs and traitors. Free.

Lying there in his arms, he could feel the trembling of little Will Samuelson coming back from the other side. He wasn't dead after all. In this version of his *lucky life* he would live, mostly deaf in his right ear, but still alive; alive in a world that did not care.

292

By the time Dallas got Will on his feet and moving toward the safety of the shadows, the two faculty chaperones were on them with their stupid questions and self-serving directions.

"What happened to the boy?" Harriet Tisdale (English I and II) shouted down at Dallas just as Prince began to profess his deep love to someone wearing a *Raspberry Beret.*

Dallas looked up at the confused large lady in the dark blue pant suit and replied in his most confident voice, "I'm not exactly sure. I think he fell and hit his head."

Peering down to look into Will's glazed eyes, Harriet asked, "Can he speak?"

"Sure," Dallas lied. "He just got the wind knocked out of him."

Will Samuelson's problems began when the rotational force from Goon Gordonski's vicious sucker punch created such a rapid acceleration in his little cranium that the squishy cerebrospinal fluid (the gooey stuff that surrounds the brain like Jell-O) was unable to properly cushion the meat from the bone. His *concussus,* (L. "action of striking together.") initiated both chemical and electrical chaos to the nerve cell's tiny membranes. When the potassium (K, atomic #19) from within those bazillions of nerve cells started migrating out of the membranes and into the gaps, the glutamates (the traffic cops of neuroscience) were all set free to try to calm the crowd and stifle any additional nerve activity. Reinforcements were soon needed to restore balance to the depleted glutes, so, naturally, the sodium-potassium ion pumps kicked-in. This sounds both helpful and impressive, except it caused an excessive consumption of adenosine triphosphate, which, unfortunately, permitted lactate to pool-up and slow the flow of blood; the boy's brain was having an energy crisis.

"What's his name?" Gretchen Safeway-Henderson (Home Economics and Typing) shouted.

Dallas instantly recognized a promising advantage. Even though Will Samuelson had lived in Freeland his entire life, and had spent more than three years in the same building as Henderson and Tisdale, neither of these women had the faintest idea who he was or what had happened. This remarkable lack of data offered the perfect opportunity for Dallas to fill in the gaps and ultimately then leave them satisfied.

"This is Will, Ms. Tisdale. You remember Will Samuelson?"

Harriet Tisdale bent down to take another longer look into the freckled face, and then grimaced at either her bad memory or Will's condition.

Either way, Dallas had her on the ropes.

"Maybe we should fill out a form or a report or something?" Dallas suggested to the English teacher. "It's probably no big deal, but, you know, you're in charge."

The two women looked at one another like they'd been told they needed a root canal.

"We were just outside in the hallway and really couldn't hear the commotion over the music," Safeway-Henderson said mostly to Harriet Tisdale. Both women bent down again to look at little Will who was vacantly staring off into space; a look that was not entirely new or unique. Then speaking directly to Dallas, Harriet Tisdale asked, "Will you take him home, or should we call his parents?"

The beautiful boy recognized that the answer to this question would be the single most important response he'd ever provided his former English teacher. To say, "Yes," implied he would drive Will home, which solved his problem with the teachers, but probably ended his date with Debbie. But, to say, "No," made him seem selfish and uncaring; qualities that could kill his credibility with the chaperones, as well as his new relationship with the Dorsett's, who were just now reappearing from the shadows. Watching closely as the brother and sister approached, he remembered something Grandma Jo had once said, "If you have to choose between the truth and a lie, go with what they want to hear."

"I guess I can take him home... if you want," Dallas said, knowing that this solution would satisfy the two teachers, Goon Gordonski, and Douglas Capernick. How it would play with the Dorsett's remained to be seen.

Now that Will had perked-up enough so that he didn't look like he was going to vomit or die, most of the spectators were satisfied to wander back to the party. Still peaked and plenty woozy, the kid sat silently in the same chair that Dallas had provided when they first came off the floor. Nearby, the worried chaperones continued to pace back and forth, wringing their tiny little well-oiled hands, and whispering to one another. It was obvious that their solution was for Will Samuelson to recover enough so the "Albright boy could take him home," thereby removing the two of them from any further responsibility.

"How's Will?" John Dorsett asked without looking at him.

As the taller boy approached, Dallas automatically stood to face him which allowed Debbie to sit down next to Will. Her face seemed more relaxed, her hands had stopped shaking, and there was even the slight hint of a smile. As she reached out and gently touched Will's shoulder, Dallas also thought he recognized genuine concern for the little guy who had so bravely come to her rescue. It was not difficult to imagine what Goon Gordonski might have done had Will not spontaneously decided to throw himself into the breach.

Dallas measured John Dorsett carefully before he spoke, knowing that any future he hoped to have with his sister likely hinged on how he managed the next few minutes.

"I'm not really sure. It seems like he's coming around. I got the blood wiped off before those two showed up," he said, pointing toward the chaperones.

John nodded as if he were considering the news, but then added, "You've got some pretty weird friends, you know. What's wrong with that guy?"

Dallas shrugged his shoulders, "I don't know. He's no friend of mine."

"Well, somebody said that he was on drugs."

Alarm bells went off in Dallas' head. Given John's accurate assessment of Goon Gordonski's condition, it wasn't going to be much of a mental leap to link him with the reprobate. If Dallas wanted to have any chance of salvaging the rest of the night with Debbie, not to mention any possibility for one in the future, he needed to quickly redirect and get the girl involved.

"It's like I said, John, I don't really know him." Then turning back to face Debbie and Will, he bent down and asked the boy, "How you feeling, buddy? You want us to take you home now?"

Tisdale and Safeway-Henderson were behind him hanging on the answer to the question.

"Yeah," mumbled Will, "guess I am kinda tired."

Satisfied that the crisis was averted, the two teachers took a final self-satisfied look at Will. Of course, had they taken time to seriously examine the kid, they would have noticed that the right side of his face was starting to swell, while his eyes remained distant and unfocused.

"Now, William," Harriet Tisdale added with a shake of her finger. "You be sure to tell your mother that you fell and hit your head. You can't be too careful when you hit your head."

With a dismissive smile and pat to the top of his head - the same kind of treatment she would have given her cocker spaniel if he'd peed on the kitchen floor - the teacher turned back to her colleague and suggested, "Maybe we should call Principal Greenway?"

Safeway-Henderson had already walked away and was headed for the food table. She stopped just long enough to reply, "It's late. Probably better if we don't."

When Harriet Tisdale nodded in agreement, Dallas knew that he'd won. That is until John Dorsett announced, "Maybe it's best if we go home, Debbie."

Dallas wasn't sure if it was disappointment or concern that he saw in her sad face, but it was clear she would do as he commanded. Resigned to this unexpected outcome, Debbie Dorsett turned to consider her foolish hero, before lightly stroking his head. Standing to accept her brother's outstretched hand, she tried a smile.

"I'm so sorry, Dallas," she whispered without catching his gaze.

As he watched them walk away, a debate raged in the beautiful boy's head: "Should I argue with John and try to convince him that I was the one she'd asked to the dance, and that it was me who should be taking her home; or, is it smarter to lose tonight and play the long game?"

From behind him, Mr. Electric whispered, "Let's make this one a ladies choice." as Paul Young offered his thoughts on *Every Time You Go Away*.

Chapter Fourteen

Murder and Hope

"There is no terror in a bang, only in the anticipation of it."
The Dark Side of Genius - Alfred Hitchcock

School on Monday was especially weird. From the minute he walked through the door it seemed as if everyone was looking at him, studying him like he was some form of new mutant life.

At first, he was put-off by their unwanted intrusion into his personal life. It was true that he'd gone to school with most of them since those first days at kindergarten, but he claimed none of them as friends. He contentedly ignored most of their school functions, took part in no extracurricular activities, and generally avoided any kind of personal contact that required a sustained conversation. His indifference made it clear that he had nothing to say to them and sincerely wanted to be left alone.

So what had changed that would account for these whispers behind his back? Why was it that every nobody he didn't want to know had suddenly developed such a keen interest in how he was going to react to the Valentine's Day Dance, especially the part between him and Debbie Dorsett?

Almost as frustrating as this new and unwanted interest in his personal life was the matter of what was going to happen when he first saw her. He'd spent most of Sunday working up a kind of speech, but each attempt was rejected for being too obvious, too meek, too aggressive, or too stupid.

Then somewhere around midnight, he realized he'd been looking at it wrong; his wasn't so much a problem of how, it was more about what - what exactly did he want? Did he want to see her again? Was there some expectation that they become boyfriend and girlfriend? As for the dance, was she expecting an explanation for something he couldn't explain? What was the deal with her brother? If they did go out again, was he going to be there? What about her folks; how did they feel about their daughter being molested by a drug-crazed lunatic, especially since he seemed to have some kind of ambiguous connection to the boy who'd taken her to the dance in the first place?

By third period English he was as worthless as a wooden watch. The nagging uncertainty about his personal life and general disinterest in school had insured he was the last one through the door, slipping in just as Mr. Carling asked, "I trust you all had a good weekend?"

Greasing down the aisle past the second seat in the second row, Debbie Dorsett did not look up as he took his usual spot three desks behind and one row west of hers.

Strike one.

Casually leaning on the corner of his desk, Mr. Carling waited for the mumbling voices to finally soften before holding aloft a book.

"Ladies and gentlemen, please... I'd like to introduce you to your next opportunity to shine. In my hand, I hold one of the finest works of English literature. I am, of course, referring to Charles Dickens' masterpiece, *Great Expectations*."

An audible groan came from the back of the classroom, but Mr. Carling continued on undaunted.

"I expect high school juniors all around the country are making that same unpleasant sound, but I can assure you that two weeks from now, when we are finished and you have all demonstrated your deep understanding and genuine love for this great work of fiction, you will recognize what an ill-mannered and ignorant perspective that truly is."

After collecting a stack of books from his desk, he began walking up and down the aisles handing each student a copy.

"As you will come to discover, *Great Expectations* is a story that can be read on several levels. Take the title, *Great Expectations*. One question that you can anticipate on a future test is how the book's title is reflected in the plot and character development. Who, I wonder, will have these great expectations? Are they fulfilled?"

Handing Dallas a copy of the book, he added, "You are about to meet some of the most fascinating characters in all literature. For example, there's an old spinster named Miss Havisham. What a horrible and wonderfully manipulative old dame, she lives with her adopted daughter, Estella. Dickens cleverly draws this girl as a kind of haughty young girl, which I don't suppose is all that special, but what makes her interesting is that she's been taught by old Miss Havisham to be this vicious shrew, sworn to break the heart of every man she meets.

Great Expectations is known as a *bildungsroman*; does anyone know that word, *bildungsroman*? Well, okay, here's your vocabulary word for the day, and it will be on the test. A *bildungsroman* is German, obviously, and it refers to a literary genre; it means a 'coming of age story.' This one is mostly about a young boy, Phillip Pirrip, or Pip, and not to get too far ahead, but this is Pip's growing up story."

Mr. Carling had distributed all the books and was now standing in a spot directly between Dallas and Debbie Dorsett. The teacher paused just long enough to catch his full attention before closing with, "As you might have guessed from my enthusiastic introduction, *Great Expectations* is one of my personal favorites. I suppose part of it is Dicken's wonderful use of language, but mostly it's the characters. To me, the most interesting part of the story will be Pip's love, his first love, for the beautiful Estella. To lean on a corny expression, it is an unrequited love."

Pausing only a moment, Mr. Carling added, "Okay then, turn to page seventeen, Chapter One of *Great Expectations*, please."

"My father's family name being Pirrip, and my Christian name Philip, my infant tongue could make of both names nothing longer or more explicit than Pip."

The bell rang and Debbie Dorsett bolted from her desk and out the door before anyone else was able to get out of their seats.

Strike two.

It was impossible to think about Debbie Dorsett and not consider how he was going to deal with Douglas Capernick and Goon Gordonski. Lunch seemed the most reasonable and safest.

His tray now loaded with a deeply bruised apple and an over-sized helping of lumpy-gray chicken n' noodles, Dallas surveyed the lunchroom crowd, easily spotting the antagonists at their customary corner table. Their domain was clearly more subdued than usual, and even showed a special empty chair where Will Samuelson - the human punching bag - normally sat. So far there'd been no sign of the little guy, which made Dallas wonder if that was good or bad.

"Hey, Dallas. How's it goin?"

Douglas Capernick pulled the seat beside him back away from the table, inviting the beautiful boy to sit down. Goon Gordonski did not look up from the mound of food on his tray, but continued shoveling in the gruel like it was coal for a steam engine. Extending his right hand toward the seat, Douglas pushed his own tray of half-eaten food out of the way, and offered, "Sit down, man. Everything's good."

Everything wasn't good, but Dallas accepted the offer, eager to finally get on with it.

Taking a long pull on his box of milk, Douglas finally nodded his head as if approving something, and then started, "I just wanted you to know how much I appreciated Saturday night. Gordon and I, well, we were kinda out of it, I guess. Anyway, I hope we didn't wreck your night with Debbie."

Goon Gordonski slurped and fumed but did not look up from his tray of food.

"In a perfect world," Dallas thought to himself, "Goon Gordonski should choke on a bone in that swill. And then while he's coughing and spitting, the whole school, teachers too, can circle around that asshole and watch as he turns blue. Then just before he dies a horrible, frightening death from asphyxiation, he'd look up and realize that no one was going to help him, that there wasn't a person on the planet who cared that this human miscarriage had taken his last breath."

"No problem," the beautiful boy replied.

From the smirk on her face, Ms. Jessica Aldonetru seemed to be thoroughly enjoying herself as she distributed the graded quizzes she had so mercilessly dispensed two weeks before.

"It gives me real pleasure to say that almost all of you received a passing grade. Hopefully, this will encourage the rest of you to pay closer attention, and to read the assigned chapters. Now as we were discussing on Friday…"

Dallas Albright turned over his paper, the same one that he'd been handed right after his dodge ball concussion, the one where he answered only one-third of the questions, the one with the small red "F" in the corner, and then happily turned off the switch to his attention.

"Okay. Fine," he thought. "That's just perfect. I get my brains scrambled, and for what, an "F." A failure, yeah, that's about right. Well, they can all stuff it. To hell with it."

The bell finally rang but he was in no hurry to move on to his last class of the day; what was the point, he had no intention of doing any of the work he'd been assigned. Like everything else he could think of school was irrelevant, a complete and utter drag; a charade in which he could see no advantage in delaying the inevitable? There was nothing, or no one, that made any difference.

"Dallas," said Jessica Aldonetru, "shouldn't you be going to your next class?"

The room was empty now as the little bird woman offered one more inconsequential peep in a world full of unwanted noise. Since she no longer meant anything, he leisurely collected his books and backpack before offering an empty smile and wandering out the door.

In stark contrast to his indifferent disposition, the current in the hallway was flowing frantically back-and-forth like supercharged electrons; students were bouncing off the walls and into each other as they wildly raced to avoid being late for something. Then just as the first bell began to ring, the stream unexpectedly shifted forcing the beautiful boy to sidestep a clingy hippie couple causing a chain reaction that ended with a second geeky maniac gracelessly dumping his tall stack of books.

"You wanna watch where you're goin', man?" the nameless boy stammered.

It was intensely satisfying to know that in a matter of seconds all of these inconsequential atoms would be locked up in their little rooms somewhere, captured by the gravity of promises and threats, while he, now free of the foolishness, floated above it all.

As the flood receded doors slammed shut. Chairs could be heard scrapping across dull hardwood floors. The drone of meaningless juvenile conversation finally subsided. The little universe had returned safely to a steady state.

But then out there on the edge, on the event horizon, walking straight toward him was the one face - the only face - that could offer him anything.

Debbie Dorsett stopped in front of the beautiful boy, opened her small leather purse, and handed him a lavender-scented envelope. Before he could speak, she whispered, "I'm so sorry. Please think about it."

Dear Dallas:

I am so sorry about the way Saturday night turned out. It was all wonderful, and then... Well, I want you to know that it wasn't my idea to leave you and Will, and I feel terrible about it. John meant well, but it was wrong for us to leave. Will has to be all right. I've been praying for him, but I know that God doesn't always answer my prayers like I want.

Sunday was hard. With everyone so excited to hear about how the night went, I felt like I had to tell them about Gordon and Douglas. My father is trying to be understanding, but mother is absolutely manic. If it were up to her I'd never be allowed to go out again. John hasn't been much help.

I know that this may be difficult for you, I mean, I've already asked so much, but I really want to see you again. I can't explain it. We just seemed to click, don't you think? So I'm going to suggest something that may be a little bit sneaky. That sounds crazy, I know, especially coming from me.

Anyway, I'm helping as one of the stagehands for the school play. I was thinking that you could talk with

Miss Aldonetru, she's the director, and maybe you could offer to help. We certainly need it. And since there's lots of time where the actors are busy and we're not, we might have a few minutes to talk. Who knows, maybe in a couple of weeks this will all be old news and we can try another date. I'd like that.

So think about it, please. I hope you do.

Your friend,
Debbie

P.S. The play is a murder mystery called Death Trap and it's really good, and it's not going to be a lot of work. Besides, there will be a big cast party after we close.

Will Samuelson came back to school on Wednesday, the same day that Dallas Albright became a stagehand for the annual spring play. In Will's case, he was forced to return to a place where no one knew that he was ever gone. As for Dallas, he reported to a job hoping no one knew he was there.

For the next three weeks, Dallas Albright did all he could to encourage his classmates and teachers to believe that on Monday, Tuesday, and Thursday evenings he was a stagehand for the school's production of Ira Levin's, *Death Trap*. In reality, he was as false and devious as the characters in the play. His entire *raison d'être* for this meaningless lie was so he might anticipate those perfect moments when everyone was too busy to notice, then he would quietly appear next to Debbie Dorsett and pretend to help her with whatever it was she was doing. The unanticipated consequence of this deceitful behavior was that their new relationship would be built on a foundation of furtive looks, whispered promises, and repressed infatuation.

Debbie Dorsett had no aspirations to be an actor; she was perfectly content to play any supportive role that was needed. In this case, it was as the scenery and props manager, which for *Death Trap* (a two-act play with five characters and a single set) meant hardly any work at all.

On the other hand, Dallas Albright had no interest in either acting or stagecraft. His single unspoken motive was to be as near to this girl as

302

possible without drawing suspicion. Obviously, when a devious, testosterone-driven teenage boy and a repressed and conflicted adolescent girl are asked to work in such close physical proximity for more than three weeks without accommodating the need, it screams for resolution.

Twenty years before, when she was a student at Freeland High School, Emily Krist was also a quiet and reserved kid with few friends and no obvious interests. That all changed the day she discovered her passion for the theater. But unlike the dysfunctional relationship she had with her own mother, Emily Krist-Albright cared a great deal about her son's indifference for building relationships; a behavior she mistakenly attributed to some undiagnosed anxiety, one possibly linked to his physical size.

Emily was as wrong about the symptoms as she was the disorder. Had he been professionally analyzed, her son - her genetic prize-package - would have most likely been diagnosed with some form of antisocial or narcissistic personality disorder; the ultra-confidence and utter lack of regard for others all pointed to a person who imagines himself superior to the rest of the human population.

So it was with great excitement and hope for her son's mental health that Emily first broached the subject of the school's upcoming theater production.

"Well, Dallas," she began, as she passed the bowl of steaming mashed potatoes to her younger son. "I was coming out of the grocery store today when I ran into your teacher, Ms. Aldonetru, and she told me the news. She was so pleased that you had volunteered to be a stagehand and would be helping with the spring play."

There was an uncharacteristic silence as the other two Albright men considered this surprising announcement.

Dallas rolled his eyes and sighed. He had hoped that this discussion wasn't going to be necessary, but given the excited and meddlesome look in his mother's eyes it now appeared obligatory.

"Well," he began, laying down his fork on the plate, "yeah. I thought it might be a good thing to help out with the play. It seemed like something that could be fun." He then quickly added, "Weren't you big in the theater when you went to school Mom?"

This subtle shift in direction was a brilliantly played gambit; by redirecting the conversation and making his mother the focal point of the discussion, he could take himself off the hook, which it did. For once, Emily Albright was invited to share with her family one of the more successful and exciting aspects of her youth. Until that moment there had been no reason to ever mention that in her day she had been both a successful playwright and a capable actor, a distinguished thespian who had attended a prestigious school on a full scholarship. For that brief moment she was back in the spotlight, and it felt good. Looking across the table at her husband, the only man she knew that had ever seen her work, and in this case not necessarily her best work, she hoped that the expression on his face was one of pride; the kind he once expressed so enthusiastically.

"So you can imagine how excited I was when Ms. Aldonetru told me that you were helping as a stagehand. I'm sure you're going to have a wonderful time. Oh, Charles, we all must plan on being there opening night, don't you think?"

By the final week of rehearsals the combination of his mother's relentless enthusiasm and the incessant coaching of the actors had worn thin with Dallas Albright; so thin that he no longer made any effort to be helpful. Reverting back to his well-established behavior, he became a pensive solitary figure hidden deep in the shadows - stage left. In his mind he had agreed to a plan where he and Debbie Dorsett would secretly be off somewhere quiet and private... talking. Instead, the evenings were mostly filled with her running errands, building sets, and acting like a property master, which, of course, was what she was. As it became clear that nothing was going to change, Dallas recognized the flaw in their agreement: If he wanted the girl to believe his motives were sincere and his efforts genuine, he would need to continue reporting to the endless rehearsals with a smile. Such is the price a young man must pay.

Principal Arlan Greenway and Mrs. Marion Christensen (Freeland's current School Board President) startled little Jessica Aldonetru when they suddenly appeared from out of the shadows in the back of the gymnasium. Ms. Aldonetru had failed to notice the interlopers when they first appeared because she was intently watching the closing moments from the third scene in Act One, and was considering the possibility of re-blocking the actor's movements so that the dead wife would collapse closer to the audience.

"Miss Aldonetru, may we have a moment, please?" demanded the principal.

Motioning for her to join them near the corner of the stage (stage left) the three converged on what they assumed was a more private location, ignorant that Dallas Albright stood in perfect silence only four feet away on the other side of the curtain.

"Jessica," the Principal began, "it has been brought to my attention that our play here is a, well, perhaps a little controversial."

Jessica Aldonetru was a tiny almost miniature blond with a large screechy voice, a private confusion about her own sexual identity, and a fanatical infatuation for modern murder mysteries. Since her graduation from the University of Northern Iowa only two years before, she had with youthful enthusiasm been attempting to teach the mostly disinterested children of Freeland High School the prerequisites of American History and Civics. Her new role as a theater director had come about solely because of her own determined eagerness. After a year of handwritten notes and tireless hints, Principal Greenway finally agreed to expand Ms. Aldonetru's job description to include, "Drama Coach." In this instance, "Coach" was a word Greenway both understood and felt comfortable endorsing to the School Board.

"I don't understand, Mr. Greenway. What is controversial?"

Fidgeting anxiously, Marion Christensen could no longer contain herself. Rolling her considerable shoulders, she stepped forward to address the young teacher.

"This is a dirty play," she proclaimed in a hiss. "It is inappropriate for the students of Freeland High School, and we are here to close it down." The last three words in her concluding declarative statement were enunciated with such clarity and conviction that they took twice as long to deliver as the rest of her entire speech.

"I don't know what to say, Mr. Greenway," the flustered young teacher replied. "I told you last fall that we wanted to do *Death Trap*. You assured me that you'd read it. You said it would be okay. I don't understand how we can get to a place four days before our performance, and then decide it's, what did you call it, 'a dirty play?'"

Dallas could not see the characters in the unfolding mini-drama, but thanks to his ringside seat he could clearly hear the dialogue. Given the conversation's shifting direction, it appeared that the good Principal Greenway was now up against the ropes. In a tentative voice that none of the students at Freeland High would have recognized, Principal Greenway stuttered, "Well, ladies, perhaps it would be best if we continued our discussion in the hallway."

As the adult actor's exited stage right, Debbie Dorsett emerged from across the stage looking both concerned and confused about the curious absence of Director Aldonetru. Lifting her arms in exasperation, she suddenly turned and walked straight to where Dallas Albright was standing back in the shadows.

"What do you suppose that's all about?" she asked.

It was the first time all night that the two of them had been alone and finally near enough to touch one another. Dallas remained silent, smiling, content with just her presence; that is until he realized she was anticipating an answer.

"Well, it seems like the school board lady is hot about the play. I know it sounds crazy, but she seems to think that it's a dirty play. I'm not sure, but maybe she found out that the gay lovers kill off the wife at the end of the first act." He smiled, and then added with only a hint of condescension, "You think that might be her problem?"

Offering a sigh and a quick glance to the heavens, Debbie turned to look back at the other kids who were now mindlessly milling around the stage.

"I can't imagine," she replied. "I guess my mother was pretty weird about it when she found out. But it's a play, a really good play, and it's supposed to open in four days."

Standing there secretly enjoying Debbie's gentle curves in profile had electrified every nerve in his body, and left him vibrating like a plucked string. They were so close that he could feel the charge between them, magnetic, pulling him deeper into alien space. His heart screamed, "Touch her. Touch her." But to touch her now would certainly end the world.

"What is it?" she asked turning back to face him.

So here it was at last. The only moment, the truth; he had to say what was burning a hole in his head.

"I want to see you… alone."

The shadows almost hid her smile.

"Yes," she whispered, lightly touching him on the hand. "Will you please take me home after the cast party."

It was a statement and not a question.

"That is if we have a play to celebrate," she added with a frown.

Part 1 – *Agreement for the Production of Death Trap – Freeland Community School District and Dramatists Play Production, Inc. November 23, 1986.*

Section III: Conditions for Presentation:

(1) The play must be presented only as published in the Dramatists Play Production, Inc. authorized acting edition, without any changes, additions, alterations or deletions to the text and title(s). These restrictions shall include, without limitation, not altering, updating or amending the time, locales or settings of the play in any way. The gender of the characters may not be changed or altered in any way, e.g., by costume or physical change. The play must be performed with women playing the roles intended for women and men playing the roles intended for men, unless the author has specified flexible casting possibilities.

After a school signs the standard theatrical licensing agreement, along with the book and rights to produce the play comes an unspoken understanding that some modest changes can be made to accommodate the local facilities and technical needs. Had either Ira Levin or the good people at Dramatists Play Production, Inc. somehow magically appeared on opening night at the Freeland High School gymnasium to see the rewritten version of their award winning drama, they might have considered stern legal measures.

Finding herself mercilessly trapped between President Marion Christensen, a self-righteous, do-nothing school board, a principal only

306

fourteen months from retirement, and a handful of wonderful children who wanted nothing more than to unselfishly entertain the people of Freeland, Jessica Aldonetru reluctantly agreed to the impossible: to illegally rewrite approximately fifty percent of *Death Trap* by eliminating any suggestion, spoken or implied, of homosexuality, and then to somehow redirect the student's efforts, helping them to relearn their parts and positions, and to do it all in ninety-two hours.

Starting with the shocking close of Act I, and all of Act II, Jessica Aldonetru savagely purged every reference or hint that the two lead males were gay lovers. Then with brazen disregard for copyright or artistic integrity, she wildly twisted the plot so that instead of despicable homosexual criminals, the two antagonists were merely friends, friends with a devious plan to frighten the one man's wife to death. Standing in the school's administrative office watching as the rewritten script ca-chunked-ca-chunked out of the copy machine, Jessica Aldonetru understood that she too was guilty of committing her own version of a brutal murder.

Half-an-hour before curtain the gymnasium was overflowing and the custodians had to be sent to find more chairs. Word had gotten round town that the students of Freeland High School were putting on a "dirty play" and naturally everyone wanted in on the drama. Marion Christensen had melodramatically staged her own production by insisting that six front row seats be reserved for the other school board members. However, on this night the seats would go unused; no one, especially the longtime board members, wanted anything to do with this potential bombshell.

As the audience flooded into standing room only gymnasium, Jessica Aldonetru did her best to calm her anxious cast and crew. Most of them, especially Dallas Albright, were certain that the show didn't have a chance of coming off.

But it did.

This remarkable production of *Death Trap* succeeded largely because there wasn't a soul in Freeland who had ever seen or heard of the play. For the good people of Freeland, Iowa, drama was mostly limited to those Broadway musicals that had been made into a film, or the occasional town production of a silly, old-time melodrama.

On this remarkable night no one would ever suspect that the deceit they'd just witnessed had almost nothing in common with Ira Levin's original intentions. Once the curtain went up there were enough missed cues and muffed lines to immediately divide the audience into two distinct camps: those misguided folks who'd come anticipating something tawdry, and those whose children were performing. For the first group, the imagined "dirty play" had turned into a typical student production filled with children attempting to play the role of adults, many many fumbled lines, and a constant string of technical snafus. By intermission the extra chairs were no longer needed. As for the other smaller group, they happily enjoyed their children's earnest efforts to entertain, overlooking the uneven qualities of the dialog and ignoring the suspicious motivations of the two leading men.

Later at the cast party, Jessica Aldonetru put on a brave face and did her best to celebrate with her ecstatic students. Sadly, her paranoia had left her in such a state that she spent most of the evening checking back over her shoulder, anticipating that at any moment the School Board President would appear with papers in hand, demanding the resignation of a young teacher foolish enough to cast high school students as homosexuals.

As his classmates happily celebrated their peculiar version of a success, Dallas Albright remained utterly apathetic to anyone's assessment of *Death Trap*.   Like a prisoner who'd just finished doing his time, the beautiful boy's interests were now entirely prurient. When he and Debbie Dorsett had stood in the shadows - stage left - and agreed that he, and only he, would be taking her home after the cast party, in his mind that agreement constituted a legal contract, one that was as binding as any lawyer had ever drawn. The next four days of testosterone-fueled anticipation were spent awaiting the implied consent to something real, something physical. By the second curtain call, Dallas Albright felt certain that if it came to trial there wasn't a judge in the land who wouldn't side with him in the matter of: *Dorsett v. Albright.*

The Camaro's wide console and stick shift now seemed an insurmountable barrier between him and Debbie Dorsett. Never before had the chrome and vinyl seemed so imposing, so treacherous to climb.

As he slowly motored down the gravel strip of road leading back into the quiet dark of Ehrmann Park, Don Henley pleaded with Stevie Nicks,

> *"You in the moonlight with your sleepy eyes,*
> *could you ever love a man like me?"*

"Can I ask you something important?"

Turning the Camaro off the gravel and onto a patch of brown grass under a stand of still leafless oaks, Dallas reached over and twisted the stereo to a whisper.

"Sure, anything," he replied, while anticipating the worst.

"Do you think people, I mean the kids at the party, do you think they know we're here?"

"What does she want to hear," he wondered? "It wouldn't take much for that group to assume we're together. Besides, people all want to imagine the worst. Sure. Yeah, they do, but what does she want to hear?"

The beautiful boy strategically turned off the headlamps, but left the engine running along with the Camaro's bright yellow running lights and red tails. When he turned to answer he could see that she was bone rigid and staring straight ahead, her right hand on the door knob as if she might jerk it open and flee into the night.

"Are you scared? I mean, of me?" Dallas asked.

Her shoulders slumped and her chin fell down to rest on her chest.

"No... I don't know. Not you, but it's everybody and what they're going to say."

She took a gulp of air then turned to face him.

"I've always been this girl who does the right thing, you know? It's like I don't know how to do what I feel and not hurt everyone."

The girl's heartfelt confession was thoroughly unexpected and outside anything he'd ever considered. One of the first things that Grandma Jo had taught him was the value of telling people what they wanted to hear. He'd learned early on that a well-placed lie would placate the adults in his world and make life so much easier. The stupid notion of caring about what other people thought or wanted was irrelevant, a minor inconvenience that was easy to ignore. But for someone like Debbie Dorsett, a girl who had an audience every day of the week, especially on Sunday, there were obviously very different expectations. What others thought was always going to be important to her, except now it was stifling.

The green glow of the dashboard lights had produced in the glass a soft unfocused reflection of her beautiful face. When she turned away he could see the long thin lines of black mascara that now streaked her cheeks.

"After the Valentines dance my father asked me if I liked you," she continued, still looking out the window. "I said, 'yes.' I thought you were nice to me, and smart."

Turning sharply back to face him, her sad smile had turned to a frown.

"But my mother didn't ask. She just said that it would be better for everyone if I waited until I went off to school before I started dating. It would be easier for my father. It would be one less thing for people to wonder about."

She considered Dallas for a split second before continuing. "Well, I knew it wasn't about my father. This isn't about making his life easier. This is all about her. This is about her being afraid."

A second or two passed before she added in a softer but equally impassioned voice, "What's makes me so angry is that she's not afraid for me, she's afraid of me, and what I might do."

Without warning Debbie Dorsett lunged across the center counsel and deeply passionately kissed Dallas Albright full on the mouth.

It was the kind of kiss that had he suffered a massive cardiac arrest and instantly died, he would have died satisfied. Long, eager, and utterly amateurish, the kiss continued on and on until the salty black tears from her cheeks were smeared across both their faces.

Life on Earth could end.

Nothing could ever take him higher.

His heart might explode, "But please don't stop."

Laughing with a childlike joy, she reached out and wiped away the black steaks of make-up from his face.

"Do you remember when you kissed me in kindergarten?" she whispered. "Do it again."

Softly, faintly in the radio background, Paul McCartney could be heard to suggest, *"You're the only woman who could ever help me…"*

It was nearly midnight when she finally broke away from him long enough to say, "It's time for me to go home."

His first reaction was to protest, but he understood that along with their new relationship she was now going to have to face a different one at home, one that remarkably included him. Given their bumpy start it only made sense to capitulate; if he'd learned anything from Grandma Jo it was to play the percentages and be patient. It's true that patience and matters of the heart are naturally in conflict, but on this most amazing night he would wait - for now. With her head resting peacefully on his shoulder, the beautiful boy automatically reached out to engage the gear shift only to realize that the stick in his pants was as hard as the one in his hand.

For the first time, he wished that the Camaro was a bit quieter. The dual exhaust was throbbing perfectly, but even at such low rpm's it was considerably louder than most other cars, and certainly loud enough to announce their arrival. As if to confirm his fears, a lamp in the front window snapped on as he pulled into the church parking lot next to Debbie's house.

"I want to see you tomorrow."

Debbie Dorsett kissed him again and smiled.

"Yes, of course. Come to the house tomorrow night after supper. There's a social at the church that I should help with, but I'll be ready at seven. So come and get me," she laughed, and then joyfully kissed him on the cheek.

Chapter Fifteen

I adjure you O' daughter of Jerusalem

"The final mystery is oneself...
who can calculate the orbit of his own soul?
De Profundis - Oscar Wilde

Debbie Dorsett and Dallas Albright instantly became the talk of the town. Along with the label of "young love" came the busybody's gossip regarding the matter of "will they" or "have they?" It would be this topic that Mrs. Lecia Buhl-Dorsett dreaded most.

It had been Lecia Dorsett who had turned on the lamp in the front window. She'd been sitting alone in the dark drinking her third cup of black coffee and waiting anxiously for her daughter to come home from the school cast party. Earlier that evening, she'd been surrounded by the buzz of the children's excitement, and had patiently provided each with her own personal congratulations for their diligence and good work. Only he was there, too; standing away from the others, dark, intense, and purposefully concealed in the shadows. He appeared to be quite alone and curiously unaffected by all the stir and busyness around him. When their eyes met, it was she who looked away first. Then later, as she sat alone in the dark room anticipating the worst, it finally arrived in the form of a dangerous black Chevy Camaro and a gleeful daughter. As she predicted, when pressed to the point her middle child could only vaguely describe the festivities and friends attending the party, but there was no hiding the glow in her cheeks, the rasp in her voice, and the need to be excused for bed. Lecia Dorsett's greatest fear had been made real, and its name was Dallas Albright.

Like Debbie, Lecia was also the daughter of a Methodist minister.

In the fall of 1967, Pastor Arne Buhl welcomed into his parish and home a freshly ordained minister, one who had just graduated from the Lutheran Brethren Seminary in Fergus Falls, Minnesota. This serious and sincere young man promptly altered the trajectory of Lecia Buhl's *lucky life*. In this particular iteration, the chain-smoking Pastor Buhl would succumb to lung cancer just six short weeks after the arrival of his new colleague. Buhl's unexpected passing would leave the door wide-open for Pastor Stephen Dorsett to assume the ministerial duties of the Nodaway Valley Methodist Church. Ten months later, Stephen Dorsett and the nineteen-year-old Lecia Buhl would be married in that same church; Lecia was confident that her father both approved and enjoyed the ceremony.

When Lecia prayed her secret nighttime prayers she would always take time to especially thank Him for bringing her Stephen Dorsett. A good man, a quiet man, humble husband, inspired minister, and loving father; Stephen Dorsett had been the best partner she could have hoped for. After eight years in the tiny Nodaway parish, their aspirations and dreams would bring them to Freeland, a place where they both felt called and needed. Together, they successfully managed both the politics of the Freeland Methodist Church, and the challenges of a large family. On the night of their engagement, Lecia solemnly promised her future partner to support and honor his calling, to manage their children, and, of course, to live God's will. After all, what could be more important to a man like Stephen Dorsett? People looked to him as a model, an ecumenical guide for how to live one's life in God. How could her husband be expected to preach the word on Sunday without his own family living an exemplary Christian life on Saturday?

As she placed the plate of steaming pancakes in front of Aaron, (her second son) Lecia Dorsett turned back toward the stove where Debbie was pouring more batter on the hot skillet. In a measured maternal voice, she remarked, "That's quite a nice car that Dallas Albright drives."

Setting down the bowl of milky batter before reaching over to prod the sizzling bacon, Debbie replied in a light and positive tone, "Yes, I guess it is."

"Well, it was good of him to bring you home," Lecia pushed back, just as her husband Stephen Dorsett entered the tiny kitchen and took a seat at the wooden table.

Smiling at his beautiful family, Stephen Dorsett put on his reading glasses, shuffled his papers, and asked in his customary distracted tone, "How is everyone this morning?"

"Just fine… I think," Lecia offered. Then setting down a cup of black coffee in front of her husband, she coolly added, "Although some of us were up a little later than others."

"Oh," he replied with a casual acknowledgement. "Were the thespians celebrating into the wee hours of the morning?"

Lecia Dorsett nodded, "Something like that."

With a wad of half-chewed bacon still in his mouth, Aaron Dorsett eagerly added, "Debbie had a date last night. It was that Dallas Albright."

Reaching across the table to deliver the plate of food to her father, Debbie purposefully flicked the back of her younger brother's ear with her forefinger.

"Shall we pray," Pastor Dorsett commanded his family.

"Heavenly Father, thank you for this meal that we are about to receive. Please bless this family in all of their good works. Keep us safe and steadfast in serving your will. In Jesus name we pray. Amen."

Debbie knew that she would find her father in his office.

Peeking through the half-open door she could see him fiercely pacing back and forth, whispering to himself as he earnestly considered the typed pages of highly edited sermon notes.

To Debbie this special little room just across the hall from the sanctuary was a paradox of both the familiar and the mysterious. Along with the rich imbedded smells of candle and coffee were the shelves of books, the just-so stacked papers, and all the symbolic trappings of her father's great work. Like the man, the space seemed a contradiction; a warm welcoming room filled with mystery and the intangible connections to things greater than she.

It was a longstanding tradition, one closely observed by the Dorsett children, that on Saturday mornings their father was to be left undisturbed so he might concentrate exclusively on the next day's sermon. Knowing she risked her mother's displeasure, Debbie also recognized that once behind those closed doors she would have him to herself. With the privilege of privacy she would become more than just his daughter, she would be someone seeking his counsel and advice.

The door to the study was open just enough so that Debbie was able to poke her head into the room without entering.

"Dad," she asked in a whisper, "can I talk to you for a minute?"

Pastor Stephen Dorsett was startled by the intrusion, but as his focus returned to reveal that it was his middle child and daughter, he smiled cheerily and replied, "Sure, honey. Please, come in."

"Mind if I close the door?" she asked while pulling it shut behind her.

Stephen Dorsett (the father) was not especially surprised by the request and casually motioned for his child to take a seat in one of the two tired armchairs that rested in front of his tidy, well-oiled desk. Then after taking a seat, he reached out to hoist the cup of cold coffee that rested next to the well-worn Bible.

Rocking as regularly as the clock's pendulum while tenderly considering his daughter's anxious expression, Stephen Dorsett finally asked, "What's on your mind, Debbie?"

She began her well-rehearsed speech saying, "I would like to ask your permission…"

There came an unexpected and utterly aggravating knock, immediately followed by the door opening to reveal Lecia Dorsett's face.

"Stephen, I wanted to remind… Oh, I'm sorry. I didn't know you were in here, Debbie."

It felt to the girl as if the temperature in the room had just dropped below freezing. Looking at her father's unaffected face, she imagined the coffee in his cup was now ice.

"Anyway," she continued, "you promised to stop by Old Oaks this morning and pay a call on Beatrice Ringold, remember? It would be best if you went out before eleven so that you don't interrupt their meals. You know how difficult it is when you're there and they should be eating."

Pastor Dorsett nodded patiently. This was hardly the first time that his wife would consider it her responsibility to manage his time - his life. Absently drifting away as she chattered on, he understood that he would need to play his role of the absent-minded pastor, the fellow who desperately needed her help to do his job.

"She would like that," he thought, and felt relieved when she smiled.

"Yes," he said. "I can be ready in twenty minutes, or so." Then with a grateful smile, he added, "Would you mind putting the mail together so I can take it to the post office, and maybe a thermos of coffee, please?"

Lecia Dorsett nodded, satisfied with his reply. Slowly closing the door, she added through the crack, "Not too long, Debbie. Your father has a busy morning."

It felt to Debbie as if everything she'd rehearsed had just been tossed out of the window, now scattered and lost in the crisp March morning breeze. She'd done it on purpose, of course, waited for just the right second to interrupt and steal her moment. Thanks to her mother's scheming intrusion she was now flustered and angry and anxious, not at all the person she needed to be if she was going to gain her father's trust.

As he busied himself with his briefcase and papers, all the while watching her intently and waiting for her to speak, he finally had to press her, "You wanted to ask my permission for something, I believe."

"Yes, Sir," she began, trying to regroup her speech. "I would like to ask your permission to see a boy, regularly, I mean."

She paused here to try to judge his immediate reaction, but the distraction of the shuffling papers and briefcase masked any initial feedback.

"Well, you've met him. Dallas Albright, I mean."

Then going off-script, she improvised, "It's not like we're going steady, or anything like that. It's just that Mother thinks it would be better if I didn't go out with any boys until I go away to college, but, well, I don't think that's fair, or right. I mean, I've tried to be a good daughter. I haven't caused you any problems, have I? All I'm asking is that you trust me, and let me spend some time with this boy."

Stephen Dorsett (the father) smiled and nodded.

"She is a good girl," he thought, "and like her older sister and brother, she's done everything we've asked."

As he considered his middle child, he realized that they'd had a very different experience with the oldest girl, Rachel. Understanding that a father is the worst person to judge, he knew Debbie's older sister as a caring and lovely person; it was also true that she was a very serious and talented student who had graduated a year early from high school.

"Yes, Rachel might come off a bit bookish, maybe even a little snobby, but the idea of dating boys never came up."

Before he knew it, Rachel accepted a scholarship to Creighton University where she was now only a semester away from completing her undergraduate degree in pre-med.

On the other hand, their oldest son, John had occasionally dated, but he couldn't remember there being much fanfare or concern from his wife about the boy.

"But then that's the point, isn't it. John's a boy."

Stephen Dorsett knew that it didn't make it right, it just made it true.

"Now it's Debbie's turn. After the Valentine's Dance, Lecia had certainly made her opinions on the subject of Debbie's dating quite clear; she was against it, especially if it involved the Albright boy. She believed that it was he and his friends who had caused the, what would you call it, a stir... fuss... hullabaloo, maybe. Anyway, she was convinced that something far worse would have happened had she not insisted that John stay and keep an eye on his sister. But I remember thinking that maybe she didn't have all the facts; Debbie, for one, never wavered from her story, or blamed the Albright boy. There's something to be said for that, certainly."

She was sitting there now patiently waiting for his desire, his declaration.

"She's just sixteen," he remembered. "What a harsh and difficult age. A time where there is so much to protect, while you instinctively want to open yourself to the world."

Stephen Dorsett (the minister) began, "I think it's good that you want to make special friends. And it is true that you and your brother and sister have all worked hard and done as we've asked. I am very proud of you. Sometimes it's difficult for me to separate my job as the father from the one of minister, but when you were talking about dating I remembered a Proverb that tells us to *"keep our heart with all vigilance for from it flows the springs of life."* Probably a bit melodramatic, but still..."

"Dad," she smiled, "I just want to go on a date with a boy. I don't want to marry him."

"She is so beautiful," he thought. "To say no would only be unkind. There's nothing that she's done to warrant keeping her from this important experience. Besides, how many times have I advised people to trust their children? You can't do it for them."

He stood and again became the father.

"Come here, child," he asked, holding out his long arms.

She was there before he knew it, with her arms wrapped around him and her head on his chest. "Thank you, Dad," she whispered. "Thank you."

For the first time in years he lost himself in her embrace. Then looking down on her smiling trusting face, he remembered but did not speak the Song of Solomon's warning, *"I adjure you, O' daughter of Jerusalem that you not stir up or awaken love."*

As for love, Debbie Dorsett loved the idea of dating a boy like Dallas Albright; in him she found everything that she thought she needed. Here was a handsome bright kid with a fabulous car that she could move with a simple smile. A boy that did not fit the model people expected from the Methodist minister's daughter. And best of all, Dallas Albright was someone who set her mother's teeth grinding. All of that, plus the electric thrill that rushed through her whenever they kissed, made her pray her special "lucky thank you prayer" every night before she went to sleep. "Thank you, God. Thank you for this boy; he's so… amazing. And please, please, just this once don't let her ruin it."

In the coming weeks, Debbie Dorsett would thoroughly strain her commitment to the fifth commandment so that she might orchestrate the complex dance between her parents and the boy.

It began by painting a picture of her relationship with Dallas Albright as only a casual association, a kind of relaxed friendship where they would occasionally take in some public venue, like the movies or a school function. To try to further deflect her mother's obvious trepidation, Debbie would delicately phrase hints that suggested that they were accompanied by other couples. This charade was partly true, they did enjoy going to the movies, but they never went with another couple, and rarely saw much more than the trailer before taking advantage of the theater's dark corners. As for double-dates, Debbie would create opportunities for her girlfriends to join them, only to have them cancel at the last minute, feigning an illness or a fictional family matter. For the next two months, these little deceits allowed the young couple the kind of solitary experimentation that caused Lecia Dorsett's blood pressure to rise so precipitously that her fretful doctor reluctantly prescribed a heavy dosage of Mevacor.

Chapter Sixteen

The Decision Made from Passion

"I am fortune's fool."
Romeo and Juliet - William Shakespeare

Sixty-three days after Debbie and Dallas' first kiss, the Freeland High School class of 1986 graduation exercises took place. Along with the afternoon's traditional cap and gown ceremony, there were also two important but undeniably dissimilar evening celebrations.

The first were the pleasant respectable parties. These were the ones where graduates and their parents would parade between homes, popping in for a short tribute and to offer the appropriate pleasantries, while the guest of honor would proudly announce his or her choice of colleges. Once all the "T's" were crossed, the venue would shift and the process repeated until all those envelopes filled with checks were distributed.

The second celebration was more informal. This one took place in a secret location, remote and difficult to find, and strictly limited to an exclusive subset of graduating seniors. There were no speeches made at this ceremony, no cake or sandwiches were provided, the only beverage came from a well-iced, sixteen-gallon keg of beer. For the past twenty-nine years, graduation night in Freeland, Iowa was also the time in which young men standing for membership in the next year's Posse were given their initiation at an event known as The Wilding.

John Dorsett quietly graduated from Freeland High School that afternoon along with one-hundred and eighteen other anxious children. His mother insisted that they celebrate his momentous achievement with a party in the basement of the church. Along with the punch and potato salad came the nearby relatives; in this case, an aunt on Stephen's side, Lecia's mother, Arianna, and two cousins, also on Lecia's side. Besides John's kin there was also a modest sampling of the church's more dependable families, and a handful of his school friends.

The well-worn basement of the Methodist church, with its dark wood-paneled walls still proudly displaying the children's drawings of their Savior's resurrection, three long lines of battered metal tables covered by white paper tablecloths, and, of course, the ever-present five gallon coffee pot, provided a predictable degree of utility and familiarity, ideal for John's swan song.

The handwritten invitation announced that the party would begin at three-thirty; by quarter to four most of John's guests were enjoying the cake and punchbowl, unaware that a shiny-red, 1985 Cadillac Eldorado had just pulled into the church parking lot. The occupants of this remarkable automobile were Lecia Dorsett's older brother, Thomas Buhl, and his exotic wife, Donella.

The adjectives "remarkable" and "exotic" are fitting since the people of Freeland seldom encountered a woman of color, particularly one as "exotic" as Donella Tachyano-Buhl. What added a rich and provocative quality of drama to the Buhl's unexpected appearance was that Thomas and Donella had, at best, been infrequent guests in the Dorsett' home; the last time they were in Freeland had been four years before when they'd come to participate in the christening of the Dorsett's youngest daughter, Judith. Like their previous visit, most of the folks now enjoying John's hospitality were both surprised to see them and slightly intimidated.

Upon his graduation in May 1963, Thomas Buhl would receive both a high school diploma and his father's enthusiastic blessing to join the United States Army. Seven months and six days later, the Private from Nodaway Valley, Iowa would depart for Da Nang Air Force Base as a member of the 196th LIB (31st Infantry Division, Fourth Battalion).

In spite of the harsh climate and inherent dangers of jungle combat, Army life agreed with Thomas Buhl's need for uncomplicated, highly structured work. As a boy, it was his father who made sure he understood the value in a chain of command, (which he did) and respected the prime directive to never question an order (which he never did). Then after five years and two tours of combat duty, the now Sergeant Thomas Buhl found himself pinned down by the North Vietnamese just outside Tan My, a mostly burned out village in the Quang Tin Province only a few clicks south of the DMZ. At the time, (November 20, 1968) the Pentagon and the President's advisors were unwilling to believe that it was, in fact, the North Vietnamese who had just crossed the border for the first time. Had they been able to ask Sergeant Buhl, or the dozens of dead and dying Americans still trapped on the side of that mountain, they would have quickly recognized the error in their reconnaissance.

It was earlier that afternoon, as he looked out across the rocks and the blood and the bullets, the Angel of Death spoke to Thomas Buhl. This turned out to be a noteworthy development. Despite five hairy years of jungle combat, this would have been the first time that Sergeant Buhl had ever spoken with an ethereal courier. For this occasion, the Angel's message was especially short and focused: "Trust in God, but do not stay here."

Obviously, Death outranks all of Buhl's mortal superiors, but Thomas and four other GIs were ordered to charge up a steep rocky embankment in a bold attempt to rescue their fallen comrades. Under fierce enemy fire, each of the men we're able to retrieve one of the wounded and return to safe cover. It was only when the First Lieutenant - another southwest Iowa boy - and Sergeant Buhl were sent back up the hill that the same nest of snipers, the ones who had somehow managed to miss them the first time, drew better aim and shot them to pieces. The First Lieutenant died on that hill. Sergeant Buhl would lose his left leg. But in this particular version of Thomas Buhl's *lucky life,* it will be the precision strafing from the Air Force F-4 Phantom's, and a heroic nighttime helicopter evacuation that successfully carries out the Angel's directive.

The Army provided Thomas Buhl with a Purple Heart, a prosthetic left leg, and a business degree from Drake University. After finishing school, Thomas begins what turns out to be a highly successful career as an agent for the Northwestern Mutual Life Insurance Company. It was there, sharing the gospel of a term-life insurance policy with anyone who would listen, that he found his calling. "What could be more important," he would ask as he teetered precariously on his prosthetic, "than to make sure those you leave behind are financially secure." Given Sargent Buhl's deep conviction and unsteady gate, it was rare when his clients did not appreciate this perspective and purchase his products.

Unlike the other guests Dallas Albright did not want to attend John Dorsett's graduation party.

It was both true and obvious: John Dorsett did not approve of his sister's relationship with Dallas Albright. Whether it was at school or the Dorsett's home, John Dorsett would purposefully hold his sister's suitor at arm's length, generally offering little more than insincere tolerance or one-word replies. Of course, this treatment meant nothing to Dallas; anything chummier would have been seen as disingenuous and unnecessary. But as a barometer for what to expect from the rest of the Dorsett's, John's message was both informative and easy to understand - interloper.

As the beautiful boy wheeled the Super Sport around the corner of East Fifth and Harding, and then directly into the Methodist Church parking lot, he discovered that the only available space was between a nondescript '82 Ford Escort and a remarkable red Cadillac flashing Polk County plates. Having now spent a considerable amount of time appraising the local automotive competition, and contentedly finding it wanting, it appeared that there was a guest that Debbie had failed to mention.

For Dallas to join the festivities unnoticed was a simple matter of discreetly sliding through the unlocked side door, and then slipping down the back steps to the basement kitchen. From his obscured vantage point behind the large silver coffee pot, he could leisurely observe the scene before making any strategic decision on when and how he might appear.

On a table nearest the kitchen was all that remained of a sheet cake. In what Dallas mistook as irony, the broken dessert's bright blue script spelled out the remarkable configuration of letters: ***Con rat Jo n.*** Smiling at the unexpected anagram, he assumed that the cake's fractured sentiment was intended as congratulations to the graduate, and had nothing to do with either the common pest (*Rattus Rattus*) or his personal feelings about his girlfriend's brother. After all, John Dorsett and his graduation meant less than nothing to the beautiful boy; the only reason he was there stood across the room near the main entrance.

Lecia Dorsett had assigned Debbie the role of greeter, a task in which she was now fully engaged by a doddering older couple; he with a fat black cane and oversized hearing aids, and she lugging a massive purple purse draped like an anchor over her thin white arm. Lightly touching Debbie's forearm, the tiny lady beamed as if she might have touched an angel, a sensation Dallas understood and appreciated. Then kindly nodding some affirmation, the old woman placed her white envelope among the others on the nearby card table, the one covered with a small stash of similar envelopes and small wrapped packages.

Commanding the left side of the space was John Dorsett and a group of other Freeland High School students, none of whom the beautiful boy could place with a name. He watched for a moment, amused as the trio mindlessly giggled at the autographs and corny comments scrawled in the back of their yearbooks.

"What is it they could write in that book that will make any difference a year from now?" Dallas wondered, but only for a second.

His attentions were abruptly pulled across the room toward the last group of guests, the ones who had come together in the corner of the basement near an ancient upright piano and the Sunday school's overflowing box of worn toys. As the group began their noisy and extended farewells, it was obvious that the strangers in the red Eldorado had become the focal point. Standing beside the smiling Pastor Dorsett was an especially well-groomed man in a Brooks Brother's blazer and sharp gray trousers. Along with a wide confident smile and booming voice, he enthusiastically offered farewell handshakes to anyone willing to accept one. Beside him a woman, an amazing woman in black slacks and a blood-red cashmere sweater, one purposefully cut to reveal her well-defined cleavage and perfect brown skin, nodded graciously and smiled for all the highly attentive men. Their grim-faced spouses stood silently a step behind them eager to leave. Given their obvious impatience, it seemed likely that they would soon have much more to say once they were in the car.

In among all that drama was Lecia Dorsett. As she worked the room, shaking hands and thanking the departing guests, the minister's wife suddenly noticed the beautiful boy casually lurking in the kitchen behind the silver coffee pot. Her icy reaction confirmed her feelings toward him, except this time, the first time since that night at the school play, she did not look away. Instead, Lecia Dorsett sustained what he imagined was a taunting, perhaps mocking gaze. The standoff continued until she was distracted by a departing guest. Then finally turning away from Dallas to face them, she cheerfully pasted on a warm *faux* smile and returned to her world of flattery and fawning.

"You might wanna wear some shitty shoes you don't care about."

Douglas Capernick looked down to admire his immaculate black Tony Lama's before peering into the truck window. In just those few seconds, Goon Gordonski had lost his focus on the "shitty shoes" and was now drifting off with the boys from Metallica as they stridently voiced the possibilities for an alternative champion to the *Leper Messiah.*

Generally speaking people hated Goon Gordonski's '79 Bronco; this was especially true of Douglas Capernick. Besides its lack of reliability (the engine had been "modified" by the shop boys last semester and was never quite the same) the thing was too loud, too obvious, and worst of all, it was filthy both inside and out. The front seat (the only seat because there was no rear one) was a patchwork nightmare of recognizable stains that included: spilt beer, animal guts, blood (some human), motor oil, dog feces, and dribbles of Copenhagen.

"What do you mean... shoes?"

Goon returned to Earth and smiled, showing off his Neanderthal collection of broken enamel.

"I told you, man. As part of the initiation, last year's guys always pee on the shoes of this year's guys. It's a tradition."

"Sounds stupid," Douglas Capernick thought to himself. "The whole god damn thing is stupid."

Douglas offered a half-hearted smile and a wave of acknowledgment, "Yeah, that's right, I remember."

He turned away from the truck and was walking up to the front door of his parent's house when out of the Bronco Goon Gordonski shouted, "You gonna drive yourself, or you wanna ride with me and Slayer?"

The idea of being trapped with Goon Gordonski and Billy "Slayer" Stetson was impossible. Climbing the six steps two at a time, Douglas Capernick did not turn, but waved his hand as he replied, "I'll meet you there."

"Okay. Nine o'clock. You can't be late or they gotta kill ya."

Douglas Capernick had already closed the door behind him.

For some, initiation into the Posse would be one of their *lucky life's* proudest achievements. After all, the Posse was an ultra-select group of the toughest, hard-hearted bastards in the Freeland High School senior class; to hold one of those five coveted spots was something that many desired, but few could achieve.

In a politically correct world the Posse was about as undemocratic as you could get. From day one this tribal society had never held a vote or cast a ballot. Its membership was entirely self-selected; local popularity was irrelevant and a pretty face did nothing to help your chances. What did count was stones. Any young man who thought that he had what it takes could show up at the appointed place and time to take his chances; if somebody wanted your spot and could take it, well then all the better for them.

Word about who was planning to stand usually got around before the night of the Wilding. This kind of insider's dope was gold since it cut down on the number of tentative applicants and guaranteed that only truly serious badasses would bother to throw in. Maintaining tradition was essential; nobody wanted the kind of shame and humiliation that would go along with being Freeland's first pussy Posse.

In those early days the initiation ceremony was conducted in private. The idea behind the secrecy was that a society designed to act as police, judge, and executioner needed mystique; it was important that the membership be appreciated for more than just their savagery. In order for the Posse to enforce tradition without constantly resorting to violence meant that that the five had to find ways of separating themselves from everyone else. Fear would work for a while, but by adding a dash of mystery, maybe a hint of class, those first Posse's were able to maintain tradition and still keep the number of physical confrontations down to a manageable minimum.

But times change; since the late '70's the Posse had enjoyed greater notoriety by forfeiting its integrity. Head bangers, drug heads, and fully tweaked degenerates were now the highest order in Freeland. The Posse that once ruled by the threat of action had been commandeered by one that lived for it. There had been a time when community officials and law enforcement tolerated the Posse, but today the annual initiation ceremony signaled that a new class of antagonist had been set loose on the streets. It was time to update the books.

It was after eight o'clock before Debbie and Dallas had the church's basement suitably cleaned and made ready for the next day's Sunday school classes.

After the last of John's guests had finally departed, Lecia Dorsett hooked her brother by the arm and announced, "Let's walk back to the house and have a last cup of coffee. Debbie and her friend have promised to take care of the cleanup. Haven't you, dear?"

Debbie nodded, but said nothing; it was impossible to interpret her reaction from the expression she offered her mother.

As the two worked at cleaning the kitchen and rearranging the furniture, Debbie hardly looked at him and spoke only to give directions. Despite his limited experience in dealing with the many moods of women, it was clear something had happened that was troubling her. The two questions on his mind were straightforward and seriously self-serving: had he done something to offend, and if so how would it manifest itself later when they were alone?

When they finally finished their chores, Debbie quietly excused herself and went back to the house to change her clothes. The evening's ruse was to tell her parents that they were going to visit some of the other graduation parties around town. Of course, they expected to be "home early."

Leaning back against the warm hood of the Camaro, Dallas Albright let his mind drift. Overhead massive broken clouds were building in the west; the sunset's fabulous deep orange and red rays were crashing between the brilliant blue cracks in the sky. It was a marvelous show that reminded the beautiful boy of those old-timey prints he'd seen hanging downstairs in the Sunday school classrooms. There was an especially creepy one of old man Abraham posed with his right arm and knife suspended uncertainly over the boy he'd been told to slaughter; behind him a furious sky had opened to reveal God's two terrible angry eyes. In another, Noah and his family cheerfully greeted a long and wonderful parade of animals as they marched two-by-two into the arc; the dark and ominous clouds left no doubt about the forecast. But the best one, the angriest one, was of Christ on the cross. As the miserable redeemer hung precariously for the entire world to watch, a troop of ridiculous Roman soldiers jeered and laughed, ignoring the truly portentous storm clouds that gathered in the distance. Positioned at the foot of the cross were Jesus' mother and Mary Magdalene, left alone to weep for their suffering son and Savior. In a familiar role, the dwindling clutch of terrified disciples once again demonstrated their dubious commitment by cowering in the background and anxiously pointing at God's fractured firmament. In spite of the fading colors and the dime store frames, it was clear that the artists wanted you to appreciate that God - the great and powerful - was about to pour his full wrath out of those violent clouds; angry, vengeful, and straight down onto the pathetic people of Earth.

Shifting gears he remembered Debbie's mother and the weird way she'd looked at him earlier in the basement. What had gotten into her with this full-out antagonism? She hated him, for sure, but there'd never been anything as dramatic as this before. No idea, but who cares.

Next he considered John Dorsett and the kid's future. Debbie said he was thinking about going to divinity school, that he wanted to be a preacher like their father, only the knucklehead hadn't even picked a school. What kind of a life would that be anyway, always trying to get people to believe in something that you could never know for sure? What was the point?

Off in the distance, a car horn sounded down on Main. Beside him was the powerful red Eldorado, a potent symbol of power, wealth, and utter disdain for other's opinions. It was impossible to imagine anyone in Freeland driving such a fine automobile. Obviously, the owner of this bad machine lived by his own rules.

"Was it ironic," he wondered, trying to remember just how the word 'ironic' was supposed to be used, "that the guy who drives this car is Lecia Dorsett's brother? Is that ironic, or just amusing? Debbie's uncle and aunt, right? That's quite an aunt. Funny weird, I don't have any aunts, or uncles."

His mind had wandered off the tracks.

The light in the window came on just as the front door opened. Debbie stepped out still talking to someone inside while nodding her head in some form of agreement before finally pulling the door closed.

She had changed her clothes all right, but these were considerably different from anything she'd worn before; the jeans were much tighter, and there was a remarkably snug cardigan sweater that only partly covered a thin, light blue T-shirt. She walked quickly down the sidewalk, arms across her chest, clutching her tiny handbag as if it might try to escape. Knowing they were being watched, the beautiful boy gallantly opened the car door for the girl. Then after she was safely inside, he turned back toward the house and returned his best false smile.

Turning the key ignited the Super Sport's Cherry Bomb mufflers. The pleasant baffled rumble splattered off the church and all around the neighborhood; a beautiful sound that Dallas knew would tweak Lecia Dorsett like a banjo string. Given the circumstances, he couldn't think of a better way to start the evening.

By the time they made Main Street tears were streaming down Debbie Dorsett's cheeks. She stared straight ahead, but said nothing. She just cried. Unsure of his role, the beautiful boy turned down the music (Dire Straits, *Brothers in Arms*) and waited for instruction. It didn't take long.

"Can you turn off here, please?" she sobbed.

Dutifully confused, he steered the Camaro around the corner and headed north up Crestwood Avenue until she whispered, "Stop here."

324

After pulling his car over to the curb and engaging the parking brake, he sat quietly and waited. Again, it didn't take long.

"Something terrible has happened," she began. "I can't believe they've agreed to make me go, but..."

Debbie Dorsett looked over at the beautiful boy, swallowed a gulp of air, and blurted out, "They're sending me away for the summer."

"What is she saying," he wondered, "sending her away? That can't be right. They send people away in books. Nobody sends their kid away, do they?"

In what was becoming an automatic reflex, Dallas reached across the console to take her hand, but she refused his empathy and instead pulled her knees up to hug her chest.

Trying for the first time, really trying, he opened himself and asked, "I don't understand. Sending you away? That doesn't make any sense to me."

Frustrated and furious, Debbie Dorsett turned on Dallas, and shouted, "They're sending me to Des Moines to stay with my uncle and his wife. They've got it all planned out so that I can work at his insurance...whatever...his office during the day, and then stay at their house. They say I can make money for college. They think it'll be good for me to learn about living in the city. But they didn't even ask me. That's why they're here. Not for John's graduation. They came to take me with them... tomorrow."

With tears streaming down her face, Debbie pawed through her purse until finally locating a wadded-up gob of Kleenex. Dabbing at her black eyes, she continued, "I thought it was weird when they said Uncle Thomas was coming to the party, but it all makes sense, now. This is my punishment. They're getting back at me for you."

Fighting back his first instincts of anger and resentment, Dallas put the car in gear and slowly, very slowly, motored up the long hill. His mind was focused on just one clear image: Lecia Dorsett's expression at the party, the one he couldn't translate. It was easy, now. It was victory. It was her way of saying, "I've won." Lecia Dorsett was looking at him with an unmistakable combination of satisfaction and conceit.

By the time they crested the hill the rhythmic drubbing of the engine had steadied his nerves and helped squash down the emotions.

"Let it go," he whispered to himself.

He knew enough to let go and focus instead on the moment. It was back to something Grandma Jo had said, "Forget 'em, Dallas. Don't ever look back. No regrets. Focus your energy forward to the future. Start with how you can take advantage of it. When people get emotional there's gonna be spaces in their thinking; time when they're not focused. That's time you can use to your advantage."

"So, hey," he thought, "if the decision is final and all the arrangements have been made then there's no point in being broke-up; it's only two months. Yeah, it's going to be different without her, but once she gets back we can pick it up again. It's not the end. She leaves tomorrow, so we've got tonight."

With a quick glance over at the girl, Dallas Albright, the beautiful boy, reached between them and popped open the console, deftly extracting a small plastic box, an audio cassette of REM's *Document*. The guitars began their steady drone as Michael Stipe cried,

> *"The time to rise has been engaged,*
> *You're better best to rearrange*
> *I'm talking here to me alone*
> *And listen to the finest worksong."*

Mr. Stipe was right. The mild spring air felt especially good when the Super Sport topped ninety on its way out of town and toward the last red rays of a fractured sunset.

Douglas Capernick was not especially surprised by the long line of cars that were now strewn like jackstraws along both sides of the gravel road. After all, the location for the Posse's initiation ceremony was one of the most poorly kept secrets in town.

It should come as no surprise, but if you build a giant bonfire, conduct a secret initiation ceremony, and provide a keg of free beer, obviously, you're going to attract a substantial crowd. However, if you were like Douglas Capernick and seriously averse to taking unnecessary risk, a large crowd of underage kids and gallons of free beer offered the very real possibility for police intervention. The thought of calling his father to inform him that he had just been arrested at a party with thirty other nitwits where there was underage drinking, well, that would probably not be the best way to start his senior year, especially since his arrest would mean that he'd already broken most of his father's rules. At this point, a great deal of time and energy had gone into perfecting his physical and psychological skills as a football player, so standing around a keg with a bunch of drug heads and drunken cheerleaders was not how Douglas Capernick imagined the end of his grid iron career.

Anticipating the worst, he drove on nearly half a mile further up the narrow gravel road to a wooded spot that he'd scouted earlier in the afternoon. There, tucked in behind one of the area's many abandoned farmhouses, he could safely hide the escape pod: his mother's new 1986 convertible Chrysler LeBaron. His plan was simple: stay out of the beer, away from the open bonfire, and hope that when they came with their red lights flashing and sirens blaring he could slip off into the woods unnoticed. With any kind of luck, he could then run across the freshly planted fields to the woods and the safety of the hidden car. Given his current physical condition and daily workout regimen, Douglas was certain that he could sprint the half-mile at a full-out dead run, something it seemed unlikely that any of the local men wearing a badge were capable of matching.

The Omega Chrono-Quartz said it was **9:10 P.M.** If he was lucky he could catch a ride with what had become a steady stream of kids headed that direction; if he was really lucky they would have already started and someone else would've taken his place.

Fishing around in the back seat, Douglas Capernick grabbed his light London Fog coat. After carefully folding it, he then neatly laid it on the passenger seat beside him. He knew it wasn't cold enough to warrant a jacket, but under the circumstances he didn't really have any other inconspicuous place to keep the gun.

The beautiful boy pulled off the dark county road and into Aldo Rooney's driveway much faster than normal; for an added effect he impulsively snuffed the headlights.

In this *lucky life,* Dallas Albright will spot the tractor and corn planter that are parked in the center of the deserted lane; making a snap-turn to the right lets the back-end of the car slide in the loose gravel, narrowly avoiding the corner of the massive machine. While the dust settles around the pulsing car, the beautiful boy glances over to see that Debbie Dorsey is now smiling. In this version of reality things are going his way.

Since the beginning he and Debbie had been coming to park near the deserted house. Dallas especially liked to go there because it was both close to town, but still owned the spook story about an old man's ghost that refused to move on. The beautiful boy did not believe in ghosts, but taking Debbie there gave the experience the extra advantage of melodrama, the kind that let him wear his more courageous and manly face. Naturally, he never shared with her any of the stories from his youth, in particular what might be found at the bottom of the well next to the collapsed barn. It seemed unlikely she would appreciate the cunning.

Only there was no reason to think about that tonight, it was their last night, and it was already off to a fine start. The Camaro had done everything he hoped, and more.

Although he had promised under the very real threat of forfeiting the car forever that he would not exceed the posted speed limits, tonight he had completely ignored that vow and instead gave the car its head. At one point on a long flat stretch of empty highway between Elan and Granville, he let loose the power of all 325 horses, pushing the black metal machine well beyond intelligent speeds and on toward a trajectory capable of flight. When they reached 120 miles-per-hour, he could feel that even the slightest touch to the wheel would send the car rocketing out over the deadly ditches and into the night sky. But was there more, did the Camaro have even more to give? Yes! At 130 it was as smooth and pure as pouring water from a pitcher, one long thin sweet stream of power. 135 felt close, but not topped out; there was more. Finally, the tachometer red-lined at 7,000 rpm's, 140 miles-per-hour, and for once it felt like that was enough.

Anxious for Debbie's reaction, he quickly glanced to his right expecting the girl to be frozen with fear, but it was the polar opposite. At some point, she'd pulled off the black elastic band that held her hair; then throwing back her head she released the fabulous mane to the wind, her eyes full wide open, and her mouth shouting silently over the crush of wind. What she was thinking he could not say, but what she felt was obvious.

"Why did you bring me here?" the girl asked in a tone that expressed quite clearly that she already knew and approved the answer.

From one of the many magic plastic boxes arranged alphabetically in the Camaro's deep console, the beautiful boy produced another cassette. Then nodding with a self-satisfied expression, he encouraged the ancient voice of Jack Bruce to sing to them.

> *"It's gettin' near dawn,*
> *when lights close their tired eyes.*
> *I'll soon be with you my love,*
> *To give you my dawn surprise.*
> *I'll be with you darling soon,*
> *I'll be with you when the stars start falling.*
> *I've been waiting so long*
> *To be where I'm going*
> *In the sunshine of your love."*

Although he would have had no specific knowledge, or interest, in the anabolic steroid C19H2802, the one that was now playing havoc with his brain and genitals, the beautiful boy was certainly conscious of its effect. As for his mental condition, his normally well-trained amygdala had shifted into overdrive and was now force feeding the hypothalamus a staggering number of inputs and stimuli.

In a well-rehearsed response, the two instantly fell entangled into a Gordian's Knot, all mouths and arms, intertwined in a clumsy naive dance made even more challenging by the car's uncompromising topography. The console and stick shift had become an unkindly divide of metal and leather,

328

a space that offered no natural or comfortable pose to facilitate the desired horizontal arrangement.

Still, this shared moment was all that existed in space and time. There was no other reality in this *lucky life*, nothing but untapped and voracious desire; the first chance to willingly fall into the deep.

His left hand timidly touched her breast through the soft cotton shirt and found it joyfully different. She had let him touch her there before, but only for a moment and on those occasions there was always another garment protecting the prize. But tonight she wore only the thin blue shirt. In his mind her greedy kisses and stuttered breathing seemed to be urging him forward. Pushing up the flimsy garment, he placed his hand under her gorgeous breast and allowed his thumb to touch the dark skin of the areola and the hardened nipple. There was a deep intake of air followed by what he believed to be encouragement.

They were now both occupying the same seat, twisting and turning like Houdini on a wire, pulling on each other's clothes and whispering their novice overtures of love. Somehow the boy freed his right arm and forced it down along her taut stomach and past the tight waist band of her jeans; in return, the girl lightly touched the hard pole in his pants sending a scream of pleasure up his spine and then deep into the amygdala.

More, there was more, had to be more. The flood of dopamine, prolactin, oxytocin, and phenyl ethylamine were now overwhelming the androgen receptors in his brain, demanding that they accept nothing but the consummation of the moment.

Only somehow, deep inside Debbie Dorsett's equally overwhelmed limbic systems a spark of panic fired and was miraculously detected in the higher levels of her neocortex. Flashes of reason struggled against the over-drugged amygdala until "the good girl" worked its way back up against the pounding current.

"No," she whispered to the boy who could not hear her.

"Please," she spoke louder now. "Please, no. I want to stop."

"She's saying something," he thought, "but the voice is so weak, like it's far away. I can't hear it. I don't want to hear it."

A rigid tension, like the metal wires on great bridge, had caused the girl's arms and legs to freeze in a twisted and inflexible position, but in spite of his partner's uncooperative posture, the beautiful boy had yet to comprehend the change in her emotional direction; all of his mental machinery was still being instructed to proceed – enthusiastically. The whole idea of shutting down the systems now seemed wrong. Perhaps the girl only needed to re-boot and then they could continue.

The boy tenderly offered his embrace hoping that by continuing his advancements the next phase of the mission might be saved.

"No, this isn't what I want. Please, we shouldn't."

He could hear her now; she sounded as if he she was talking from the bottom of a deep hole. Mildly surprised when his speech systems worked, he replied, "Yes. Yes we can. We can. I want to."

The anxious girl tried pushing back against the boy hoping to slide out from underneath him, all the while saying, "No. Please, stop."

In a desperate effort to make her understand his desire, he deftly pinned her left arm at the wrist above the seat, and with his free hand pushed the blue T-shirt up under her chin.

"No." She screamed this time. "Stop it. You're hurting me."

The beautiful boy's cerebrum was being ignored, so its normal hearing functions went unnoticed. With his free hand he roughly grabbed at the waist of the girl's jeans and started tugging them over her hips.

Lunging forward the girl blindly, ferociously, clawed at the first skin she could touch – his face. Deep searing pain redirected all mental faculties. An instant later, the beautiful boy released the girl's arm and wickedly slapped her above the right eye. The sound of skin on skin, bone on bone, was horribly audible, even over the rock band's loud guitar work.

Almost as quickly came the first cogent thought that Dallas Albright had had in some time: "I just hit my girlfriend who I was trying to rape. I am going to jail."

Three wildly inebriated girls, juniors, maybe, but kids he only knew by their first names, had stopped their Volkswagen Golf to offer him a lift. While the three babbled over each other about how "cool it was that he was going to represent '87 on the Posse" and how "pumped they were for football to start next fall," Douglas Capernick carefully counted the number of barbwire fences between where they'd picked him up and where he'd left his car. If these children were any indication of what to expect it was certain that the local police department was about to have a field day.

"Now where exactly is this party?" Tina What's-her-name, the driver and drunkest of the three demanded in a giggled slur.

Despite the dim light, Douglas noted that this Tina had certain physical charms that on another occasion might warrant deeper investigation; assuming, of course, that she made it to another night. Casually reaching across the front seat, Douglas grabbed the steering wheel and redirected the little car back into the right lane, just as a pickup full of kids headed in the other direction sped by.

Pointing out across the dark field to where a stand of timber could be seen on top of the distant hill, he offered, "Over there. See the bonfire?" Then quickly adding, "But you can let me off here. Your best bet's going to be to park along the road here and walk the rest of the way."

Without warning, Tina wildly slammed on the brakes, sending the two squealing passengers in the back bouncing off the front seats. A cloud of dust was rising up around the little car when Tina laughed and pointed, "Get out, Mister Capernick. You can walk if you must, but my friends and I are expecting the valet to park our vehicle. "

Without a word or any hesitation, Douglas took advantage of the moment and quickly opened the car door. No sooner had he set his well-worn tennis shoes on the ground, than the drunken Tina tromped down on the accelerator, sending both Douglas and gravel flying. As the little car fishtailed down the gravel road, a head popped out of the backseat passenger window.

"See you later, Mr. Capernick." the girl shrieked into the night,

"I doubt it," Mr. Capernick muttered as he jumped the fence to hike across the freshly planted bean field toward the stand of oaks.

Stepping out of the circle of trees and into the clearing, Douglas Capernick was surprised by the ridiculous number of kids who had somehow managed to make their way to what was supposed to be a secret location. Among this asinine mob were people of all ages: stumbling-drunk newbies, utterly inebriated seniors, freshly stewed graduates, along with a handful of the local twenty-something badasses, who from their solitary position among the dark timber apparently preferred the camouflage of the shadows.

"Times change," Douglas thought, "but I can't believe that this is what the guys who started this thing had in mind."

At some point early in the evening someone had smashed open the padlock on the metal gate at the bottom of the hill. This simple act of petty larceny had allowed more than thirty vehicles to make their way along the rutted dirt lane next to Raymond Troyer's freshly planted bean field. Although it was unlikely that anyone in this crowd would have considered such things, but in the eyes of the law that little moment of thoughtless vandalism seriously upped the ante. To participate in this Wilding meant you were now guilty of full-out trespassing, which in Iowa is a misdemeanor punishable by thirty days in jail.

A great bonfire had been built in the center of the grove, one that was throwing flames fifteen, twenty, thirty feet into the air, and brightly illuminated the clearing. Like an industrious column of ants, a steady stream of gleeful kids wandered in and out of the woods, arms fully loaded with fuel for the pyre. For these persistent pyromaniacs, enough was clearly not going to be enough.

The focal point of the action was a new Ford F-150 pickup that had been parked near the back edge of the clearing under an impressive century maple. A sizable line of revelers now stretched from the shiny silver hood around to the tailgate where three kegs of beer had been tapped. Both doors were left wide open and Aerosmith's chestnut *Toys in the Attic* was being played loud enough so that it was audible back in town. Scattered around the grassy clearing, small noisy groups of inebriates shouted inane challenges and drunken nonsense at one another. The one thing that everyone seemed to have in common was the ubiquitous red cup.

Thanks to the gentle warming of the planet twelve thousand years before, the last of the great North American glaciers (the Wisconsian) had rapidly receded north out of Iowa, and left behind what would one day become the richest and most valuable farmland in the world. Those humans that facilitated the modern metamorphosis from vast open prairies to vast fenced farmland occasionally spared these little island pockets of oak and maple forest from the plow. Sadly, the incredible diversity of Iowa's ecosystem, and the remarkable fact that it still flourished in the middle of this one hundred and eighty acres of freshly planted black soil, was entirely overlooked as a topic of party conversation.

"Where the hell you been?" growled the familiar voice of Goon Gordonski. Then shoving a red cup half-filled with beer at Douglas Capernick, he added, "Here, you got some catchin' up to do."

The backlight from the bonfire plainly revealed the deeply inebriated condition of both the giant kid and two other prospective initiates, Slayer Stetson and the moronic Jarhead Wheeler.

Douglas ignored the red cup as Jarhead stumbled forward and mindlessly belched, "S 'bout time you showed up, man. People are pissed. Where you been, anyway?"

Everyone agreed that Jarhead Wheeler was perfect for the Posse.

Although a bit smaller than the giant Goon Gordonski, Jarhead had a reputation for being both highly volatile and impervious to pain, a combination common among many of the recent Posse initiates. Besides a notorious family history filled with petty crime and drug abuse, Jarhead had miraculously walked away from two horrific car crashes before his seventeenth birthday; a combination that had earned the juvenile an especially prominent status among area law enforcement.

The first "accident" took place just south of town and involved excessive speed and an unfortunate deer. By the time the County Sheriff arrived on the scene, Jarhead had extracted himself from his mashed-up (but still running) 77' Dodge Dart, and was gamely attempting to tie the bloody carcass onto the damaged hood. Both Sheriff Brayton and the emergency room nurses were impressed that the thoroughly inebriated boy had somehow managed to lift a one hundred and twenty pound doe with a separated shoulder.

The second crash happened just three weeks before the Wilding. In this *lucky life*, Jarhead apparently fell asleep at the wheel and drove off an eight-

332

foot embankment straight into Frog Creek. Although the water was shallow and slow moving, when the inebriated boy was awakened by the Highway Patrol the stream had filled the cab of his stepfather's pickup above his ankles. Not appreciating the extent of his injuries, Jarhead managed to stumble out of the truck and up the steep bank before recognizing that his right shoulder and wrist were both broken. There were those around town who believed the kid's lousy judgment and dysfunctional pain center might be the result of his youthful enthusiasm for huffing glue, others attributed his iffy mental capacities to the frequent beatings he'd received from his currently incarcerated stepfather.

While Jarhead's sloppy condition likely came from the free beer, Slayer and Goon had clearly been in the medicine. You could see it in their eyes; an unmistakable clarity, uncompromising, a malevolent sharpness that guaranteed plenty of unchecked hostility, and a very short fuse. Douglas Capernick knew this as a fact; it hadn't been that long ago that he'd personally spent a few wired weeks with the same demon. Now backlit by the raging bonfire, his blue and bloodshot eyes flashing, it was clear that Goon Gordonski was wrapped very tight and would require close watching.

"Hey! How 'bout some help?"

From the other side of the bonfire four drunken kids stumbled out of the woods and into the clearing while trying to maneuver an absurdly oversized tree branch. After an unproductive effort that smashed one nitwit's finger and scorched another's tennis shoe, the four maniacs finally discovered that by standing the tree trunk on end they could shove it over and into the fire. Sparks flew into the cold black sky like a million fireflies, prompting a howl of laughter and cheers from the rowdy crowd.

Behind him a drunken female voice announced, "We found the valet, Mr. Capernick." Sliding up behind Douglas, and then throwing her arms around his neck, was Tina What's-her-name with the chest.

"Now all we gotta do is find him when we wanna leave," she screamed.

As Tina and her two dimwit friends howled at their own drunken notion of a joke, Douglas Capernick glanced over at the Goon. From the lecherous look in the big kid's eyes, it appeared that he was thrown off the trail and seemed satisfied that Douglas new "friends" were adequate reason for the late start.

Grabbing both of the dimwits around the waist, Goon Gordonski howled, "Come on. Let's go find Topper and get this thing goin.'"

In a single tremendous lift, both girls suddenly found themselves perched on his massive shoulders. They, of course, squealed with delight.

"So, Goon, there's just five of you?" asked Topper Milton - Posse Class of 1986.

The angry tone in Milton's question was easy to understand; "just five" meant just five. Since there were only five initiates there would be no confrontations, no conflict, and no fights. Like the spectators at an air show who go hoping for a crash, most of those attending the Wilding had come to see the fights. Although it was uncommon for a class to come to their initiation with only the minimum number of candidates, technically, five was all that was required; the tradition could be maintained. But given Topper's obvious lack of enthusiasm, it was clear that he didn't believe this new group had the kind of manic appreciation for tradition that the previous Posse's had shown. In '85, for instance, twelve guys had stood for induction. With no clear winners, or quitters, a ferocious brawl broke out that lasted more than twenty minutes, until only five bloody combatants were left standing.

"Guess that's what the thugs back in the shadows were hoping for," Douglas Capernick thought to himself.

It was true that Gordon "Goon" Gordonski had never so much as led a class in the Pledge of Allegiance, and though there was technically no official leaders or officers in a Posse class, it was necessary to have a spokesman. Goon had enthusiastically volunteered.

When the "class of '87" finally stumbled forward to face their initiation, Goon Gordonski understood that this group, his group, was not going to live up to past Posse standards. Along with himself, Jarhead, Slayer, and Douglas, the fifth and weakest wheel on the wagon had come as a complete surprise to everyone.

Tony Odam was a short swarthy kid with no real physical presence, bad teeth, and a permanent muddle of unkempt greasy hair. The fifth of seven, Odam was known for two things: he had grown a remarkably full mustache in the sixth grade, and he was a thief. After his last official run-in with the law, one where he was found so guilty of boosting Mayor Patrick Krammey's pride and joy, his 1968 Corvette, most people were surprised to see Tony Odam walking the streets of Freeland and not in residence at the Anamosa Juvenile Detention Center.

If there was a positive thing to be said about Odam, it was that he was an opportunist. In this case, when he learned that there were only four guys standing for initiation, he took a chance and showed up. Despite a serious lack of leadership experience, Goon was smart enough to know that the shit was going to hit the fan if he produced only four initiates. Did he want Tony Odam? No. But at the moment his options were fairly limited. Besides, there was no reason that someone a bit more robust couldn't be recruited to challenge Odam *post hoc*. This kind of personnel management was something that could be easily handle later on, but tonight they needed to stand as one, as the class of 1987.

334

Without any recognizable program or fanfare, Douglas Capernick and the other initiates were instructed to stand at an equal distance apart facing the bonfire. On someone's silent command, the '86 Posse stepped directly behind one of the inductees.

"Hands behind your back," ordered Topper Milton. "Now!"

Staring straight ahead into the fire, someone crudely tied a red bandana over Douglas' eyes. A moment later, a thin piece of raw bailing twine was used to crudely bind his hands.

"Get this over with," Douglas said to himself. "I'm blind, trussed, and screwed if the cops show up now."

From behind him, the voice of Topper Milton announced, "I'm gonna count to five. When I'm done, turn around and face your enemies."

"One... two... three..."

"God damn it. Don't come now," Douglas pleaded to no one.

"Four... five. Turn around, assholes."

From the excited reaction of the crowd he knew that the other four had done as commanded. But as the initiates turned away from the fire, a roar of wild laughter and inebriated shouting erupted from the crowd. When Douglas finally capitulated and turned he could feel a warm wet spot growing on his ankles.

The shouts and hysterics grew louder, accompanied by such witty banter as, "Soak 'em down, Duke" and "Piss on him, Topper."

Goon had told him to expect it, but it just seemed so stupid, so juvenile, that Douglas Capernick had forgotten the outgoing Posse made pissing on the legs of the new initiates a formal part of the program.

"Very little," he thought, "is worth this."

A moment later the blind folds were ripped away to reveal that the five members of the '86 Posse had been replaced by five of Freeland's more notorious young ladies. When his eyes clicked back into focus, Douglas recognized his partner's slinky frame as that of Brandi Homer, a suggestible, easy-going gal that he'd dated a time or two with considerable success.

"Ladies," Topper Milton laughed, "do your duty,"

Out of nowhere someone switched on Donna Summers' breathy tune, *Love to Love You, Baby.*

Brandi was apparently pleased to comply, which says a lot about four lines and half-a-bottle of Jack. Wearing only ridiculously short shorts and a tank top that left nothing to the imagination, Brandi slowly approached Douglas Capernick with a wink and a drunken come-hither smile. For one so young, but clearly so skilled, Brandi Homer used Douglas' sturdy body as a dance pole, sending the already hysterical crowd into a frenzy.

Encouraged by Brandi's lascivious performance and the mob's rowdy reaction the other four dancers made the most out of their four minutes of tawdry fame. If anyone had been paying attention they would have noticed that none of the '86 Posse were laughing now.

When the music finally played out, Topper Milton stepped forward. After a grateful bow to the dancers, followed by a round of applause from the wildly enthusiastic crowd, he shouted, "The Posse of '86 has only one more thing to say. Eat shit, losers."

The mob went mad at the proclamation, throwing their trash and beer cups toward the fire, the new Posse, and the girls. As Douglas Capernick struggled with the twine that still tied his hands, Brandi Homer eagerly offered herself and a long wet kiss.

The class of 1987 was now the official Posse for the town of Freeland.

It was at that exact moment when the jubilation and abandon had reached their zenith that both Freeland police cars and the County Sheriff roared into the clearing with their sirens screaming and red lights flashing. Like he'd been shot from a gun, Douglas Capernick turned back into the woods and began to run as fast as he possibly could.

It seemed strange to Dallas that the streets of Freeland were deserted at only eleven o'clock, but, apparently, between the Wilding and all the button-down graduation parties everyone was still engaged. Debbie Dorsett, his ex-girlfriend, the one he'd just slugged in the face, the one with the black eye and ugly bruise was curled-up in the seat next to him in a fetal position quietly sobbing into her hands. The Methodist Church and her house were only five blocks east of downtown. If something was going to be said it needed to be soon.

On the drive back from Old Man Rooney's, Dallas had tried his best to consider it from every angle, but facts were facts: No matter how you spin it, he had lost his mind and viciously struck the girl with whom he was trying to have sex. Rape was the uncompromising word that kept coming to mind, and even though that wasn't exactly how it happened, whatever he would say was going to sound like an excuse. Sure, he was a partner, a willing and enthusiastic partner, but she wasn't an innocent here. She was just as into it as he. Who wore the tight jeans and T-shirt with no underwear? Who urged him on with her kissing? And who said over and over, "I love you. I love you?"

All that was true, but it meant nothing, it was just a preamble to the inevitable final act, a climax that could be anticipated in her swollen face and blackened eye.

When he pulled the Camaro into the Methodist Church's parking lot the house was dead-black except for the ever-vigilant lamp in the window. As the beautiful boy considered that light, a steadfast, sixty-watt bulb under a dime-store shade, it unexpectedly morphed from the familiar and unassuming welcome home glow into a searching lighthouse beacon, a piercing signal that relentlessly screamed out a warning to the neighbors to stay vigilant because the girl was not yet home.

"Do you want me to go in with you?"

Since he'd punched her in the face for not having unprotected sex with him in the front seat of his car, the beautiful boy had been thinking about what to say, and sadly this was the best he could come up with. Yes, he understood that this hopeless admission of guilt meant his doom, but what did it matter, all that was left was the inevitable?

It was weirdly quiet in Freeland. Debbie Dorsett was no longer crying, but had yet to turn and face him. The gray sweater she'd brought along, the one that had spent most of the night in the backseat now lay wadded-up in a ball on her lap. Why she hadn't put it on was a mystery, the thin blue T-shirt revealed plenty in the cool of the evening. Surely she didn't want to face her parents looking so inviting.

When Debbie finally turned to look at him, he could see for the first time what a mess he'd made of her beautiful face. The right eye was now swollen mostly closed and encircled by a deep purple bruise. Even though the high cheek bone was covered by her long hair, he knew that it too would be discolored, maybe fractured.

"No," she said looking past him and into the night. "I don't want to do this with you there."

Dallas instinctively reached out to touch her shoulder, but stopped short.

"Why?" he asked. "I'm to blame here. It's me that they're going to come after. I might as well face it now."

A single tear from the open eye ran down her cheek. Her lower lip quivered as she sobbed, "You don't understand. This isn't going to be about you. This will be about me, my sins, and my disobedience. I'm the one God blames, not you."

Surprised and confused by Debbie's reaction, the beautiful boy automatically shut down the Super Sport. In those sixty-three days that they had been together, sixty-three days as a couple, the minister's daughter had never once mentioned either God or her father's work. In all that time there'd been plenty of conversation about the normal things kids talk about; it could've been school, or some new music, sometimes a film that they'd both seen. But as he sat there in the dark waiting for the world to end, he realized that other than the trivial automatic conversations everyone has there really hadn't been that much to talk about.

"So now what's all this about 'sins and disobedience,'" he wondered? "Where did that come from?"

Given their uncompromising situation, not only was Debbie's confession unexpected, it was also outside anything Dallas had ever experienced; it had been, after all, a very long time since he'd given any thought to either of his Fathers.

"Well," he started, "that may be right, but your mom is still gonna go nuts, and I'm the one that she'll blame. It's me that she'll call the cops on."

With an unexpected fierceness, Debbie turned on Dallas.

"That won't happen."

"What do you mean? I'm the one who took you to Rooney's. I'm the one who hit you."

"You don't get it, do you?" she asked. "It's what she wanted all along. This is what she told my father would happen, and see, she was right. Imagine what people would say if they knew? 'Oh, Pastor Dorsett's daughter was out having sex in the front seat of a car. And look how she was punished.'"

Debbie paused to turn away, but then continued in a quieter voice, "She has everything now, everything she wanted. It's perfect for her. She won't call the police. She doesn't need to."

The girl pulled the handle and opened the door, but before she got out of the car Debbie Dorset added, "See, this isn't about you at all. It's about me and how I failed my father. How I failed God. I'm so sorry, Dallas. I'm sorry it was you."

There was a moment - a flash - when the miserable stillness of the spring night flooded through the car windows. It would be in that split second between his history and the future that the boy first sensed the hurt in being alone.

Then the car door closed.

As she turned to walk away he knew that he was no longer welcome in this world. The wall was quickly being built between them, leaving them once again alone and isolated.

The beautiful boy watched as Debbie Dorsett slowly walked along the sidewalk, then up on the porch, before finally disappearing inside the tiny house. For the first time since that night of the school play she did not turn to look back and wave.

"She might be right about some of it," he thought, "but there's one thing that's for sure: Lecia Dorsett's gonna find some way to get back at me."

Running as hard as you can through a freshly planted field in the dead of night is a remarkably difficult thing to do. Not only is the ground deeply rutted and rough, but the loose soil makes it feel sticky like you're running in a nightmare. Douglas Capernick was counting on this handicap as he sprinted away from the Wilding and out into the darkness.

His count was correct; there were eight fences between the grove of trees where he'd started and the car. By the time he jumped the fifth fence his hands had begun to shake and it felt as if his lungs would explode, which he took as a good sign. After all, he knew what kind of physical shape he was in, and given the distance and difficult terrain it seemed unlikely that any of the local law could keep up.

Yes, the escape plan was working perfectly, except as he plowed across the black field - as black as if it had been burnt - there was a surprising flash of regret for the drunks and knuckleheads who would soon be calling their parents to let them know that they'd been arrested.

"Who, exactly, did they hurt," he wondered? "What was it they'd done that was going to make any difference to anyone but themselves? Fools and idiots for sure, but really, they're just a bunch of kids out in the middle of nowhere doing the exact same thing that their parents were doing back in town. Who cares?"

His empathy didn't last long, there was far too much at stake to waste energy worrying about the others. For him to remain sparkling clean all he had to do was lay low for an hour or so, and then when the time was right take the side roads back into Freeland. They may have arrested half the school in their stupid raid, including most of the starting football team, but at least he was free and clear.

Chapter Seventeen

The Ghost, the Goon, the Player, and the Beautiful Boy

"One cannot predict future events exactly
if one cannot measure the present state of the universe precisely."
Stephen Hawking

It is important to keep in mind that a *lucky life* has no conscience or plan. When coincidence occurs there should be no cry of foul play, or complaints of a stacked deck; *lucky life* is utterly unemotional, unbiased, and impartial. Just because something happens in one reality does not mean that it will happen the same way in another; or better yet, just because something didn't occur doesn't mean it won't. What seems fantastic or impossible in one version of *lucky life* is merely the alternate application of an infinite number of variables aligning themselves perfectly as an endless string of possible realities.

It was just after eleven o'clock when Douglas Capernick rolled back into town. His escape from the local law had been perfect. The way he saw it there was nothing that could directly link him back to the Wilding or the Posse. To avoid any potential contact with the police, Douglas had wandered the unpaved back roads of Benton County for almost two hours until finally ending up in Galton, a tiny berg fourteen miles south of Freeland. By taking old Highway 6 back up through Greer and Exira, he motored into Freeland secure that there was no possible way he could be connected with his inebriated classmates.

There was only one thing left to do before heading home, one little task that would permanently insure his innocence: wash the evidence off the car. The time that he'd spent aimlessly driving the gravel roads of southwestern Iowa had left his mother's new Chrysler caked with dust. Taking the white car home in such a condition was sure to draw both her attention and ire. Besides, once the news of the arrests broke it was possible that she'd put two-and-two together and then start with the questions. A quick run through Haviland's carwash wouldn't take that long, and then once the car was clean he could be safely home by eleven-thirty. No problems.

As usual the lamp in the window had been left on for Debbie. To accommodate his aunt and uncle, John Dorsett had gladly given over his bedroom. Still wide awake on the living room sofa, anticipating his sister's return, he passed the time concentrating on the familiar sounds of his quiet home: the constant hum from the refrigerator motor, the soft stealthy gate of their cat Jinx as he crossed the hardwood floor in the adjacent dining room, and the steady breathing from his brother Arron who lay asleep on the floor beside him.

Lying like a corpse with both hands over his heart, John Dorsett considered the pleasant steady drumming of his own pulse. The rhythm was as soothing as the knowledge that after church tomorrow his beautiful sister would be leaving town for the rest of the summer. He would miss her horribly, of course, but at least this way she would be far away from Freeland and the Devil - Dallas Albright. Given the situation, he couldn't imagine a better solution for his sister's poor judgment than to keep her from it. He admired his mother's cleverness, and had even told her so on two separate occasions.

"We all want what's best for her," John had earnestly declared, knowing that Debbie's reaction to the plan would be one of anger and disappointment. But then she was in no position to judge, was she, her emotions had made her blind to what was really going on. Thank heavens, by this time tomorrow she'd be gone, along with his friend's constant carping about, "what Dallas Albright really wants." Once she was away from Freeland and safely in Des Moines, he'd no longer be forced to listen to their whispering about what was really going on out there in the dark.

Of course, he could never speak of it, their sins and badness, but John Dorsett understood exactly what Dallas Albright had in mind. He knew what the Devil wanted because he also felt it in his own heart, and those places good boys never mention. He knew it because he shared his own version of those desires.

For more than a year now the struggle between his own pulsing biology and feeble conscience had kept him in a tense and conflicted place. How many times had he secretly watched as girls like Gracie Lovell or Marjorie Stetson, the popular pretty girls with the cherry-red lips and those too tight sweaters, swished by, apparently oblivious to his presence? Only he was there, lurking back in the dark corner; John Dorsett, the harmless ghost. Their smell, the soft bouncing hair and exciting curves left him speechless and pleasantly uncomfortable. Sometimes, after Aaron was asleep, his desires would sneak into the room and overwhelm his better judgment. Then afterwards, as he lay in his bed sticky and frustrated from both the act of sin and his lack of courage, he would promise God to do better, but he didn't.

At the first familiar sound of the Camaro outside in the parking lot, John Dorsett looked over at the clock on the Sears VCR; it read: **11:38**.

"Well, at least she's home," he thought. "That's the end of that."

When the front door silently opened, John rolled over on his side pretending that Debbie had awakened him; even in the confusing shadows it was clear that she was surprised to see him there on the sofa. Instantly turning away from both her brother and the light, the girl said nothing, but moved quickly toward the stairs.

"You okay?" he whispered.

"Shhh... I'm fine," she replied. "Go back to sleep before you wake everyone."

John Dorsett pushed back the quilt and sat up.

"Something's wrong. I can hear it in your voice."

Turning to face her brother and the lamplight, Debbie insisted, "No, it's nothing. Please."

The uncompromising illumination of a sixty-watt bulb can make ugly things appear even worse than they are. Debbie had turned to climb the stairs, and in that short transition the right side of her face was momentarily exposed. Brother John had only a glimpse, but in that heartbreaking instant he could see that her beautiful face was horribly damaged. There was no question how it happened.

"Did he do that to you?" John asked in a louder voice.

"Be quiet," she insisted. "I did this."

From the top of the stairs, Lecia Dorsett whispered, "Is that you, Debbie?"

"Yes, Mother. Go back to bed, please. John and I were just saying goodnight."

Even though it had only been a matter of seconds, John Dorsett knew what he was going to do. Throwing back the covers, and then carefully stepping over their sleeping brother, he considered his sister before repeating his question in a voice loud enough for his mother to hear, "Did he do that to you?"

He did not wait for her answer. Moving even closer, he forced himself to take a good long look at what the Devil had done; he did not wish to forget or forgive. Whatever was said between his sister and his mother was lost as he closed the door to the tiny bathroom.

He was dressed and out the back door before the two women had moved from their places on the stairs. Without any real plan other than to find and punish him, John Dorsett - the ghost - climbed onto the back of his bicycle and started pounding toward downtown Freeland.

Dallas Albright had forty-six dollars in his wallet and half a tank of gas in the Super Sport. He was not going far.

Since he'd left Debbie to face her family alone, the beautiful boy had been struggling with the unfamiliar emotions of guilt, anxiety, and fear. As they washed over him, gooey like a marshmallow, he thought he could hear his Grandma Jo cursing at him for his sentimentality and weakness.

"Don't wallow in it, boy. You've got to accept what's done and make a new plan. Besides, nobody can prove anything. It'll be your word against hers. She's gone tomorrow. By the time she gets back it'll be settled and you'll have moved on. Don't get sentimental and weak, Dallas. It's what broke my back."

"Yeah, well I feel sentimental and weak," he said out loud, but Grandma Jo had already provided her best advice.

Without much thought or purpose, Dallas Albright let the Super Sport choose its own direction. Since leaving Debbie's house, he and the car had covered most of the little town's side streets and alleys until finally returning to Main. As far as he could tell it made as much sense to turn right as it did left.

The only other car on the entire deserted street pulled across the intersection in front of him and headed west; it was Douglas Capernick in his mother's new LeBaron. Recognizing both the car and driver, Dallas acknowledged Douglas' "follow me" hand signal and turned in behind the dusty white car.

Dallas Albright and Douglas Capernick had known one another for almost twelve years; twelve years since that first day of school, twelve years of close personal interaction, twelve years of knowing one another's thoughts and feelings. But then just knowing someone, even knowing them well, doesn't always mean that you are friends. This was true of Dallas and Douglas.

For Dallas the problem was simple: it was impossible to trust Douglas Capernick. The foundation for trust is built on consistency, a confidence that you can predict another's behavior with such accuracy that there is no fear of a false or disingenuous act. In this case there had been too many occasions where his "friend" was not. With Douglas Capernick you never knew what you were going to get; one day cold, the next sullen, dispassionate, angry, even hateful. Still, the thing that Dallas wanted, the only thing he ever wanted, was to have Douglas Capernick's friendship.

Going all the way back to that first day on the playground, the beautiful boy had gone to school with the hope of making a best friend. A special person he could count on; a guy who'd have his back. It never worked out that way. The minute that Dallas let down his guard and trusted their friendship, Douglas would turn cold and unpredictable, abandoning any loyalty to their shared history. No matter how hard he tried or rationalized, this was a harsh and bitter pill he could neither explain nor swallow. So to stay safe, to stay clean, Dallas Albright had learned to live with his disappointment by avoiding any kind of commitment or sense of loyalty.

Although he would never admit it, Douglas Capernick was afraid of Dallas Albright; the fact that he was eight inches taller and seventy pounds heavier was irrelevant. What made Douglas afraid was that he could imagine a day when Dallas Albright would kill him.

As neurotic as that may sound, his anxiety was built on two connected realities.

First, Dallas Albright was never afraid. From the first day they met, the beautiful boy had demonstrated a kind of self-confidence that informed the world that whatever he wanted, whatever he did, was the only thing to do. Douglas accepted the fact that Dallas was smarter than he was; in fact, Dallas Albright was smarter than anyone he'd ever met. He was the brains. Obviously, he didn't concern himself with school, but that was the point wasn't it; school provided nothing of value. Whenever he wanted, Dallas could see through people for what they truly were. He only used what he wanted, only took what he needed. Who else does that at ten? No one but the smartest person in the world, that's who.

Then there was a day when they were much younger. Dallas had invited him into his bedroom under the guise of showing him something special, something he'd never seen before.

"Hold out your hands," he told him.

From a nearby bookshelf, Dallas pulled out a jigsaw puzzle box that he then placed in Douglas waiting hands.

"Open it," he demanded.

Inside the box was a silver revolver, the one that Dallas had stolen from the police car only the day before. For a reason he couldn't really explain, Douglas knew that this small boy would one day shoot him with that gun. That is, unless he found a way to take it away from him.

Now, thankfully, that gun was hidden in the coat pocket of his jacket, which lay innocently in the passenger seat of his mother's car.

Haviland's Car Wash was on the far western outskirts of town and shared a potholed parking lot with Haviland's Best Used Cars and the Dairy Treat. The ice cream shop had closed and turned off their lights at ten-thirty, the two adjoining lots were also dark and deserted. Dallas Albright pulled in behind the LeBaron and shut down the engine. Douglas Capernick was already out of the car and coming toward him shaking a hand-full of coins.

"How's it goin'," Douglas asked as he approached the open window.

"Okay, I guess."

"Debbie gone home?"

"Yeah."

Douglas nodded. "It's been a long day."

"Hey, how'd the Posse initiation go? Did you make the team?"

Douglas Capernick looked surprised, but replied, "You haven't heard?"

"No. Heard what?"

"Well, the cops raided the Wilding and busted probably a hundred people. Can't say I blame them, it was getting out of hand; lots of beer and drugs, plenty of stupid people. Anyway, they'd just finished pissin' on my shoes when Brayton and the County Sheriff decided to cancel the party. I figured the streets would be lined with cars waiting to bail their kids out of jail, but the whole town's deserted."

Dallas whistled softly, and then added, "That's a drag, but how come you're here and not in jail?"

Turning back to the car wash bay, Douglas began feeding quarters into the machine. When the pumps kicked in and water gushed out of the long black hose, he shrugged his shoulders and replied, "Let's just say that I went prepared."

Dallas had four minutes to consider what that last sentence meant.

When the water eventually shut down, he got out of the Super Sport and walked up to where Douglas was shoving the long handled wand into a hole in the wall.

"Really, how come you're not with the others, or are you just bullshittin' me?"

"No, man, would I do that?"

Dallas smiled at the comment knowing full well that he had, and would.

"Okay. I figured something like that was bound to happen. Hell, everybody in town knew where it was gonna be. I just stashed the car down the road, and then when the cops busted in I took off. The only thing any of them ever saw was my back running into the dark. Not much you can do with that," he added with a smile. "You want to ride around for a while so I can dry off the old ladies' car?"

"Sure," said the beautiful boy, "I got nowhere to go."

As the back door slammed behind the son and brother, the first thing Lecia Dorsett said to Debbie was, "Let's get some ice on your eye."

The kitchen was the largest room in the Dorsett's house, which wasn't saying terribly much, but it was also Debbie's favorite spot. More than her bedroom, more than the sanctuary, even more than her father's office, the kitchen was the friendliest most constant space she'd ever known.

The Dorsett's kitchen was an everyday kind of kitchen that featured two rectangular windows positioned long-ways over the sink, and draped on both sides by dusty lengths of cream-colored muslin. The worn windowsills were constantly covered with broken debris in need of repair, an unmatched single earring, half-a-dozen expired coupons, the grubby gray stub of a candle kept handy for when the electricity failed, and, always, Lecia's African violets. Next to the ancient enamel sink sat a tired Amana refrigerator left in a permanent state of glaciation and constantly wanting for a defrosting, an adventure that would take four pans of boiling hot water and the investment of two good hours before you could finally loosen the encrusted ice. Inconveniently located on the far side of the room next to the back door sat the stove; a tiny enamel box with a broken pilot light and four burners, a surface so small it could hardly manage much more than a single pan. And in the center of the room, the kitchen table; a worn wooden rectangle that when fully occupied left no space for anything or anyone else. It was in this tiny crazy kitchen that Debbie had known her happiest moments. It was here that she was most connected to her family. Here in this warm safe wonderful place she felt closest to God.

Lecia Dorsett returned from the bathroom with an empty ice bag and a mood that was hard to read. As she went to turn on the light over the sink, Debbie quickly sat down on the opposite side of the table so that the injured side of her face was turned away from her mother. She was prepared for the inevitable, but hoped that the shadows might temporarily disguise the extent of her injury.

Cracking open the tray of ice, Lecia filled the rubber bladder with most of the cubes and then indifferently handed it to her daughter. Still silent, she refilled the tray and placed it back in the freezer before finally crossing her arms over her chest.

"Did Dallas do this to you?"

"No," Debbie replied, shattering the fifth commandment.

"No?" Lecia countered in a tone of disbelief.

Debbie winced as she put the icy cold bag to her cheek.

"No," she answered calmly, "I did it."

There was an anxious pause before Lecia finally asked the obvious, "How did you do this to your face?"

Debbie firmly pressed the bitter cold bag against her swollen eye, setting free a thousand harsh needles that seemed to pierce the skin and bring fresh tears to her open eye.

She had come into the fight as a gambler's long shot with no real history of success against this opponent and very little chance for an upset. All she had in her corner was anger and indignation, righteous anger and indignation. Shifting the ice bag recharged the pain receptors in her damaged nerves. The sharp sensory overload straightened her back and fortified her courage enough to look at her affronted mother.

"I did this to myself."

"I see," Lecia said, and then moved around the table toward her daughter. As she approached, Debbie pressed the bag tighter against her face as if it were something precious she feared might be taken away.

Lecia Dorsett reached out and touched her daughter on the damaged side of her face, gently turning it toward the light and into her view. A flash of sadness crossed the mother's eyes, but was quickly replaced with her more natural stern and focused expression. Pulling the ice bag away from her daughter's face, Lecia Dorsett tenderly touched the battered cheek before lightly placing the cold bag back on the wound.

"I expect that the swelling will go down in a day or two, but it's going to hurt for some time," she said in a way that left Debbie wondering if she meant her cheek or her heart. "Perhaps it would be best if you missed Sunday school and church tomorrow. I'll let your father know. Then after lunch, you can still go with your aunt and uncle as we planned."

Lecia turned her back on the girl and reached into the cupboard above the sink for two glasses. Filling them with water from the tap, she placed one on the table in front of Debbie. Reaching into the pocket of her robe, she pulled out a small green bottle of aspirin and offered two of the white pills to her daughter before taking two for herself.

"Cheers," she said flatly before swallowing the bitter pills.

As Debbie looked down on the two little white tablets that now lay in her open palm, she realized that her head was throbbing in time with each beat of her heart. The steady pound, pound, pound of blood rushing through her body and brain left her feeling like a damaged machine, one that had been running too fast for too long.

"Did he rape you?"

"No. He didn't rape me," Debbie answered in a calculated tone that took full advantage of the maddening lack of information her statement provided.

Lecia Dorsett took a second long slow swallow from her glass before counterpunching in her own dispassionate parental voice, "Well, that's good."

"And what's good about that," Debbie instantly fired back.

"I'm just referring to your virtue."

"Yes, Mother, I know what you are referring to."

The pain in her head had peaked at intolerable. The sound of her voice and the incessant pounding made it feel as if someone inside was trying to beat his way out. Then gritting her teeth, Debbie Dorsett aimed and fired, "But I would ask you, what's so good about that? Perhaps we did have sex. Maybe it wasn't the first time. Maybe I liked it."

"Stop it," Lecia whispered in a hiss through clenched teeth. "I don't want to hear that kind of comment in my kitchen. You may think that you have some knowledge about what you're saying, but I can assure you that you do not. Someday, maybe, when you are much older and have met and married the right kind of man, we can continue this conversation, but until then we are finished."

"You're right. I believe we are finished."

Debbie stood up from the table and found the room was moving around her. She steadied herself on the corner of the table before adding, "We will never talk of this again."

As Debbie Dorsett made her way toward the kitchen door, her mother's voice took on a mocking juvenile tone, "And what is it that you have to remember about this special boy?" There was a short pause, followed by, "That he tried to rape you? That he struck you. That he didn't even have the courage to stand up to his responsibilities?"

Debbie had now passed through the door but did not turn to look back as her mother added, "Martyrs are always so pathetic and lonely."

Chapter Eighteen

Air Vibrates with Their Intent

Broken lines broken strings, broken threads broken springs
Broken idols broken heads, people sleeping in broken beds
Ain't no use jiving, ain't no use joking, everything is broken.
Bob Dylan

"What kinda dumbass would be ridin' a bike down Main Street at midnight?"

Given the hour and mode of transportation, Goon Gordonski had posed a reasonable question. In this case, it was only John Dorsett.

For the past twenty minutes, John Dorsett had been mindlessly wheeling his bicycle up and down Main hoping that somehow his demon, his enemy, Dallas Albright would miraculously appear. What he planned to do should such a weird twist to his *lucky life* actually transpire was unclear.

Like the twenty-eight other underage kids arrested at the Wilding, Goon Gordonski was free on his own "temporary recognizance." Since there had been so many more drunken children than even the optimistic Freeland police had expected, pretty much all they could do was to charge each of them for possession of alcohol by a minor, public intoxication, and then issue a citation that required the minor's presence in court on an "unspecified future date." It was nearly midnight before the three lawmen sorted out the minors from the majors and dispensed their paperwork.

"That's weird," added Slayer Stetson, "but I think that's John Dorsett. God damn, what's that idiot doin'? Must be drunk or somethin'."

"Watch this," Goon laughed, as he whipped the Bronco across the street and up onto the curb, narrowly missing the unsuspecting John Dorsett.

Although surprised by the radical driving maneuver, Slayer Stetson nonchalantly wiped the spilt beer from his hands on his shabby blue jeans before shouting out the window, "Hey, Dorsett, what you doin' out here?"

Under normal circumstances these three young men would have never been in such close proximity, let alone conversing at midnight on the Main Street of Freeland, Iowa. But as John Dorsett looked at the beaten truck and its inebriated occupants, a plan - a very bad and miscalculated plan - began to take shape.

"Hey, guys," John Dorsett offered. "How's it going?"

"How's it going," thought Goon Gordonski? "What a dumbass."

Pushing Slayer Stetson back out of the way, Goon looked across the cab of the truck and out on the face of what was now a clearly uncomfortable John Dorsett.

"What are you doin' out here Dorsett?"

Incredibly, Goon Gordonski had just posed his second cogent question in less than sixty seconds. To be fair it was largely a restatement of his first inquiry; still, Goon was beginning to experience the new and heady feeling that came along with being the self-proclaimed leader of the Posse. Until tonight, he'd been perfectly happy enforcing his will on the innocent by intimidation and excessive force. But now, thanks to the power of this new high office, he was beginning to sense the potential in the dialectic. Obviously, if enlightened discourse should fail, he could always revert back to his more familiar and physical form of persuasion.

Peering in at the hulking face of the same ogre who had only two months before attacked his sister at the Valentine's Dance, John Dorsett recognized that he was rapidly moving outside his element. In the eyes of the world he was seen as a good boy, a minister's son, and until that very minute he had been able to successfully avoid all of life's conflicts and controversies. He had never, not once, gotten into a fight, caused a soul any kind of distress, or offered anyone a reason to distrust him; he had played his role of eldest son with consistent precision. For boys like Goon Gordonski and Slayer Stetson, however, John Dorsett was invisible, a nothing - an unremarkable ghost.

Boldly stepping out onto the wire, John spluttered, "Yeah. Well, I've been trying to find somebody, see." Then bending down to peer in at the two dull faces, he plunged forward, "Must seem sort of weird, but have you fellows seen Dallas Albright, lately?"

"Where's your sister?" Goon asked. "Ain't they always together?"

From where he stood straddling the bicycle, John could see that inside the filthy truck both boys were holding open cans of beer. A curl of smoke from Slayer Stetson's cigarette drifted out of the window along with the dull thud of heavy metal music. Given their notorious history of lies and cheap tricks, John understood that it would be a mistake to put any trust in either of these degenerates. Besides, what was he going to tell them, "I'm looking for the guy who raped my sister?" Clearly that kind of information was not something that should be spread around Freeland. But then who else was going to help him in his quest to find the Devil? Who else could help him punish Dallas Albright?

"Yeah, well, there's kind of a problem and I need to talk with him right away."

Goon Gordonski could smell a rat.

"Okay. What do you need to talk with him about?"

350

John Dorsett was a good boy, and a terrible liar; in fact, he hadn't told a lie since the time when he was six and had secretly taken two silver dollars out of his own piggy bank to buy a toy car at the local five-and-dime. That time he got caught, felt bad, and learned his lesson. Only this was nothing like that. This situation required that he tell a lie, a big and complicated lie.

So in the chill of an early spring morning, standing alone under a focused streetlight, a light that seemed to be shinning straight down from heaven, Stephen and Lecia Dorsett's son screwed up his courage and announced, "I've got to find him because, ahhh... because he stole some money from the church. That's right, he stole some money, and I need to get it back.

"Hmmm," grunted Goon Gordonski as he stroked the stubble of baby whiskers on his chin, "sounds like maybe you need the Posse. Leave the bike and get in."

Traffic on Main was beginning to pick up as the unhappy partygoers filtered back into town after their arrest at the Wilding. Along with the kids in their cars, the two local police and County Sheriff were also back and making a considerable effort to stay as visible as possible. Douglas Capernick anticipated the tension that the police presence on Main was likely to cause and chose instead to motor out into the quiet western side streets.

"So," Dallas laughed, "let me get this right. There's Slayer and Goon, Jarhead Wheeler, Tony Odam, and you. Now that's a distinguished group."

Douglas Capernick nodded his head and rolled his eyes before adding, "I'm so proud." Underneath the conversation the radio was offering Creedence Clearwater Revival's best effort,

> *"Some folks are born silver spoon in hand,*
> *Lord don't they help themselves."*

"Well, shouldn't you be hangin' out with your buddies in the Posse? I mean, isn't there some freshman somewhere who needs a beating?"

Douglas glanced over and shook his head before replying, "Are you kidding? Those dumb bastards are probably in jail. No thanks. I'm just fine."

"Bet your dad is real proud. What did he say when he heard you were joining the Posse?"

"Say? I don't know. I can't remember the last time I talked to him?"

Douglas glanced up at the rear view mirror and loudly added, "Shit."

They had just turned the corner from Second to Hilltop when the County Sheriff hit his cherry tops.

"Shit," was all Douglas Capernick said. "Shit! Shit! Shit!"

Douglas dutifully pulled the LeBaron over to the side of the street and slammed the car in park.

"Listen," whispered Douglas, "if you can do it in way that numb nuts back there won't notice, see if you can get my coat from the back, and then shove it under your seat."

Without asking why, Dallas turned so it gave the appearance he was facing the driver. Warily glancing into the back seat to locate the jacket, he could see out of the window that the officer had just opened his door and was now starting to pull himself up out of the car. This would be the only moment when he was not focused on the LeBaron. With a swift inconspicuous move, Dallas deftly reached back behind the driver's seat, and with a snap pulled the jacket between the bucket seats, over his lap, and then down on the floor where he could kick it under his seat.

"What's in the coat?" he asked.

Douglas looked straight ahead, both hands strangling the steering wheel, but offered only, "Just an old friend."

County Sheriff Tubs Tully was a hard-ass unhappy man who after sixteen years as a cop, eight of them as the County Sheriff, had come to the point in his career where he hated everything and everyone associated with his job, especially his constituents in Freeland.

Tubs Tully (aka, Sheriff Thomas Albert Tully) was only forty-four, but thanks to his shaved-head, a deeply lined, weathered face, and an intimidating gravel voice he came off as much older.

Born and raised in the nearby town of Templesberg, Tub's father and uncle's operated the local Farmer's Co-op. Also stout surly people, the Tully family was well-known among the local farm community for being no-nonsense business men; hard people who managed their operation strictly by the ledger. In a trade of scales and weights no favors were offered, and none were ever given. The office and plant was tight, nothing was out of place. The brothers had no time for anything that didn't conform to their hard design.

Like his kin, Tubs was known as an aggressive hard-hearted kid. His only notable divergence from the family plan was that this youngest Tully would enjoy some modest success as a basketball player. His achievements on the hardwood weren't necessarily built upon skill or determination, but relied almost exclusively on his natural physical strength, and a well-developed aptitude for intimidation. If he could manage to stay in the game and not foul out, which was not a given, Tubs aggressive, mean-spirited play generally got the better of the league's weaker boys.

It would be during his senior season at the Southwest Iowa sectionals that Thomas Tully experienced one of his worst *lucky life* disappointments, one especially relevant to the two Freeland boys in the clean Chrysler LeBaron.

Coming into the finals, the successful Spartans from Templesberg were undefeated and about as overconfident as a team could get. Since they'd already clobbered the Freeland five - twice - there was really no reason to believe that Tub's and his boys wouldn't soon be on their way to Des Moines and the State Tournament. Except in this *lucky life* the cocky kids from Templesberg go cold in the second half, which allows the red hot Freeland five to sneak back into the game.

Despite being played on an allegedly neutral court, the referees had been giving Tubs a free pass to commit murder under the boards. Then with only twelve-seconds left and a one-point Templesberg lead, Tully finally got called for flagrantly shoving the Freeland center to the floor. The stunned Spartan crowd exploded, cursing and threatening the official for what they all believed to be an impossible injustice. But it was possible, and if this boy from Freeland made both of his free throws the unimaginable could happen. Heaven forbid, but after all the investment of time and emotion that the Templesberg fans had channeled into these unreliable high school boys, there was a very real chance that they might just lose – and to Freeland.

As both teams assumed their places around the free-throw line, the slow steady surge of human noise made it feel like somebody in that little cracker box was steadily cranking the volume from medium to full blast. Along with their hostile shrieks and nasty catcalls, the anxious homer crowd was sending out a sinister and threatening pulse; the kind of dark energy that left anyone not from Templesberg anxious to locate a nearby exit. Sadly, on this cold Tuesday night in March, it wasn't church or some civic responsibility that had these decent Iowa parents screaming their lungs out; no, the issue, the enemy, was a mild sixteen-year-old farm kid named Eric Ringsted.

When the Freeland center's first shot clanked off the back of the rim, popped up into the air, and then miraculously flopped through the net, all four hundred and twelve Templesberg fans reacted as if they'd been told there was a death in the family.

Like the wave, a surge of panicked whispers raced around the gymnasium.

"He'll miss this one for sure," somebody said. "Yeah, then we'll get 'em in overtime," added someone's mother. From further down the row, someone who should have known better coldly muttered, "They'll never get out of here alive."

Everyone was holding their breath as the short round referee handed Eric Ringsted the ball. "One more shot, fellas," he shouted. But he needn't.

In the startling silence everyone could hear the echo of the boy bouncing the ball on the floor once… twice… three times. Then suspended in time, the ball arced gracefully toward the orange rim before confidently ripping the cords.

Panic ensued.

Now down by one, the Templesberg coach was on his feet screaming at his boys to "set up the diagonal one"; further down court, the Freeland coach was hollering for his guys to fall back and "Don't foul"; the Templesberg fans were demanding that someone, anyone, get the ball to Tubs Tully for a last winning shot; the band was too excited to play; the cheerleaders were gnawing on their fingernails; if anticipation could be converted into electricity they could've powered the building.

Everyone did what they were supposed to do. It went just as they had practiced. The ball quickly moved around the court from guard to forward, and then down the lane to Tubs. With three-seconds left on the clock, Thomas Tully pivoted to face his man: the skinny farmer, Eric Ringsted. All night long, Tully had been making bank on the smaller center, but as he took the last winning shot, the one that he'd made countless times in practice, the shot that would send the people of Templesberg up to Des Moines and their first State Tournament, Eric Ringsted timed his jump just right and miraculously tipped the ball, misdirecting the shot so that it clanged pointlessly off the rim. As Tub Tully's hopes for a state championship sank into a "what if," his irrational and lifelong hatred for anything associated with Freeland, Iowa became a "what is."

Slowly approaching the LeBaron from behind, Sheriff Tully paused to shine his flashlight into the backseat hoping to spot some telltale sign that these two Freeland boys were doing things they shouldn't. After the killing they'd made earlier it felt like these two kids in their fancy new car might just be dumb enough to be carrying alcohol; except the back seat was disappointingly barren of anything incriminating.

Before he'd even looked in at the driver, Sheriff Tully croaked, "Pretty late for you fellas to be out drivin' around."

Douglas and Dallas said nothing.

Bending down to peer into the car, the big man was breathing loudly through his nose and making a sort of "*thmpf*" with each snort. Shining the bright light directly into Douglas' eyes, the County Sheriff said with undiluted condescension, "Driver's license, please."

Douglas Capernick reached back into his hip pocket, produced his wallet and license, and then handed it to the officer without making eye-contact.

The sheriff turned the flashlight onto the blue piece of paper, and then asked, "You Douglas Capernick?"

Douglas had returned both his hands to the wheel and was now lightly drumming on the hard plastic. "Yes, Sir," was all he said.

"Hmmm… your dad run the bank?"

"Yes, Sir."

"Does he know you're out here after midnight?"

"I don't know, Sir. I didn't seem him before I left the house."

Sheriff Tubs Tully said nothing, but instead turned and walked back to the rear of the LeBaron, where he stood for what might have been two minutes.

"You wanna come open up the trunk, please."

Before pulling the car keys from the ignition, Douglas glanced over at Dallas in a way that said everything was "cool" in the trunk. All that Sheriff Tully was going to find in the back of Mrs. Capernick's new Chrysler LeBaron was the spare and a collapsible pink umbrella.

"You can get back in your vehicle," Tully said before returning to his patrol car.

As he climbed back in behind the wheel, Douglas Capernick muttered under his breath, "What an asshole."

For the next ten minutes, Sheriff Tully did nothing but sit in his car with the motor running and bright lights shining in the back window of the LeBaron, all in an obvious attempt to get a rise out of the young men from Freeland. Only he had nothing. He'd stopped them for no other reason than the hope of finding they'd been drinking, but clearly they were clean. The car was registered to Mr. Stanley P. Capernick and showed no prior problems. The boy hadn't been speeding, and didn't appear to be intimidated. He had nothing.

Finally, the boys heard the officer's car door slam and watched as the flashlight bobbed toward them.

"Okay, Douglas Capernick. I was just wondering if you were the same kid who played football."

Douglas was surprised by the direction of questioning and hopeful that Tubs Tully was about to lighten-up.

"Yes, Sir. I was a linebacker last year."

"Linebacker, huh. Were you any good?"

"I did okay, I guess."

Sheriff Tully took another short snort of air - *"thmpf"* - then turned the flashlight back on Douglas face.

"Is that so? Well, I don't 'spose you know where your team was tonight? No? See, Sheriff Brayton and his deputy and me, we arrested most of them along with about fifty other drunken idiots out on Ray Troyer's place. But what's funny is that you weren't there. Why is that? You're a good lookin' kid. Ain't you popular?" Tubs peculiar pronunciation of the word "popular" had more in common with a species of flowering deciduous tree than an adjective describing one's social status.

While lightly drumming his fingers on the steering wheel, Douglas considered several pointed replies, but wisely said nothing.

"Well, that got me thinking about something Sheriff Brayton said. He said when we rolled in to break up that kegger, he saw a couple of kids runnin' back out through the trees. It was dark, and he could've been mistaken, but then maybe a big strong football player like you might just have been there. And then when we showed up, well, maybe you took off. S'pose that's possible?"

Sheriff Tully turned the light away from Douglas eyes, then immediately switched it onto Dallas.

"Maybe it was you that he saw?"

Dallas Albright blinked at the harsh light, but continued to stare straight ahead.

"Well, Douglas Capernick, I'd suggest that you and your little buddy here go on home. I'm kinda tired and cranky, and let's face it… I don't like kids from Freeland. So here's what we're gonna do. I'm goin' back and get in my nice warm car, but, if I see you two again tonight, I promise that we're gonna go see your daddy's, and I 'spect you don't want that, do you."

"How did I get myself into this?"

Wedged between Goon Gordonski and Slayer Stetson in the front seat of a filthy noisy truck, John Dorsett tried again to explain to the two reprobates why he needed to find Dallas Albright and retrieve the make-believe money he'd stolen from the church.

"Want a beer?" Slayer Stetson asked. "Might calm you down?"

"No. No, thank you," John replied. "Say, have you guys even seen Dallas tonight?

"Relax, bro."

Slamming the Bronco's metal stick shifter from first to second gear, Goon Gordonski turned and gave John a nod of reassurance.

"Freeland's a pretty small town. We'll find him if he's still out. Now tell me again about this money?"

From the menacing tone in his question, John Dorsett was fairly certain he'd made a mistake including these drunken delinquents in his quest. Trapped by his own deceit, and with no obvious way to escape, he did what liars do: he went ahead and told more lies.

"Well, see, I heard my father say that there was some money missing from the collection plates. And then my mother, she said that she thought she saw Dallas in the hallway to the office. So they asked me to come out and find him, you know, to bring him back to the house, I mean, so we can ask him about it."

Goon Gordonski just shook his giant head; this new version of the kid's story was even more confusing than the first.

356

The problem was that John had no practical experience at lying. As any liar will tell you, if you want someone to accept your story as the truth it has to be believable, and that requires consistency. In the first version of his lie, John had told Goon that *he-John* needed to find Dallas Albright to "get the money back" which implies that *he-Dallas* had stolen it, and possibly had it with him. In this second version, John had made the story unnecessarily complicated by adding his mother and father into his overplayed mix. To make matters even worse, *he-John* claimed that *they-his parents* wanted *he-John* to "bring Dallas back to the house to ask him about the missing money" at midnight.

From their confused expression, John knew that if he was going to have any chance of finding Dallas Albright, and then getting one of these two thugs to hold him, or better yet, beat him, it was going to rely on the miscreant's state of inebriation and taste for blood. John reckoned that both were highly elevated, and in this he was correct.

"I think I've had enough," Douglas Capernick said as he turned the LeBaron out onto Main heading west toward the car wash and Dallas' Super Sport.

Dallas Albright agreed. He'd been trying to imagine what it was going to be like waking up in his parent's house, only to have to tell them the unhappy story of his previous evening. There was no question how they were going to react: it was going to be bad, guaranteed bad, and would certainly include them taking back the Super Sport.

Absently pushing his hand out the open car window and into the cool evening air, he wondered, "Should I wake them up, or wait for breakfast? Maybe Debbie's mother will have called before I even get home. What if the Sheriff is there waiting for me?" The situation and his nerves were rapidly getting out of control.

"I know Debbie's being sent away, but let's face it, this is the kind of story that's going to get around. After all, it's Freeland. It's what people do here. And this is Debbie Dorsett, the minister's daughter that they're going to be talking about."

An unexpected vision of his mother's sad face flashed through his consciousness. Just the thought of how she was going to react to this news gave him a headache.

Then his father was there. It usually didn't take much to light his fuse, but this was liable to burn him to a crisp. Like some kind of comic book character, Dallas imagined his father engulfed in bright orange flames, a bubble of dialog about "his responsibilities to your family and yourself," suspended over his blazing skull.

Taking inventory of the sad facts revealed few options: he had no money, absolutely no excuse for his repulsive behavior, and nowhere else to go. Add them up and all they amounted to was an extremely questionable future. Without really trying, it seems that Dallas Albright had achieved his one true desire: to be left alone.

"Yeah, that's good. Just drop me at the car," the beautiful boy mumbled.

There was a part of him that desperately needed to confide this horrible new secret with Douglas Capernick; if there anyone who might understand or offer the slightest sympathy it might be his old partner in crime. Only Douglas Capernick had never been the kind of person who suffered other people's problems. In the twelve years that they'd known one another, Dallas could not remember an occasion where he'd provided a single word of kindness or encouragement to someone with a problem. It wasn't, as they like to say, "In his nature." Add on all the new pressures of football and the Posse, it was unrealistic to hope he'd become something he never could.

"Hey, hey, hey," shouted Slayer Stetson as he smacked John Dorsett in the shoulder. "There's Albright's Camaro over in Haviland's lot."

Goon Gordonski nodded in agreement, and added, "Alright, now we're gettin' somewhere."

Jerking the Bronco off the highway and into the shadows behind the Dairy Treat, Goon added in an ominous tone, "We'll just sit here for little bit and wait for our friend to come to us. Shouldn't be too long… besides," he added, leaning back over the seat to rummage through the cooler, "we got beer."

Knowing that he had only a short amount of time to drop Dallas at his car and then get the LeBaron home before Tubs Tully came looking for him, Douglas Capernick drove the most direct route out to the west side carwash. The radio remained unnaturally silent and there was no conversation.

When they arrived the parking lot was dark. The Super Sport was still where Dallas had parked it next to the Dairy Treat. To save a buck, Mr. Dwight Haviland - the Haviland of Haviland's Used Cars - had recently installed a timer that would automatically shut off the main lights around his car lot at midnight. Sheriff Brayton had strongly protested this decision, reminding Dwight of the difficulty they were going to have policing a dark lot. But like so many of the local Freeland businesses, Haviland's Used Cars was suffering financially from the opening of yet another new dealership in the nearby town of Alton. After acknowledging the Sheriff's good counsel, Mr. Haviland countered with the indisputable observation that very few people considered buying a used car after midnight. In this *lucky life* every penny counted.

When Douglas pulled up next to the Camaro, the only illumination for the entire parking lot was the interior lights from the carwash and a small 60-watt bulb over the office door; everything in the Dairy Treat was black.

Intending to keep the conversation short, Douglas pulled close to the Super Sport and announced, "Guess we better keep movin'. Tubs' is still out there waiting for us."

"Yeah," Dallas agreed, "I'll talk to you later."

"Later," Douglas replied, and started rolling before Dallas had a chance to close the door.

"Maybe," Dallas said to himself.

So utterly distracted by the question of "Where do I go now," Dallas Albright did not notice the three dark figures standing behind him as he unlocked the door to his car. From out of the shadows, an ominous presence voiced a variation to the same question.

"Where you goin', Albright?"

Completely taken by surprise, Dallas spun around, instantly recognizing the giant Goon Gordonski and his nitwit companion, Slayer Stetson. But the third face, the one still hovering back in the shadows was the one that confused him. Finally, after a second hard look, Dallas recognized that the slender boy standing behind the two delinquents was, unbelievably, John Dorsett. It was in every way impossible, but there he was cowering in the dark, a clueless doof of a kid, standing in Dwight Haviland's dark parking lot, at midnight, with two of the nastiest people in Freeland, Iowa.

"John? What are you doing here?"

It was a good question, and one that John would certainly have given his full consideration had he not already been engaged with the more pressing concern of how to extricate himself from his own nightmare. The image of his beautiful sister's battered face had provided a powerful motivation to find and hurt the person that had hurt her. Only now that he had done it, now that he had foolishly involved these two villains, his rash plan needed a serious change in direction.

Goon Gordonski stepped out of the darkest shadows and into a place where Dallas could see his face.

"Hey, Albright. Good to see ya. We been talking to John here, and he says you been busy tonight."

Stunned to think that the minister's son had been out on the streets talking about what he'd done to his sister, the best Dallas could offer was a "What?"

Scurrying like a shifty rodent from behind the goon, Slayer Stetson suddenly darted from out of the darkness and in behind Dallas. In what he must have imagined as a very threatening gesture, the skinny punk repeatedly slapped his fist into his palm. Then with a breath like mustard gas and weaving badly from the combination of medicine and free beer, Slayer mumbled, "Yeah, Shorty. He says you been a bad boy. He says his parents wanna talk to you."

"I don't know what you guys are talking about, but, John this is not a good place for you. Get in the car and I'll drive you home."

Before he could even consider opening the car door, both Goon and Slayer took another intimidating step forward; in such close quarters the two thugs reeked of stale beer and urine.

The big kid leaned forward and whispered near Dallas' ear, "Tell me 'bout the money. How much you get? You got it in the car?"

If John Dorsett had heard it once he had heard it a hundred times, "Be careful what you wish for, it might come true." It was one of his father's favorites; a saying so overworked that he mostly ignored it thinking it trite. Until that moment, his father's expression had meant nothing because it never happened; John never got what he wanted. And he certainly wanted things: important things like good looks, money, girls, and confidence. The kind of stuff everyone seemed to have, everyone, that is, but John.

Be careful what you wish for...

Except that was thirty minutes ago. Now the scene was exactly what John Dorsett had wished for. Like a movie script, he had wanted, needed, someone powerful and ugly to punish Dallas Albright for his sins. Of course it had to be someone stronger and meaner than he would ever be, someone that could abuse the Devil the way he'd hurt Debbie. Only he'd forgotten about his father's advice, and now these two thugs were about to seriously hurt Dallas Albright for something that did not involve them in anyway. Taking a step back into the shadows, John Dorsett became so overwhelmed with remorse and fear that he did something he often did, but always regretted, he began to cry.

Before he pulled out of Haviland's parking lot, Douglas Capernick reached into the back seat, grabbed his jacket, and then casually threw it on the seat beside him.

"Lucky thing Albright was in the car when Tub's pulled me over," he thought. "I doubt he would have understood about the gun."

For whatever reason, perhaps gratitude, in this particular confluence of events - this *lucky life* - Douglas Capernick will glance into the LeBaron's rearview mirror just in time to see three shadows come out from behind the Dairy Treat.

"Listen, man," Dallas Albright offered the big kid, "I don't know what you think happened tonight, but this guy's parents do not want to talk to me…" The beautiful boy glanced down at his watch: **12:18**. "…especially not at this time of night."

Dallas pulled the handle on the car door, and added, "Think about, Gordon."

Goon Gordonski tried to think about it, but the staggering number of variables that this version of his *lucky life* had just strung together was too great for the big kid to calculate. The dangerous combination of frustration and intoxication had left him overwhelmed and without a way to mentally organize a plan. Unfortunately, Goon Gordonski's historical fallback from such a dilemma was not in Dallas Albright's best interests.

Douglas Capernick's mind was racing. "Why would three people be coming out from behind the Dairy Treat at, shit, it's almost twelve-thirty."

He was just passing the empty parking lot in front of the Aldi's Food King. "Come on, man. It was probably just the people closing up to go home." Through the passenger window, he noticed the first lights blinking on in the back of the Daylight Donut shop. "The only problem is that the place closes at 10:30." On the corner, the Freeland Bank's **Time and Temperature** sign had just flashed from **12:29** to **53** degrees. "For Christ sake," he wondered. "Who would want anything from Dallas Albright?"

Making a tight U-turn in the bank's drive-thru, Douglas Capernick decided, "This is stupid."

The beautiful boy pulled open the door to the Super Sport, but knew better than to ever stop looking directly into Goon Gordonski's eyes.

"Always know the leader," Grandma Jo had said, "and stay focused on him. He'll tell you what's going to happen next."

In spite of the parking lot's sketchy lighting and the worrisome grimace on the giant kid's face, it was clear that the new "leader" of the Posse was struggling to sort through all the variables in his current story problem. Unfortunately for Dallas Albright, this failed exercise was rapidly becoming another unpleasant reminder of how Gordon Albert Gordonski was made to feel at school: ignored. Since he started middle-school every single person at the Freeland Community schools was delighted to ignore him. No one ever called on him, asked for his ideas, or considered his feelings. His teachers assumed he didn't do the homework, assumed he didn't know the answer, and worst of all, they assumed he didn't care. It was in the dull solitude of the back row that the imposing "problem kid" was left alone to mindlessly doodle his cars and machine guns into an empty notebook, while forever falling further and further behind.

"Come on, John. I'll drop you off," Dallas said to the ghost hovering near the corner of the building.

Pushing the car door closed, Goon demanded, "Just hold on a second. Do you got the money you stole from the church, or not?"

"Get in the car, John," Dallas repeated while trying to open the door that the Goon now held closed with his giant paw. "I told you, Gordon. I don't know what you're talking about. And I don't have any money. It's late. This kid should be home before his mom goes nuts and calls the cops."

Dallas could see past his immediate problem to John Dorsett who was now stumbling out of the shadows, wiping his face with his hands. What he did not see was the wicked sucker-punch to his right kidney from Slayer Stetson, the boot from Goon Gordonski to his ribs, or the flash of headlights from Helen Capernick's Chrysler LeBaron.

Douglas Capernick did not need to be reminded that he was now living on borrowed time. Until that moment, everything he thought and did had been carefully calculated to keep him out of the reach of the law, everything but this. For complicated reasons he did not take time to consider, he was now putting himself in a spot where he might soon be arrested, beaten, or worse.

Steering the LeBaron off the highway and into Haviland's lot he could see one of the shadows viciously punch the smallest of the three in the back, while the other taller one followed up with a boot to the side. Presuming that it was Dallas Albright who was now on the ground, it was not difficult to imagine the identity of the two assailants. What was difficult to imagine was why?

Pulling the LeBaron up beside the two leering thugs and the motionless body that now lay helpless on the cold asphalt, Douglas Capernick heard himself ask in a remarkably casual voice, "What's goin' on?"

Dispensing a final brutal kick to the beautiful boy's back, Goon Gordonski looked up from his work with the same dull expression you would expect from someone digging a hole. Apparently being caught dead-to-rights beating a smaller man meant nothing to either of the two newest members of the noble Posse.

"Where the hell you been?' Goon asked, wiping the dirty sleeve of his T-shirt across his mouth.

"Nowhere," Douglas Capernick answered.

The lump on the ground lay motionless.

"What's with Albright?"

Wasted beyond understanding and still battling a head full of super-charged demons, Slayer Stetson stumbled around the motionless body cursing and mumbling under his breath.

"Hey, Capernick," the freak hollered, "where'd you go, man? We got busted."

"Sorry to hear that. How come you're beatin' on Albright?" he repeated.

Something like a sated jackal, his jowls still smeared red with blood, Goon Gordonski coolly stepped over the legs of his victim and walked up to put his giant paws on the side of the clean white car. After what seemed an especially long pause for such a straightforward question, Goon finally blurted out, "Posse business. He's a thief. We're servin' justice."

"You're kidding," Douglas Capernick laughed. "You think Dallas Albright is a thief? Come on, pal. That guy's rich. He's got all he needs, and more. Besides, what'd he steal?

Like a mistreated gorilla that sits silently and stares through the glass at his abusive handler, Goon Gordonski slowly lowered his ugly mug closer to the open window. Despite his serious inebriation, the vicious expression on his face made it clear that he did not appreciate the tone of the question.

"Step out of the car, asshole," he whispered, "I'm gettin' sick of your attitude. Come on, man. What are you waitin' for? You always think you're so goddamn smart. Well, come on out and let me introduce you to the new leader of the Posse. That's right, me. From now on everyone is gonna be takin' orders from me; you, Slayer, everyone. So you can cut the shit, man, or I'll mess you up just like I did Albright."

Straight or stoned, Douglas Capernick did not want to fight Goon Gordonski. Even if he could get out of the car and strike first, it was far from certain that he could hurt Goon bad enough to take him down. Like the incensed gorilla, the only way to stop him was going to mean killing him.

Under the flimsy pretext of "bulking-up for football," Douglas had seen the fool ingest a drugstore of suspect narcotics and cheap steroids. Emboldened by the dubious success he'd gained from the medicine, Goon began to experiment with even more harsh and painful regiments; frightening dangerous workouts which he proudly wore like a badge.

Sadly, there was no one who ever questioned why he wanted to lift those oversized pieces of indifferent metal until his nose bled. Instead, it was now a common scene to find high school wannabe's cheering Goon on as he snatched four hundred and fifty pounds, all in a pitiful effort to fulfill some twisted macho need for acceptance. But in spite of the coach's timid warnings and feeble protests, Goon Gordonski had finally discovered his niche, a place where no one "assumed" anything, and he reigned supreme.

"Easy there, fella," Douglas replied as he reached over to the passenger seat and retrieved his jacket. "You better believe the Posse needs you to take over. This is our year. '87, man. We need a bad mother like you to kick it hard. It won't be me. No way. Forget about Slayer, or the other two. It's you, Gordon. We need you to lead the Posse."

Through the soft rich cloth of his coat, Douglas Capernick could feel the ominous shape and extra weight that lay waiting patiently in the pocket.

Dallas Albright was now conscious, but did not immediately open his eyes. He knew that he was hurt, bad: broken ribs, maybe, a deep sickening pain in his back and right kidney, an ear that was ringing like a fire bell, knuckles skinned raw and bleeding, and a thoroughly scrambled brain. There was a flash where he considered the possibility he might die and wondered if it would hurt, but it passed quickly and left him feeling even worse knowing that in this sad *lucky life* he was all alone.

"So," he wondered, "where are all the people who were so ready to tell me how to live my life? Where's the old hag who had me convinced that stealing for her was such a good thing? That's a laugh. All we ever accomplished was to give her some kind of bitter satisfaction over people whose only crime had been to ignore her.

Where's my genius father with all of his threats and advice? That all worked out, didn't it, Dad? Funny how everything you told me was planned to build me into another version of you."

As feeling began to ebb back into his body, Dallas recognized that the ground was bitter cold. He hurt everywhere, even his heart. There were voices, but it was difficult to understand what was being said. The only thing that his damaged brain could make clear was the undeniable fact that no one was coming to help him. He was alone.

And what a thought it was to be alone. How many times had he wished to be left alone? How many times had he ignored everyone around him, hoping that they'd just go away?

As he lay there wondering if he was going to die, Dallas Albright understood that he had achieved his life's one great desire; it was true, in this version of the beautiful boy's *lucky life* he had attained his one constant wish, his only aspiration: to be left alone.

Although a *lucky life* has no provision for a paradox and is ignorant of irony, in this version of Dallas Albright's reality he is finally and inescapably all alone; an easy thing to want when you're surrounded by life's complex human interactions, but perhaps not as welcome when you're lying broken and empty on the cold cold ground.

"Hey, Dorsett, come 'ere."

John Dorsett had been considering his chances of escape. Although he'd never been any kind of an athlete, once, to pass his P.E. class and silence an unpleasant teacher, he had run a mile without stopping. "Maybe," he thought, "if this crazy Goon is chasing me, I could do it again."

Only it was more than a mile to the safety of his house, and someone was calling his name.

From deep in the shadows, John - the ghost - watched as the two giants easily defeat the smaller one. Despite his trepidations it had been an especially sweet and satisfying moment when Satan fell to the ground, utterly vanquished and left for dead. As remarkable as it seemed, he had achieved his goal; he'd revenged his sister's pain. The Devil finally got his due.

Only it didn't last long; something sad and familiar had interrupted the celebration - guilt. Since this was his first time in the revenge business, John had no idea that guilt was going to show up. What had been an intoxicating feeling of triumph was rapidly evaporating. Satan had been too easily overpowered. He'd put up no fight. Lying there on the ground next to his car, that hateful place where his sister had been abused, the Devil stopped being the Devil, and once again became a person. The ghost could actually feel his moment of satisfaction fading as he slipped backwards into the familiar coward he mostly hated.

"Hey, dumbass, come here."

The horrible hateful energy in the Goon's command drifted past him and out into the cool night air where it was eventually consumed by the massive indifference of the universe.

"Come here," Goon repeated, as he walked over and grabbed John Dorsett by the arm. "I ain't gonna hurt you," he said calmly. "Just tell Capernick here about the church and the money."

Douglas Capernick remained behind the wheel, but purposefully left the car idling.

"Get out of here," he told himself. "If you're lucky you can still get home before you get busted."

For a reason he couldn't have explained, Douglas Capernick opened the door and got out of the car. As he stood, the body on the ground trembled slightly and appeared to try and roll over. The extra weight in the jacket pocket reminded him that he was still holding the coat, and its heavy cargo. Tossing them back onto the driver's seat, he walked the few steps to where Dallas Albright lay on the pavement.

Kneeling next to the beautiful boy, Douglas Capernick whispered, "Lay quiet for another minute, then we'll get you out of here."

"What are you doin', man?"

Crouched low and madly bouncing from one foot to the other like a crazed baboon protecting its kill, Slayer Stetson had crept in behind and planted himself between Douglas and the car.

Quickly leaping to his feet and making a fast confident move in Stetson's direction," Douglas commanded, "Lighten up, dude."

Douglas Capernick understood that Slayer Stetson could not be taken lightly. Although he wasn't as physically intimidating as Goon, Billy "Slayer" Stetson was just big enough, and loud enough, to be a successful bully.

It was back in the fifth grade (after he'd thoroughly throttled the current Alpha-male, Ronnie Taylor) that his status jumped from run-of-the-mill troublemaker to full-on class bully. Thrilled with his dubious distinction and hopeful he could maintain it, young Billy Stetson desperately employed two new offensive strategies: First, he glossed himself with what he imagined an imposing nickname – Slayer; it wasn't especially, but it did stick. Second, whenever there was a need to bolster his sagging status he would judiciously assault a smaller weaker boy; he favored the blind sucker-punch to the kidney.

It was during the transition from elementary school tuff to middle school victim that Slayer Stetson tumbled to the value in numbers. To avoid unwanted conflict from the other tougher troublemakers, he enthusiastically glommed on to a group of sixth-grade reprobates that included Gordon Gordonski. It was in that environment of the gang that he first assumed his current role as toady.

Turning away from the startled and temporarily derailed Slayer Stetson, Douglas shouted, "Hey, Gordon. It looks like Albright might be hurt pretty bad. What's your plan?"

In spite of the dim light and deep shadows, it was obvious that the big kid was seriously frustrated. Spewing a raw and steady stream of profanity, Goon Gordonski had turned his back on the scene and was now manically pacing between the used cars, viciously pounding his thighs with his fists.

Douglas Capernick kept up the pressure.

"Come on, Gordo. Unless you plan on leaving him here, you better come up with something soon. Old Tubs Tully can't be far off."

"Shut up," Goon shouted, and began rubbing his giant forehead as if the answer might come off on his hand.

"Let's just get out of here," Slayer whined.

Douglas Capernick noticed that Dallas' eyes were now open. He hoped he wouldn't move or try to speak.

"That works." Douglas offered. "You guys cut out. I'll deal with Albright and John."

"Yeah, that's good," Slayer volunteered, while cautiously pulling on Goon's shirtsleeve.

Immediately turning on Slayer Stetson, Goon Gordonsiki furiously grabbed the smaller bully by the front of shirt and began to shake him like a rag doll.

"Shut the fuck up," Goon hollered down into his face. "We gotta have a plan. People are gonna start askin' how his face got all messed up. We're in deep shit if he talks."

The giant carelessly dropped Slayer to the ground. With eyes pinched tight in frustration, Goon continued to mutter under his breath while furiously pulling on his unkempt greasy hair. A long minute passed before a new and frightening expression spread across his ugly mug, signaling some kind of intellectual triumph.

"I got it," he laughed. "This is too good."

In a sinister combination of amusement and menace, he added, "I know what we're gonna do."

Reaching down to pull the smaller punk to his feet, he continued, "Slayer, my man, we'll tell 'em it was Capernick that did this to his little buddy. Oh, yeah. We're gonna tell 'em Douglas Capernick went ape shit and beat Dallas Albright."

"What?" Douglas was stunned by the absurdity of Goon Gordonski's plan. "That's crazy," he protested. "Nobody's going to believe I did this."

"Sure they will," Goon laughed confidently. "This guy here, John, yeah, he's gonna tell 'em that you and Albright got into a fight, and that you pounded him. Me and Slayer, we're gonna say the same thing. Yeah, it was two old friends fightin' over somethin'. And we got here just in time to stop you from killin' him."

"That's a hell of a plan, Gordo. But I'm betting that when Albright wakes up in the hospital, he's going to tell them it was you that put him there."

"Oh, yeah, man," Slayer Stetson stuttered. "He's right. Albright's gonna tell 'em."

"Slayer, it don't matter what he says, 'cause it's gonna be three against one. And one of us is a preacher's kid."

Thrilled to the bone by his original solution, Goon Gordonski had regained both his confidence and swagger. Bigger, louder, and now fearless, he grabbed John Dorsett around the shoulders like they were best of friends, and continued, "It's like John said. We had to stop Capernick from killin' the little guy. Hell, it took all three of us to hold him back. That's how come Capernick got all bloodied up."

Goon and his captive slowly approached where Douglas Capernick was standing next to the body.

"See, we just had to kick his ass to keep him from hurtin' poor Shorty anymore."

Squeezing the skinny kid around the shoulders, Goon Gordonski gave John Dorsett a terrifying smile, one so strange and frightening that it seemed a better fit for the Angel of Death than a high school reprobate.

"That's just the way it went down. Ain't that right, John? Nod your head," Goon commanded. "That's a good boy."

He couldn't feel the parts of his body that didn't hurt.

Even though Douglas had whispered for him to lie still, from what he could make out of Goon Gordonski's twisted plan, Douglas Capernick was in one hell of a spot. If he could stand, which was uncertain, there was almost nothing he could do to keep Slayer and Goon from ganging-up on the only person in the world who could help him.

"I need to get up," he thought. "I need for Goon to understand that this stupid plan won't work no matter what he gets John to say. They're not going to believe him. They can't."

"What would my mother do," John Dorsett asked himself.

It was impossible to imagine his father ever being in such an evil place, but his mother, well, perhaps. In so many ways she was the stronger of the two, always able to think for herself, always in control of the family, the church, the congregation. She would never admit it, but his mother always had a more practical perspective on life; the problems in her world were never solved by quoting the Bible or some meek display of supplication. She was always his harshest critic, but the first to celebrate with praise. While his father dwelt in the future, on a plane balanced somewhere between heaven and earth, it was Lecia Dorsett who lived in the present with both feet firmly on the ground.

"What would she say?" he wondered. "One thing she wouldn't allow is someone trying to tell her what to do, that's for sure. She wouldn't lie for someone. She would stand her ground, I think."

The door to the LeBaron was open. Douglas Capernick could see his jacket lying innocently on the front seat. In the pocket was his only hope to avoid catastrophe.

He could feel it as Slayer Stetson slithered around behind him, but he maintained his focus forward on the slowly advancing hulk, Goon Gordonski. In that clear awful moment, he wondered which was going to be worse: the bloody beating he was sure to take from the Posse, or the ongoing damnation from his father.

Either way, Douglas Capernick was not afraid to fight, he wasn't even afraid to be bloodied. Since those first days back on the school playground, he had developed a serious reputation as someone both willing to fight, and someone with considerable success. In that time he had learned fighting

368

was as much about experience as it was skill. It had been his "experience" that made people afraid to fight him. Their fear left them tentative, which put them at a terrible disadvantage.

"I can't win if I fight Goon," he thought. "My only hope is to take Slayer down and then try to talk some sense into him."

Without further debate, Douglas Capernick turned on Slayer Stetson.

In a mad rush like a linebacker storming the quarterback, Douglas made first contact with Slayer, driving his shoulder into the boy's chest, and then forcing him backwards, always back, until they crashed into the rear of the LeBaron. Douglas could hear the crack from the boy's skull slamming into the side of the car as the wind sailed out of his lungs in a rush. With a single blow to the face he could end any possibility for Slayer Stetson's future participation. But before Douglas could raise his fist, he heard Goon Gordonski bellow like an injured bull. While still on his knees, Douglas turned and shouted, "Wait!"

Goon Gordonski's rage kept him from hearing Douglas Capernick's demand. When they collided, the giant rolled over him like a metal wind, his sole purpose to crush what he saw as an enemy. With the throttle thrown wide open the engine tore ahead at the only speed it understood - victory or annihilation.

The beautiful boy struggled over onto his aching side just as Douglas Capernick and Slayer Stetson crashed into the back of the LeBaron. A second later, Goon Gordonski roared by at full-speed on his way to smashing into both Douglas and Stetson.

The tremendous force from the collision left all three either stunned or unconscious on the ground. The only one still standing, but now frozen and silhouetted against the arc of the LeBaron's headlights, was the ghost, John Dorsett. Between them was the open car door. The bright interior lights perfectly illuminated Douglas Capernick's jacket.

Lucky life cannot affect behavior, in fact, *lucky life* is strictly a human contrivance employed to cope with the passage of time; it has no memory, or motivation, no desire, no interest in human affairs. In this version of Dallas Albright's *lucky life,* he will remember the gun that he'd stolen from a police car four years before, the same gun that Douglas had demanded from him one afternoon in a hot and dusty shed, the gun that had stayed invisible until tonight that now lay quietly waiting in a jacket pocket.

Goon Gordonski was the first of the three to regain his senses, and the first to re-engage the attack. Once the giant could get to his knees, he began a brutal assault on Douglas Capernick's helpless head and chest. A second, a third, a fourth blow to the boy's handsome face was quickly turning it in to a bloody pulp.

The beautiful boy had gotten to his feet and was limping toward the open car door when John Dorsett stumbled forward.

"Run, John," Dallas demanded before falling hard against the side of the LeBaron. "Get the hell out of here."

John Dorsett could now clearly see both the injured Devil and the crazed giant who was savagely beating on the other boy's face. It felt like Satan had said something to him, something that made him think he should run away; but he didn't. Instead, the real and grotesque horror on the ground, with its unnatural sound of flesh-on-flesh and the smear of black blood pouring from the nose and mouth, stunned the boy's meek sensibilities, freezing him to the spot. Until that second, John Dorsett's life had been so remarkably sheltered that his only reference point for such a nightmare came from books, mostly comic books, and the Holy Bible. The revolt and self-pity he experienced caused a synapse to fire, a memory directly linked to Matthew's impossible lesson, *"But I say to you, Love your enemies and pray for those who persecute you."*

John wondered if Matthew had ever seen this much real blood.

When Dallas Albright grabbed the jacket from the front seat of the LeBaron and felt the extra weight of the gun in the pocket, he experienced an extraordinary combination of relief and empowerment. Without hesitation the beautiful boy stepped up behind Goon Gordonski, still on his knees mindlessly flailing away at his helpless victim, and cocked the pistol, immediately placing the bright silver barrel against the giant kid's head.

In a few seconds everyone would be safe again.

There are a handful of sounds instantly recognizable to most humans. A teakettle on the boil, the breathy whisper of a true love, and the hammer of a pistol being cocked; these are all unmistakable sounds that become real the moment that the air vibrates with their intent.

As the vibrations from the pistol's hard metallic "click" tickled the fibers of the auditory nerves inside Goon Gordonski's cochlea, an army of electrical signals were immediately dispatched to the sensory area of his temporal lobe. After a brief expedition through the boy's poisoned brain stem, where the busy neurons were trying desperately to deliver some of the more basic auditory data like duration and frequency, the signals then moved into his thalamus; an ovoid mass of gooey grey matter at the base of the cerebrum. It was there that Goon Gordonski's affected sensory system was attempting to integrate the bazillion-and-one messages into some form of motor response.

Goon Gordonski heard the sound of the pistol's hammer at the same moment he felt the cold hard steel on the back of his neck. He instantly stopped hitting Douglas Capernick in the face, but made no other movement.

"Get off," the beautiful boy demanded as he pressed the muzzle even deeper into the back of monster's shaggy mane.

Slowly, and now with a noticeable quiver in his hands, Gordon Gordonski slid off Douglas Capernick's chest, but remained on his knees beside the bleeding boy.

"Turn around and look at me. I want to tell you something, first."

As Goon Gordonski slowly pivoted on his knees to face his accuser, Dallas continued, "This only matters to me because you'll be dead. Still, it needs to be said. You can't possibly understand, but this is for all the kids you've abused, for all the people you've ripped-off, or lied too, or hurt. You need to die, Gordon."

Dallas Albright let those harsh and final words linger in the cool morning air, then added, "It won't matter much, but it still matters. It matters to me."

With his hands folded like a child in prayer, Goon Gordonski pleaded, "Listen, Albright. Please, please don't shoot me. I don't wanna die here. Please."

"Sorry, Gordon," the beautiful boy replied as he took a step closer to the whimpering giant.

When Dallas Albright pressed the silver pistol against Goon Gordonski's right temple, enjoying one long last satisfied look at the whimpering giant, four unique but significant events simultaneously take place.

In this version of the protagonist's *lucky life*, County Sheriff Tubs Tully will steer his giant Dodge police cruiser into Haviland's parking lot and come to a skidding stop right in front of the still unconscious bodies of Douglas Capernick and Slayer Stetson. "Drop the gun, kid," he will bark as he opens his car door and draws his own weapon.

The sound of the car sliding to a stop near Douglas Capernick's injured head will demand that the boy's thalamus initiate a series of muscular contractions that ignite the appropriate nerves and muscles, thereby making it possible for his body to roll over on its right side away from the sound.

Now in the presence of not one but two handguns, each pointed at different human targets, John Dorsett becomes emotionally overwhelmed and chooses the path of least resistance. Sitting down next to the still idling LeBaron, the ghost puts his head in his hands and returns to weeping.

For Dallas Albright there is no confused or tragic internal dialog, he has decided that everything in his life, his *lucky life*, has led him to this moment. It was, in the end, necessary to terminate Goon Gordonski's miserable existence by discharging the weapon and lodging its bullet deep inside the monster's broken brain.

Without remorse the beautiful boy pulls the trigger on the .38 caliber police revolver, hears the fatal click from the falling hammer, but does not feel the recoil in his hand or the sound of the report. Squeezing the trigger a second, a third, and even a fourth time, Dallas Albright sadly realizes that there are no bullets in the gun.

As the pistol's hammer strikes metal on metal, Goon Gordonski will not feel a bullet enter his skull. The gears turn and he wonders why he is not dead.

Through vision blurred by tears, the miserably naive John Dorsett understands that something that should have happened didn't.

And, stepping out from the protection of his car door, County Sheriff Tubs Tully breathes a sigh of relief knowing that tonight no one is going to die.

Chapter Nineteen

Parents Day

"The only reason people want to be master of the future is to change the past."
Laughter and Forgetting - Milan Kundera

Emily Albright sat bolt upright in bed before the phone could finish its first ring. She knew that this was the phone call, the one she'd expected and dread since the night they agreed to let the boy have the Super Sport. Given the late hour there was no question that something horrible had happened. Out there somewhere, her son was either broken into pieces, or cold dead on the road.

"Charles," she whispered as she shook his shoulder to wake him, "it's the phone."

"Hello," he mumbled into the receiver. "What? What? Where is he now? Okay, we'll come right away. Thank you."

Assuming the worst, Emily asked, "What's happened?"

Charles Albright swung his legs over the side of the bed and then stood before finally answering.

"He's at the hospital. He's hurt, but not in the emergency room."

Emily managed a breath before she replied, "I thought he was dead."

"No," Charles said, switching on the lamp beside the bed. "But he's under arrest."

The remarkably efficient, but professionally distant staff at the Freeland Hospital's emergency room would reveal only the room number where Emily and Charles Albright could find their son. Turning the corner to the hospital's West Wing, they could see halfway down the dim and noiseless hallway to where Deputy Sheriff Alan Plimsol slouched against the door to what they presumed was room 116. As the anxious couple approached, the weary lawman stood a bit more erect and nodded a professional acknowledgement.

"Hello, Alan," Charles Albright offered. "Is he inside?"

Looking a little like the kid who didn't want to say anything but knew he must, the deputy uneasily replied, "Evenin' folks. Sheriff Brayton said you were on your way."

"Can we go in?" Emily asked before he'd finished.

It was obvious from the tired eyes and droop to his shoulders that the deputy was exhausted. Nodding his acknowledgment, he added, "Sure, go ahead. The Sheriff will be back soon, but he's, well, he's got other things he's doin,' so it may be awhile. He asked me to make sure that you stayed until he comes back."

On the right side of what was normally a double-room (half now left dark and vacant behind a drawn curtain) Emily and Charles found their son asleep. From above the bed a dull fluorescent glow produced so little light that it left no shadows but somehow still revealed the distressing dark bruise on the left side of the boy's face. An intravenous drip had been patched into his thin white arm. Nearby an ominous-looking electronic box silently monitored the quiet breathing and steady heart rate.

Emily moved silently around to the side of the bed, unsure whether to wake him. Instinctively reaching to touch the boy's battered face the mother noticed a brief flash of reflection from the silver handcuff that now effectively secured her son's small left wrist to the guard rail of the bed. It was painfully clear that her first born was now a prisoner of the law.

"Mom?"

The beautiful boy's long lashes fluttered and then opened.

"Is that you?"

Emily turned back to consider her husband who had remained just inside the door. Despite the heavy shadows she could see that his arms were crossed like a shield, his expression a dour and impenetrable scowl.

"Yes, dear; your father and I are both here," she whispered.

As she had done so many times before in his young life, Emily Albright automatically reached out to offer comfort by taking his hand. Only this time, instead of the reassurance of his warm skin, she felt the cold ugly finality of a metal manacle.

"How do you feel?" was the best she could offer.

"I don't know. They gave me some pain drugs," he replied in a dreamy far-off voice. "The car's okay, though. You don't need to worry about that."

Behind them the door opened hitting Charles in the back. The night nurse, Randi Olsen glided past Charles who mumbled an apology before repositioning himself even further from the patient. Without additional comment the two parents helplessly watched as the nurse went about her duties. After she'd made her last notation on the clipboard, she turned directly to the groggy patient and said, "The doctor's still with your friend, but he'll be back to see you before too long. Sleep if you can, okay?"

Finally, as Nurse Olsen turned to leave, Charles asked, "Randi, can you tell us about his injuries?"

In what seemed to Charles a professional but empty reply, Randi Olsen only offered, "Yes, well, he has some internal injuries along with the bruises on his hands and face. I can't tell you much right now, but I know that Doctor Stilwill has seen him. They've taken some x-rays, and he's been given Demerol to ease the pain. I just don't know how much longer the doctor will be with the Capernick boy before he can get back here. We're kind of understaffed this morning, so it could be an hour or so."

Charles responded mechanically, adding, "Thanks, Randi. We appreciate what you're doing for the boy."

Randi Olsen then provided the Albright's with her practiced smile and instantly left the room without another word.

In a voice that seemed to resonate with a remarkable tone of suspicion, Emily asked, "Do you know her?"

Surprised and put-off by the implication, Charles snapped, "Yes. She and her husband Brad live in Exira. We remodeled their kitchen last fall. Remember?"

Emily Albright nodded as if she remembered, but, of course, she did not.

The boy had fallen back asleep and was again breathing peacefully. The mother had turned away from her angry husband to focus on the innocent countenance on the beautiful boy's battered face. The quiet and dark of the hospital's lighting would effectively mask the husband and wife's emotions as they drifted away to consider their own version of this *lucky life*. When the door opened forty minutes later neither had moved, nor spoken.

"Charles, can I talk to you outside?"

Ray Brayton was a good man; well-liked, a solid Republican in a place rich with solid Republicans, a two-term deacon at Saint John's, and for the past nine years the Chief of Police for Freeland, Iowa. As a local born and raised, people around Freeland naturally liked Ray Brayton. He was one of them. As the face for local law enforcement there was more than just a little Andy Griffith in his approach, but people liked that, too. What crime that did happen in Freeland usually got sorted out without much fuss or fanfare.

The West Wing's public waiting area was just across the hall from the nurse's station, but when the Sheriff motioned for Emily and Charles to take a seat none of the staff were anywhere to be seen.

"Well, sorry about all this," the Sheriff began, "but we got a couple of problems that we need to talk about. I s'pect you know the County Sheriff. Tom, this is Charles and Emily Albright. Anyway, earlier tonight your boy had some trouble with a couple of other kids. A couple of, well, problem kids, I guess."

Before the Sheriff could continue, Emily slid the metal chair she was occupying around the edge of the table and closer to her husband. When she reached out to take his arm, Charles Albright glanced over at his wife of seventeen years with a look that made her feel as if the act was an intrusion.

In a clear but noticeably hostile voice, Charles Albright asked, "Ray, my boy is handcuffed to a bed. Has he been arrested for something?"

Tubs Tully wasted no time; his mood was obvious.

"Not yet, Sir," the big man replied. "But your boy is being held here before being charged. It seems he got himself involved in a fight with some other local kids. You might know Douglas Capernick? Right now, he's down the hall being treated for some pretty bad injuries. Then there's these two other guys, Gordon Gordonski and a William Stetson. Apparently, there was some kind of disagreement and your boy and the Capernick kid took the worst of it."

Emily Albright couldn't restrain herself any longer, "I don't understand what you're saying. Dallas is lying in a hospital bed, and he's under arrest for fighting?"

It was clear from the reaction on his face that Sheriff Tubs Tully did not like to be interrupted.

"Miss Albright, your boy was involved in some kind of fight tonight. I don't have that all figured out yet, but I will. We're holdin' him here until we can get a bit more information, but my plan is to charge him with theft and attempted murder."

The last two words went off like a bomb had exploded in the small waiting room.

"This is crazy," Emily argued. "How do you know he tried to murder somebody?"

"I saw him," was all Tully said.

"You saw him," Emily asked? "How?"

"It's been a long night Miss Albright, and we've had lots of problems here in Freeland, but I know what I saw."

Sitting up in his chair and fixing his eyes directly on Charles Albright, Tully continued, "I was making my last sweep through town before headin' home and spotted what looked like trouble in Haviland's car lot. When I pulled up, your son was standing over this Gordonski kid with a gun in his hand. When I told him to drop it, he looked up at me and then calm as you please turned back to this kid and pulled the trigger."

Emily Albright cried, "Oh god, no. Is the boy... dead?"

The Sheriff melodramatically pushed his chair back from the table before answering,

"No, ma'am. There was no ammunition in his gun."

"What," Charles interjected in a louder more anxious voice, "he had a gun, but there were no bullets? You said he tried to kill a boy, but with a gun that had no bullets?"

Ray Brayton gently put his hand on Charles arm before quietly suggesting, "Hold on, Charles. I know this is kinda strange, but Sheriff Tully here believes that Dallas intended to shoot the Gordonski boy."

"Why would you think that?"

The Sheriff gently placed his fat hands on the tabletop. After snorting a gulp of air, he answered, "It's like I said before, your boy looked me in the eye, and then turned back to the other kid before he pulled the trigger."

Charles interrupted, "But maybe he knew there were no bullets in the gun. Maybe it was some kind of stupid game."

"No, sir, I don't think so. You see he didn't just pull the trigger once. When his weapon didn't discharge, he didn't quit. He pulled the trigger three more times. I saw him. He wanted to shoot that boy in the head."

"Maybe you could explain it to me. I know everyone here thinks I'm the dumbest man on Earth, but try me again. Why did you put a gun to that boy's head and pull the trigger, four times?"

It was nearly three o'clock on Sunday afternoon. The beautiful boy had been released from the hospital and into his parent's custody with a pair of deeply bruised ribs, a mild concussion, and some undiagnosed damage to his right kidney. They had driven home in silence, but once ensconced in the familiar family kitchen, Charles Albright began his cross-examination with the pointed statement: "How could you be so stupid."

This sentence was purposefully not structured as a question.

In the past, whenever Dallas wanted to avoid discussing his behavior with his father, he would tactfully stall and procrastinate until Charles lost his patience and stormed off. Ordinarily, this did not take long. Although the boy didn't fully appreciate the psychology, it was self-evident that his father had little patience, preferring to solve the problem himself rather than deliberate or wait until his son got around to complying. This technique had been especially successful at dodging work, communicating his poor grades, or the most common complaint - ignoring his mother's requests. The stakes were higher this time, but the gambit would be the same: "If I can stall long enough, the old man will give up and leave me alone." Perhaps not the wisest approach, considering the seriousness of his predicament, but it was certainly one that fit Dallas Albright's disposition and history.

"It's complicated," the boy offered with an utterly straight and expressionless face.

"I don't know what that means," Charles demanded. "Are you suggesting that I'm not smart enough to follow your complex story? Are you incapable of communicating this complicated story? Or is there something I'm missing?"

"Well, yes," the son offered. "It's complicated."

"Please don't use that word again."

An especially tense protracted moment passed before Charles Albright was certain he would not explode in rage. Through gritted teeth, he demanded, "We are owed an explanation."

"You're not going to like it," the beautiful boy answered with such a frightening level of detachment that Charles thought he heard his grandmother's voice.

"I already don't like it," the father shouted.

"Why kill Goon Gordonski? Where should I begin? Who do I include and incriminate? How much detail is necessary?"

These were all important questions, but he was running out of time. He had clearly pushed his father as far as he dared. If he was going to keep his family out of this nightmare, but somehow not alienate them so completely as to be disowned, he was going to have to satisfy some quantity of his father's questions.

"This goes back awhile," he began.

Choosing his words and the principal actors carefully, he began by revealing how it had been Grandma Jo who had taught him to steal. Back in the quiet of the hospital, he had decided that since she was now long dead and there was nothing anyone could do to her, he would throw her under the bus. By forcing everyone's attention on to the bizarre story of the crazy grandma, it might be possible to deflect some of the guilt away from himself and avoid involving either Douglas or Will. As he revealed more and more of the back-story, including the essential moment when he'd stolen the Sheriff's gun, Dallas made certain to heap as much of the responsibility as was plausible on the old woman. Although she'd never so much as left the house, by the time Dallas was done it sounded as if she was not only the brains behind the operation, but that she'd even driven the getaway vehicle. When his mother asked, "What possessed her to do such a thing," he coldly dismissed the question by saying, "She had demons. Everyone knows that... right?"

Then he switched gears to Debbie Dorsett. This was a far more complicated and delicate part of the story, a double-edged sword that could easily destroy his already shaky credibility.

Even though it wasn't fair or right, Dallas knew that Debbie would take the fall for her injuries. Of course, they would look at her beautiful damaged face and demand that she tell them the truth, the whole truth, and nothing but the truth. Except in this version, she would only mention her behavior, her mistakes; the boyfriend would be treated as a non-essential player in a horrible misunderstanding. Nothing would be said about his actions or bad judgment either before or after he'd smashed her in the face with the back of his hand.

Her father would naturally be angry and disappointed, but she would deliberately tell the story in such a way that made her a willing partner, and not the victim. That kind of revelation would expose a different person than the daughter he thought he knew. In his line of work, Stephen Dorsett understood a lot about martyrs, but did he know one when he saw one?

Lecia Dorsett, on the other hand, was much easier to predict. No matter what Debbie said, her first reaction would be to protect the family's reputation, especially her husband's. Even though she would thoroughly enjoy seeing her daughter's ex-boyfriend suffer, the necessity of avoiding any public awareness for this "lack of judgment" was clearly the first priority.

It would go just like Debbie predicted. Lecia Dorsett would stoically refrain from the, "I told you so," and then hide her daughter away until the afternoon when they would quietly load the big red Cadillac with her bags and baggage. Without any dramatic fanfare or farewells, the aunt and uncle would help Debbie get into the back seat, and then quietly drive off to the safety of the city. As the Dorsett family stands on the porch waving their goodbyes, Lecia will suppress the satisfaction she gets from knowing her plan had worked so perfectly. By the time her willful daughter returns in the fall, the bruises on her face will have faded along with any memory of the boy who gave them to her.

His relationship with Douglas Capernick and the decision to kill Goon Gordonski was especially "complicated." And even though the word accurately described the situation, it was clear that this particular adjective would not be the best way to start. Instead, he offered, "Goon Gordonski is a plague. He's a disease. He was out of his mind on drugs. If I didn't do something he would have killed Douglas. I knew that the gun was in his coat pocket."

The boy patiently waited for his mother to catch up before adding, "It was the only way to keep Goon from beating my friend to death."

Like a seasoned actor, Dallas Albright purposefully lingered over the noun "friend." He was counting on the scene's inherent drama to sell them that his decisions were at a minimum noble, and possibly heroic. The calculated use of the word "friend" had been planned to further amplify what he knew people were going to want to hear.

With tears now streaming down her face, Emily Albright sobbed, "But did you intend to kill the boy? Please."

Playing his trump, the beautiful boy meekly replied, "I had to do something to help Douglas. Can't you see that?"

Like someone had thrown a switch, Charles Albright leapt from his chair, pounding his fist into his palm, and shouting, "Stop it. You didn't answer the question. All you did was provide an excuse for your act. These are meaningless words; words that you're using to confuse us, or to keep from admitting the truth."

Leaning across the kitchen table, Charles turned to his wife and said, "It's insane, but Emily, I believe that if there'd been bullets in that gun our child would have killed that boy. Just because he can't or won't admit it doesn't make it any less true."

The gambit was almost played out. There was one more line that had to be delivered before he could be certain of his father's complete separation.

"Okay," the boy said defiantly, "I don't want to be a problem for you. I can manage this myself."

As planned, Charles Albright exploded, "Manage? You can't manage anything. You are likely to go to jail, probably for a very long time. A boy with a gun... what the hell has happened here?"

"This is my problem, not yours," Dallas yelled, knowing that his father had reached the point of no return and he had won.

"Stop it! I can't hear another word. You are a stranger to me. How could you live in this house for sixteen years and understand nothing of who we are?"

The boy remained silent, but maintained constant eye contact with his father.

"Manage this yourself," Charles continued, "manage what? Do you seriously think that you could walk away from your mother and me? Who will hire your attorney? Who will stake your bail? Who will suffer most in this community? Not you little man. It'll be your mother and me. It's our business, our reputations that have been destroyed. And now you want me to... what, forget you tried to kill another person."

Charles Albright stopped and turned around to place his shaking hands on the kitchen table.

"It is impossible for me to understand, but for no other reason than there were no bullets in that gun, you would have murdered another human being."

Except for the steady hum from the refrigerator motor and an incessant "click-click-click" of the clock above the doorway, the familiar family kitchen was finally silent.

The mother of the beautiful boy was still sitting beside him. She had been there, bolt-upright, in the heavy oak chair for more than ninety minutes. Her vacant expression revealed no emotion or feelings.

Across the table sat the boy, his son. His hands rested neutral in his lap, his posture relaxed. The child's bruised face revealed nothing, but remained blank and expressionless; Charles Albright incorrectly interpreted this look as indifference.

It was nearly five o'clock. For the first time since they'd sat down Charles' concentration flagged. In that private second he left behind his personal nightmare and had managed to focus his attention on the dozen framed pictures on the wall behind his son. Right there, along with the traditional stiff school photographs of the boys (the ones that were you to open the back of the frame you'd find a stack of the same smiling, self-conscious pictures from the year before, and the year before…) there were a dozen of the more candid moments from their lives, his life, all permanently trapped under the glass of a 4 X 6 frame.

"It's funny," he thought, "but these are just the kind of moments you never imagine ending. We must have a thousand just like them, hanging on a wall or stuffed away in a scrapbook somewhere. Then a new one comes along and it gets slipped into the frame, burying the one left behind, covered up and forgotten."

Charles' gaze travelled absently to the lower right-hand corner of the collection to one of his favorites, a grainy photo that he'd taken of Emily and the two boys as they proudly displayed a pitiful stringer of three undersized fish; three fish that had taken their Indian guide seven hours and two hundred-fifty dollars to help them capture. Above and to the left of the fish was the one taken at Disney World by an agreeable stranger who had somehow managed to keep the family in focus, while cutting off most of Goofy's green hat. There next to the giant cartoon character was the most recent photo to grace Emily's wall, the boy and his date - Debbie Dorsett. Too dark and poorly composed the photo presented two anxious children as they nervously paraded arm-in-arm into the high school gymnasium.

"That's crazy," he thought, "but the boy is actually smiling in this one."

These beautiful pictures, Emily's sweet snapshot smorgasbord, had a common quality: they were all photos of the family, his wife and his sons, all but one. Surrounded by Cub Scouts, science fairs, baseball games, and family vacations, all of these pictures were of the same four people, all but one. That exception was placed inconspicuously in the lower left hand corner closest to the refrigerator.

In its ancient silver 3 X 5 frame was a deeply faded black-and-white photograph. The picture featured two men standing side-by-side, and a small boy perched precariously on their shoulders. Looking at it now, with its maddeningly off-kilter composition, Charles remembered how his mother passionately defended it as a *bona fide* "keeper." Her emphatic point of view was based on both her enthusiasm for the men's wide gaping grins and the historical importance of the moment. On the back, Charys had lovingly inscribed in her perfect hand,

First day in our new home - April 30, 1952.
Gordon – Charles – Bill Albright

In spite of the photo's inferior size, and that thirty-five years had faded the grays to brown, this small picture stood out as clear and focused as any on the wall; for Charles it now dominated the space and made all the others seem vague and withdrawn.

"Look at those two," Charles Albright thought. "What a pair. My father is so young and filled with possibility. And Grandpa Bill, he's already there, successful and respected. These are great men. These are men who accomplished so much in their lives."

As he drifted in the history of the picture, Charles tried to imagine what the two would say about the problems facing his family. How would they have reacted? What would they have done in such a spot? Would they have known something that he couldn't know?

"Maybe it doesn't matter. After all, neither of them would have ever gotten themselves in such a mess. Right?"

As he continued to study the two patriarchs there seemed to be some kind of change in their expression, something that wasn't there before. Was it possible that those steady smiles were now mocking him? Like Marley on the doorknocker, could their faces somehow have shifted into, what? No, it couldn't be, but was that disappointment he saw in their eyes?

"I don't blame you. This is my fault. I let you both down. You did so much for me, and what have I done to thank you... only this boy, this wicked, self-centered boy who is about to bring us all down.

I honestly don't know how this happened. It's been so long since he's let anyone in, since I could connect with him."

Desperate to erase the condemnation in their eyes, he asked his father, "How was it that I avoided something like this? How did you keep me on course? What did I see that he doesn't?"

Dallas Albright was confused by the shifting expressions on his father's face, but wary of interrupting. It seemed like the rage had drained away and left behind something softer and more relaxed.

"What is he looking at, anyway? Is it something behind me?"

The beautiful boy turned to look over his right shoulder, but saw nothing out of the ordinary.

"I am so sorry for what the boy and I have done."

The father then turned his gaze away from the picture to the problem across the table. Now back in the familiar kitchen, Charles Albright had returned and brought with him his family's disappointment and resentment.

Broken and humbled, he pronounced his own version of a verdict.

"Here's where I stand," the father's voice cracked. "You want to manage this yourself... then fine, you're on your own."

His heart broken and all patience lost, Charles Albright reached out and carefully took down the photo from the wall.

"You've taken all there is. I have nothing more to give."

Chapter Twenty

Tongues of Fire

"It isn't the fear of God, but the upholding of one's own honor and conscience."
The Diary of a Young Girl – Anne Frank

The turnout for the ten-thirty worship service was conspicuously smaller than usual.

Storm clouds heavy with rain had rolled in just before dawn leaving the air feeling thick and dull. Standing out in their yards and fields, the good people of Freeland looked to the sky with high hopes that those great gray sponges might open up and provide a needed spring soaking. But they didn't. Instead, the atmosphere remained loaded with the disconcerting quality of anticipation, apparently ignoring any possibility for cheerfulness.

For those faithful few in attendance there were signs that their Pastor Dorsett might be out of sorts.

For one thing, the late service religiously began at ten-thirty sharp; except on this restless morning the two acolytes wouldn't finish lighting the Disciple's Candles until almost ten forty-five. Then during the call-and-response to the Pastor's Prayer, the normally precise Pastor Dorsett lost his place and had to restart the passage in Psalms about, *"He makes winds his messenger and flames of fire his servants."* This canonical kerfuffle produced its own domino effect, sending those folks still engaged in the exercise scrambling to relocate their parts.

But the most telling sign that something was not quite right with Pastor Dorsett came during the singing of *Holy! Holy! Holy*, which, as they all knew, was one of his personal favorites. The familiar hymn started out fine, but somewhere in the second verse his normal booming tenor mysteriously trailed-off to nothing. Sadly, the blessing of the trinity was left to the weak and distracted efforts of the congregation.

So when it finally came time for the sermon, all the adults, all thirty-three of them, were watching with great interest as their pastor and spiritual leader mechanically rose from his wooden chair behind the pulpit and ascended to the podium.

Lecia Buhl-Dorsett understood why her husband was having trouble concentrating on his work; her hope, however, was that by providing as much smiling normalcy as possible they might all get through the day without further incident, or deeper scrutiny. For those paying attention, and in that small crowd there were several paying very close attention, Lecia and her children (that is, John, Aaron, and Judith) were all seated in their usual Sunday spot, second row on the right side nearest the aisle. In keeping with Dorsett tradition, all were wearing their Sunday-best and sporting their customary thoughtful smiles; the one's intended to be both inspiring to the congregation and supportive of their father.

On this morning, also sitting between Lecia Dorsett and her children (and adding an unanticipated bit of noteworthy melodrama) were two remarkable visitors. In this case, the beautiful and exotic dark-skinned woman was Lecia Dorsett's sister-in-law, Donella. Sitting beside her was a handsome confident man, Lecia's brother, Thomas Buhl. Like the return of Halley's Comet, the mysterious and fantastic Buhl's had come back to shine their fabulous alien light on the curious congregation of Freeland Methodists.

For those keeping score, and there were those who also kept close score, only daughter Debbie was unaccounted for. This fascinating development prompted all kinds of speculation, the most interesting of which was the possibility that there was a causal link between the ministers less-than-stellar performance, the mysterious absence of his middle child, and the unexpected appearance of the remarkable strangers.

"Good morning."

Pastor Stephen Dorsett looked down at his sermon notes and began to read, slowly, "In the book of Acts, the Acts of the Apostles, Luke writes, *'When the day of Pentecost came they were all together in one place. Suddenly, a sound like the blowing of a violent wind came from heaven and filled the whole house where they were sitting. They saw what seemed to be tongues of fire that separated and came to rest on each of them. All of them were filled with the Holy Spirit and began to speak in other tongues as the Spirit enabled them.'"*

After an especially long pause, Pastor Dorsett finally removed his reading glasses and then carefully folded them before laying them on his notes. Apparently going off-script, he continued, "Since I was a young boy, the Pentecost story has been both a mystery and a comfort to me. I'm especially fond of this story because of the extraordinary way that God reveals his Holy Spirit through a miracle, a miracle that I personally find inspiring.

It's no surprise that the celebration of the Pentecost has been going on for a very long time. It is, in fact, one of the oldest festivals in the Church. Originally known as the Jewish Feast of Weeks, its significance was that it always took place fifty days after the Passover, fifty days after God gave Moses his Ten Commandments.

Pastor Dorsett paused long enough to look out over the congregation, then continued, "So, if we jump ahead fourteen hundred years, God's son, our Savior, will die on the cross. Then after the miracle of his resurrection, Christ will return to Earth where he will spend the next forty days with his disciples. Forty days where he will teach them all they need to know to carry on his great work.

I think we can all agree that Jesus return to the living would have made for some fantastic and exciting times. And under the circumstances, it's easy to understand why the disciples would've been a little anxious about doing what he commanded, which was, of course, to 'Go forth and teach all the nations by baptizing them in the name of the Father and the Son.'

Teach the world. Now that is indeed a daunting task. How would you go about that when there are so many different people, so many different traditions and languages? And to make thing even more complicated, the disciples are expected to do this without getting arrested by the Romans.

I was just a boy the first time I heard my pastor, Pastor Viedenbach, tell the Pentecost story. Oh, this man was such a marvelous storyteller. You see, he had this way of making things seem to come alive, and this particular story is so very dramatic. I could imagine from his description that the disciples had gathered together a small congregation, people from all over the area, people that had heard about Jesus and wanted to celebrate the Shavuot. Then suddenly roaring down the chimney and into this little room was this fantastic storm..."

Pastor Dorsett paused to allow his audiences' imagination to catch up before adding, "It was there, you see, in that room that the Holy Spirit first appears. The Holy Spirit, the indispensable Holy Spirit, appears to these people in the form of the tongues of fire, floating there above their heads as both its purpose and power. Thanks to the presence of the Holy Spirit, all of these people could suddenly understand one another. Miraculously, they could all speak the same language. They could hear one another and the message of God.

I do appreciate that sometimes it can be difficult to understand God's will, but not here, not in the Pentecost story. It was the presence of the Holy Spirit that made it possible for Christ's disciples to reach out to the people of the world, each in their own language, and each in their own way."

There was a brief pause before Pastor Dorsett added, "It all seemed so very dramatic to me back then, the possibility for everyone, no matter what language they spoke, no matter where they were from or what they believed, it was now possible for them to hear and understand the message of God. From that moment forward, Jesus was no longer the only one who could understand God's will. Now we too can understand, and our voices can spread the Spirit of that understanding.

For many years I preached the Pentecost story from the perspective that thanks to the Holy Spirit we can now all receive God's gift, his clear promise of a life after death through Jesus Christ. But this morning I am conflicted. I came prepared to share with you the promise in the Pentecost, but I am also obliged to say a word about our children, and the choices that they make.

Last night many of our children turned their back on the collective wisdom of their mothers and fathers. Somehow their conscience, their internal voice, the flame if you will, was extinguished. Covered up by vanity, or as Solomon observed, *'Feet that are quick to run into mischief.'*

Many of them chose the darkness, a path that they certainly knew in their hearts was wrong.

Why, I wonder?

If God's Holy Spirit has a flame and light for each of us, why would they choose to ignore it?

John said in 3:19 *"Men love darkness, rather than the light."*

But why, why do we love the darkness? Is it because it's fun? Is there some kind of pleasure in that darkness? Or, perhaps, it's because we are unable to see the immediate consequences of our actions? After all, God doesn't directly intervene in our lives, does He? Perhaps He doesn't really care? Maybe… maybe He doesn't even exist?

I appreciate that questions like these are challenging, and to some may even seem sinful. Is it wrong to question God's purpose or existence? No, I don't believe it is; in fact, it's important because your decision demands that you make a choice; a choice between believing and trusting in God's promise, or choosing your own voice, your inner voice, your self.

From the moment that a child is born, that first joyful frightening moment when we welcome them into our lives, we begin to teach them about God's most important message, the message of love. As parents we know that it doesn't take very long before they begin testing themselves against our rules. Sometimes we see their willful behavior as a personal challenge, a defiance of our own experience about what is right and what is wrong. It is easy to become frustrated by these persistent challenges, and so we start devising punishments and reprimands that we hope will get them to do what we want. We'll administer small disciplines like a time-out or more chores, we are always very quick to lecture them, and sometimes we'll even dispense a good old-fashioned spanking. Thankfully, this combination of love and persistence is enough to guide most children through those demanding times.

But not always; sadly, there are those who will not, or cannot, abide by the rules of family and society. For a child to understand and embrace these standards is one of life's most important lessons. Yet, without life's experiences to guide them, without our love, without our patience, this Christian idea of freedom can place an especially heavy burden on the young.

Sometimes children will ask me, 'If God is there, if He cares, why doesn't He tell me so? When I scream at Him, at the top of my voice, where are you? why doesn't He answer? Why does God hide from me?'

These are also important questions and they deserve thoughtful intelligent answers. Without any touchable tangible proof of His existence, it is easy to forget, or ignore, what God has taught us. Without clear and consistent rules it's not too difficult to believe that you can do whatever you want, whenever you want, and with no consequence. After all, God doesn't seem to care, He never says anything. If you want to extend that line of thought to a frightening conclusion, then maybe it's because He's just not there?"

Pastor Stephen Dorsett glanced down on his small congregation and hesitated long enough to second guess his last comment, after all, his own children had just made choices that fit the example. The boy with his head held low in contrition, and the daughter closed off in her bedroom, had exercised their freewill in ways that had caused tremendous misery and permanent consequence. By following their own intuition they had hurt themselves and deeply injured others.

"They were lucky," he thought. "They took an adult-dose of life's harshest medicine and no one had died."

He began again, "This question of taking responsibility for our lives is one that you have heard me talk about many times before. As Christians it stands to be the single most important question of our lives. So when we give it time and serious thoughtful consideration, it is always best to consult those whose own life experiences can communicate the deepest meaning.

Doctor Viktor Frankl survived the death camp at Auschwitz. His personal story, and how he has used that horrific experience to teach us about finding meaning and truth in our own lives, can be a powerful inspiration. I want to share with you something he said. It is difficult to hear this and remain unaffected."

"And so the last day in camp passed in anticipation of freedom. But we had rejoiced too early. The Red Cross delegate had told us that an agreement had been signed, and that the camp must not be evacuated. But that night the SS arrived with trucks and brought an order to clear the camp. The last remaining prisoners were to be taken to a central camp...to be exchanged for some prisoners of war. They were so friendly, trying to persuade us to get into the trucks without fear. Telling us we should be grateful for our good luck. Those who were strong enough crowded into the trucks while the sick were lifted up with difficulty. My friend and I stood in the last group, from which only thirteen would be chosen for the next to last truck. The chief doctor counted out the requisite number, but he omitted the two of us. The thirteen were loaded and we had to stay behind. Impatiently

we sat down and waited with the few remaining prisoners for the last truck. We waited a long time. Finally, we lay down on the mattresses in the deserted guardroom, exhausted.

The noise of rifles and cannons woke us; the flashes of tracer bullets and gun shots entered the hut. The chief doctor dashed in and ordered us to take cover on the floor. Then we grasped what was happening: the battlefront had finally reached us.

Many weeks later we found out just how uncertain human decisions are… I was confronted with photographs which had been taken in a small camp not far from ours. Our friends who thought they were traveling to freedom that night had been taken in the trucks to this camp, and there they were locked in the huts and burned to death."

Pastor Stephen Dorsett looked up from his worn and dog-eared copy of the Frankl manuscript to survey the reaction of his congregation.

"It would seem," he continued, "but for some exceptional good fortune, some kind of *lucky life*, Doctor Frankl survived.

When I think about that moment, that crucial instant when Doctor Frankl and his friend do not get into the truck, but instead stay behind, stay behind to live, I start thinking about all the possibilities that make a moment. For instance, how many different versions of that place and time were possible? How many unique alternatives could there be; one's that either keep him off the truck, or send him to his death?

Imagine the consequences from even the smallest most insignificant change to that moment. Perhaps someone in front of them falls down and is unable to get into the truck. What if one of the soldiers changes his mind and forces Doctor Frankl to get on the truck with the others? Maybe it starts raining and the soldier becomes distracted?

I wonder: Are there an infinite number of possibilities to this one critical moment, small insignificant variances that would have changed the outcome and the fate of this man? "

"Well," he added with a weary smile, "that brings us back to the question, the one that has confounded us since the original sin: In a life that seems to be filled with an infinite number of possibilities, why would God give us this great gift, the gift of freewill? In a universe with an unlimited number of opportunities, why would He do this when we are so often drawn to those choices that are wrong and hurtful?"

Those faithful few Methodists scattered around the familiar sanctuary could not appreciate the personal context of Pastor Dorsett's remarks; at least not yet. But in those quite seconds that followed, most folks understood that there had been something important in their minister's message, something essential, maybe. In that remarkable moment something palpable and profound had just happened. After all, it wasn't every day that the people of Freeland Iowa took time to consider God's plan for the universe; there was work to get done, bills to pay, and kids to care for. But on this unremarkable morning in May, it felt as if something extraordinary might have just happened.

Through the open windows a puff of warm spring breeze mingled with the noise of someone starting a lawnmower. The candles flickered, children stirred impatiently, and Pastor Dorsett offered this hopeful conclusion.

"My friends, when we face life's challenges, especially those of family and faith, good or evil, right from wrong please remember that God does not cause bad choices... but he does permit them. When we understand that distinction, that difference, then we must use this gift of freedom to choose a path that strives for goodness, understanding and love."

* * *

Kirk Brocker grew up in small town Iowa where his stories and heart still live. He is now a retired nonprofit executive with more than twenty-five years of service to science, art and the cultural community.

His epitaph will read: *He was prompt.*

Lucky Life is his first novel.

Made in the USA
San Bernardino, CA
28 February 2017